Puerto Rican Students
in U.S. Schools

Sociocultural, Political,
and Historical Studies in Education
Joel Spring, Editor

Puerto Rican Students in U.S. Schools

Edited by

Sonia Nieto

LAWRENCE ERLBAUM ASSOCIATES, PUBLISHERS
2000   Mahwah, New Jersey   London

Lawrence Erlbaum Associates, Inc., Publishers
10 Industrial Avenue
Mahwah, New Jersey 07430-2262

Cover photograph from the Historical Archives of Puerto Rican Migration to the United States, Centro de Estudios Puertorriqueños, Hunter College, CUNY.

Cover design by Kathryn Houghtaling Lacey

Library of Congress Cataloging-in-Publication Data

        p.   cm.
    Includes bibliographical references and index.
    ISBN 0-8058-2764-1 (cloth) 0-8058-2765-x (paper)
    1. . 2. . 3. . I. . II. .
    LB2822.82.B65 1996
    371.2'00973—dc20   96-18769
                                                     CIP

Printed in the United States of America
10   9   8   7   6   5   4   3   2

This book is dedicated in loving memory of María Engracia Rodríguez de Sánchez (1927–1999), one of the pioneers in educating Puerto Rican students in U.S. Schools. She made us laugh and made us think, and she taught us many things. Her wisdom and courage are an enduring model to all who knew her.

Contents

                                                              vii

Introduction and Overview

Sonia Nieto

Puerto Rican students are no strangers to U.S. schools. As is seen in the chapters that follow, Puerto Ricans have been living in the United States in substantial numbers for about a century; they were in New York City and a handful of other U.S. cities even before then. So, if they are not newcomers, why write a book now about Puerto Rican students in U.S. schools? There are a number of reasons that I began this project several years ago. First, although Puerto Rican students have been attending schools in the continental United States for a significant part of this century, by and large they have not done well. Their achievement levels tend to hover around the lowest in the country, and the drop-out rate from high school tends to be among the highest of any other group. Longevity does not seem to make a major difference.

In addition to dismal educational outcomes for the group as a whole, the case of Puerto Rican students also needs to be studied because of the unique relation between Puerto Rico and the United States. In an age when colonialism is not in vogue, and in fact is downright contemptible in many quarters, Puerto Rico continues to be a colony in almost every way but name (it is officially called a "commonwealth" by the United States). The centenary of the invasion of Puerto Rico by the United States

(1898–1998) seemed a fitting time to take stock of the relation that has existed between them and to assess critically how Puerto Rican children have fared in U.S. schools. This is a major reason for this book.

Puerto Ricans are U.S. citizens and they can travel freely to and from the States. This makes the case of Puerto Ricans unlike that of any other group of immigrants who left home, in most cases never to return. The nearly 3 million Puerto Ricans who currently reside in the United States are a fluid group: some are third or fourth generation, some will arrive tomorrow; some speak only English, some only Spanish, and most a degree of both; some are here to stay, and others go back and forth frequently depending on the economic situation. U.S. citizenship and the back-and-forth migration leave an indelible mark on the experience of Puerto Rican children. Moreover, in an era when the "melting pot" ideology has come under increased criticism, the case of Puerto Ricans stands in sharp contrast to that of other groups who were pressured to assimilate, in the process losing most vestiges of their native languages and cultures. Puerto Ricans are an example of a group no longer willing to trade in its native language and culture for new ones, and it is important to analyze the impact of this situation on their experiences in U.S. schools. Additionally, the cultural fusion that is typical of the Puerto Rican community—where Spanish, English, and combinations of both are used, and where native Puerto Rican culture both melds with and changes U.S. mainstream and U.S. youth urban culture—also needs to be considered. Neither the melting pot nor the "salad bowl" are adequate metaphors for the cultural synthesis occurring in the Puerto Rican community.

Puerto Rican students in U.S. schools have been studied for decades and, as is seen in the chapters in this book, there have been numerous explanations for the relative lack of success they have experienced. And although a number of books have focused on Puerto Rican students, this volume is the first in which so many of the authors are themselves Puerto Ricans, many having had experiences similar to those they write about. My desire to make these personal and professional experiences visible was a basic motivation for undertaking this project.

OVERVIEW

In this book, both scholarly chapters and personal reflections tell the story of Puerto Rican students in U.S. schools. In addition to research studies and policy analyses, a number of short essays are also included. Written by Puerto Ricans from the ages of 15 to 50 who write firsthand about their experiences as students in U.S. schools, these reflections give voice to the many students who have not been given the opportunity to describe what it is like to be a Puerto Rican student in the United States. In Part I, the historical and sociopolitical context of Puerto Rican students in the United States is developed. This section begins with a short poem by el Cortés that describes the experience of one Puerto Rican student. In chapter 1, I give a brief educational history of Puerto Ricans in the United States. I consider a number of recurrent themes in the literature and conclude with implications for teachers, other educators, and policymakers. Chapter 2, by Xaé Alicia Reyes on return migrant students, those who return to the Island after having studied here in the United States, is a fascinating study that demonstrates the kind of discrimination Puerto Rican students face even when returning to the place they may call "home." It also shifts responsibility from just teachers in the United States to island-based teachers to care for Puerto Rican students. In her essay, Gillian Rivera, a high school student, puts a human face on the impact of mobility from the Island to the U.S. mainland and also within cities and towns in the United States. Chapter 3 is a personal and political perspective on educational change in New York City by Luis O. Reyes, a long-time activist and a former member of the New York City Board of Education. His chapter represents the latest stage in the long road of political activism and change in the New York Puerto Rican community.

Identity is an essential issue that repeatedly comes up in the literature on the education of Puerto Ricans, and Part II concerns identity as it is manifested through culture, language, and gender. This section begins with a moving essay by Hipolito Baez on the need to develop a strong sense of self in order to succeed in school. In chapter 4, Catherine Walsh focuses on another aspect of identity, the *imagined community* and how it is developed and maintained by Puerto Rican students and their families. She focuses her analysis on "Mill City," a small northeast city with a large Puerto Rican community. The role of language, whether English or Spanish, has always been a pivotal issue in the education of Puerto Ricans, both in the United States and in Puerto Rico, and it is laden with political and personal meaning. Chapter 5, by Maria V. Zavala, centers on a study among college students concerning the influence of language on Puerto Rican identity, and it confirms that the impact of language continues to be felt even among second and third generation students. Race too has been a central question among Puerto Ricans, and Carlos Mills de Jesus' essay is a poignant reminder that racism continues to exist, both outside the Puerto Rican community and within it as well. Although gender is a key component of identity, the voices of women have been silent in most research about Puerto Rican students. Carmen Rolón bases chapter 6 on her study of young Puerto Rican high school females and how they talk about themselves, their school experiences, and success. In another study focusing on females, Nitza M. Hidalgo (chap. 7), whose work on mothering strategies is well known, extends her research to consider the role of grandmothers on the academic success of Puerto Rican children. Both of these chapters should help educators and policymakers as they think about ways to help young women succeed in school.

Social activism has been an essential characteristic of the Puerto Rican community in the United States for many years, and political action centering on education has been especially evident. The chapters in Part III concentrate on how social activism is manifested in schools and its impact on students' lives. It begins with an essay by Alicia M. López, my daughter, who is now herself a teacher, as she reflects on her experience as a student in "a different kind of school," one that was decidedly political and multicultural. In chapter 8, Diana Caballero, a well-known activist and educator, documents the history and lessons of the Puerto Rico/Latino Education Roundtable, an advocacy group that helped change the educational landscape in New York City. In chapter 9, Melissa Rivera and Pedro Pedraza discuss educational reform in New York City in general, and focus on implications for Puerto Rican students. They offer as a concrete example the local small school reform initiative, and they describe a school that has garnered considerable support in the Puerto Rican community, El Puente Academy for Peace and Justice, in Brooklyn.

Part IV delves more specifically into classroom- and school-based studies and initiatives, and it begins with a poem by "Shaggy" (a.k.a. Jaime Flores), a poet who lives in Massachusetts and whose poem is a facetious reminder that the intelligence of Puerto Rican students is sometimes unacknowledged by teachers and other staff members. In chapter 10, Milga Morales and Elvira R. Tarr, colleagues at Brooklyn College, describe the social action projects they design for students who are being prepared to teach in New York City schools. Through numerous examples, they explain how and why they engage in these projects with their students, and the changes that have occurred as a result. José Manuel Caraballo, a 14-year-old student who attends school in Massachusetts, contributes his perspective that "teachers don't care," and he explains why he has reluctantly concluded that this is so. In contrast, in chapter 11, María Torres-Guzmán and Yvonne Martínez Thorne describe what can happen when students' voices are heard. In an ethnographic study, they provide moving documentation concerning the impact of school policies and practices that encourage student engagement. Elizabeth Capifali follows up with her essay on teachers who did care and how important they were in her life as a student in the South Bronx in the 1950s. Finally, Carmen I. Mercado and Luis C. Moll (chap. 12) conclude the section with two examples of research that builds on the knowledge that students and their families can bring to bear on their education. These cases demonstrate that, although there is no easy answer to improving the education of Puerto Rican students, there are examples of transformative experiences that help students become academically successful.

In Part V, Janice Petrovich Beiso, reflecting on all of the previous chapters and essays, offers her analysis and points to some promising directions for the future.

As educators, we know that many Puerto Rican youngsters have fared poorly in U.S. schools. We also know that some Puerto Rican students have been extraordinarily resilient despite poverty, discrimination, and the other obstacles they may face. What makes the difference? Is it a strong sense of self that helps them withstand the odds? Is it having one teacher who believes in them? What is the impact of particular policies and practices in schools? Has bilingual education helped or hurt? What has been the role of the educational reform movement of the past several years? Do students' families make the difference? If so, how? Puerto Ricans are incredibly diverse, and as is shown in this book, there are no easy answers to these questions. But the insights and findings discussed by this group of talented authors provide partial answers to this very complex problem. What is undeniable is that much more needs to be done than is currently the case. Too many Puerto Rican students are still dropping out and disengaging from school. Most of them are capable of becoming successful learners as well as productive citizens and leaders of their communities and of the United States. In order for this to happen, teachers, schools, and communities all need to respond to the grave challenges ahead.

ACKNOWLEDGMENTS

As often happens, this book took much longer to complete than I ever expected. Organizing a group of educator-activists is no easy task, and it became even more difficult when I was thousands of miles away on sabbatical. But this was a project about which we all felt passionate. The lives of the authors—Puerto Rican or not, young people or seasoned activists, students, teachers, or researchers—are written into the chapters because we know what it is like when schools give up on Puerto Rican youngsters or when Puerto Ricans themselves give up on education. We also know the terrible toll that this takes on our society. I want to thank all of the authors for staying the course, for writing and rewriting and rethinking and rewriting again. I know that their words will be an inspiration to a new generation of Puerto Rican students and to all those who believe in and work with them. I am also grateful to all the Puerto Rican and non-Puerto Rican pioneers from the early decades of the 20th century to the 1970s—those teachers and writers, activists, and scholars—who gave voice to the struggles of the Puerto Rican community and their children, and who paved the way for those of us who continue their work.

I also want to acknowledge the assistance of Elizabeth Capifali, who was tremendously helpful while I was on sabbatical, and Lori Mestre, reference librarian at the University of Massachusetts W.E.B. DuBois Library, who helped me find many of the resources I needed. As always, I give special thanks to my compañero, Angel, who brings so much light to my life, and to my children and grandchildren, who are the inspiration for my work.

I

HISTORICAL
AND SOCIOPOLITICAL CONTEXT

I Remember

by el Cortés

I remember kindergarten
I remember having to say good-bye to Mami
I remember crying
I remember not understanding the teacher
I remember the English lessons with pretty Miss Powell
who made the boxy words fit just right in my mouth without pain
I remember the teachers who said, "You don't look Puerto Rican,"
expecting to hear me say thank you very much
I remember overhearing some saying Puerto Ricans
don't care about their children, Puerto Ricans aren't clean
I remember the heat of shame rising up, changing the color of my face
I remember praying no one heard what the teachers said, praying
no one see my hurt red as a broken heart
I remember Mr. Seidman in the 4th grade and how he chose
me for a big part in the school play
I remember feeling important
I remember memorizing all those lines and Mami helping me
I remember both Mr. Seidman and Mami smiling, proud—
looking at me!—the night of the performance
I remember making the audience laugh and the applause
I remember moving to Flatbush from Fort Greene—
from a fifth floor walk-up to our very own house
I remember going from Girls' High to Erasmus Hall
I remember going from smart to borderline in one day
I remember the bio teacher, Miss Nash, calling me stupid
because I didn't know how to use a microscope
I remember Mr. and Mrs. Hamberger
I remember how I laughed when I heard I was getting
one for political science and the other for economics
I remember being amazed when they made learning a wonder-filled adventure
I remember working hard for them both and the faith each had in me
I remember the A's I got in their classes
I remember being Puerto Rican in Erasmus Hall High School
because I was the only one—until my sister followed—on the academic track
I remember the guidance counselor advising me to be
a bilingual secretary because I certainly was not college material
I remember Papi, with his third grade education, saying,
"Lidin, tu puedes hacer lo que quieres. Yo te apoyo en todo. Siempre."

3

1

Puerto Rican Students in U.S. Schools: A Brief History

Sonia Nieto

School systems that don't care, no matter their expertise, are hardly school systems at all, because very little "schooling"—teaching and learning—occurs within them. Things will get no better until the schools face up to their obligations and decide that what needs improvement is not their image but their performance. Meanwhile, they forfeit their responsibilities, just as the children forfeit their hopes and the nation forfeits its future. We are all the losers.

—Margolis (1968, p.15)

Written over 30 years ago, this rather bleak assessment of schools' responses to Puerto Rican students still rings true today in far too many cases. In spite of the many changes that have taken place in the intervening years, many schools remain alienating places for Puerto Rican youngsters, who continue to fail and drop out at alarming rates. Unfortunately, many educators in the United States are still unaware of their Puerto Rican students' history, experiences, dreams, and strengths and of how they might be used to teach these children more effectively.

Who are the Puerto Ricans and what are they doing in U.S. schools? How long have they been here and how have they fared? And why is it important for teachers, other educators, policymakers, and the public at large to know these things? Given the recent centenary of the takeover of

Puerto Rico by the United States as a result of the Spanish–American War (1898–1998), the colonization of the Island, and the subsequent massive diaspora of the Puerto Rican people to the United States during this century, it is a particularly appropriate historical moment in which to investigate these and related issues.

In this chapter, I attempt to answer the preceding questions by briefly reviewing the history of Puerto Ricans in the United States in general and in U.S. schools in particular. First, I explain how colonization and migration have affected the education of Puerto Ricans in the United States. The chapter also provides a historical and critical context within which to understand the remainder of the chapters in this book. (Readers interested in delving into this history in depth are urged to read more comprehensive accounts such as Walsh, 1991, and Nieto, 1995). I conclude the chapter with educational implications for teachers, other educators, and policymakers.

COLONIALISM, MIGRATION, AND EDUCATION

No matter what one's ideological or political stance may be, the history of the Puerto Rican people is U.S. history because the two nations have been intertwined for over a century. Yet virtually nothing is taught in most U.S. schools about the Island's history, its formal relationship with the United States since 1898, or the reasons for the massive migration of the Puerto Rican people. Because Latino[1] children are the fastest growing ethnic group in U.S. public schools (National Center for Education Statistics [NCES], 1995), this information is crucial if these children are to be well served by the schools. Colonialism, migration, and education are inextricably linked in the case of Puerto Ricans, and this connection needs to be analyzed.

According to the U.S. Census Bureau, Puerto Ricans represent about 15% of the total Latino population, second only to Mexican Americans. In 1990, Puerto Ricans living in the United States numbered 2,651,815 (Institute for Puerto Rican Policy, 1992). By 1996, the number was estimated to be 3,123,000, a dramatic increase in just a few years (Institute for Puerto Rican Policy, 1998). Put another way, nearly one half of all Puerto Ricans now live in the United States, probably one of the most dra-

---

[1]In this chapter, the terms Latino and Hispanic are used at times to designate the broad category that includes Puerto Ricans, Mexicans, Mexican Americans, Cubans, Dominicans, and Central and South Americans. Because much of the data about Puerto Ricans are not available separately, I sometimes use data that refer to Latinos/Hispanics in general. Whenever possible, however, I use data specific to Puerto Ricans.

matic diasporas of any people in the world. But no matter where Puerto Ricans reside, they are all U.S. citizens. According to sociologist Clara Rodriguez (1991), since 1898 all Puerto Ricans can be considered to have been "born in the U.S.A." This is true whether they live in Puerto Rico or in the United States because they have been subject to U.S. policies as a result of the change of sovereignty from one colonial power, Spain, to another, the United States.

The Impact of Colonial Status

The colonial status of Puerto Rico implies that all Puerto Ricans, even those on the Island, have been educated in U.S.-controlled schools since 1898. The mandate by the U.S. Congress that Puerto Rican children learn English and the "American way of life" (Negrón de Montilla, 1971; Osuna, 1949) became apparent in schools on the Island soon after the takeover: U.S. ideals were, and continue to be, instilled through U.S. textbooks, materials, methods, language policies, and teacher preparation practices and through the celebration of U.S. holidays, including, paradoxically, United States Independence Day. According to Juan José Osuna (1949), shortly after 1898, the average Puerto Rican child knew more about George Washington, Abraham Lincoln, and Betsy Ross than the average child in the United States.

Given its status as a colony of larger world powers for almost 500 years, Puerto Rico has always been at the mercy of policies and practices over which it has had little control. This experience has left its mark on the educational experiences of Puerto Rican students as well. John Ogbu's theory concerning the nature of voluntary and involuntary immigration is helpful in understanding this phenomenon (Ogbu, 1987). Ogbu characterized Puerto Ricans as *involuntary minorities* because of Puerto Rico's relationship to the United States as a colony. According to his theory, a group's political situation in the host society and its perceptions of opportunities available in that society influence its educational achievement to a far greater degree than simple cultural differences. Hence, the major academic problem for U.S. Puerto Ricans is not that they possess a different language, culture, or cognitive or communication style, but rather the nature of the history, subjugation, and exploitation they have experienced together with their own responses to their treatment. Research with newly arrived Puerto Rican and Mexican students seems to confirm this theory: These students are significantly more academically successful and have higher self-esteem than those born in the United States (Adams, Astone, Nuñez-Wormack, & Smodlaka, 1994). However, Ogbu's theory fails to explain why some students succeed whereas others do not. Issues such as race and social class, among others, are also at work. That is, because Puerto Ricans are racially mixed, racism in the U.S. context has consistently influenced their educational experiences. Moreover, most Puerto Ricans are poor, and they live in deteriorating inner-city neighborhoods where their children are confined to poorly financed and overburdened schools (Orfield, Bachmeier, James, & Eitle, 1997).

The colonial experience has led to a circulatory migration, creating what have been called "the students in between," those who spend time on both the Island and the mainland (Quality Education for Minorities Project, 1990). For example, between 1969 and 1973, 51,000 Puerto Rican youngsters went from Puerto Rico to New York City, and another 63,000 traveled in the opposite direction. In addition, about 30% of all New York City Puerto Rican students reported between one and four changes in schools between Grades 7 and 9 (Quality Education for Minorities Project, 1990). Special programs and policies to help ease the transition from the Island to the mainland or vice versa have often been suggested (Gallardo, 1970; Morrison, 1958; Rivera-Medina, 1984; Santiago-Santiago, 1986), although they have never been fully implemented.

Uniqueness of the Puerto Rican Migration

The history of Puerto Ricans in the United States is different from that of all other groups. It cannot be understood without considering the reasons that brought Puerto Ricans here in the first place. Puerto Rico and the United States are connected through colonial ties, and this gives the migration a unique character. According to Clara Rodriguez, that Puerto Rico and the United States were joined as a result of "an act of conquest" is frequently overlooked or minimized in the literature, with Puerto Ricans generally perceived as simply one of the latest newcomers in the traditional conception of the immigration experience (Rodriguez, 1991). But given the unique status of Puerto Rico, the migration of Puerto Ricans has been unlike any other (History Task Force, 1982). For one, they represent the first group of newcomers to arrive as citizens. Most often the term *migration* rather than *immigration* has been used to describe the Puerto Rican experience (although some writers prefer the term *[im]migration* because of its unique hybrid character; see Marquez, 1995). Second, Puerto Rican migration was the first "jet-age" movement to the United States. Travel to and from the Island was relatively easy and inexpensive with the increasing accessibility of air travel beginning in the 1940s, the period that has been called "the Great Migration" (Sánchez Korrol, 1983). Third, the major Puerto Rican migration occurred at a time when technical and professional skills were becoming far more important than had been the case with previous immigrants. As a result, Puerto Rican migrants' low levels of education placed them at a unique disadvantage (Fitzpatrick, 1971/1987). In addition, because Puerto Rican migration is defined by a back-and-forth movement, it has been dubbed "the revolving door," "circulatory migration" (Bonilla & Campos, 1981), or "a process of Puerto Rican commuting" (Fitzpatrick, 1971/1987).

Puerto Ricans were made U.S. citizens in 1917. (However, citizenship was neither requested nor particularly desired by the Puerto Rican people. In fact, both houses of the Puerto Rican legislature had previously asked that the Puerto Rican people be given the right to choose their own destiny; see Wagenheim & Jímenez de Wagenheim, 1973). As U.S. citizens, Puerto Ricans can travel freely to and from the United States and they have come in large numbers since the beginning of the century to seek better economic opportunities for their families (Fitzpatrick, 1971/1987; History Task Force, 1982; Sánchez Korrol, 1983). All Puerto Ricans have been affected by the migration: At least one third of the population at one time or another has lived in the continental United States, most of them for periods of less than 10 years (Cafferty & Rivera-Martínez, 1981).

As a group, however, Puerto Ricans are not new migrants; they have lived in the continental United States for well over a century. By 1830, there was a Sociedad Benéfica Cubana y Puertorriqueña (translated at the time as the Spanish Benevolent Society) comprised primarily of Puerto Rican and Cuban merchants in New York City (Sánchez Korrol, 1983). An important segment of the early Puerto Rican community consisted of political activists, especially those supporting independence for Cuba and Puerto Rico and dedicated to an Antillean federation. A small group of these activists found their way to New York City by the 1860s, where they published newspapers and started political and civic organizations. By the early 1900s, skilled craftspeople and unskilled workers, particularly in the tobacco industry, had migrated to Florida and New York. Thus, even before they officially became U.S. citizens, Puerto Ricans resided in the continental United States. By 1910, there were already over 1,000 Puerto Ricans living in 39 states and Hawaii, and by 1920, Puerto Ricans could be found in 45 states (Puerto Rican Forum, 1970; Sánchez Korrol, 1983). By 1957, 550,000 or a quarter of all the Puerto Rican people lived in the United States (Rand, 1958).

Overpopulation on the Island has been the conventional explanation for Puerto Rican migration to the United States (Fitzpatrick, 1971/1987), but this has more recently been discounted as too simplistic (Rodriguez, 1991; Sánchez Korrol, 1983). Other explanations include the impact of dramatic structural economic changes that virtually destroyed traditional patterns of individual land ownership and consolidated the domination of large corporations from the United States. This situation has persisted: at present, 70% of Puerto Rican industries are owned by U.S. corporations (Hidalgo, 1992). Structural changes have resulted in high levels of unemployment and the growth of a marginal work force on the Island. Puerto Rican migration to the United States has been more accurately described as a "push–pull" phenomenon, and the U.S. economy has acted as both a "pull" and a "push" factor. A 1950 study, for instance, documented that the ups and downs of the U.S. economy and the waves of migration from Puerto Rico had been highly correlated since 1908 (Mills, Wright, & Goldsen, 1950).

An example of a pull factor has been the direct recruitment of Puerto Rican workers to the United States and elsewhere. Early recruitment efforts resulted in Puerto Ricans settling as far away as Hawaii where, in 1903, 539 children were enrolled in Hawaiian schools (History Task Force, 1982). Many Puerto Rican communities in the United States began as a result of former agricultural workers remaining and bringing other family members with them (Cordacco & Bucchioni, 1968; Fitzpatrick, 1971/1987). The contract farm worker program that began in 1940 was another important source of migrants, resulting in an average of 20,000 workers coming every year to harvest crops in such diverse states as Michigan, New Jersey, Connecticut, and Massachusetts. These arrangements continued into the 1970s in formal contracts, and they still occur informally.

Although many Puerto Rican migrants came as agricultural workers, most Puerto Ricans have lived in urban areas, primarily in the northeast. New York has more Puerto Ricans than any other city in the world. Only 37% of Puerto Ricans who lived in the United States at the beginning of the 20th century were concentrated in New York City, but by 1940, 85% were residing there (Sánchez Korrol, 1983) and most were living in East Harlem, also known as El Barrio or Spanish Harlem. By 1948, some 200,000 Puerto Ricans lived in New York City. Although they were largely concentrated in New York City between 1940 and 1960, Puerto Ricans have dispersed throughout the northeast since then. By 1955, as many as 175,000 Puerto Ricans were estimated to live in cities outside of New York, with another half million in New York City itself (Padilla, 1958). In 1990, over 60% of all Puerto Ricans in the United States resided outside of New York State (Institute for Puerto Rican Policy, 1992). Although the actual number of Puerto Ricans in the United States has increased steadily throughout the century, return migration has sometimes surpassed the numbers coming into the country (Meléndez, 1991).

Consequences of Circulatory Migration

The circulatory migration of Puerto Ricans has had two major consequences. First, because Puerto Ricans are already citizens and because of the ease of getting back and forth, there has been no need to sever ties with the home country, contrary to the experiences of most immigrants. This experience has provided a cultural and linguistic continuity not afforded previous or even more recent immigrants, and it has been manifested by a practical need for continued use of the Spanish language and the maintenance of cultural patterns. Examples of this cultural maintenance abound. For instance, the first major study of bilingualism among Puerto Ricans based on a series of interviews with community leaders revealed that they placed great importance on maintaining and speaking Spanish and identifying as Puerto Ricans (Fishman et al., 1971). A more recent study focusing on bilingualism among Puerto Ricans in New York City concluded that there is tremendous allegiance to maintaining the Spanish language as a marker of identity (Durán, 1983).

Another effect of the circulatory migration for Puerto Ricans has been to redefine immigration from "a single life-transforming experience" to "a way of life" (National Puerto Rican Task Force, 1982). Circulatory migration has been disruptive in terms of schooling and mobility, but it has also reframed migration as a normal experience in which cultural patterns are renewed, transformed, and recreated, and it has redefined Puerto Ricans not as traditional immigrants but as "a community in movement" in "a process of commuting" (Fitzpatrick, 1971/1987). Although for the majority of Europeans immigration was a new beginning, for many Puerto Ricans migration has tended to be a series of periodic movements to and from the Island. Consequently, what Puerto Ricans as a group expect of U.S. schools is not assimilation, but rather accommodation to, and even the protection and maintenance of, their language and culture. Although many Puerto Ricans dream of returning to the Island, and in fact many do move back and forth, Puerto Ricans as a community are in the United States to stay. Therefore, it is necessary for teachers to study and become aware of the unique characteristics and experiences of Puerto Rican students.

EDUCATIONAL EXPERIENCES OF PUERTO RICANS IN THE UNITED STATES

As a subgroup in the United States, Puerto Ricans have fared worse than Whites and African Americans in educational outcomes and among the worst compared to other Latino groups, and this has been true for many years (Carrasquillo, 1991; Latino Commission on Educational Reform, 1994; Meier & Stewart, 1991; NCES, 1995). It is necessary at this point to note a shortcoming concerning the available data: Because Puerto Ricans are usually categorized within the larger framework of Hispanic or Latino rather than through their particular national origin, data specific to

Puerto Ricans are often hard to find. A graphic example of this problem
will suffice: Although more than a third of all Latino children, compared
to just one eighth of White children, live in poverty, Puerto Rican children
have the far greatest risk of being poor of any other Latino group, with an
extraordinarily high 58% living in poverty (ASPIRA Institute for Policy
Research, 1993; National Council of La Raza [NCLR], 1991, 1993). This
situation is primarily due to the fact that for Puerto Ricans, there are more
households headed by single mothers than is true for any other group of
Latinos.

General data concerning Latinos can nevertheless be helpful because
they provide a glimpse into the distressing conditions faced by the entire
community, regardless of national origin. For instance, many Latinos live
in poverty, and the relationship between poverty and schooling tends to
be very strong. Because many Latino youngsters are poor, their educational outcomes also tend to be quite low. For example, the NCES (1993)
found a significant correlation between social class and dropping out of
high school: Among high-income students the dropout rate is 6%, among
the middle-income it is 23.3% and among the poor it is 41.3% (NCES,
1993). Furthermore, less money is spent on Latino students than on other
groups of students in the United States. Large urban school districts,
which are 27% Latino, tend to be chronically underfunded, spending an
average of $5,200 per pupil in 1991, compared with $6,073 for suburban
schools (ASPIRA Institute for Policy Research, 1993). And because most
Latinos live in large and impoverished urban centers, they are now significantly more segregated than African American students. As a result, they
experience more concentration in high poverty schools than any other
group of students (Orfield et al., 1997). The impact of social class on Latinos was summed up by Earl Shorris (1992, p. 216): "No matter what else
influences the educational lives of Latino children, class is almost always
the determining factor."

Thus, despite many differences among them, some issues affect a great
many Latinos regardless of their specific national origin. In addition, the
longer that Latinos live in the United States, the more likely they are to
develop a pan-Latino identity. This is true for several reasons, not the least
of which is increased mobility among all Latino populations. That is, it is
no longer true that Mexican Americans live exclusively in the southwest
or Puerto Ricans in the northeast; now there are Mexican American migrant farm workers in Massachusetts and a growing Puerto Rican community in Los Angeles. This mobility, along with the impact of
Spanish-language mass media, interethnic marriages among Latinos, and
common experiences and problems, has created a greater identification
with a pan-Latino identity among many, especially younger, Latinos. For

these reasons, although data on educational outcomes for Puerto Rican students were largely disaggregated in the early years of their experiences in the United States, this has not been the case in the past several decades.

Early Experiences

That Puerto Ricans have faced tremendous problems in U.S. schools has been recognized for many years, but how these problems have been identified and defined over the years has varied. For example, much of the early literature was replete with references to the "Puerto Rican problem," thus placing the blame squarely on the background, culture, family, language, and social class of Puerto Rican students (Nieto, 1995). The existence of the Puerto Rican problem was defined as early as the 1930s, with the claim of a report from the New York City Chamber of Commerce in 1935 that Puerto Rican children were "slow learners" based on the results of an experiment in which 240 Puerto Rican children were given intelligence tests (Sánchez Korrol, 1994). The release of this report was met by fierce rebuttals from the community, and this became, according to Sánchez Korrol, a primary issue addressed by Vito Marcantonio, the much loved Italian-American politician who represented Spanish Harlem for many years. In what was probably the first challenge to the discriminatory effects of standardized tests for Puerto Rican youngsters, Marcantonio concluded that the tests made inadequate allowances for the social, economic, linguistic, and environmental factors of Puerto Rican children's lives. Until the 1960s, Puerto Ricans were almost invisible in the many commissions, reports, and studies carried out in their name. In addition, during the first years of advocacy for Puerto Rican students, most Puerto Ricans who were hired filled low-level, low-status, and substitute positions. For example, the first major report on Puerto Ricans in the New York City schools recommended creating the position of 10 such positions city-wide. Other teaching personnel (OTPs) who were hired to teach English to Puerto Ricans, and Puerto Rican coordinators, teachers at the junior high school level, were added to these specialists and they numbered 50 city-wide by 1954 (Morrison, 1958).

The Puerto Rican Study was the next significant report to address the educational progress of Puerto Rican students in New York City. A massive project conducted from 1953 to 1957, *The Puerto Rican Study* investigated the education and adjustment of Puerto Rican students in the public schools, who by that time numbered over 53,000 (Morrison, 1958). The major objectives of the study were to gather accurate data on the number and characteristics of Puerto Rican pupils in New York City schools and to determine the most effective methods and materials for teaching them

English. As a result of this extensive, $1 million study, six reports and 16 resource unit volumes were generated, and 23 short- and long-range recommendations, many of which were to be repeated in the next 40 years, were made. The lack of Puerto Rican voices in the study no doubt affected how problems were defined as well as the recommendations that were made. *The Puerto Rican Study* had only one Puerto Rican among the 17 advisory panel members (Morrison, 1958). Nevertheless, one of its major accomplishments was to upgrade the teaching of English as a second language (ESL), setting the stage for the increase of Puerto Ricans in the schools as aides, community liaisons, teachers, and counselors. Their appearance in the schools marked the first time that a real Puerto Rican presence—especially of women—could be felt in the New York City educational system (Sánchez Korrol, 1994).

The growth of Puerto Rican organizations in the 1950s was an early indication of the community's efforts to self-define. Self-help and advocacy groups invariably centered on education. In the mid-1950s, a group of young Puerto Rican professionals established the Puerto Rican–Hispanic Leadership Forum (now the National Puerto Rican Forum), a community-wide organization to promote their interests in New York City (ASPIRA Association, 1991; Fitzgerald, 1971). Chief among them was Antonia Pantoja, called the "inspiration and guiding spirit" of these early movements (Fitzgerald, 1971). A Puerto Rican social worker, Pantoja was born in Puerto Rico and raised and educated in New York City, working her way up as a factory worker, artist, student, and teacher (ASPIRA Association, 1991). Many educational and social reform efforts of the past 4 decades can be traced to her vision, and she has remained a formidable model of strength and perseverance in the Puerto Rican community.

The Community Develops its Voice:
The 1960s and 1970s

A primary example of the kind of organization that reflected the growing self-awareness and incipient spirit of self-determination of these years was ASPIRA. Deriving its name from a Spanish word meaning "to aspire," ASPIRA was founded by the Puerto Rican Forum in 1961 to promote education among Puerto Rican youths. As the primary agency promoting the educational rights of Puerto Ricans in the United States, ASPIRA motivates countless youths to continue their education by providing educational guidance and leadership in schools and communities. ASPIRA has also been instrumental in promoting higher education for Puerto Rican youth through the establishment of clubs in high schools (where student members become *Aspirantes*) and many Puerto Ricans who have become leaders in their communities trace their success to their involvement with ASPIRA. With national headquarters in Washington since 1985, ASPIRA has affiliates in six states and Puerto Rico and has expanded its services to other Latinos besides Puerto Ricans, and even to non-Latinos in the neighborhoods it serves (ASPIRA Association, 1991).

Other grass-roots, educational, and political organizations that have emerged over the past 3 decades echo the theme of self-determination begun in the early part of the century (Sánchez Korrol, 1983, 1994) but most evident in the 1960s. These include the National Puerto Rican Coalition in Washington, D.C., and in New York City, which is still the location with the largest and most influential Puerto Rican community, the Institute for Puerto Rican Policy; the Puerto Rican Educators Association; the National Congress for Puerto Rican Rights; the Puerto Rican/Latino Education Roundtable; the Puerto Rican Legal Defense and Education Fund; and El Puente. The National Council of La Raza and the Hispanic Policy Development Project, both located in Washington, D.C., although not focused exclusively on Puerto Ricans, include them in an important way.

In spite of the growth and visibility of the Puerto Rican community, however, educational outcomes worsened. For example, by 1960, only 13% of Puerto Ricans 25 years and older had completed high school and more than half had less than an eighth-grade education (Puerto Rican Forum, 1970). A 1961 study of a Manhattan community found that fewer than 10% of Puerto Rican children in third grade were reading at grade level or above (Puerto Rican Forum, 1970). In 1963, a minuscule number of Puerto Ricans graduated from New York City high schools with academic diplomas (331, or 1.6% of the 21,000 academic diplomas granted), this at a time when the total Puerto Rican school population was over 150,000 (Fitzpatrick, 1971/1987). Of these 331, only 28 went on to college (Cafferty & Rivera-Martínez, 1981). Outside of New York City, the situation was even worse. For instance, between 1966 and 1969, only 4 Puerto Rican students graduated from the Boston public schools (Cafferty & Rivera-Martínez, 1981). A 1972 study in Massachusetts estimated that at least 2,500 Puerto Rican children in Boston were not attending school and that a third of all students in one Springfield junior high school quit before going on to high school (Massachusetts State Advisory Committee, 1972). The educational condition of Puerto Rican students was thoroughly documented in an important early edited volume (Cordasco & Bucchioni, 1968).

The worsening educational situation for Puerto Ricans changed how these issues were addressed in the community, and this was apparent in three major ways. First, educators and community activists began to challenge more aggressively the melting pot and "cultural deprivation" models and other negative characterizations of their community. As a result, boycotts and other protests for quality education became common during the 1950s and 1960s, especially in New York City. Second, there were initial although somewhat tentative demands for programs such as bilingual education, ethnic studies, and cross-cultural education because a new paradigm of cultural and linguistic inclusion was beginning to form. Third, demands were made to involve more Puerto Rican educators, parents, and policymakers in the educational decisions that would impact Puerto Rican students.

The First Citywide Conference of the Puerto Rican Community had substantial community involvement and took place in April 1967 in New York City (Office of the Mayor, 1968). Thirty-two recommendations, many similar or identical to those made previously by *The Puerto Rican Study,* were submitted to the mayor of New York City. The new recommendations reflected the changes in the political climate of the 1960s and the larger Puerto Rican membership of the conference. Among these were bilingual programs and courses in Puerto Rican culture, literature, and history. Bilingual and ethnic studies education was also a feature of the ASPIRA Symposium of 1968, *Hemos Trabajado Bien* (ASPIRA of New York, 1968), a conference on the education of Puerto Ricans and Mexican Americans that received widespread national attention and for which an investigative report was commissioned (Margolis, 1968). Titled *The Losers,* the report served as a common starting point for understanding the status of the education of Puerto Rican youth. Visiting 16 schools in seven cities with large Puerto Rican communities, Margolis found high drop-out and low attendance rates, poor academic achievement, and teachers and administrators who were uninformed and unsympathetic to the plight of Puerto Rican students. The report signaled a new emphasis in parent involvement, an issue that was to become a hallmark of all subsequent efforts that centered on the education of Puerto Ricans. The report's findings concerning poor record keeping, biased and uninspired teaching, and low expectations of Puerto Rican students were compelling. The report concluded that the longer Puerto Rican children attended public school in the United States, the less they learned.

Even though leaders in the Puerto Rican community had rejected the melting pot ideology by the 1960s, schools continued to reflect the conventional wisdom that the assimilation of Puerto Rican students was essential for their academic achievement. A 1965 ethnographic study by Eugene Bucchioni revealed in devastating detail the daily and consistent pressures toward assimilation that took place in schools in New York City with large Puerto Rican populations (Bucchioni, 1982). The researcher undertook extensive observations in a number of classrooms, and he used the case of "Miss Dwight" for detailed analysis and discussion. In her classroom, assimilationist pressures were evident in curriculum content, teaching methods, and other messages to children about the inherent lack of worth of their experiences and culture. These negative messages included admonitions about not speaking Spanish, choosing the best students to be "Mr. and Mrs. America" for the morning pledge to the flag, and a discussion about what constitutes a nutritious diet (in which no Puerto Rican foods were included), among other lessons. During the 1960s, it was becoming clear to many educators that the cumulative effect of such practices could be disastrous for young people struggling to maintain a sense of integrity in a hostile dominant culture.

The messages in both the expressed and the hidden curriculum emphasized that everything associated with the lives of Puerto Rican youth—their native language, foods, lifestyles, music, and even their parents—was somehow lacking and deficient. Children's literature is a good example: Research on the images of Puerto Ricans in children's books and school textbooks documented that especially those published before the 1980s tended to be full of stereotypes as well as racist, sexist, and assimilationist themes (Council on Interracial Books for Children, 1972; Nieto, 1983, 1997). Puerto Ricans from the Island were not exempt from the belief that simply learning English would by itself solve the educational problems of Puerto Rican youngsters. A conference on the education of Puerto Rican children living in the United States that took place in Puerto Rico in 1970 exemplified this stance (Gallardo, 1970). The conference organizers, largely educators from Puerto Rico, presented a viewpoint of great naiveté, suggesting that within the next 25 years Puerto Ricans would know English sufficiently well that bilingual programs would no longer be needed (Gallardo, 1970). These educators were clearly unprepared for the more militant Puerto Rican educators from the mainland, who demanded that the format of the conference be changed to include their perspectives because educators from the Island were unaware of, and in some cases unsympathetic to, the reality of Puerto Ricans in the States.

Later in the decade, the U.S. Commission on Civil Rights conducted a series of regional studies and open meetings and issued a far-reaching influential national report on the condition of Puerto Ricans in the United States (U.S. Commission on Civil Rights, 1976). This report was noteworthy for a number of reasons. First, it represented the first time a federal government agency other than the Census Bureau had focused specifically on the mainland Puerto Rican population. Second, it was the first report to accurately document the tremendous poverty and high levels of unemployment among Puerto Ricans. Third, the report was the first to comprehensively document the educational status of Puerto Ricans in the entire country. Specifically, the report found a severely undereducated population and an educational establishment that consistently failed to respond to the needs of the Puerto Rican community. The report also documented the catastrophic drop-out problem among Puerto Ricans, including a dropout rate of over 70% in Chicago (U.S. Commission on Civil Rights, 1976).

This report was notable in its insistence that school policies and practices contributed significantly to the failure of Puerto Rican students, rather than using the traditional explanation of "cultural deprivation" to explain such failure. It joined other early attempts to redefine the problem of Puerto Rican children's underachievement in a more comprehensive way (ASPIRA of New York, 1968; Cordasko & Bucchioni, 1968; Margolis, 1968). It documented how tracking, I.Q. and achievement tests, assignment practices, little support for parent and community involvement, and insensitive teachers and counselors unfairly jeopardized Puerto Rican students, and it highlighted how Puerto Rican and other low-income students had unequal access to quality education compared to middle-class and wealthier students. A focus on school policies and practices represented a fundamental shift from the "blaming the victim" paradigm (Ryan, 1972) that had been the norm, and it signaled a new systemic way of looking at the problems that Puerto Ricans were having in school. The U.S. Commission on Civil Rights report was also significant because it redefined language and cultural differences as potential assets rather than liabilities.

Examples of Militancy During the 1960s and 1970s

The growing educational militancy that developed in Puerto Rican communities can be understood as part of the larger civil rights movement in the country. In what follows, I use two examples to help illustrate these developments. The first concerns the struggle for equal educational opportunity through decentralization in two cases in New York City, and the second describes the prominence of bilingual education in the Puerto Rican community's struggle for civil rights.

The Struggle for Equal Educational Opportunity in New York City. The decentralization battle began in Intermediate School 201 in Harlem and District 1 on the Lower East Side (Fuentes, 1976; Gittell, 1972; U.S. Commission on Civil Rights, 1976). Along with African Americans, Puerto Ricans had demanded two-way integration since the 1950s.

Intermediate School 201, a new school built in 1966 in Harlem, was to be the setting for this long-awaited integration. But because they feared an exodus of White students from the public schools, neither the mayor nor the Board of Education pursued integration and this set the stage for parent demands to control the school to guarantee quality education.

The boycotts and prolonged community activism that followed led to the establishment of three experimental school districts in New York City: I.S. 201, Two Bridges, and Ocean-Hill Brownsville. Parents and other community members were to have a major voice in the educational decisions affecting their children in these districts (Gittell, 1972). Puerto Rican students were a significant population in each of these schools. The combined power of the Board of Education and the United Federation of Teachers was able to largely crush these grass-roots movements, but they nevertheless left an important legacy. For example, one of the first bilingual programs established without federal or state support was set up as a minischool in Ocean-Hill Brownsville in 1968 (Fuentes, 1980; Rubinstein, 1970; Wasserman, 1969). Although the federal government had bilingual education legislation on the books for 2 years, this program was established largely due to parent demands. Parents also helped select the staff and determine the focus of the curriculum (Rubinstein, 1970).

Two Bridges, a community in lower Manhattan, was the setting for another important educational movement in the early 1970s in which Puerto Ricans were well represented (Fantini & Magat, 1970). This neighborhood, known as Community District 1, became the setting for one of the longest and most bitterly fought campaigns for the rights of Puerto Rican and other community students and parents (Fuentes, 1976, 1980). Once parents and other activists secured control of the majority of seats on the school board, they made immediate changes, including hiring Luis Fuentes (the principal in the Ocean-Hill Brownsville school who had begun the bilingual program a number of years before) as community superintendent. They also hired more Latino, African American, and Chinese American personnel and instituted educational programs such as bilingual education and a systematized reading program (Fuentes, 1976).

The teachers' union, the United Federation of Teachers (UFT), greeted these changes with skepticism and fear. The UFT claimed that because of the campaign waged by the community, the schools had become "arenas of political extremism, racism and patronage" (Shanker, 1973, p. E11). Although the UFT-backed coalition called itself the "Brotherhood Slate," it ran in the 1973 and 1974 elections a total of 17 White and only 1 Black candidate, despite the fact that the district's pupil population was 73% Puerto Rican and only 6% White. In addition, none of these candidates had children in the public schools. Grass-roots elements of the local

Puerto Rican community organized an opposing parent slate that consisted of 4 Puerto Ricans, 2 African Americans, 1 Chinese citizen, and 1 White citizen, all parents of children in the district's public school system. This slate was termed "separatist" by the opposition (Fuentes, 1976).

The UFT spent more than $100,000 to the parent slate's $4,000, and by 1974, the community school board was restored to a White majority and the controversial Luis Fuentes, who had been supported by most residents of the community, was fired. Despite these setbacks, District 1 had struggled and in some ways even flourished as an educational experiment as new and innovative programs were started, including hiring bilingual Chinese and Spanish-language teachers, the development of interviewing and hiring committees that included parents and students, and a school lunch program selected and supervised by parents (Fuentes, 1976).

Bilingual Education in the Puerto Rican Community.   Integrated schools remained the primary focus for achieving educational equality in the African American community, but this was not generally the case for Puerto Rican and other Latino communities. Integration was viewed as a largely Black/White issue, and Puerto Ricans and others who did not fit neatly into these categories were often excluded from consideration. In addition, language maintenance was becoming a much more central issue to most Puerto Ricans. As a result, bilingual education became the cornerstone of educational equality for Puerto Ricans and other Latinos (Báez, Fernández, Navarro, & Rice, 1986). Most language minority communities began to view bilingual education as their major civil rights issue because it represented the best guarantee that youngsters who did not speak English would be educated in a language they understood. Moreover, parents, community activists, and educators began to fear that through the hidden and expressed curriculum and the educational power of the media, young Puerto Ricans were being taught to reject the values of their own communities, including their language and culture. For most Puerto Ricans, getting a good education and remaining who they are have always been equally important goals.

Activism concerning bilingual education in the Puerto Rican community resulted in programs in specific schools such as Ocean-Hill Brownsville and P.S. 25 in the Bronx, the first bilingual school in the northeast, established in 1968 (Fuentes, 1976; LaFontaine et al., 1973). At the national level, protests and demands among activists in the Mexican American, Puerto Rican, American Indian, and other language minority communities led to the passage of the Bilingual Education Act of 1967 (part of the Elementary and Secondary Education Act of 1968), which provided funding for a small number of demonstration projects throughout the country (Bilingual Education Act of 1967, 1968). This act provided for a program of instruction that would enable students to achieve equal proficiency in English and their native language, develop pride in and awareness of their cultural heritage, and increase their academic achievement. State-level activism on the part of Puerto Ricans and others in Massachusetts led to the passage of Chapter 71A, the first state law to mandate bilingual education, which in turn became the model for virtually every other state-mandated law in the country (Bureau of Transitional Bilingual Education, 1971).

State and national legislatures, and the local and federal courts, became key arenas for the political demands of the Puerto Rican and other linguistic minority communities. In 1969, plaintiffs representing 1,800 Chinese-speaking students sued the San Francisco Unified School District for failing to provide non-English-speaking students with an equal chance to learn. Although the case was lost at the state level, by 1974 it had reached the Supreme Court. In the landmark Lau v. Nichols case, the Court, recognizing the relationship of language to equal educational opportunity, ruled unanimously that the civil rights of students who did not understand the language of instruction were indeed being violated (Lau v. Nichols, 1974). By 1975, the Office for Civil Rights and the Department of Health, Education, and Welfare issued "the Lau remedies," which provided guidance in identifying, and assessing language abilities and providing appropriate programs for students with a limited proficiency in English (Office for Civil Rights, 1975). This document has served as the basis for determining whether school systems are in compliance with the findings of Lau v. Nichols. In most school systems, bilingual programs became the common remedy.

One of the most important campaigns in the history of the Puerto Rican community for educational equity through bilingual education took place in 1972 when the Puerto Rican Legal Defense and Education Fund (PRLDEF), ASPIRA of New York, Inc., ASPIRA of America, Inc. (now the ASPIRA Association), and other organizations representing the educational interests of Puerto Rican youngsters sued the New York City Board of Education on behalf of 15 schoolchildren and their parents (ASPIRA Association, 1991; Santiago-Santiago, 1986). The suit, a landmark case in the history of bilingual education because it involved the largest school system in the country and the largest class of plaintiff children (over 80,000), was based on evidence that Puerto Rican students of limited English proficiency were being denied equal educational opportunity. After a great deal of litigation and negotiation, the suit was resolved in August 1974 and resulted in the *ASPIRA Consent Decree* mandating bilingual education in the New York City school system (ASPIRA Association, 1991).

According to Santiago-Santiago (1986), the ASPIRA Consent Decree, and in general bilingual education in the Puerto Rican community, needs to be placed in the context of the sociopolitical relationship of Puerto Rico to the United States, particularly given the special citizenship status of Puerto Ricans. Although the reasons for bilingual education may be just as urgent in other language minority communities, the case of Puerto Ricans is unique in that they are not immigrants but citizens who are as free to move within national borders as any other citizens. Given these reasons, it is understandable that bilingual education became inextricably linked with demands for equal educational opportunity in the Puerto Rican community.

The 1980s and 1990s: Redefining Complex Issues

The 1980s represented a period of retrenchment and retreat from the more liberal educational policies of the 1960s and 1970s, and this mood was no better defined than in the educational reform movement that officially began with the publication of *A Nation at Risk* (National Commission on Excellence in Education, 1983). During the previous 2 decades, educational concerns had focused on educational equality by challenging the deficit theories popularized in the 1960s and through strategies such as busing, integration, ethnic studies, and bilingual, cross-cultural, and multicultural education. The new reform movement reflected a much more conservative agenda and was characterized by a concern that equity had been won at the expense of excellence. This led to calls for raising standards, reinstating the classics, returning to the "basics," and forging a common cultural experience for all students (Hirsch, 1987; National Commission on Excellence in Education, 1983).

For Puerto Ricans, bilingual education remained a key ingredient in all calls for reform, but their educational agenda of the 1980s and 1990s expanded to include a more serious look at other policies and practices leading to educational failure among Puerto Rican youths. For instance, in a review of the *ASPIRA Consent Decree* over a decade after it was implemented, Isaura Santiago-Santiago (1986) suggested that one of the *Consent Decree's* shortcomings was that it would not ensure equal educational opportunity for the 60% of Puerto Rican students in New York City who were *not* enrolled in bilingual programs. Puerto Rican advocacy groups began to focus specifically on shortcomings of the schools attended by Puerto Rican children (Caballero, 1986; National Puerto Rican Coalition, 1991). For example, in a move to counter the prevailing conservative ideology of the reform movement, the National Commission on Secondary Education for Hispanics (1984) was created to explore not the failures of students but the failure of many inner-city public high schools to educate Latinos. The major thrust of the report was on academic achievement and, in a marked departure from most reports and studies carried out in the previous 2 decades, the commission chose not to get into the "acrimonious debate" over bilingual education. Instead, the report concluded that there were two major language needs at the high school level for Latino students: to teach them English efficiently and effectively, and to foster biliteracy and bilingualism as much as possible (National Commission on Secondary Education of Hispanics, 1984).

By studying data concerning dropouts, placement practices, test scores, and tracking, among others, the commission chronicled the failure of schools to educate Latino students. For example, the report revealed that 40% of all Latinos in the United States who drop out do so *before* tenth grade, information useful to drop-out prevention programs, which are generally targeted for high school students and are too late to be of any help. The commission also found that 25% of all Latino students who entered high school were overage for their grade, and that 45% of Puerto Rican students who began high school never finished. The effects of tracking, testing, and low expectations of students were found to be severe for Latino students, with 76% of those who took the High School and Beyond Achievement (HSAB) tests scoring in the bottom half of national results and 40% of all Latinos in a general track (National Commission on Secondary Education of Hispanics, 1984). Not surprisingly, the major findings of the commission centered on the importance of the quality of life in schools, suggesting that personal attention, contact with adults, and family involvement with the schools are the keys to improving the performance and retention of Latino students.

During the 1980s, evidence mounted that Latino students were becoming the most segregated of all students in the nation (Orfield, 1986). By 1995, segregation was even more pronounced, and it continues to be most severe in the northeast, where the vast majority of Puerto Ricans live. For example, over 75% of all Latinos now attend schools with majorities of Black or Latino students (Orfield et al., 1997). But segregation is not the only problem in urban schools, as revealed in an extensive analysis of 142 U.S. school districts undertaken to explore inequities in Latino education (Meier & Stewart, 1991). Although the authors agreed that Latino students were more segregated than African Americans, they argued that more subtle methods than segregation were equally effective in denying equitable access to education. These included ethnic disparities in discipline (for example, dress codes that are more rigidly enforced among Latinos) and academic grouping (through special education, curriculum tracking, ability grouping, and segregated bilingual education). Coined "second-generation educational discrimination" (Bullock & Stewart, 1979), these kinds of strategies can lead Latino students to drop out of school. Meier and Stewart (1991) also found that school districts with greater Latino representation on school boards and among teaching faculty experienced significantly less second-generation discrimination.

The most recent report specifically chronicling the education of Puerto Ricans in New York City was released in 1994 by the Latino Commission on Educational Reform. The Latino Commission was formed in October 1991 to examine issues of concern to the 334,000 Latino children in the New York City public schools. Latinos now represent 35% of the student body in the public schools, about 50% of whom are Puerto Rican. Chaired by board of education member Luis Reyes, the commission included 35 Latino leaders representing community-based organizations, colleges and universities, and government agencies, as well as students, parents, and teachers (see chap. 3 by Reyes, this volume, for a history of the commission). Latino student voices were also represented through a series of surveys and interviews carried out by Latino college student researchers from Fordham University working under the supervision of the sociologist Clara Rodriguez.

Low academic achievement remains a serious issue in the Puerto Rican community specifically and in Latino communities throughout the United States in general. Academic achievement levels among Latinos have improved since the 1970s, but they continue to lag behind national averages. For instance, although only 37.7% of Latinos are enrolled in algebra or accelerated math classes and only 4.7% are enrolled in calculus, they are twice as likely to be enrolled in remedial math classes as Whites (ASPIRA Institute for Policy Research, 1993; NCES, 1995). Also, the percentage of Latino teachers and other professionals is exceptionally low: although Latinos were 11.3% of all elementary school students and 10.4% of all high school students in 1990, only 3% of teachers were Latinos (ASPIRA Institute for Policy Research, 1993).

Reinterpreting Causes of Failure

As the 1990s approached its midpoint, the research on Puerto Rican students had increased dramatically from its beginnings in the 1930s and had expanded beyond its traditional New York City borders (Hidalgo, 1992; Rivera & Nieto, 1993). The nature of the research has also changed a great deal; newer perspectives on the causes of failure and underachievement among Puerto Rican students have emerged in the past decade. I will use the drop-out crisis as an example of these changing perspectives.

Dropping out of high school has been a constant and recurring dilemma in the educational experiences of Puerto Ricans documented since the 1960s, although it probably existed even before then. The data are not firm, but anecdotal and other sources suggest that the drop-out dilemma has been evident since Puerto Rican students began attending U.S. schools (Cafferty & Rivera-Martínez, 1981). Contributing to the early drop-out crisis no doubt were practices such as placing students behind their peers or in "special" classes (such as those for students with mental retardation or those classified as slow learners) because they were Spanish speaking (Sánchez Korrol, 1983). In one of the first reports on the educational status of Puerto Ricans commissioned by ASPIRA, the drop-out crisis was identified and although the data were described as "murky" and accurate statistics could not be provided, the author concluded (Margolis, 1968, p. 3), "The public schools are like a giant sieve, sifting out all but the strongest, the smartest, or the luckiest." Low high school completion has been dismally similar over the years wherever Puerto Ricans go to school, with drop-out rates of 71% reported in Chicago (Kyle & Kantowicz, 1991; U.S. Commission on Civil Rights, 1976); 70% in Philadelphia and 90% in Boston (Cafferty & Rivera-Martinez, 1981); 80% in New York City (Fernández & Vélez, 1990); and 72% in Holyoke, Massachusetts (Frau-Ramos & Nieto, 1993).

Depending on the measures used, data differ widely concerning the drop-out crisis, but the fact remains that Latinos in general, and Puerto Ricans in particular, have one of the highest drop-out rates of any group. Although the situation improved slightly during the late 1970s and mid-1980s, by the early 1990s more Latinos were dropping out than ever: In 1991, 35.3% of Latinos were high school drop-outs, compared to 34.3% in 1972 (ASPIRA Institute for Policy Research, 1993). Although the rate has declined in recent years, it is still much higher than for White students, and it is complicated by the fact that many Latino students drop out before even reaching high school (NCES, 1995). Data reported as late as 1996 indicated that the high school completion rate for Latinos aged 18 to 24 stood at only 56%, compared to approximately 77% for African Americans and 82% for Whites (Carter & Wilson, 1996).

Tackling the vexing problem of drop-outs has been on the Puerto Rican agenda for decades. A number of theories explaining the drop-out crisis have been formulated over the years. The National Council of La Raza, for example, described a combination of factors that place many Latinos in a high-risk category for dropping out: Single-parent family status plus low family income and low parental education plus limited English proficiency are reported as two significant combinations. Among Puerto Ricans, 40.8% are more likely to have two or more of these risk factors than are other Latinos. The numbers of Puerto Rican children living in single-parent households (33%) and those living in families headed by females (29%) are greater than that of any Latino group (NCLR, 1990).

Although data such as these are interesting and the resulting theories may help explain some of the drop-out phenomenon, many Latino students from single-parent households and with other so-called risk factors are nevertheless successful in school. Relying simply on family structural issues to explain school failure is inadequate given the complex issues involved. In addition, this reliance implies that the problem lies in the students, their families, or their culture, with little attention paid to larger structural issues that may actually promote failure. Also, such deficit explanations provide few solutions. The policies and practices of schools attended by Puerto Rican students need to be viewed more critically, as began in the research carried out in the 1980s. That is, traditional research was called into question for failing to look more deeply into the role that schools play in actually promoting failure (Wehlage & Rutter, 1986).

More recent research has suggested that school policies and practices themselves rather than simply family, personal, and socioeconomic characteristics, negatively influence Latino students' academic performance, behavior, and decision to stay in or leave school. For instance, Latinos tend to have higher drop-out rates than their non-Latino peers *even when they do not fall into the risk categories* (Fernández & Shu, 1988). That is, they have higher drop-out rates even if their grades are better than those of other students, they are in academic rather than general tracks, they are not from poor families, they do not have parents with less schooling, or they do not have problems with their teachers. The only possible clue these researchers uncovered to explain this situation was that Latinos expressed more negative feelings about their schools than did other students.

IMPLICATIONS OF THE EDUCATIONAL EXPERIENCES OF PUERTO RICANS IN U.S. SCHOOLS

Although a small number of Puerto Rican students have fared very well academically and some have expressed gratitude for opportunities they were given in U.S. schools that they might never have had as poor, working-class children in Puerto Rico (see, for example, the comments of many of the writers interviewed by Hernández, 1997), the great majority of Puerto Rican students have not been as fortunate. Most Puerto Ricans have had difficult and unsatisfactory experiences in U.S. schools, characterized by low levels of academic achievement, severe ethnic isolation, and one of the highest drop-out rates of all groups of students in the United States. A number of interconnected and contrasting themes have been evident in the research on the education of Puerto Rican youths in U.S. schools, and I will mention them briefly before presenting some of the educational implications that emerge from this review. (In another article, I included the fiction literature as well and presented these and other themes in more depth; see Nieto, 1998.)

Puerto Ricans' cultural and linguistic diversity and how these have been perceived and treated by teachers and schools have been a major thread throughout the history of the education of Puerto Ricans in the United States. The responses of teachers and other educators have ranged from denial of cultural differences (being "color-blind"), to insensitivity, to outright discriminatory practices, and in happier cases, to the affirmation of students' differences. The inability to accept cultural differences was evident in much of the early research concerning teachers of Puerto Rican youngsters. In *The Losers* (Margolis, 1968, p. 7), the author explained: "Because [the teacher] subscribes to the great American abstraction that 'prejudice is bad,' she abhors the more barbarous symptoms of bigotry and allows herself the luxury of feeling tolerant. The tolerance often turns to condescension." But prejudice denied inevitably leads to overlooking real differences among students as well, and this happens especially when teachers are unaware of differences. Attitudes reflecting ignorance and lack of awareness are not limited to the 1960s: Research as late as the 1990s echoes a continued lack of awareness. Antonia Darder and Carole Upshur, for instance, found that a significant number of the teachers they interviewed in four Boston public schools felt that their academic preparation was inadequate with respect to the educational needs of Latino children (Darder & Upshur, 1993).

The conflict between marginalization and belonging is another key theme that has emerged from the history of Puerto Ricans in U.S. schools. When students feel welcomed in school, they can develop an identity that helps them want to succeed academically, but this has not usually been the case with Puerto Rican students. For example, Virginia Zanger found that even high-achieving, college-track Latino students in one high school in Boston felt excluded, invisible, and subordinate to other students (Zanger, 1993). In the words of one student, "They want to monoculture [you]" (p. 172).

A third consistent theme found in the research concerning the education of Puerto Rican students in U.S. schools is the struggle to maintain their identity in the face of the pressure to assimilate. For instance, the 1976 report of the U.S. Commission on Civil Rights found that a primary reason for dropping out of school as identified by young people themselves was schools' unresponsiveness to their cultural backgrounds. One way in which assimilation is promoted is by mythologizing what Ellen

Bigler (1997) called "ethnic success stories" (p. 9). The model for these Horatio Alger–type success stories is the struggling European immigrant who makes good by learning English and adapting to the cultural mainstream. In the middle school that she studied in upstate New York, Bigler found that the teachers and other residents who perpetuated this "ethnic success story" had no awareness of how Puerto Rican migrants differ from earlier European immigrants. In the words of one of the teachers in the study, "Why are these kids doing this? Why are they not speaking English when they can? Why aren't they trying to fit into the mainstream? They're no different than earlier waves. They worked, they learned the language, and that was your key to success" (Bigler, 1997, p. 9).

Resisting the push for assimilation, Puerto Ricans as a group have always attempted to claim and maintain their identities, even within the school setting. That is, in the Puerto Rican community, there has been an insistence that one can be *both* Puerto Rican and a good student, *both* English and Spanish speaking, in other words, one can be bilingual *and* bicultural. Although assimilation has been rationalized by schools on many grounds, recent research on cultural and linguistic identity has challenged the long-standing wisdom that in order to get ahead one must sacrifice one's identity. Ana Celia Zentella (1997), studying language practices among Puerto Rican children growing up in a low-income community in New York City, found that the most academically successful students in the study were also the most fluent bilinguals. They also happened to be in bilingual rather than monolingual classes.

There are lessons to be learned from the struggle of Puerto Ricans for equal and quality education in the United States. These lessons, described in what follows in four broad contexts, can be found throughout the extensive literature covered, and they are presented briefly with examples from additional research.

The Need to Build on Family Strengths

The family has been a major force in the education of Puerto Ricans throughout their history in the United States. Whether through parent involvement, the community control movement, or inclusion of family perspectives in the curriculum, the family has had a positive impact on students' attitudes and achievements (see Hidalgo, chap. 7, this volume). But although the literature is replete with evidence of the high expectations that Puerto Rican parents have had for their children, it has also shown that they have received little support from schools for promoting their children's success (Díaz-Soto, 1988; Hidalgo, 1992).

Particular strengths of the Puerto Rican community are close family relationships, the concept of community responsibility, and resilience in the face of adversity. It is crucial that these be used in any strategy to improve the education of Puerto Rican students. One example of using family strengths of Puerto Ricans and other children as the core of the curriculum was described by a teacher, Joanne Wilson Keenan, working with two professors, Jerri Willett and Judith Solsken, in an elementary school in Springfield, Massachusetts. They explained: "Unlike other approaches that focus on changes the families must make to support schools, we begin with ways that schools must change to support families" (Keenan, Willett, & Solsken, 1993, p. 57). Through classroom visits by families of culturally diverse backgrounds, the researchers vividly documented the wide range of knowledge, skills, and teaching capabilities that parents use with their children at home that can be used to enrich their education in school as well.

Research such as this documents how students' experiences, culture, and language are important sources for curriculum development and, thus, for their academic achievement and are a promising practice for other schools working with a culturally diverse population, including Puerto Rican children.

The Importance of Promoting Cultural and Linguistic Maintenance

Throughout much of the history of the education of Puerto Ricans in the United States, cultural and linguistic maintenance has served both as a defense against a hostile environment and as a nonnegotiable demand for educational improvement. Even during periods of "Americanization" and other assimilationist pressures, Puerto Ricans in general have insisted on retaining Spanish and their cultural roots while at the same time learning English and becoming biculturally adept.

An example can be found in research by Jeannette Abi-Nader (1990), who described how one high school teacher found a way to improve the learning conditions of Latino students by using their language and culture to help them envision college as a possibility rather than a dream. This college preparatory program for Latino students, located in the bilingual program of a large inner-city public high school in the northeast, is characterized by a 15-year record of success with a college admission rate of 65%. What Abi-Nader found significant about this program was not so much the teaching methodology or the class activities, but the creation of a learning environment where the bilingual and bicultural backgrounds of students are affirmed in every aspect of their learning. From Latino art in the classroom to constant references to cultural values and the advantages of being bilingual and bicultural, the teacher strengthens students' identities as young Latinos during their adolescence, the most critical time of identity formation. That is, by learning in an environment where students feel comfortable speaking two languages, and where they are encouraged to express and explore the behaviors reflecting the heritage of both cultures, students are able to better shape their self-identity. Of all the cultural elements in this program, the value that Latinos place on the family deserves special consideration. The title of her article ("A house for my mother") is an example of how the central motif of family in the lives of Puerto Ricans is used in the program.

The Need to Reform School Policies and Practices

Much research on the education of Puerto Ricans has either directly or indirectly emphasized the need to reexamine the impact of school policies and practices on academic achievement and high school completion. These have included inequitable school funding (ASPIRA Institute for Policy Research, 1993; Meier & Stewart, 1991), overcrowding (Orfield, 1986), ability grouping (National Commission on Secondary Education for Hispanics, 1984; Valdivieso, 1986), retention (Fernández & Vélez, 1990; Margolis, 1968; Orfield, 1986), testing (Mestre & Royer, 1991), curriculum reform (Latino Commission on Educational Reform, 1994), disciplinary policies (Wehlage & Rutter, 1986), and the need for work–study programs (Hispanic Policy Development Project, 1990; Valdivieso, 1986).

Research suggests that rather than continuing to focus on students or their families as "the problem," schools and teachers need to look at their own policies and practices in order to improve the education of Puerto Rican students (Nieto & Rolón, 1997). Although this in no way means minimizing the responsibility that Puerto Rican families and communities must have in the process, it simply reaffirms the traditional responsibility that U.S. schools have to educate all students, not just those from English-speaking, middle-class, and highly educated families. Rather than focusing on issues about which they cannot do anything—issues such as poverty, low parental educational levels, or single-parent family structure—schools need to focus on what they *can* change. At the same time, Puerto Rican families and communities need to feel that they have an important role in the education of their children, and partnerships need to be formed among families, schools, and the larger community to tackle the plague of underachievement and high drop-out rates.

Care Can be Demonstrated in Numerous Ways

One truth has emerged from this review above all others: The care or rejection experienced by Puerto Rican students in U.S. schools can significantly impact their academic success or failure (Nieto, 1998). The focus on caring is not new; for many years, "care" has figured prominently in research about the education of Puerto Ricans and other Latinos in the United States. Hearings held by the National Commission on Secondary Education for Hispanics (1984), for instance, found that "Hispanic students almost unanimously identified 'someone caring' as the most important factor in academic success" (p. 13). In fact, Latino youngsters often explicitly mention "love" as the factor that can make or break their experience in school. In the previously cited research by Virginia Vogel Zanger, one young Latina described the experiences of Latino students in this way: "They just feel left out, they feel like if no one loves them, no one cares, so why should they care?" (Zanger, 1993, p. 176).

What does it mean to care in the context of schools? Martha Montero-Sieburth (Montero-Sieburth & Pérez, 1987) documented the strategies that a bilingual teacher used in relating to her Latino students, and she identified *cariño* (affection or endearment) as a key element in the success of Latino students. Marla Pérez, the bilingual teacher in whose classroom Montero-Sieburth did her research, described herself as "teacher, friend, mother, social worker, translator, counselor, advocate, prosecutor, group therapist, hygienist, and monitor" (Montero-Sieburth & Pérez, 1987, p. 183). Similarly, one of the Latina teachers in research described by Carmen Mercado and Luis Moll (1997) spoke of her profession in this way: "It is not an 8:40 to 3:30 P.M. job but an extension of my life, as if it were part of my family" (Mercado & Moll, 1997, p. 31). Nancy Hornberger (1990), reporting specifically on the successful development of biliteracy among a group of mostly Puerto Rican children, drew a similar conclusion: The teacher in the classroom that she studied openly displayed tenderness and affection, as well as a "motherly concern" for her students. The importance of this kind of interpersonal support was explained by Nitza Hidalgo: "Students have to feel liked by the teacher; they gain strength from their relationship to their teacher" (1992, p. 36).

CONCLUSION

Caring can be demonstrated in many ways. As we enter a new millennium, we need to expand what it means to create a caring community for Puerto Rican students. Caring is not revealed simply in outward shows of affection. It is not just a matter of hugging children more often, or of including their cultural traditions in the curriculum; by themselves, these gestures do little to guarantee that Puerto Rican youngsters will be more academically successful. Care is demonstrated most powerfully through high expectations and rigorous standards, and in teachers' beliefs that students are worthy and capable. At the institutional and societal levels, care is most evident in schools staffed with competent and respectful teachers. In the most effective examples of research we have seen, caring has included not only providing affection (*cariño*) and support for students but also developing strong interpersonal relationships with students and their families, learning about and from them, respecting and affirming their language and culture, and building on these to support learning.

Caring also implies that policies and practices need to change dramatically if schools are to be perceived by Puerto Rican youngsters as places where they belong and where they are valued. Policies and practices that need to be transformed include curriculum, pedagogy, tracking and testing policies, counseling services, and the professional development of teachers, all of which have largely undermined Puerto Rican students' hopes of educational achievement. And because Puerto Rican students have an unfortunate legacy of attending inequitably financed schools, care is demonstrated most effectively through the provision of adequate means to ensure that learning can take place. A process that includes work at all three levels—personal relationships, institutional policies and practices, and societal priorities and expectations—is the only solution to the longstanding troubled history of Puerto Rican students in U.S. schools.

The negative impact of this history has been felt both by Puerto Ricans and by society at large. Puerto Rican youngsters have paid through unfulfilled dreams of educational success, but our nation in general has also been affected. In the words of Richard Margolis (1968), whose quote from *The Losers* I used at the beginning of this chapter, we are all "the losers": "The children are losing all hopes of learning or succeeding; the schools are losing all hopes of teaching, and the nation is losing another opportunity, perhaps its last, to put flesh on the American dream" (p. 1). Yet there is hope, as some glimpses of success in particular programs and schools have shown. Puerto Rican youngsters, just as all others, are capable of great things once the barriers to their progress are removed. Although schools can do little to remove barriers related to poverty, they can create spaces where students can learn at high levels and demonstrate the tremendous promise that they have. When that happens, we will all be the winners.

REFERENCES

Abi-Nader, J. (1990). "A house for my mother": Motivating Hispanic high school students. *Anthropology & Education Quarterly, 21,* 41–58.

Adams, D., Astone, B., Nuñez-Wormack, E., & Smodlaka, I. (1994). Predicting the academic achievement of Puerto Rican and Mexican-American ninth-grade students. *The Urban Review, 26*(1), 1–14.

ASPIRA of New York. (1968). *Hemos trabajado bien. Proceedings of the ASPIRA National Conference of Puerto Ricans, Mexican-Americans, and Educators.* New York: Author.

ASPIRA Association. (1991). *The ASPIRA story: 1961–1991.* Washington, DC: Author.

ASPIRA Institute for Policy Research. (1993). *Facing the facts: The state of Hispanic education, 1993.* Washington, DC: Author.

Association of Assistant Superintendents. (1948). *A program of education for Puerto Ricans in New York City.* Brooklyn: New York City Board of Education.

Báez, T., Fernández, R. R., Navarro, R. A., & Rice, R. I. (1986). Litigation strategies for educational equity: Bilingual education and research. *Issues in Education, 3*(3), 198–214.

Bigler, E. (1997). Dangerous discourses: Language politics and classrooms practices in Upstate New York. *Centro, IX*(9), 8–25.

Bilingual Education Act of 1967, U.S. Code 20 (1968).

Bonilla, F., & Campos, R. (1981). A wealth of poor: Puerto Ricans in the new economic order. *Daedalus, 110*, 133–176.

Bucchioni, E. (1982). The daily round of life in the school. In F. Cordasco & E. Bucchioni (Eds.), *The Puerto Rican community and its children on the mainland* (3rd rev. ed., pp. 201–238). Metuchen, NJ: Scarecrow Press.

Bullock, C. S. III, & Stewart, J., Jr. (1979). Incidence and correlates of second-generation discrimination. In M. L. Palley & M. B. Preston (Eds.), *Race, sex, and policy problems* (pp. 115–129). Lexington, MA: Lexington.

Bureau of Transitional Bilingual Education. (1971). *Two way: Bilingual bicultural is two way education.* Boston: Department of Education.

Caballero, D. (1986, June 5). *New York School Board elections: A fight for the future of our children.* Testimony presented by the Puerto Rican/Latino Education Roundtable at the New York State Assembly Public Hearing on School Board Education Reforms.

Cafferty, P. S. J., & Rivera-Martínez, C. (1981). *The politics of language: The dilemma of bilingual education for Puerto Ricans.* Boulder, CO: Westview Press.

Carrasquillo, A. L. (1991). *Hispanic children and youth in the United States: A resource guide.* New York: Garland.

Carter, R., & Wilson, D. (1996). *Minorities in higher education. Fourteenth annual status report.* Washington, DC: American Council on Education.

Cordasco, F., & Bucchioni, E. (Eds.). (1968). *Puerto Rican children in mainland schools.* Metuchen, NJ: Scarecrow Press.

Cordasco, F., & Bucchioni, E. (Eds.). (1982). *The Puerto Rican community and its children on the mainland* (3rd ed.). Metuchen, NJ: Scarecrow Press.

Council on Interracial Books for Children. (1972). Special issue on Puerto Rican materials. *Bulletin, 4*(1 & 2).

Darder, A., & Upshur, C. (1993). What do Latino children need to succeed in school? A study of four Boston public schools. In R. Rivera & S. Nieto (Eds.), *The education of Latino students in Massachusetts: Issues, research, and policy implications* (pp. 127–146). Boston: Gastón Institute for Public Policy and Development.

Díaz-Soto, L. (1988, April). *The home environment and Puerto Rican children's achievement: A researcher's diary.* Paper presented at the annual conference of the National Association for Bilingual Education, Houston, TX.

34 NIETO

Durán, R. P. (1983). *Hispanics' education and background: Predictors of college achievement*. New York: College Entrance Examination Board.

Fantini, M., & Magat, R. (1970). *Community control and the urban school*. New York: Praeger.

Fernández, R. R., & Shu, G. (1988). School dropouts: New approaches to an enduring problem. *Education and Urban Society, 20*(4), 363–386.

Fernández, R. R., & Vélez, W. (1990). Who stays? Who leaves? Findings from the ASPIRA Five Cities High School Dropout Study. *Latino Studies Journal, 1*(3), 59–77.

Fishman, J. A., Cooper, R. L., Ma, R., Hoffman, G., Casiano, H., Terry, C., Greenfield, L., Findling, J., & Herasimchuk, E. (1971). *Bilingualism in the barrio*. Bloomington: Indiana University Press.

Fitzpatrick, J. P. (1987). *Puerto Rican Americans: The meaning of migration to the mainland*. Englewood Cliffs, NJ: Prentice-Hall. (Original work published 1971)

Frau-Ramos, M., & Nieto, S. (1993). "I was an outsider": Dropping out among Puerto Rican youths in Holyoke, Massachusetts. In R. Rivera & S. Nieto (Eds.), *The education of Latino students in Massachusetts: Issues, research and policy implications* (pp. 147–169). Boston: Gastón Institute for Public Policy and Development.

Fuentes, L. (1976). Community control did not fail in New York: It wasn't tried. *Phi Delta Kappan, 57*(10), 692–695.

Fuentes, L. (1980). The struggle for local political control. In C. E. Rodriguez, V. S. Korrol, & J. O. Alers (Eds.), *The Puerto Rican struggle: Essays on survival in the U.S.* (pp. 111-120). New York: Puerto Rican Migration Research Consortium.

Gallardo, J. M. (Ed.). (1970). *Proceedings of conference on education of Puerto Rican children on the mainland*. Santurce, Puerto Rico: Department of Education.

Gittell, M. (1972). Decentralization and citizen participation in education. *Public Administration Review, 32*, 670–686.

Hernández, C. D. (1997). *Puerto Rican voices in English: Interviews with writers*. Westport, CT: Praeger.

Hidalgo, N. M. (1992). *"I saw Puerto Rico once": A review of the literature on Puerto Rican families and school achievement in the United States* (Rep. No. 12). Boston: Center on Families, Communities, Schools and Children's Learning.

Hirsch, E. D. (1987). *Cultural literacy: What every American needs to know*. Boston: Houghton Mifflin.

Hispanic Policy Development Project. (1990). *A more perfect union: Achieving Hispanic parity by the year 2000*. New York: Author.

History Task Force. (1982). *Sources for the study of Puerto Rican migration: 1879–1930*. New York: Centro de Estudios Puertorriqueños, Research Foundation of the City University of New York.

Hornberger, N. (1990). Creating successful learning contexts for biliteracy. *Penn Working Papers in Educational Linguistics, 6*, 1.

Institute for Puerto Rican Policy. (1992, June). The distribution of Puerto Ricans and other selected Latinos in the U.S.: 1990. *Datanote on the Puerto Rican Community, 11*. (Available from the Institute for Puerto Rican Policy, 99 Hudson Street, New York, NY 10013).

Institute for Puerto Rican Policy. (1998, February). Puerto Ricans and other Latinos in the United States. *IPR Datanote, 19*. (Available from the Institute for Puerto Rican Policy, New York).

Keenan, J. W., Willett, U., & Solsken, J. (1993). Constructing an urban village: School/home collaboration in a multicultural classroom. *Language Arts, 70,* 56–66.

Kyle, C., & Kantowicz, E. (1991). Bogus statistics: Chicago's Latino community exposes the dropout problem. *Latino Studies Journal, 2*(2), 34–52.

LaFontaine, H., Colon, E., Hernandez, M., Melendez, G., Orta, A., Pagan, M., Perez, C., Quiñones, N., & Rivéra, S. (1973). Teaching Spanish to the native Spanish speaker. In J. W. Dodge (Ed.), *Sensitivity in the foreign-language classroom: Reports of the working committees* (pp. 63–86). Northeast Conference on the Teaching of Foreign Languages.

Latino Commission on Educational Reform. (1994). *Making the vision a reality: Final report of the Latino Commission on educational reform.* Brooklyn: New York City Board of Education.

Lau v. Nichols, 414 U.S. 563 (1974).

Margolis, R. J. (1968). *The losers: A report on Puerto Ricans and the public schools.* New York: ASPIRA.

Marquez, R. (1995). Sojourners, settlers, castaways, and creators: A recollection of Puerto Rico past and Puerto Ricans present. *Massachusetts Review, 36*(1), 94–118.

Massachusetts State Advisory Committee to the U.S. Commission on Civil Rights. (1972, February). *Issues of concern to Puerto Ricans in Boston and Springfield.* Boston: U.S. Commission on Civil Rights.

Meier, K. J., & Stewart, J., Jr. (1991). *The politics of Hispanic education: Un paso pa'lante y dos pa'trás.* Albany: State University of New York Press.

Meléndez, E. (1991, September). *Los que se van, los que regresan: Puerto Rican migration to and from the United States, 1982–1988.* New York: Commonwealth of Puerto Rico, Department of Puerto Rican Community Affairs.

Mercado, C. I., & Moll, L. (1997). The study of funds of knowledge: Collaborative research in Latino homes. *Centro, IX*(9), 26–42.

Mestre, J. P., & Royer, J. M. (1991). Cultural and linguistic influences on Latino testing. In G. D. Keller, J. R. Deneen, & R. J. Magallán (Eds.), *Assessment and access: Hispanics in higher education* (pp. 39–66). Albany: State University of New York Press.

Mills, C., Wright, C., Sr., & Goldsen, R. K. (1950). *The Puerto Rican journey: New York's newest migrants.* New York: Harper & Row.

Montero-Sieburth, M., & Pérez, M. (1987). Echar pa'lante, moving onward: The dilemmas and strategies of a bilingual teacher. *Anthropology & Education Quarterly, 18*(3), 180–189.

Morrison, J. C. (1958). *The Puerto Rican study, 1953–1957.* Brooklyn: New York City Board of Education.

National Center for Education Statistics. (1993). *Dropout rates in the United States: 1993.* Washington, DC: U.S. Department of Education.

National Center for Educational Statistics. (1995). *The educational progress of Hispanic students.* Washington, DC: U.S. Department of Education, Office of Educational Research and Improvement.

National Commission on Excellence in Education. (1983). *A nation at risk: The imperative for educational reform.* Washington, DC: U.S. Government Printing Office.

National Commission on Secondary Education for Hispanics. (1984). *"Make something happen": Hispanics and urban school reform.* Washington, DC: Hispanic Policy Development Project.

National Council of La Raza. (1990). *Hispanic education: A statistical portrait, 1990.* Washington, DC: Author.

National Council of La Raza. (1991). Hispanic child poverty: Signs of distress, signs of hope. *Agenda, 10,* 2.

National Council of La Raza. (1993). *Moving from the margins: Puerto Rican young men and family poverty.* Washington, DC: Author.

National Puerto Rican Coalition. (1991). *A blueprint for change: A Puerto Rican agenda for the 1990s.* Washington, DC: Author.

National Puerto Rican Task Force. (1982). *Toward a language policy for Puerto Ricans in the U.S.: An agenda for a community in movement.* New York: City University of New York Research Foundation.

Negrón de Montilla, A. (1971). *Americanization in Puerto Rico and the public school system, 1900-1930.* Río Piedras, Puerto Rico: Editorial Edil.

Nieto, S. (Ed.). (1983). Puerto Ricans in children's literature and history texts: A ten-year update [Special issue]. *Bulletin of the Council on Interracial Books for Children, 14* (1 & 2).

Nieto, S. (1995). A history of the education of Puerto Rican students in U.S. schools: 'Losers,' 'outsiders,' or 'leaders'? In J. A. Banks & C. A. M. Banks (Eds.), *Handbook of research on multicultural education* (pp. 388–411). New York: Macmillan.

Nieto, S. (1997). We have stories to tell: Puerto Ricans in children's books. In V. J. Harris (Ed.), *Using multiethnic literature in the K-8 classroom* (pp. 59–93). Norwood, MA: Christopher-Gordon.

Nieto, S. (1998). Fact and fiction: Stories of Puerto Rican students in U.S. schools. *Harvard Educational Review, 68*(2), 133–163.

Nieto, S., & Rolón, C. (1997). Preparation and professional development of teachers: A perspective from two Latinas. In J. J. Irvine (Ed.), *Critical knowledge for diverse teachers and learners* (pp. 89–123). Washington, DC: American Association of Colleges for Teacher Education.

Office for Civil Rights. (1975). *Task force findings specifying remedies for eliminating past educational practices ruled unlawful under Lau V. Nichols.* Washington, DC: Department of Health, Education, and Welfare.

Office of the Mayor. (1968). *Puerto Ricans confront problems of the complex urban society: A design for change* (Community conference proceedings). New York: Author.

Ogbu, J. U. (1987). Variability in minority school performance: A problem in search of an explanation. *Anthropology and Education Quarterly, 18*(4), 312–334.

Orfield, G. (1986). Hispanic education: Challenges, research, and policies. *American Journal of Education, 95*(1), 1–25.

Orfield, G., Bachmeier, M. D., James, D. R., & Eitle, T. (1997). Deepening segregation in American public schools: A special report from the Harvard Project on School Desegregation. *Equity and Excellence in Education, 30*(20), 5–24.

Osuna, J. J. (1949). *A history of education in Puerto Rico.* Río Piedras, Puerto Rico: Editorial de la Universidad de Puerto Rico.

Padilla, E. (1958). *Up from Puerto Rico.* New York: Columbia University Press.

Puerto Rican Forum. (1970). *A study of poverty conditions in the New York Puerto Rican community.* New York: Author.

Quality Education for Minorities Project. (1990). *Education that works: An action plan for the education of minorities.* Cambridge, MA: Author.

Rand, C. (1958). *The Puerto Ricans*. New York: Oxford University Press.

Rivera, R., & Nieto, S. (Eds.). (1993). *The education of Latino students in Massachusetts: Issues, research, and policy implications*. Boston: Gastón Institute for Public Policy and Development.

Rivera-Medina, E. J. (1984). The Puerto Rican return migrant student: A challenge to educators. *Educational Research Quarterly, 8*(4), 82–91.

Rodriguez, C. (1991). *Puerto Ricans: Born in the U.S.A.* Boulder, CO: Westview.

Rubinstein, A. T. (1970). Schools against children: The case for community control. New York: *Monthly Review Press*.

Ryan, W. (1972). *Blaming the victim*. New York: Vintage Books.

Sánchez Korrol, V. E. (1983). *From colonia to community: The history of Puerto Ricans in New York, 1917–1948*. Westport, CT: Greenwood.

Sánchez Korrol, V. (1996). Toward bilingual education: Puerto Rican women teachers in New York City schools, 1947–1967 (pp. 82-104). In A. Ortiz (Ed.), *Puerto Rican women and work: Bridges in transnational labor*. Philadelphia: Temple University Press.

Santiago-Santiago, I. (1986, November). ASPIRA v. Board of Education revisited. *American Journal of Education, 95*(1), 149–199.

Shanker, A. (1973, April 29). Where we stand. *The New York Times*, p. E11.

Shorris, E. (1992). *Latinos: A biography of the people*. New York: Norton.

U.S. Commission on Civil Rights. (1976). *Puerto Ricans in the continental United States: An uncertain future*. Washington, DC: Author.

Valdivieso, R. (1986). *Must they wait another generation? Hispanics and secondary school reform*. New York: Clearinghouse on Urban Education, Institute for Urban and Minority Education, Teachers College, Columbia University.

Wagenheim, K., & Jímenez de Wagenheim, O. (Eds.). (1973). *The Puerto Ricans: A documentary history*. New York: Praeger.

Walsh, C. E. (1991). *Pedagogy and the struggle for voice: Issues of language, power, and schooling for Puerto Ricans*. New York: Bergin & Garvey.

Wasserman, M. (1969, June). The I.S. 201 story: One observer's version. *Urban Review, 2*, 3–15.

Wehlage, G., & Rutter, R. (1986). Dropping out: How much do schools contribute to the problem? *Teachers College Record, 87*(3), 374–392.

Zanger, V. V. (1993). Academic costs of social marginalization: An analysis of Latino students' perceptions at a Boston high school. In R. Rivera & S. Nieto (Eds.), *The education of Latino students in Massachusetts: Issues, research, and policy implications* (pp. 170–190). Boston: Gastón Institute for Public Policy and Development.

Zentella, A. C. (1997). *Growing up bilingual: Puerto Rican children in New York*. Oxford, UK: Blackwell.

2

Return Migrant Students: Yankee Go Home?

Xaé Alicia Reyes

When I returned to Puerto Rico at the age of 12, the warm memories of the Island I had cherished as a young child became a somewhat confusing reality. Everything seemed smaller and not as welcoming as I had expected. My grandmother's apartment did not have the palatial, long tiled hallways I remembered from my infancy. Some of my cousins now looked at my sister and me as if we were from another planet because our Spanish was faltering and our behaviors differed from theirs. In spite of our parents' continued efforts to maintain our language and customs, we were not familiar with many expressions and did not know the right songs, nor did we read the *fotonovelas* that our peers so enjoyed. My sister and I found comfort in maintaining ties to the U.S. culture we had been immersed in by speaking English with each other while we began to relearn Puerto Rican cultural norms and language nuances. We were fortunate to attend bilingual Catholic schools for the first 3 years after our arrival. Academically, we were successful because English was (and still is) valued cultural capital in most of the Island's private schools. It was a completely different story when we had to attend public school for the last 2 years of high school. The dynamics we confronted then were similar to those with our extended families previously described. What eventually made our experiences bearable enough to succeed academically were the other "bilingual" students we connected with and a wonderful English teacher, Mrs. Noboa, who organized us into what was known as the English Club, which provided the *bilingües* with opportunities to socialize and feel successful. I credit these two factors, and the incredible support and encouragement from our parents, for our being able to overcome the difficult transition of return migration.

Many years later and after several returns to the United States for reasons of work and school, I stumbled upon an article by Eduardo Rivera-Medina (1984) aptly called "The Puerto Rican Return Migrant Student: A Challenge to Educators." I was immediately drawn to the article out of curiosity over what the state of affairs might be for "return migrants" more than 10 years after my own return migrant experience. The article piqued my research interest, and I selected it as my doctoral dissertation topic in order to ascertain what, if anything, was being done to meet the challenges presented by return migration as articulated by Rivera-Medina (1984) and the circumstances that had been so familiar to me. The longitudinal study I conducted from 1992 to 1994, which is the subject of this chapter, concerns student perspectives of their own processes as Puerto Rican return migrants in the public school system in Puerto Rico. My original study was prompted by the need for additional research in the area of return migrant students (Rivera-Medina, 1984; Vivó, 1982).

Return migrants in the school system were divided by the 1980 census, in Puerto Rico, into three categories: return migrants who were born in Puerto Rico, moved to the mainland, and returned to the Island; circulatory migrants who were children of Puerto Rican parents and who had traveled from the Island to the mainland several times; and migrants born in the mainland of Puerto Rican parents but who had returned to the Island in search of their roots. In 1982 to 1983, the Department of Education established a Migrant Education Program to provide services for students who returned from the mainland with little or no knowledge of Spanish; however, Cafferty and Rivera-Martínez (1981) indicated that this group is not served well by either the mainland educational system or that of the Island. Furthermore, Colón (1988), in a profile of return migrants, reported that many drop out of high school in Puerto Rico because of language problems and behaviors and attitudes perceived by Islanders as incompatible with Puerto Rican culture.

The constant flow of students affects the educational system in Puerto Rico in many ways. Vivó (1982), in a review of the literature on migrant students, concluded that there was a need for improved data collection and analysis. In addition, she found that many problems related to language difficulties, cultural adjustment, and reinsertion had been objects of some discussion but that relatively little research had been done.

Vivó also mentioned that education planners and policymakers were particularly interested in obtaining data on the turnover of school-age children on the Island, surveying language teacher in-service needs, and setting a preliminary agenda for research. More recent research (Hamilton, 1987; Prewitt-Díaz & Seilhamer, 1985; Vázquez, 1989), relying mostly on surveys and questionnaires to collect data, has addressed these issues to some degree. Vázquez (1989) and Prewitt-Díaz, Trotter, and Rivera (1989) recommended that ethnographic methods be used to more thoroughly study the needs of this population. The needs of students who flow in and out of the system are related to problems that need to be addressed in each individual classroom, rather than in a comprehensive pproach on a school-wide or society-wide level (Rivera-Medina, 1984). Bilingual programs come and go, and no truly concerted effort has been implemented to deal permanently with the needs of this population.

In this study I used ethnographic methods to analyze students' perceptions regarding their interactions with staff and other students in their new environment. The focus of the study was the transition of return migrant students into Puerto Rico's educational system. On a deeper level, I looked at issues of identity as perceived by migrants and the community: Did the migrants no longer feel Puerto Rican? How did they report their identity? Were these feelings a result of their interactions in the school? In what ways, if any, did the school environment contribute to these feelings of self? Did the students describe their transition to the Puerto Rican schools as successful or difficult? My concern was that the feelings of inadequacy these students experience may push them out of the system by encouraging them to either drop out or return to the mainland, where they are often unwelcome.

In this chapter I address first the literature on the migration of Puerto Ricans to the United States mainland. I will then review the literature concerning the effects of migration on schooling, paying particular attention to its effects on Puerto Rican return migrant students. A discussion of the study I conducted in two Puerto Rican high schools highlights issues of conflicting interactions between return migrant students and their peers and teachers in the schools, their misunderstanding of school policies, and the need for a support system for return migrant students. I conclude with recommendations on how to better serve the return migrant student population in Puerto Rican schools.

THE PUERTO RICAN MIGRATION EXPERIENCE

The literature on migration within the United States focuses on seasonal and field workers in agricultural settings and in assembly line manufacturing in some U.S. cities. In Puerto Rico, the term migrant is embedded in the patterns of mobility from the Island (Puerto Rico) to the mainland (United States). This population flow is comparable to the patterns of interstate movement observed on the mainland when job conditions and economics appear more promising in some states than in others. The major similarity between the majority of interstate migrants and Puerto Rico's return migrant population is the notion of already belonging to the dominant culture. Return migrants share the belief that the Island's culture and language are known to them. The terms in this chapter are used according to the nuances they have in the Puerto Rican literature and discourse on migration.

If we consider difficulties faced by migrant groups on the mainland to be overwhelming, we can appreciate how difficult it is for individuals to undergo the migration process repeatedly. The situation is even worse when we consider that Puerto Ricans often nurture idyllic memories and unrealistic views of their homeland, known as "la isla del encanto" (isle of enchantment). Upon returning, children of migrants often find that the dream no longer exists (Robles, Martínez, & Moscoso, 1980). As Pilar Beléndez-Soltero (1994) poignantly stated,

> Either by deliberate action or by omission, we [Puerto Ricans], as a nation, are subjecting the return migrants to a prejudice which is nearly as cruel as that which they are subjected to in the United States, crueler if we consider that Puerto Ricans, as a whole, proclaim themselves as being above the prejudiced Americans. Perhaps it is not as evident as it is in the United States, but what makes it crueler is that it [the attitude of Island Puerto Ricans] denies return migrants their national identity, an identity which they clung to when fighting the prejudice they encountered during their stay in the United States. (p. 291)

Despite efforts to preserve their ethnic identity and vernacular language, Puerto Ricans who return to their native land are seldom viewed by Island residents as "real" Puerto Ricans. If they show evidence of U.S. customs and English language use, they are called *bilingües* (bilinguals), "Neo-Ricans," or "Newyoricans," and they are often rejected by the greater Puerto Rican community (Pacheco, Wapner, & Lucca, 1979; Prewitt-Díaz & Seilhamer, 1985; Ramos Perea, 1972; Rivera & Medina, 1984).

In spring 1986, an article in the *Wall Street Journal* described the difficulties faced by return migrants and used the expression "children of the skies" to describe their sense of belonging to neither the mainland nor the Island but rather to the skies, where they are on a seemingly constant flight to and from the Island. The article described how migrants are rejected by older and more conservative family members who view all return migrants as too savvy or streetwise and females, in particular, as too liberal. Puerto Rico is a patriarchal society where women are still expected to fulfill the traditional roles of mother and homemaker and to work outside the home only if necessary (which is increasingly the case). Hence women are expected to be submissive and dependent. The feelings that return migrants experience of belonging to neither the United States nor to Puerto Rico (Wapner & Pacheco, 1979) affect their sense of identity and their possibilities for academic success. For example, perceptions of return migrants by teachers responding to a study of the National Institute of Education (NIE, 1981) included lack of knowledge of language and culture, disrespect toward teachers and Puerto Rican values, and an overall attitude of viewing their new environment as inferior to the United States. These perceptions affect communication between teachers and return migrant students, and in turn, academic achievement is affected by the communication barriers resulting from these perceptions.

Return migrants have been exposed to and influenced by U.S. society, with its emphasis on competition and success (Alers & Montalvo, 1985). Although *anomie,* a feeling of rootlessness (Durkheim, 1965) might result from migration, Puerto Rican migrants are immersed in the quest for success and competition among North Americans, and this is replicated by return migrants in Puerto Rico. Puerto Ricans on the Island are generally considered more "laid back," and many settle into their jobs and are not as concerned with promotions as they are with making a living. Influences of the media and of U.S.-educated employees have altered some traditional behavior patterns. Observations conducted by college students in business settings in Puerto Rico's metropolitan area in fall 1993 uncovered "dog-eat-dog" competitive behaviors in Island subsidiaries of Big Six companies. In these environments, older and better educated return migrants thrive and are viewed as having an edge because of their understanding of U.S. culture and language.

The experiences of return migrants vary depending on their families' socioeconomic status and employment opportunities. If one has access to private education for one's children or finds employment in an English-speaking environment, the return migrant experience is less traumatic for the family. The situations of the students in my study reflect the realities of a return migrant population with limited resources. Stereotyping by teachers led to misunderstandings, rejection, and alienation of students in classrooms and schools, which contributed further to the negative perceptions held by the communities in which these students interacted.

MIGRATION AND SCHOOLING

Educational ethnography has helped identify the problems involved in the schooling of ethnic minorities (Spindler & Spindler, 1987). Unfortunately, little has been done in practice to reduce the marginal position of these groups. Most of the literature on immigrant groups focuses on how they address and react to the pressure to assimilate into American life (Campa, 1989; Fitzpatrick, 1989; Gordon, 1964). It is important also to study interactions among migrants and nonmigrants to assess the counterassimilation pressures involved in return migration. That is, we must look at the dynamics of exclusion and inclusion of individuals as they participate in a social setting such as a school. For example, migrants think of themselves as insiders only to discover they are viewed as outsiders and excluded from participation unless they reverse the assimilation process. Return migrants have been forced to assimilate to mainstream culture once, and they are now pressured to disengage from it to be granted membership. Furthermore, educational research has provided valuable evidence regarding the effects of social context on academic success (Trueba, 1989). For learning to occur, the students' language and culture must be taken into account and connected to teaching and learning so that interactions will be meaningful and relevant (Freire, 1972; Macías, 1987; Nieto, 1996). The context in which the interactions take place will contribute to or impede progress to optimum development. Thus, characteristics of return migrants should be looked at not to justify their failure to thrive in Puerto Rican public schools, but rather to understand what must be addressed so that they may thrive.

Migrant students' needs are often not addressed by the Puerto Rican educational system. Their interactions in schools replicate those of migrants in the greater society. That is, students may feel marginal; they may feel they are caught between two or more cultures, including the culture of the home, the culture of the school, and the culture of their peers. They may also experience anomie, a sense of rootlessness, over the uncertainty and anxiety engendered by competing norms and beliefs.

Studies of other migrant groups have shed light on the complexities of migration. Gibson (1988, 1991) explored cultural differences between Punjabi and mainstream youth in the United States and social problems encountered by Punjabis. She reported patterns of differential treatment of boys and girls in Punjabi homes. By high school, most of the Punjabi students she studied had learned to behave differently at home and at school (Gibson, 1988). Girls had the most difficult time reconciling their two worlds because they were caught in a conflict between two cultural systems. An Americanized Punjabi was one who had forgotten her roots and adopted the lifestyle of White peers. Schools were more concerned with having Punjabis conform to mainstream patterns than pursue academic excellence. Family backgrounds and strong cultural traditions allowed Punjabi students to achieve academic success in spite of the pressures they confronted in school to conform to mainstream culture. Gibson (1988) reported that the Punjabis' sense of pride in their accomplishments was tied to bringing honor to their families.

Discontinuity in the enculturation process, described as "an abrupt transition from one mode of being and behaving to another" (Spindler, 1974, p. 308), was the focus of Macías' (1987) study of Papago children in Arizona. He found that children sometimes rejected school experiences that seemed foreign to them. Papago parents, for example, model and gesture for their children and use brief comments and directives. So, the children are minimally verbal in the school setting. Macías investigated the benefits of the PECHS (Papago Early Childhood Head Start) program to mitigate cultural discontinuity. The program employed Papago teachers and used culturally appropriate teaching behaviors and strategies to encourage children to be verbal in contrast to what they were taught at home. According to Macías, Papago teachers have developed their own Papago "hidden curriculum" by strategizing to minimize the effects of cultural discontinuity. Here again we are reminded of the work of Freire (1972). On one hand, the curriculum must be based on knowledge already acquired by students before they enter the school, and on the other, there is a need to identify facilitators or mediators to mitigate cultural discontinuity. Ideally, the teachers and or teachers' aides participating in the program should be able to identify ethnically and experientially with the students.

An interesting perspective on return migration was discussed by McConnell (1988) concerning Japanese children who return to Japan after attending schools in the United States. McConnell referred to a 1980 *New York Times* article that reported that when these children go back home, they are often ostracized by their teachers and peers, who resent them for their command of English and for interpersonal traits that are seen as abrasive within the Japanese cultural context. Special schools have been established for reentering children, but McConnell argued that although these schools may ease the psychological trauma of readjustment, they may place the children at an educational and occupational disadvantage in Japan because their reentry is made difficult by their inability to "speak and act in a culturally appropriate manner" (p. 4). He cited vignettes of classroom attempts to acculturate Japanese children such as a teacher's insistence that a Japanese child look at her as she spoke.

While in the United States, Japanese parents attempt to preserve their culture and vernacular (McConnell, 1988) including everything from prohibiting the use of English to creating a "Saturday school" for practicing Japanese skills and behavioral patterns. In spite of these efforts, when the children return to Japan they have been influenced by their participation in U.S. schools. Teachers often say that the children do not act like Japanese children who have grown up in Japan. The differences pointed out by teachers in Japan are similar to those mentioned by teachers in Puerto Rico comparing return migrant students to nonmigrants. In my study, teachers repeatedly pointed out that the return migrant students did not act like Puerto Ricans. While in the United States, most Puerto Rican migrants also have social environments at home and in their communities that reinforce their cultural values and identities. McConnell's (1988) powerful conclusion questions the socializing power of the family when it is not reinforced in the schools and community.

The schooling of migrant students in the United States has relied heavily on assimilation into the majority culture and has assigned a superior status to the host culture, language, and behaviors. This stance almost inevitably implies that other cultures are inferior, other languages undesirable, and other behaviors inappropriate. Once this lesson is learned, reentry may seem contradictory and can be interpreted as a step backward or as a form of regression, especially by school-age children. The students' sense of marginality and anomie may produce both frustration and intragroup conflict. Although return migrants may feel entitled to participate in their native group's interactions based on their ethnicity, their language and cultural differences create barriers that eventually push them out of the school environment and force them to fend for themselves.

PUERTO RICAN MIGRANTS

Before beginning any discussion of the plight of return migrant students, it is important to consider the general experiences of Puerto Rican migrants to the mainland and their specific educational experiences in the United States. There is a respectable amount of literature in both areas, some discussed in other chapters of this book. Hence, I have selected accounts based on data collected through interviews and life histories, because they are more compatible with the methodological approach I consider most appropriate for studying this phenomenon.

In an early ethnographic study, Bucchioni (1973) integrated accounts from observations and field notes into one representative school day for

Puerto Rican migrant elementary school students in New York City. Teachers' conversations centered on their disappointment with the Puerto Rican children; one teacher felt that trying to teach them was a waste of time. As in McConnell's (1988) account of Japanese children in American schools, migrant students' pronunciation was constantly corrected. One teacher protested a child's addressing her as "teacher" in English (following the appropriate title used in Puerto Rico, *maestra* or *maestro*) because teachers in the United States expect to be addressed by their title (Mr./Miss/Mrs.) and their surname. One child's comment about a home with three bathrooms belonging to someone rich was "clarified" by the teacher with a statement that its owner was not necessarily rich but rather that this was the reward for hard work. The child responded that his father worked hard every day and even some Sundays and yet they only had one bathroom for several apartments in the building. Teachers likewise stated that their Puerto Rican students were dirty and that they acted like animals. Bucchioni (1973) asserted that a plethora of statements and interactions such as these between teachers and students reflected a profound cultural misunderstanding and a total lack of interest in the students on the part of the teachers.

Alers-Montalvo (1985) studied the changes in cultural values, attitudes, and beliefs among Puerto Ricans that can result from migration to New York. For instance, he found that the types of jobs migrants obtain lower their self-esteem. He also suggested that friendships were affected by work and that they are perceived as less important in the United States than in their native land. Some migrants had trouble understanding how people could be pleasant in the workplace and then act as if they did not know you once they left the workplace. On the Island, coworkers were often considered family. Alers-Montalvo suggested that these discontinuities between well-established cultural expectations and behaviors caused migrants to experience anomie. In order to cope with an unwelcoming environment, Puerto Ricans immerse themselves in their identity as Puerto Ricans, thus distancing themselves from the dominant group.

Fitzpatrick (1971) addressed the gender-related changes of some values, indicating that work had made women independent and more involved in their communities. Once "submissive" Puerto Rican children become aggressive, competitive, self-reliant, and prone to ask "why?" they gradually can become separated from family. This, in turn, weakens extended kinships. Fitzpatrick identified three strategies for adjustment: (a) Escape from the immigrant group, disassociate from the past, and risk the danger of becoming marginal; (b) resist by withdrawing from the old culture; or (c) try to build cultural bridges by establishing oneself with the new society but identifying with those from home.

This latter strategy appears to be the one employed by a group of Puerto Rican women in New York City as reported by Torruellas (1991). Their life histories and the researchers' ethnographic observations in the context of a literacy program describe their efforts "to define themselves, to validate their culture and traditions, and affirm their collective sense of identity" (pp. 2–3). The researchers found that rather than demanding inclusion and participation, these women asserted their differences in order to contribute to society. These Puerto Rican migrants also found a sense of solidarity and support in the literacy center similar to that found in an extended family, and they referred to the literacy program as their *segunda familia* (second family). Torruellas (1991) concluded that committed policy makers or researchers can galvanize these cultural resources to produce social change.

PUERTO RICAN RETURN MIGRANT STUDENTS

Coming back is often as difficult as leaving was. Decisions to return are often made hastily with minimal planning. Many people return without having a job lined up, and without knowing where they are going to live. And returning families must often make as many adjustments as they did when they left, which ironically includes dealing with cultural shock.

—Santiago (1994, p. F5)

The literature on Puerto Rican return migrant students constantly points out that they represent a problem for Puerto Rico's educational system (Prewitt-Díaz & Seilhamer, 1985; Rivera-Medina, 1984; Robles et al., 1980). To address this issue, studies have focused on investigating which characteristics of return migrant students are problematic. Hence, researchers have looked at students' social and linguistic behavior (Albino-Serrano, 1990), their attitudes toward school (Prewitt-Díaz & Seilhamer, 1985), their identity problems (Pacheco, Wapner, & Lucca, 1979), and their adaptation problems (Ashton, 1981; Ramos-Perea, 1972). Most studies have consisted of questionnaires administered to teachers, parents, principals, and, lastly, students. The study reported in this chapter differs in that the information was obtained principally from the students themselves, although observations and feedback from teachers, parents, and staff also were used to interpret the data.

Pacheco et al. (1979) explored migration as a critical transition of an individual in an environment. The researchers explored return migrant students' perspectives within the framework of rejection by the community and adjustment to a different physical, cultural, and social environment. They compared these students to others who had never migrated. Their findings were similar to those of an earlier study by Ramos-Perea (1972), who found that return migrant students had difficulties adjusting to the demands of school. Pacheco, Wapner, and Lucca (1979) designed a questionnaire to obtain information on the transition process and quality of life of return migrants in the present environment compared to their former environment. The focus of their research was not, however, on the effects of this process on education but rather on students' language use and social interactions and the impact of these on students' adjustment to school. Students described feelings of moving from an active (U.S. mainland) to a passive (Puerto Rico) environment, and of feeling "dead" after being "alive." The researchers concluded that the effects of migration were worsened by the lack of knowledge and false expectations regarding Puerto Rican culture.

Most studies of the poor performance of return migrants have focused on teachers' perceptions of them. In 1984, a review of the research on Puerto Rican return migrant students by Rivera-Medina demonstrated that they were not well received by the educational system. He cited a National Institute of Education study (1981) based on survey data involving 807 teachers from 12 public school districts in Puerto Rico. Findings were reported according to the perceptions of English teachers and Spanish teachers. According to Rivera-Medina (1984), the concerns of these teachers pose the most serious problems for the curriculum because migrant students' problems are mostly related to language. However, Vivó (1982) also recommended Puerto Rican culture courses for return migrant students. Because the cultural values of return migrants often differ from traditional Puerto Rican values, dissonance among return migrant students and between them, their teachers, and their peers can result. In general, teachers responding to the questionnaire indicated that they had problems both in and out of the classroom with return migrant students. Some of these problems included behaviors that teachers perceived as disrespectful, such as directness when responding to or asking questions and appearing inattentive in class.

In a study of return migrant students' perceptions of teachers, school, and self, Prewitt-Díaz, Soto, and Seilhamer (1982) compared perceptions of circulatory migrants (those moving constantly to and from Puerto Rico) and return migrants who had remained in the United States for 3 or more years before returning to Puerto Rico. An inventory was administered to 117 students, and the findings included a more positive attitude toward teachers, school, and self in Puerto Rico by return migrants as compared to circulatory migrants. Meanwhile, circulatory migrants had more positive responses to schools, teachers, and self in the United States. Prewitt-Díaz et al. (1986) conceded that their findings were not consistent with the findings of other researchers. The study was conducted with students who were in their last year of high school or already in college, so the students may have had time to adapt to their new environment. On the other hand, Likert scales and inventories often lack the depth and breadth of open-ended questions and interviews that accompany longitudinal observations in a setting. Hence, studies that rely solely on quantitative data may provide limited perspectives that need to be complemented with data collected in other ways over a longer period of time.

García-Pérez's (1990) is the only study I found comparable to the one reported in this chapter. Garcia-Pérez investigated nonverbal and paralinguistic classroom interactions among teachers and students with and without migratory experiences in the United States and focused on communicative competence. The researcher used ethnographic methods such as open-ended questions, videotaped observations, and field notes. Some of García-Pérez's findings revealed assertive behaviors among students with migratory experiences. For example, in turning in their papers after a quiz or exam, students with migratory experiences had no qualms about placing their papers on top of the pile. Those with no migratory experiences went out of their way to place their papers under the rest or in the middle of the stack. Other patterns observed in females concerned the use of makeup and choice of handbags carried to school. Behaviors and artifacts exhibited by return migrants are often different from those of their peers, differences that are sometimes interpreted as deliberate rejection of local customs and styles.

A STUDY OF RETURN MIGRANT REENTRY

In this study I examined the experiences of return migrant students in two high schools in an urban setting in Puerto Rico. Preliminary research to identify schools for my study revealed little or no information on the existence of programs to address the needs of return migrant students at the high school level. One private school described a program for *continentales* where lessons are taught in English. I found nothing in writing or in school policies and practices about the socialization or affective needs of return migrant students. In what follows, I describe the methods, setting, and participants of my study. I then describe the themes that emerged from my data, and finally I discuss my findings and their implications for educational policy and curriculum.

There were four basic goals in this study. The first was to understand the social, educational, and interpersonal conditions that migrant students encounter when they go to school in Puerto Rico. Second, I wanted to determine whether the students' social and academic needs were being addressed by schools. A third goal was to find out how migrant students interpreted their academic situation in the schools, and the fourth goal was to determine the affective and pragmatic needs of this population within the social context of the school.

I selected a city in the central region of the Island because it has many of the characteristics of San Juan's metropolitan area, including an increase in home construction, schools, and amenities such as malls. However, because it retains many features common to the Island's smaller towns, people still identify with older traditions and values. Furthermore, many extended families have remained in the area. This distinguishes this city from the San Juan metropolitan area, which has become a conglomerate of housing and population sprawl similar to major cities in the United States where constant demographic turnover makes it difficult to develop a sense of community. Hence, the city chosen was appropriate for the study because return migrants presented a visible contrast to local residents.

Two high schools were selected for the study. One, Downtown High School, was the city's old high school located in the downtown area and the other, Uptown High School, was located in a middle-class urbanization on the outskirts of the city. After screening 53 students for the study, I selected 20 from Downtown High and 10 from Uptown High. Selection of students was based on referrals by teachers, students, and other school personnel who identified them as newcomers who were English speaking.

Student perspectives of their own experiences in school are as important as those of teachers and other staff members who interact with them. Students themselves can provide essential information to help others understand their needs. The 30 participants were interviewed in as naturalistic a way as possible, allowing for the free flow of conversation. Data describing the two school settings chosen, as well as the communities where they are located, were derived from my observations and from the perceptions of students, teachers, and parents, as related through interviews. I also studied peer interactions. Observations of students included interactions in the classroom, participation in school activities, and other interactions with staff and peers in the school setting. These data corroborated interview information generated by participants and descriptions of realities as perceived and reported by them and observed by the researcher (LeCompte & Preissle, 1993) to recreate the experiences of return migrants in the social contexts of two Puerto Rican high schools.

Within the framework of qualitative research, sharing cultural background and similar experiences with the group studied lends authority to the accounts of the participant observer (Atkinson, 1990). This characteristic of shared background facilitated my study. My role in this study was that of a participant observer who could relate to the experience of return migrants because I had been a return migrant myself while my father was in the U.S. Army. Hence, the students had an empathic listener. Teachers and school staff were equally comfortable with me because I could relate to the public school scenario in a number of ways: I had graduated from a public high school in Puerto Rico, and I had attended and taught prospective teachers at the University of Puerto Rico.

Many of the students initially identified for the study as return migrants had attended elementary school in Puerto Rico. Hence, they had migratory experience but were already integrated into the system. Other students in the study had left the school before the interviewing began. "Tony was too American. He even had an American last name," his teacher told me when she informed me that he had gone back to the States. After spending no fewer than 8 hours a week in each school during the fall, I selected 30 student informants in two different schools. I collected data through the academic year 1992–1993.

Secondary informants included teachers, staff, and parents. Teachers were interviewed and observed whenever their names were mentioned by student interviewees as either teachers they could work with or teachers they had problems with. In all cases, interviewees agreed to participate in the study and were assured that pseudonyms would be used when reporting the data to ensure confidentiality. Early in the study I requested permission from teachers to visit their classes and to interview them during their preparation times. Parents were interviewed when they came to school. Most of the time the counselors or social workers would contact parents for me. Because parents and guardians were inaccessible, I was unable to collect much data from parents. Inaccessibility of parents and/or guardians began with their not visiting the school and it was affected by a high turnover rate caused by moving from one neighborhood to another, or having the students move from one relative to another. As a result, the school had no way of contacting some students.

All of the students in the study had been born in the United States and educated there through junior high school. Students came from New York (11), New Jersey (6), Illinois (2), Texas (1), Florida (5), Pennsylvania (2), Connecticut (1), Massachusetts (1), and California (1). Generally, people think that most migrants come from the northeastern part of the United States, and most are labeled "Newyoricans" because of this.

All the participants had problems with Spanish language classes as well as with courses such as history and sociology, which rely heavily on language proficiency. The schools had placed all of them in sophomore Spanish although they were seniors and juniors. Return migrant students spoke English among themselves in and out of class. They usually sat together in classes when two or more were assigned to the same course. Most carried one large spiral notebook or a loose-leaf binder rather than the one notebook per class favored by nonmigrant students. Few of the return migrant female students wore makeup and those who did wore a discreet amount. Return migrant males wore their trousers baggier than their nonmigrant counterparts. Some also wore baseball caps with emblems such as Bulls or Raiders. At the beginning of my study, most of the return migrants (subsequently referred to as RMs) were loners, but near the end of the study they had bonded and sought each other out. Some of the students sat together during their free hours talking about rock, rap, and reggae music and musicians. They ate both in the school cafeteria and in small shops across the street from the school, and they chose to eat Puerto Rican staples as did non-RM students.

Five themes emerged based on the frequency with which they were mentioned by students in the study. Specifically, the themes addressed here are identity, the need for special support, criticism of school policies and practices in Puerto Rico, unavailability of extracurricular activities, and RM teachers as cultural mediators.

Identity

In an attempt to help educators address the needs of RM students, researchers have focused on the characteristics that make RM students different from non-RM students. Several profiles have been produced (Hamilton, 1987; Ramos-Perea, 1972; Vivó, 1982; Pacheco & Wapner, 1979). Rather than focusing on differences, in this study I look at how return migrants themselves feel. I found that these students felt Puerto Rican, but they also felt that others did not view them as Puerto Ricans. My observational data and interviews of teachers, other staff members, and nonmigrant peers confirmed the students' feelings.

The following quote from the Island's English-language newspaper illustrates the ambivalence many RMs experience as they begin to encounter rejection by Island Puerto Ricans. While in the United States, they asserted their ethnic identities because they were often treated as non-Americans. In Puerto Rico, the opposite happened.

Kids who come with parents returning [in a quest] for their romantic image of Puerto Rico can find themselves with prejudice on this side too. There they were told they were Puerto Rican. Here they are told they are not Puerto Rican. It can be very painful. (Santiago, 1993, pp. F2,3)

All but one of the students in this study considered themselves Puerto Rican. However, for the teachers, staff, and peers, they were not Puerto Rican but rather *gringos*, *bilingües*, and "Newyoricans." Comments were made by teachers, staff, and other students to point out the traits that, according to them, distinguished the RMs from the rest of the students. These traits included not knowing Spanish (or English) well, aggressiveness, "walking shrugging their shoulders," "having an attitude," not being interested in Puerto Rican language and culture, thinking they are better, being more liberal (girls), being ganglike (boys), and not wanting to be in Puerto Rico. Students' self-reported identities were not consistent with their identities as perceived by others. In some cases, the students were painfully aware of this, and in other cases they appeared not to care. When asked about their nationality, 29 of the 30 students immediately responded that they were Puerto Rican:

Tito: I'm Puerto Rican because that's my culture. People here don't speak to me because they think I don't know Spanish. When we get to talking and they find out I'm from the Bronx, they say it's a bad place with lots of gangs and that Chicago is better. I tell them that they are stereotyping. Labels make me feel uncomfortable because they judge me without knowing who I am.

Annie: They used to call me "gringa." I'm not "gringa." That's for the White people.

Only one student, Nitza, identified herself as American because of her citizenship. Of course, all Puerto Ricans are American citizens, but Nitza said "I'm an American citizen. My dream is to go work in the States, get married over there and do everything over there."

Confusion about their identity is seen in RMs' comments about how others perceive them. These responses, as described by current RMs, are not new, as one of the teachers in Downtown High pointed out: "I was a victim of bias when I returned to Puerto Rico and people called me 'Newyorican.' I felt like an outsider until recently." Many of the RM teachers expressed similar feelings. Knowledge of English implies, according to some residents of the Island, incompetence in Spanish and ignorance of Puerto Rican culture. For the most part, initial interactions with peers reflected identity-related misconceptions and stereotypical expectations. The media also perpetuate stereotypes when they identify a subject in a news item as a "Newyorican" and when they include comic characters in local sitcoms who mix languages and portray streetwise males and Americanized females with liberal views. Some of these perceived liberal behaviors include smoking, drinking, and premarital sex practiced by women, behaviors that have traditionally been viewed as appropriate for males but off-limits for women. Working outside of the home has become standard practice for Puerto Rican women, and many of the behaviors mentioned are considered tolerable if the woman works.

As a result of stereotyping by peers, RM students describe scenarios such as these:

Betty: When we got here this guy started talking to me and right away said 'you know what I want from you.' I didn't speak to him anymore. Guys here think that just because we came from over there we're like garbage. Some people, just because you come from the States they label you.

Berto: Here in school a guy threw some ravioli from off the floor on my tray and I dumped them on his tray. And he said that I thought I was important because I was from the States. And I told him if he had a problem we could go outside. I beat him up and he doesn't bother me anymore.

Isabel: I've been here one semester and people still look at me like I'm not from here. I can tell when I walk by and they stare at me. I think it's for the way I look. I don't wear as much makeup as the girls here wear.

Nora: I don't know anyone yet; I don't have any friends. I'm always by myself whenever a teacher is absent from school or anything. My mother insisted that I go to the field day to make friends. I marched with my group to the park but spent all day sitting next to Ms. Resto [her English teacher who is also an RM].

Linda: I think most of the girls don't like me because I speak English. It's as if they were saying. "She thinks she's big because she knows two languages." I got used to it already.

Reports such as these from the RM students were confirmed in my observations in and out of classrooms. Generally, non-RM students did not try to befriend RMs. They were stared at or ignored, which caused RMs to speculate about the reasons why this would happen. Isabel thought the curious looks she got were because she wore little makeup when in all probability she was stared at simply because she was from the States. Most of the students were loners or had found common ground with some peers who lived in the same neighborhood or who liked the same music. However, one student, Ed, explained his success with this advice: "You can't speak English, man; if you do nobody will talk to you. I only speak Spanish around school and that's how I've made friends."

This advice may be on target given what non-RMs say about bilinguals. Ileana, one of the non-RM students, said "Most are nice—not snobs or anything. Most don't want to stand out in class and some even speak English with an accent to fit in with the group." This pattern is also present among the bilingual professionals with whom I have interacted. In situations that call for speaking English, they do so with a heavy accent, even though they have native fluency, so as to protect themselves from the *gringo* label.

Some teachers and staff also expressed their views about the identities of RMs. A non-RM history teacher at Uptown High School stated "RMs have language and cultural difficulties most of all because they have been taught that the Puerto Rican language and culture are inferior."

The most negative responses came from a history teacher in Downtown High School who had never experienced migration himself. He stated *"No dan pie con bola"* (They can't get it right). *"No quieren estar aquí, sólo hablan de regresar"* (They don't want to be here, they just want to go back). A non-RM science teacher in Uptown High School said "They have an attitude, they don't know Spanish, and they think the culture and language here are less important than English and the American culture. So they don't really care."

Need for Special Support

The support staff appeared to disagree among themselves regarding RMs, as revealed by the following conversation at Downtown High School:

Social worker: Teachers misunderstand students and feel they know neither English nor Spanish. They also describe them as aggressive in class.

Counselor: That's true.

Social worker: Some come from good backgrounds.

Counselor: You have to see the teachers' side too. These students come with an attitude that everything (schools, teachers) is better in the U.S. and they want to go back.

This kind of conversation was repeated many times throughout my study. In their conversations with me and among themselves, teachers, other staff members, and administrators demonstrated confusion and a lack of information regarding issues of migration and schooling of RM students. Some teachers believed the RMs had problems adjusting to the school simply because they were not interested in school, and that their language problems and cultural misunderstandings were a matter of "attitudes." When I tried to explain that migration processes often had these effects on schooling, they reacted by saying that RMs should have not come back to Puerto Rico if that was the case. In both schools, I found the support staff, one guidance counselor and one social worker, very committed to the transition process of RM students. The social worker made home visits and took extra steps to procure a more suitable academic placement for students, one where their limited Spanish skills could get them through. The Uptown High School had a business program where English and computer skills were valued. The counselor at this school made every effort to enroll interested RM students in this program. Both of these professionals advocated for all of their students, and I found them especially helpful in accessing my students.

School Policies and Practices

Many RM students frequently compared the schools and teachers in Puerto Rico and the mainland in negative ways, stating that everything was better in the United States. Some of the features mentioned were access to computers, textbooks to take home, air-conditioned classrooms, big libraries, science labs, auditoriums, and recreational facilities. Another aspect frequently mentioned was the lack of information about team sports and other school activities and the absence of extracurricular interest groups such as clubs and organizations. Students lamented that Puerto Rican public schools do not encourage interaction on the school grounds beyond school hours. When I asked Lucy, a petite, dark-haired, dark-eyed girl with a gentle disposition, to compare her initial experiences in Puerto Rico with school in the States, she giggled sarcastically: "There are a lot of differences. Over there [in Texas] if a teacher was absent you got a sub. Here on my first day I only had one or two classes out of five because teachers were absent."

The lack of a substitute program in Puerto Rico's public education system is troubling given the number of unemployed teachers. The Education Department has traditionally stated that it has no funds for such a program. Nevertheless, costly reforms such as vouchers and community schools have recently been funded. For RMs, responding to the absence of teachers and resulting free periods requires cultural information to which they are not privy upon arrival. Tito explained:

> Here when teachers are absent there are no substitutes, and everyone just leaves saying *"adelanta, adelanta"* [literally, "move up"]. I didn't know what was going on and everyone started going to different rooms. Later I asked my English teacher and she explained that it meant to take a class you have scheduled later in the day at the period that has been freed up.

Nobody explains to these students that there is no substitute program and that there are certain practices such as *adelantar*. A possible result is a reaction such as Berto's: "Yesterday I didn't have two of my classes so I went a lot of places. I also went to Uptown School 'cause I have lots of friends over there."

The absence of substitutes affects students' perceptions about teachers and the school. According to Linda, "Here if a teacher doesn't come, there is no substitute. You just leave the class and during classes students get up and walk in and out. Over there the discipline is better than over here."

In Puerto Rico, as well as in many Latin American and Caribbean countries, students are identified with specific schools by assigning uniforms with school emblems inscribed on shirtsleeves. Uniforms are often viewed as a major restriction by newcomers:

Isabel: My parents brought us in July so we could adjust but school started in August and I was used to [it starting in] September so it was too sudden. I then had to get used to uniforms. I hate them, they are so weird and in the States I always wore pants and here I have to wear skirts. I only wore skirts when I had no choice. They make me feel naked. Here you're only allowed to wear pants if you're pregnant.

Rob: If you don't do laundry every 2 days you have to bring an excuse for wearing other clothes. I liked it better in the States where I could wear whatever I liked.

Another problem mentioned by students was the scarcity of resources. Materials and resources are lacking and fall short even when compared to students' former inner-city schools in the United States. The students in my study described their feelings about resources in several ways:

Betty: Over there I was learning word processing. Here only the business students get to use the computers.

Al: [remembering his former school] Oh man! Air conditioning, nice rooms, computers.

Tito: Here they hand out books. In New York you got to take home a book from each class.

Isabel: I had computers since eighth grade. Here there is nothing. Now I feel I'm so behind.

Problems of class placement were also described by students as setbacks. RMs are usually placed in lower tracked groups for all their classes and end up taking English classes that are below their proficiency levels.

Rob: The English class is too easy. I had everything in 7th grade.

Jenny: [shyly shows me her English notebook.] I take class with Mrs. Ramos [a non-RM teacher] and sometimes she writes sentences on the board with mistakes like no verbs and I go to her and tell her quietly and she corrects them but I don't think she likes it.

Norma: I'm taking regular English 11 because there was no room in advanced English 11. The class is so easy that the kids are always trying to copy from my paper. Some have only talked to me to ask me to let them cheat.

Extracurricular Activities

Extracurricular activities have been described as a necessary component of a well-rounded student life, but they are not emphasized in Puerto Rico's public schools. I was able to identify a Library Club at Uptown High School and I was told of basketball, volleyball, and baseball teams although I actually never saw or heard anyone talk about games. Unfortunately, RM students often enter schools at times when recruiting for these organizations has ended. There are very few extracurricular activities, and students must take the initiative to find out about them because the schools do not coordinate efforts in this direction.

Public schools in Puerto Rico lack the collegial environment promoted by extracurricular activities such as varsity sports, clubs, and organizations that exist in U.S. schools. After-school activities are implicitly discouraged for lack of security and supervisory personnel. Students who want to participate in sports must depend on the physical education teacher to close the building and secure school property, but many teachers are not willing to do this for reasons of safety (LaSemana, 1993, June 3, p. 6). Students coming from schools with strong traditions of sports teams, drama clubs, and school newspapers are at a loss when they are unable to pursue these interests. Extracurricular activities provide space for socialization among people who share interests. The unavailability of these outlets in Puerto Rican public schools slows the process of integration of the RM students. It also encourages cutting classes among all students because many have no place to socialize except on the school premises.

> *Isabel:* I wanted to play volleyball and I was told the team was formed, but they never announced tryouts or anything. And there's a field day but nobody tells you how you can get in and compete.
> *Al:* In the States I played football. Here in this city they don't have it. And if you get in any sport you have to pay.
> *Elisa:* In the States there was more order and there were extracurricular activities in school.

For brothers Wiso and Eliseo, the most frustrating experience was the lack of sports. In the States, one was in baseball and wrestling and the other was on a varsity baseball team. In Puerto Rico, facilities are scarce and the physical education program is weak. In fact, physical education, art, and music are not even required components of the regular curricula of public schools. There are a few specialized music and performing arts schools, but exposure to fine arts and sports is not considered a priority for all.

RM Teachers as Cultural Mediators

Students frequently expressed feeling marginalized or alienated by a lack of cultural knowledge of the practices in the new school setting. Certain English teachers, especially those who have experienced return migration to Puerto Rico, were described by RMs as liaisons. However, this relationship depended upon an RM being assigned to an RM English teacher's class, and this does not often happen. When they were placed with RM teachers, students expressed satisfaction that their skills were acknowledged.

> *Betty:* My teacher [an RM] calls on me a lot because I finish fast and she sends me to the board to write my answers.

One of the Spanish teachers remarked: "Berto [an RM at Downtown High] got a D in Spanish and an F in English. I can't understand this unless the English teacher is insecure in English." The English classes present special problems for RMs. Students complain that "the classes are too easy," but teachers, especially those with no migratory experience, consider the students incompetent in English. They believe that the students "overestimate their ability" and that "they only know street English and are poor spellers with bad grammar." Teachers who are RM tended to disagree. A teacher from Uptown High stated "RMs shine as readers and are wonderful resources in language classrooms." It was refreshing to hear a comment that focused on RM students' strengths.

Return migrant teachers needed to inform parents, and students themselves, about norms and practices in Puerto Rican schools. Return migrant students needed to have Spanish-language competency to perform adequately in their classes and they needed to understand that there were no special accommodations officially available. Students needed to know how teacher absences were handled and what students could do with the free periods that would result from these teacher absences. Students also had to know that in many schools they could not take books home, so they needed to complete much of the work at school and copy a lot of material into notebooks in order to review. Other needs surfaced for individual students, and others affected the entire group. For the most part, schools addressed individual and collective problems only if they were brought to the teacher's attention or passed on to another staff member. Many times the students kept to themselves about their difficulties unless they had an RM teacher.

Return migrant teachers are in a unique position to act as cultural mediators for RM students. The empathy they have for RM students is comparable to that of bilingual teachers in U.S. schools who have experienced the educational process of second language acquisition and acculturation within the U.S. school system. Bilingual teachers' experiences with the dominant culture and language enable them to relate to the anxieties and tensions that their own students' experience (Montero Sieburth & Pérez, 1987). Their role as cultural mediators is replicated by the RM teachers as they validate RM students' skills and guide their understanding of the cultural norms of their new setting. Teachers who are aware of the effects of migration stated that the system cannot address RM students' needs. Many of them claimed that there was a need to reinstate the bilingual programs that were established in the 1970s and later defunded and phased out.

CONCLUSION

I found that the needs of RM students continue to be neglected in Puerto Rico's public school system. Return migrants are erroneously perceived and stereotyped as one homogeneous group when they are in fact heterogeneous due to their different migratory experiences and backgrounds.

The complexities of return migration begin with the term itself. Many of the RMs are coming to Puerto Rico to live for the first time, some have visited in summers or during Christmas holidays, and others have only heard of the Island from their parents. These experiences may determine the degree of success with which RMs interact with Puerto Ricans who have little or no migratory experiences. Many of the teachers of RM students lack information about them, and unless the teachers themselves have experienced migration, their own educational experiences have very little to do with the experiences of the RM students. Differences in school policies, classroom dynamics, and communicative styles of teachers in the United States and in Puerto Rico are but a few of the issues unknown to educators in Puerto Rican schools. This lack of knowledge interferes with the possibility of offering high-quality education.

My conversations with teachers revealed that most of them are unprepared to teach RM students attending Puerto Rican schools for the first time. Other than those teachers who have benefited from migratory experiences or those who have been involved with the few existing bilingual programs, preservice education programs totally ignore this population. Return migrants have been the topic of several research studies, some of which have been cited here, but the findings have not influenced educational policies on the Island, nor have they trickled down to practitioners or to those who prepare teachers. For the most part, the issue has been discussed only in scholarly journals, dissertations, and academic forums.

All but one of the RM students in this study identified themselves as Puerto Rican until confronted by teachers and peers who challenged their identity. Language usage was the first criterion used for exclusion. Any student who could not communicate in Spanish or who mispronounced the language was immediately suspected of not being a "real" Puerto Rican. In the school environment, other differences surfaced once RMs were confronted with unfamiliar policies and expectations. Some of these included the use of uniforms, the lack of a substitute teacher program, and the absence of adequate programming to address Spanish-language proficiency and cultural and historical knowledge of Puerto Rico. More often than not, teacher reactions to students' difficulties in the setting were victim-blaming. Transition into the system would have been helped greatly if the teachers had some understanding of the students' experiences in U.S. schools. It would have been an enriching experience for all involved to find out more about what being Puerto Rican meant for these students and about their struggles to maintain their Puerto Rican identity, rather than making RM students feel unwelcome and non-Puerto Rican.

If students do not know about the open-door policy and the reason for it, and they come from schools where entry is restricted, they become confused. If the reasons for wearing uniforms were explained, students may even agree that they are practical. If not, they view them as a senseless imposition. A school without a substitute program may appear anarchic, but if students are informed about the practice and available options such as *adelantar* or using the time to study, they may develop time-management skills. All of these pieces of information are part of the school culture or practices and norms that are peculiar to public schools in Puerto Rico which RM students must learn about in order to behave appropriately. Not knowing this culture will lead students to behave differently and, consequently, to be stigmatized and punished.

Although I had minimal opportunities to interview parents, the few I did speak with were as confused and frustrated as their offspring. Their expectations were grounded in experiences with schools in the United States, where parent advocacy and community activists have mobilized school systems to provide services for special populations ranging from disabled students to non-English-speaking students. In Puerto Rico, these parents found no parent centers and no new student orientation processes or special programs for students transferring into the system. In each of the schools I found either a social worker (Downtown High School) or a guidance counselor (Uptown High School) and one or two teachers who went out of their way to help students. Unfortunately, the contacts between students and these few educators were coincidental or random; their interactions were not part of any organized plan to help these students. When a student was lucky enough to be assigned to a caring teacher staff person, efforts were made to enroll the student in the appropriate levels of Spanish or the higher, more challenging levels of English. If these contacts were not made, RM students, for the most part, were simply ignored by many of the teachers in their own classrooms.

Two areas that must be addressed in order to reach RM students and meet their needs are teacher preparation and parental involvement. Teacher preparation programs in Puerto Rico need to include multicultural education in the curricula. They must value the diversity of their students in the same way we expect diversity to be valued in the United States. In Puerto Rico, we too have diversity among Spanish-speaking immigrants from different countries, among people from different socioeconomic backgrounds, and among Puerto Ricans born and/or raised in the United States or elsewhere. This diversity needs to be discussed and explored in teacher education programs and courses. Preservice teachers need to acknowledge and learn about these differences and their potential impact on educational achievement. All students, not just RMs, should be made aware of the enormous impact of migration on Puerto Rican society.

Parents must also understand the differences between and within the school systems of Puerto Rico and the United States. They must be well informed in order to make appropriate choices for their children. It is important for parents to understand the impact of migration on schooling and the effects of moving in and out of different cultures. School personnel should meet regularly with parents to discuss the best possible way to meet the needs of their children, and, if possible, parents should be directed to the schools and teachers most experienced with linguistic and cultural differences. Ideally, of course, all teachers should develop knowledge and skills necessary to serve whatever student enters their classroom. Establishing parent centers and recruiting bilingual college students to work as volunteers to complete course requirements in education by tutoring and mentoring RM students in Puerto Rico's schools could also make a difference. Services need to be provided at a variety of locations and schedules compatible with the job demands of parents.

The voices of the students and teachers in this study confirm the need for special attention to the effective transition of Puerto Rican RM students into school. Those who are to work with RM students in and out of school must acknowledge the negative consequences of assimilation and the devaluation of their native cultures in the U.S. school system. Many of these students have been in classrooms where they have been met with low expectations, and stereotypical assumptions, and where even the Spanish spoken in their homes is considered inferior to that of Spain and other Spanish-speaking countries. For most of the students, embracing their ethnic identity and connecting to their ethnic communities became a strategy from which they drew strength to survive in the U.S. school system. When this process is understood, RM students will no longer be viewed as outsiders but rather as participants whose lived experiences can be shared and whose presence in Puerto Rican classrooms should be validated and nurtured.

REFERENCES

Albino-Serrano, I. (1990). *A comparative study of classroom coping behavior of return migrant and non-migrant high school students in English and Spanish classes.* Unpublished doctoral dissertation, Inter-American University of Puerto Rico, San Juan, Puerto Rico.

Alers-Montalvo, M. (1985). *The Puerto Rican migrants of New York City: A study of anomie.* New York: AMS Press.

Ashton, G. (1981). Return and re-return of long-term Puerto Rican migrants: A selective rural–urban sample. *Revista/Review Interamericana*, 1, 27–45.

Atkinson, P. (1990). *The ethnographic imagination: Textual constructions of reality.* New York: Routledge.

Beléndez-Soltero, P. (1994). Issues in educating the return migrant in Puerto Rico. In C. A. Torre, H. Rodríguez Vecchini, & W. Burgos (Eds.), *The commuter nation: Perspectives on Puerto Rican migration* (pp. 289–310) Rio Piedras: Editorial de la Universidad de Puerto Rico.

Bucchioni, E. (1965). A sociological analysis of the functioning of elementary education for Puerto Rican children in the New York City public schools. In F. Cordasco & E. Bucchioni (Eds.), *The Puerto Rican experience: A sociological sourcebook.* Totowa, NJ: Rowan & Littlefield.

Cafferty, J., & Rivera-Martínez, C. (1981). *The politics of language: The dilemma of bilingual education for Puerto Ricans.* Boulder, CO: Westview Press.

Campa, A. (1989, Winter). Immigrant Latinos and resident Mexican Americans in Garden City, Kansas: Ethnicity and ethnic relations. *Urban Anthropology, 19,* 4.

Colón, L. (1988). *La inmigración o el regreso de migrantes a Puerto Rico.* Rio Piedras: Editorial de la Universidad de Puerto Rico.

Cordasco, R., & Bucchioni, E. (Eds.). (1973). *The Puerto Rican experience: A sociological sourcebook.* Totowa, NJ: Littlefield Adams.

Dworkin, A.G. (1972). The peoples of La Raza: The Mexican-Americans of Los Angeles. In N. Gist & A. Dworkin (Eds.), *The blending of races: Marginality and identity in world perspective.* New York: Wiley.

Durkheim, E. (1965). *El suicidio: Estudio de sociología* [Sociological study of suicide] (L. Gibaja, Trans.). Buenos Aires: Editorial Schapire.

Escuelas afectadas por falta de seguridad [Schools affected by lack of security]. (1993, June 3). *La Semana,* p. 6.

Fitzpatrick, J. (1971). *Puerto Rican Americans: The meaning of migration to the mainland.* Englewood Cliffs, NJ: Prentice-Hall.

Fitzpatrick, J. (1989). Puerto Ricans as a social minority on the mainland. *International Journal of Group Tensions, 19*(3), 195–208.

Freire, P. (1972). *Pedagogía del oprimido.* [Pedagogy of the Oppressed] (J. Mellado, Trans.). (25th ed.). Ciudad de México (Mexico City), México: Siglo veintiuno editores.

García Pérez, M. (1990). *Communicative competence: Nonverbal, paralinguistic classroom interactions among Puerto Rican teachers and students with and without migratory experience in the United States.* Unpublished doctoral dissertation, Inter-American University of Puerto Rico, San Juan, Puerto Rico.

Gibson, M. (1987). Punjabi immigrants in an American high school. In G. Spindler & L. Spindler (Eds.), *Interpretive ethnography of education at home and abroad.* Hillsdale, NJ: Lawrence Erlbaum Associates.

Gibson, M. (1988). *Accommodation without assimilation.* Ithaca, NY: Cornell University Press.

Gibson, M., & Ogbu, J. (1991) *Minority status and schooling: A comparative study of immigrant and involuntary minorities.* New York: Garland.

Gist, N. P., & Dworkin, A. G. (Eds.). (1972). *The blending of races: Marginality and identity in world perspective.* New York: Wiley.

Gordon, M. (1964). *Assimilation in American life.* Oxford.

Hamilton, J. (1987). Perfil del estudiante migrante de retorno en primer año universitario (1985–86) en Puerto Rico [Profile of the return migrant university freshman]. *Revista Cupey,* 80–85.

LeCompte, M. D., Millroy, W. L., & Preissle, J. (Eds.). (1992). *The handbook of qualitative research in education.* San Diego, CA: Academic Press.

LeCompte, M. D., & Preissle, J. (1993). *Ethnography and qualitative design in educational research* (2nd ed.). San Diego, CA: Academic Press.

Macías, J. (1987). Mitigating cultural discontinuity. In G. Spindler & L. Spindler (Eds.), *Interpretive ethnography of education at home and abroad.* Hillsdale, NJ: Lawrence Erlbaum Associates.

McConnell, D. (1988, April). *Culture, school, and family: The social identity formation of Japanese children temporarily enrolled in American elementary schools.* Paper presented at the annual meeting of the American Educational Research Association, New Orleans, LA.

Montero Sieburth, M., & Pérez, M. (1987) Echar p'lante, moving onward: The dilemmas and strategies of a bilingual teacher. *Anthropology and Education Quarterly, 18*(3), 180–189.

Nieto, S. (1996). *Affirming diversity: The sociopolitical context of multicultural education* (2nd ed.). New York: Longman.

Pacheco, A. M., Wapner, S., & Lucca, N. (1979). La migración como una transición crítica para la persona en su ambiente: Una interpretación organísmica evolutiva [Migration as a critical transition for an individual in his/her environment: An evolutionist organismic interpretation]. *Revista de Ciencias Sociales, 123*–155.

Prewitt-Díaz, J. (1982). The Puerto Rican migrant student and the home–school conflict. *El Sol, 26,* 6.

Prewitt-Díaz, J., & Seilhamer, E. (1985). The social–psychological adjustment of migrant and non-migrant Puerto Rican adolescents. *Migration World, 15,* 2, 7.

Prewitt-Díaz, J., Soto, L., & Seilhamer, E. (1982). The perception of migrant students towards teachers, school and self. *Revista Cayey, 50*–51, 97.

Prewitt-Díaz, J., Trotter, R., & Rivera, G. (1989). *Effects of migration on children: An ethnographic study.* Division of Migrant Education, Department of Education of Pennsylvania.

Ramos-Perea, I. (1972). *The school adjustment of return migrant students in Puerto Rico junior high schools.* Unpublished doctoral dissertation, University of Missouri, Columbia.

Reyes, X. A. (1994). *The social environment of the Puerto Rican high school and its effect on the retention of return migrant students.* Unpublished doctoral dissertation, University of Colorado, Boulder.

Rivera-Medina, E. (1981, September). *Assessment of the in-service needs of teachers of English and of Spanish to returned migrants in Puerto Rico* (Final Report to NIE). Washington, DC: National Institute of Education.

Rivera-Medina, E. (1984). The Puerto Rican return migrant student: A challenge to educators. *Educational Research Quarterly, 8*(4), 82.

Robles, R. R., Martínez, R., & Moscoso, M. (1980). *A study of Puerto Rican return migration: Impact on the migrant and the Island.* San Juan: School of Public Health, University of Puerto Rico.

Santiago, W. (1993, May 23). Lives across the water. *The San Juan Star,* pp. F2–F3.

Santiago, W. (1994, January 23). The rough road back home. *The San Juan Star,* p. F5.

Spindler, G. D. (1974) The transmission of culture. In G. D. Spindler (Ed.), *Education and cultural process.* New York: Holt, Rinehart, & Winston.

Spindler, G., & Spindler, L. (Eds.). (1987). *Interpretive ethnography of education at home and abroad.* Hillsdale, NJ: Lawrence Erlbaum Associates.

Torruellas, R. (1991, November). *Affirming cultural citizenship: Puertorriqueñas constructing identity.* Paper presented at the American Anthropological Association meeting, Chicago.

Trueba, H. (1989). *Raising silent voices: Educating linguistic minorities for the 21st century.* New York: Harper & Row.

Vázquez, J. (1989). *Bilingual education programs for return migrant students in Puerto Rico: Perceptions of participants, parents, and teachers.* Unpublished doctoral dissertation, Boston University, Boston.

Vivó, P. (1982). *Puerto Rican migration: The return flow* (UD 022 534). Washington, DC: National Institute of Education.

Moving Around and Moving On

Gillian Rivera

When I was a child, moving around to different places was like picking a new breakfast cereal at the supermarket with my family (my mother, an older brother, and a younger sister). We moved around a lot for many different personal reasons. My mother and father had divorced a few months before I was born. My mother says that my father must have felt he should be there for me for at least one thing in my life, because she knew he was going to be a "blank page in a filled book."

In first grade, I attended Dávila Elementary School in Puerto Rico, and Sra. Muñoz was my teacher. I began the year in late September and stayed until the end of the school year. I had a wonderful time in that class even though I can remember that almost every day I would stay after school with Sra. Muñoz and she would review everything that we had learned in class that day. I had many problems understanding everything that went on in the class and nothing made any sense at all. It wasn't until the end of that year that it was discovered I had a minor case of dyslexia. But after my dyslexia was diagnosed, some family problems surfaced and we had to move back to the States. One of the biggest problems I had as a child was not making friends easily. I had a hard time saying good-bye and making all of those "I'll write to you" promises that I knew I would never keep.

Before I knew it, second grade had arrived, and I was in for one of the biggest nightmares of my life. Ms. Rodríguez was my teacher in school in Paterson, New

Jersey. I would walk to school through the toughest parts of town, but I wasn't as scared walking through those streets as I was about going to school every day and facing the "Devil," as I referred to her. I was nicknamed the "stupid little Puerto Rican" by Ms. Rodríguez and the rest of the students in that class. I was too scared to tell anyone about my dyslexia. I thought they would tell the entire school about it and then the entire school, not just the other children in my classroom, would tease me. I shut myself out from the world in school by staring blankly at the walls or the ceiling and by not talking to anyone.

If I ever needed to go to the restroom, I would just wait until I got home. I tried to avoid any confrontation with anyone in the school. Ninety out of a hundred times I was humiliated in front of the class by Ms. Rodríguez. Most of the time she would make up reasons for why I didn't know the answer to a math question. She would say things like, "She doesn't know English, that's why she can't do it." She would say things to me like, "Come on, you're not a retard, think like everybody else," while knocking on my head and making a hollow noise. I remember report card day like it was yesterday: There she stood with that devilish smile on her face as she said my name out loud and said, "Get ready for this one" as she told the class my grades for the year. Finally, after 9 tormenting months, my family and I moved away to another part of Paterson, and that meant another school.

I attended the new elementary school for the rest of second grade and it was just enough to drive me crazy. I made few friends but many enemies. Everyone in that school hated me because I looked gringa. The majority of the students in that school were Asian, Black, and Hispanic. When I arrived, I was one of the few students who was outcast for either being a gringa or resembling a gringa. I was called "sellout" because I looked the way I did, instead of being tanned or just having darker skin like the rest of the students. I attended this school for 3 months.

My family and I moved once again, this time to a rural area in Massachusetts. There, I was in third grade and attended an elementary school where I had the beginning of a good time. Then things began to take a turn for the worse. One day my older brother came home with a bloody nose and said that he had been jumped at school by a group of boys who had been calling him racial slurs for quite some time. Everyone knew that I was the little sister of "the boy that got beat up." When I got back to school, things were different. I lost a few friends and gained a few enemies, because the boys who had beat up my brother were very popular in the junior high school that my brother attended. After a few confrontations and finally realizing that the schools really weren't doing anything to deal with the problems, my family and I moved once again. This time we moved to a small city in western Massachusetts. We stayed there for an entire year of school and everything was great with the schools, teachers, and students.

After the school year had ended and finding a better place for our family to live, my mother decided to move us again, this time to a small city where we lived for 4½ years. For 3 years, I had the chance to experience for the first time a school with a great atmosphere. I had the chance to stay long enough to go straight through the last half of fourth grade, and all of fifth and sixth grades. I also had the chance to stay in the junior high school as a seventh grader for about 2 months. After having some difficulty with the landlords of the house we rented, we moved back to the town we had lived in before for another 3 years. I attended middle school for the rest of seventh and eighth grades and then attended the high school, a great school where I was taught the meaning of being open-minded about many different things in life. Then we went back to the other town, and I attended the high school, where I am now.

Experiences such as these have led me to pursue education with the strength of my family's support. Adapting to different situations has been one of the hardest things I have had to cope with. I have learned that children need to stay in one place as they grow in order to learn from their education. Having to move around to different locations as a child has given me many disadvantages, but it has also given me many advantages. I have been exposed to many people and have made many friends, but saying good-bye and keeping those "I'll call you" promises have been very difficult. Yet I have also learned to adapt to new surroundings quickly and not to become too attached.

3

Educational Leadership, Educational Change: A Puerto Rican Perspective

Luis O. Reyes

Mac, Mac. Don't turn your back. We're here today, and we'll be back.

In December 1982, these and other militant chants were voiced by hundreds of Puerto Rican demonstrators massed in front of the New York City Board of Education headquarters. The New York Coalition for Bilingual Education, an ad hoc collection of mostly Puerto Rican educators, community activists, parents, and students, had organized this demonstration in downtown Brooklyn to protest Schools Chancellor Frank Macchiarola's unilateral actions to reduce the numbers of New York City students served by bilingual education programs.

As a program administrator with ASPIRA of America, Inc., I was assigned by Mario A. Anglada, then national executive director, to assist ASPIRA of New York, Inc., the Puerto Rican youth leadership development organization that had successfully negotiated a Consent Decree in 1974 with the New York City Board of Education forcing the latter to establish bilingual and ESL classes for Latino students who did not speak English fluently. Thus, I appeared at that 1982 demonstration as a "co-coordinator" of the coalition along with two other educator–activists, Diana Caballero, of the National Congress for Puerto Rican Rights, and Guillermo Linares, a founder of the Asociación Comunal de Dominicanos Progresistas (Community Association of Progressive Dominicans) in Washington Heights, Manhattan.

From 1990 to 1998, I was a member of the New York City Board of Education, working out of that same Brooklyn building. Today, I am an assistant professor in the School of Education at Brooklyn College, CUNY. Dr. Diana Caballero has completed 14 years as the director of the Puerto Rican/Latino Education Roundtable (an educational advocacy coalition that we helped to found in 1983). She has also helped to lead the Leadership Secondary School Collaborative, which worked with school officials to establish a dual-language high school shaped largely by ASPIRA's original mission of leadership development and community service. She is now an assistant professor in the School of Education at City College, CUNY. Guillermo Linares is now a member of the New York City Council, the first Dominican in the United States to be elected to a municipal public office. He last served as a member and president of his local community school board in Washington Heights.

Although this chapter focuses on the issues of educational leadership and educational change from my personal perspective, clearly it easily could be written from others' personal perspectives or from a collective perspective. I attempt to be true to the collective vision that brought many of us together over the last 15 years to fashion a comprehensive education reform agenda on behalf of Puerto Rican/Latino[1] students. However, I speak for myself in relating and interpreting my experience of those efforts.

ENTERING THE STRUGGLE

The work of the New York Coalition for Bilingual Education was not just about mounting a successful demonstration against Chancellor Macchiarola's attempt to dismantle bilingual education. In fact, a U.S. district judge ordered the New York City Board of Education to desist from any action to implement Macchiarola's "opt-out memo," citing the Board's callous disregard for the needs of language minority students. The Coalition's deeper purpose and meaning was to rekindle the fires of the grass-roots campaign in the Puerto Rican communities of New York City for equal educational opportunity and community empowerment. That

---

[1] Although the chapter focuses on the experiences of Puerto Rican students and the role of Puerto Rican leaders in advancing educational improvements, the increasing non–Puerto Rican Latino student body of New York City's public schools and the involvement of Dominican and other Latino community leaders cannot be ignored.

campaign had succeeded in 1974 in establishing bilingual programs in New York City public schools as an educational entitlement for Puerto Rican students.

Dr. Isaura Santiago-Santiago, the former president of Hostos Community College, CUNY in the Bronx, described that process in her 1978 doctoral dissertation, *ASPIRA v. Board of Education: A Community's Struggle for Equal Educational Opportunity* (Santiago-Santiago, 1978). Issues of language of instruction for Puerto Rican students in New York City public schools were tied to a broader set of concerns and demands. Puerto Rican parents, teachers, and community leaders worked collectively along with ASPIRA of New York and the Puerto Rican Legal Defense and Educational Fund (PRLDEF) to document the school system's failure to educate Puerto Rican children, especially those who were non–English speaking.

Many Puerto Rican organizations, such as ASPIRA, PRLDEF, and the Puerto Rican Educators Association (PREA), in fact, were founded in the 1960s and 1970s to respond programmatically to the educational needs of Puerto Rican children and to the lack of responsiveness and inclusion of the educational establishment. From the very beginning, roles and statuses were blended, with college students like Josephine Nieves joining social workers like Dr. Antonia Pantoja, researchers like Dr. Frank Bonilla, and medical leaders like Dr. Francisco Trilla to found ASPIRA, Inc., in New York City in 1961. The many "alternative institutions" created by the Puerto Rican community in those years, institutions as diverse as the Young Lords Party, the Center for Puerto Rican Studies at Hunter College, and the Puerto Rican Association for Community Action (PRACA), all shared a similar underlying ideology. They all envisioned improving the life conditions for Puerto Ricans through self-reliance, community development, and advocacy vis-á-vis the larger society and its formal institutions.

Also made explicit in the mission and practice of these Puerto Rican community organizations was the commitment to the cultural self-affirmation of the Puerto Rican community (Fitzpatrick, 1971/1987; Nieto, 1995; Pantoja & Perry, 1993; Sánchez-Korrol, 1983; Santiago-Santiago, 1978), that is, a determined resistance to forced assimilation. What others defined as the "Puerto Rican problem" (Association of Assistant Superintendents, 1948; Chenault, 1970; Iglesias, 1984; Jennings, 1988; Morrison, 1958; Sánchez-Korrol, 1983; Urciuoli, 1996), our collective refusal to melt linguistically and culturally into the Anglo-American melting pot (Bucchioni, 1982; Glazer & Moynihan, 1963; Margolis, 1968; Mills, Wright, & Goldsen, 1950; Ogbu, 1978), our community leaders regarded as a means of survival (Cafferty & Rivera-Martinez, 1981; Fishman et al., 1971; Nieto, 1995; Reyes, 1981; Pérez & Torres-Guzmán,

1992). The ideology of resistance to forced assimilation led to many collective efforts to assert our right to be both bilingual and bicultural in our personal and public lives (Cafferty & Rivera-Martinez, 1981; Fishman, et al., 1971; Nieto 1996; Walsh, 1991). ASPIRA's mission of developing a new generation of Puerto Rican leaders successful in academics and committed to community service and community development was one of many examples of the marriage of ideology and praxis.

It is no wonder, then, that Fernando Ferrer, now borough president of the Bronx, should have "cut his teeth" as a political activist as vice president of the city-wide ASPIRA Clubs Federation. Along with other high school *aspirantes* (student members of the ASPIRA clubs) like Angelo Falcon, now president of the influential Institute for Puerto Rican Policy, and Digna Sanchez, vice president of Children's Television Workshop in charge of Plaza Sésamo, Ferrer presented a list of 19 demands to the Board of Education on November 19, 1969. The group's subsequent sit-in at the Brooklyn headquarters in support of bilingual education programs and bilingual teachers was a precursor to the 1972–1974 community organizing efforts that resulted in the 1974 ASPIRA Consent Decree and to the 1982 coalition demonstration (the Consent Decree, issued by U.S. District Court Judge Marvin E. Frankel, ordered the New York City Board of Education to implement transitional bilingual programs for Spanish-surnamed students with limited English proficiency). In all three efforts, a consistent pattern was at work: The educational establishment was not meeting its obligations to provide equal educational opportunity to Puerto Rican students, responding minimally, at best, after determined grass-roots pressure from the Puerto Rican community. Equally consistent in these three efforts was the combining of community research, legal analysis, mass mobilization, community education, and subsequent negotiation between Puerto Rican community leaders and educational officials. "Taking it to the streets" went hand-in-hand with going to court and negotiating compromises in boardrooms.

When I was called in to help organize the 1982 campaign in defense of bilingual education, it became clear that I would have to play multiple roles: researching the facts behind the chancellor's bureaucratic gambit as well as the details of the 1974 Consent Decree; meeting with the current ASPIRA staff to explain to a new generation of young, overworked, and underpaid community organizers the goals of bilingual education and the parameters of the Consent Decree; attending strategy meetings with fellow Puerto Rican educational activists who were university professors, school teachers, central board bureaucrats, and parent trainers; and working out principles of unity among group representatives while mapping out outreach tactics to both media outlets and our own constituencies.

As advocates of multicultural education would say today, the process is as important as the product (Banks, 1997; Nieto, 1996; Sleeter, 1991). In fact, as an administrator for a Puerto Rican nonprofit organization with a recently minted doctorate from Stanford University, I found myself learning elementary lessons daily about the educational needs and aspirations of the Puerto Rican community, about the role of intellectuals in popular struggles, about the need to balance ideological purity with the demands of coalition-building, and about the primary importance of human development and personal integrity as anchors for group process and group actions. I was thrust into an exciting educational and community battle for which I had prepared myself by studying 3,000 miles away for 7 years as an expatriate New Yorker. The biggest paradigm shift I had to make was from identifying myself as an atomized graduate student researching leadership behavior in abstraction to becoming a public community leader in the real world of New York.

DIMENSIONS OF LEARNING

In winter 1974, I had undergone a very wrenching identity crisis at Stanford University. After 16 years of Catholic primary and secondary education, I had graduated in 1967 *summa cum laude* and I had been selected to the Phi Betta Kappa chapter at the Catholic University of America. During the 6 years I taught Spanish to high schoolers in the suburbs of northern New Jersey, I also earned a master's degree in Spanish literature. All that striving and achieving led me to Stanford, at the time the premier research university in the United States in the field of education. After a semester in which I established my academic credentials with straight A's, I still was faced with barriers put up by my own educational experience. I knew little or nothing about my Puerto Rican heritage. Even my MA studies exposed me to only one Puerto Rican poet in a sea of Iberian and South American authors. My teachers' high expectations and praises for me were packaged in an unspoken message that said, "You're bright, for a Puerto Rican." For many years I had taken in that silent poison, often almost choking on its doses of self-hate, self-doubt, and resentment. Cut off from solidarity with other Puerto Rican students by geography and by my Catholic striver's upbringing, I finally rebelled. Poetry became my means of detoxification and release. Today only four lines of poetry that I wrote at that time survive intact in my memory, but they have taken on great meaning not only as a personal philosophy of life but also as an expression of ASPIRA's mission (to which I gave 10 years of my life) and as a philosophy of education:

> *Upwardly mobile*
> *Downwardly stable*
> *And inwardly fertile*
> *I want to be.*

I later added a fourth dimension, "outwardly global," in recognition of a shared humanity that is universal and calls me to act locally, but think globally, as the popular saying goes.

In my various roles as educator, advocate, policymaker, and intellectual, I have tried to actualize this multidimensional pedagogy of living and learning. I believe it integrates concepts of excellence, empowerment, creativity, and social justice. Excellence in education implies high aspirations, academic achievement, and socioeconomic mobility. I assume, then, that education can prepare individuals to be intellectual strivers who are enabled to reach the full potential of their God-given talents. Although policymakers must set a floor of certain minimal standards (content, performance, opportunities to learn), we must also have high expectations. We must set standards of excellence that are obtainable.

The second dimension of learning is its role in rooting the individual in his or her own sociocultural community. To be downwardly stable is to be grounded, not ground, to be empowered to go out into the world because one finds stability and strength in one's own experience, an experience that begins in the home and is nourished and shaped by one's community. As a Puerto Rican who has lived within and beyond the Puerto Rican communities of New York City where I grew up, I have learned not to romanticize my ethnic experience but to understand and accept it as real in order to transform it. Our problems don't go away; neither do they define us completely. They do not confine us to victimization, but rather they propel us to change our reality collectively. And so, education for empowerment, no matter what the conditions of the individual student or of specific communities, should be seen as enabling children, young men and women, and adults to take charge of their lives and to create, recreate, and transform their communities. We do not educate ourselves in a social vacuum, just for our personal benefit. Education is a tool for individual socioeconomic advancement, but it is also a tool for collective cultural and political advancement (Darder, 1991; Freire, 1970; Spring, 1993; Walsh, 1996).

The third dimension of education is that process by which each human being is encouraged and enabled to unleash his or her creativity. This goal implies that education is not just for intellectual development, not just for community development, but also for individual human development. Every human being has a unique contribution to make to the world and can only do so by learning to make personal choices, by acting as a free moral being. We did not choose our innate abilities or what racial or ethnic community to be born in, but we can and must make ethical choices. We can and should be permitted to choose our career in life. Educators have the responsibility to provide their students access to all forms of learning appropriate for their age. For Puerto Rican children, that includes access to the linguistic codes of their parents and of the larger society (bilingual proficiency) and access to the ways of knowing, doing, and being of their ethnic community and of American society (bicultural/multicultural competence).

As a people, Puerto Ricans have insisted on bilingual/bicultural education (Darder, 1991; Nieto, 1996; Rodriguez, 1991; Zentella, 1997) precisely to ensure that our children continue to exercise their God-given rights to their language, their culture, and their collective identity. They can choose to become monolingual English speakers, even to assimilate socioculturally into the great U.S. melting pot. What we resist is being forced to do so. Like the coquí, the tree frog of Puerto Rico, we are an "amphibious people". Our very survival as a people, our century-long struggle for self-determination in our island colony and in our marginalized barrios of the continental United States, is predicated on our ability to teach our young to value their linguistic and cultural heritage as they also integrate into the U.S. multicultural democracy. We refuse to choose only one.

Because our U.S. experience, both insular and continental, has taught us difficult and painful lessons about colonialism, racism, ethnocentrism, xenophobia, and discrimination, we Puerto Ricans are particularly susceptible to a pedagogy that affirms diversity and that teaches human solidarity across race, religion, class, color, language, and culture. This is not to deny that many Puerto Ricans subscribe to our own narrow "isms," including machismo and homophobia. But, as a transplanted island people whose demographic dispersion precludes us from becoming a majority group dominating other groups, we have a particular imperative to work out a place in U.S. society based on an ideology of cultural and structural pluralism. Acting locally and thinking globally leads many of us Puerto Ricans to fight police brutality, miseducation, and environmental racism in our neighborhoods, while calling on the U.S. Congress and the United Nations, no matter what our political persuasion, to grant us our rights to self-determination. These sociopolitical realities may be the last thing that a New York City teacher has in mind when she enters her classroom each September, but they are truly part of our educational vision for Puerto Rican children to be educated for the world they will inhabit at the opening of the new millennium.

Although the preceding discussion may seem like a strange philosophical detour, it is, in fact, an example of one of the necessary roles of the Puerto Rican educator: to articulate a vision for the education of Puerto Rican children and youth. My work in ASPIRA and as a member of the New York City Board of Education entailed, precisely, developing and advocating within the board for a "re-visioning" of public education to incorporate the Puerto Rican (and Latino) communities' goals and demands. My philosophy of education, as previously expressed, has been shaped not only by my personal experiences but also by my engagement in a public, collective dialogue with colleagues in the Puerto Rican community and beyond. I believe we not only have to change and transform policies and practices but also must challenge the hegemonic discourse of the educational and political power elites regarding the purpose and goals of public education. All too often our recommendations to policymakers are ignored or misunderstood because of the technocratic obsession of policymakers and the mass media with reading and math scores as the only measurement of success in public schooling.

The improvement of education for Puerto Rican students in U.S. public schools must be multifaceted, requiring Puerto Rican educational leaders to develop a comprehensive agenda for change and to play multiple roles. The Latino Commission on Educational Reform convened by the New York City Board of Education in 1991 and chaired by me between 1991 and 1994 in my capacity as a board member represents just such a change agenda and change process.

BEYOND BLAME AND BAND-AIDS

Starting with the Assistant Superintendent's Report of 1948 (Association of Assistant Superintendents, 1948), the education of Puerto Rican students has been the subject of episodic studies and reports by the public school system, by government, and by Puerto Rican advocacy organizations. The focus of these reports invariably has been the failure of Puerto Rican students to do well: a high drop-out rate, academic underachievement, a lack of English language proficiency. Although government studies have highlighted student and parental characteristics, Puerto Rican researchers and advocates have consistently argued that school characteristics are more salient and have the advantage of being subject to change and improvement by public school officials.

Puerto Rican leaders have refused to acquiesce to the "blame the victim" ideology adopted by local officials and social scientists when addressing the educational experiences of Puerto Rican students. Instead these leaders have rejected analyses that frame the question as "the Puerto

Rican problem" and have challenged the public school system and the society at large to adapt to our children's needs and to reform structural arrangements, organizational culture, and funding policies.

From the perspective of Puerto Rican researchers and educational leaders, the problems to be addressed comprehensively are as follows: the continuing and disproportionately high drop-out rate among Puerto Rican and Latino students, academic underachievement in core subject areas, the lack of guidance and support services, negligence in implementing quality bilingual education programs, the discouragement of Puerto Rican parent and community group participation, and the low representation of Puerto Ricans in the teaching and administrative ranks.

These problems were prioritized by the 35 members of the Latino Commission (most of whom are of Puerto Rican heritage) after collective reflection about the pressing dilemmas facing Puerto Rican and Latino students in the New York City public schools. Many of these problems had been addressed in previous reports by ASPIRA's Office of Research and Advocacy (A-ORA), which I established and headed from 1985 to 1990. For example, two A-ORA reports, *Su Nombre Es Hoy I* (Reyes, 1988) and *Su Nombre Es Hoy II* (Reyes, 1989), were prepared and delivered to Chancellors Richard Green and Joseph A. Fernández at the beginning of their respective administrations, each documenting a series of educational problems facing Puerto Rican/Latino students and presenting a plan of action for Green and Fernández's consideration. Previously, ASPIRA of New York had commissioned Ronald Calitri, an economist, to prepare a report *Racial and Ethnic High School Dropout Rates in New York City* (1983), which had been submitted to Chancellor Anthony Alvarado in 1983. The Puerto Rican/Latino Education Roundtable had spearheaded a community teach-in on bilingual education in 1983 flowing from the 1982 community mobilization efforts of the New York City Coalition for Bilingual Education, discussed at the beginning of this chapter.

These various research and advocacy reports were undertaken from outside the public school system, and they met with sporadic and short-lived responses. Chancellor Alvarado and then Assemblyman José Serrano obtained funding for drop-out prevention initiatives focused on counseling services by community-based organizations (initially, these community-based organizations were almost exclusively White-run entities). The Band-Aid nature of these efforts was clear to us within ASPIRA of New York, but drop-out prevention funds were the only ongoing funding stream at the time that allowed ASPIRA and other community-based organizations to gain entrance into the schools to address the symptoms of the drop-out crisis. Likewise, when Chancellor Green failed to respond to the continuing disproportionate drop-out rate of Latino students in

1988, it took political pressure by Puerto Rican community leaders on Mayor Edward Koch to convince Chancellor Green to appoint a "study group." This symbolic response was very narrowly focused and had a short life. Some additional funds were allocated for ASPIRA to expand its drop-out prevention services to a few more high schools, and some efforts were made to recruit more bilingual teachers from Puerto Rico. The lack of a systemic response was disheartening but predictable.

The Puerto Rican community had become so marginal to the policy-making process and to the power structure that in 1986 Mayor Koch was able to force Miguel Martinez, the only Puerto Rican member on the board, to resign so that the mayor could name Richard Beattie, a well-respected White lawyer, in his place. In a system where 31% of the students at the time were Latino, such a lack of representation was regarded by the Latino community as an outrageous slap in the face and as another example of disenfranchisement of the Puerto Rican/Latino community. Guillermo Linares (then a local school board member), the Roundtable, ASPIRA, the National Congress for Puerto Rican Rights, and many other groups and individuals, including high school *aspirantes,* mounted a letter-writing and media campaign in 1987. The campaign culminated in a massive demonstration in front of City Hall, on November 19th, officially Puerto Rican Heritage Day in New York City's Puerto Rican communities. The awakening of the Latino "sleeping giant" caught many politicians' attention as they jumped on the bandwagon demanding that Mayor Koch rescind his appointment and name a Latino. I decided, after much study, reflection, and heated discussion with other Puerto Rican activists, to announce publicly that I would go on a hunger strike on the day after Thanksgiving. Two other Puerto Rican leaders, Luis Garden Acosta and City Councilman José Rivera, volunteered to join the fast. In the face of almost unanimous community support for the cause of representation on the Board of Education, and faced with a public relations fiasco, the mayor caved in on Wednesday, as New York City prepared to celebrate the traditional Thanksgiving turkey feast. Eventually, Mayor Koch chose a close and loyal political ally, Mrs. Amalia Betanzos, to replace Richard Beattie after he graciously "fell on his sword."

What is most revealing about this episode was that it took 13 months and titanic efforts to coalesce very disparate sectors in the Puerto Rican/Latino community only to see a Puerto Rican political apparatchik take the seat at the Board of Education. For all her history in the Puerto Rican community, Mrs. Betanzos avoided engaging the educational activists in any meaningful or sustained way. In some ways, this episode led me to consider the feasibility and usefulness of seeking the position myself. With the election of David N. Dinkins as mayor in November 1989, the first African American to win the mayoralty (and on a rainbow coalition platform), and the naming of Joseph A. Fernández as schools chancellor beginning in January 1990, the time seemed propitious for me to seek a new venue for our collective struggles.

Whatever hopes I had of focusing on the needs of Puerto Rican/Latino students when I was named to the board by Manhattan Borough President Ruth Messinger were waylaid by two significant and intervening crises. First, the city was suffering from another impending fiscal meltdown requiring draconian budget cuts to the Board of Education. At the same time, Chancellor Fernández, who arrived in New York City with tremendous allies in the UFT teachers' union, the various newspaper editorial boards, and the philanthropic community, announced plans 3 months into my first term to expand AIDS education, to make condoms available in the city's public high schools, and to include gay and lesbian lifestyles in the board's first-grade multicultural teacher's guide. The board's attention was riveted on the budget cuts imposed by a seemingly progressive Black mayor and by the growing cultural war unleashed by the conservative right against the Chancellor's so-called "Children of the Rainbow" curriculum guide.

It was only after another annual Board of Education *Dropout Report* was released in June 1991 (New York City Board of Education, 1991), showing no appreciable improvement in the disproportionate Latino drop-out rate, that I was able to convince the new president of the board, H. Carl McCall (former state senator, ambassador to the United Nations, and now state comptroller), to convene a board commission to address not only the Latino drop-out "crisis" but also a myriad of other problems in a strategic and systematic way. I assembled a Latino Commission on Educational Reform with more than 30 members and I was named to chair the commission (over the objections of Ninfa Segarra and Michael Petrides, new members of the New York City Board of Education who had become aligned with Rudolph Giuliani and against David Dinkins).

The Latino Commission issued a series of reports between 1992 and 1994: *Towards a Vision for the Education of Latino Students: Community Voices, Student Voices* (1992) and *Making the Vision a Reality: A Latino Action Agenda for Educational Reform* (1994). These reports, with their many recommendations, reflect the understanding of the more than 30 educators, parents, students, researchers, and community leaders who made up the commission that piecemeal solutions focusing on add-ons to an unchanged school system were inadequate. Instead, the commission argued for a "revisioning" of public education to incorporate the Puerto Rican/Latino communities' demands and goals. These demands included valuing bilingualism and multiculturalism (i.e., adding linguistic diversity and cultural diversity as goals of the board's nondiscrimination policy and pedagogical instruction); empowering parents and community members to participate in all governance decisions, starting at the school level; providing students with a clear understanding of the link between school success and the world of work (career guidance, financial assistance, and employment internships); and engaging students in building community and exploring citizenship roles.

Chancellor Fernández and the members of the board responded well enough, at least rhetorically, to the commission's interim report in spring 1992. But in reality, only 4 of the 99 recommendations in the five major policy areas were implemented. Although the vision and the agenda may have been comprehensive, the response was small-scale and underfunded. Indeed, Mayor Dinkins, as well as the chancellor, came up empty-handed when requested to find funding for a limited number of the most pressing and viable recommendations. Mayor Dinkins, the first African American elected as Mayor of New York City, had been swept into office in 1989 with the support of a rainbow coalition made up of members of the Black and Puerto Rican communities. Despite the mayor's promise to serve what he characterized as New York's "gorgeous mosaic," he was unable or unwilling to deliver any significant resources. The commission members, nevertheless, insisted on continuing to work, helping to establish the Leadership Secondary School (a dual-language, college-preparatory school focusing on leadership development and community service); to obtain state funding for the Bilingual/Multicultural Institute within the board's Office of Bilingual Education; to get board support for the opening of a Migration/Immigration Resource Center for parents and children in District 10 in the Bronx (the "Welcome Center"); and to advocate for the initiation of the Math and Science Institute, which would provide Latino and African-American middle-school students with enriched instruction and test preparation to facilitate their admission to the city's specialized high schools such as Stuyvesant and Bronx Science.

Several of the initiatives recommended by the Latino Commission were implemented under the leadership of the next Schools Chancellor, Ramon A. Cortines. Cortines was named Schools Chancellor in 1993 with the support of the new mayor, Rudolph Giuliani, and the four conservative board members who had ousted Joseph Fernandez. I found myself on the losing end of that struggle, having attempted to rally support for Fernandez's attempts to address the AIDS crisis and gay–lesbian inclusion within the Board's multicultural curriculum. In fact, I had chaired the Chancellor's Multicultural Advisory Board, which helped shape the board's 1989 policy statement on multicultural education. Although sexual orientation had been included in the policy statement, most Puerto Rican/Latino educators and community advocates had focused on moving the Board of Education to include accurate information about our struggles and contributions into school textbooks and classroom instruction. Rainbow politics and the rainbow curriculum both came under attack, and these were conflated and confused in the eyes of many people in the Puerto Rican/Latino communities. Culturally conservative values, not to mention outright homophobia, came to the fore in both Latino and African-American communities, leading to the defeat of Mayor Dinkins and the election of Rudolph Giuliani, one of whose closest allies was Michael Petrides, the Staten Island board member. With Ninfa Segarra, the other Puerto Rican Board member, jumping on the anti-Fernandez and pro-Giuliani bandwagons, I became isolated in a minority of three and was unable to deliver real board support for the Latino Commission's work.

It was in this spartan budgetary climate, with its newly resurgent conservative retrenchment, that the commission delivered its final report, *Making the Vision a Reality: A Latino Action Agenda for Educational Reform,* to Chancellor Cortines and the board in March 1984. This report focused on special education, college preparation, community collaborations, and fiscal and staffing equity. We had done our homework, and we had incorporated students, parents, teachers, researchers, and many other members of the Puerto Rican/Latino educational community into our work groups. If we failed to produce systemic changes or to impel the board and chancellor to initiate strategic planning in response to our recommendations, it was not for lack of trying. Some of the criticisms that we received as a commission, or that I was subjected to as chair of the commission, included the following: The commission was all over the map; the recommendations were noteworthy but unrealistic (e.g., a salary differential for bilingual teachers, and an overhaul of the board's budget allocation to funnel more funding to poorer districts); and there was no new money available to fund even our most modest recommendations.

In October 1995, Rudolph Crew became chancellor after a protracted and heavily politicized search process. Although the commission no longer had official status, I continued to convene informal meetings periodically to inform interested members of issues affecting Latino students and to enlist their help in monitoring the school system's responsiveness to our Latino reform agenda.

In our 3 years of sustained work as a commission and the subsequent efforts to hold Chancellors Cortines and Crew accountable for implementing our recommendations, we had penetrated the inner reaches of the central bureaucratic system. We had amassed a wealth of data and analyses that represented some of the most creative, collective work ever done by Puerto Rican educators and advocates. Although some educators and activists within the Puerto Rican/Latino community dismissed the commission and my efforts as being myopic and too focused on one issue, bilingual education, a close reading of our reports reveals the comprehensiveness of our agenda. A similar fate has befallen the equally substantive report of the board's Commission on Students of African Descent during 1996 and 1997 (Commission on Students of African Descent, 1998).

Other reform efforts, particularly the creation of several "New Visions" high schools, similar in scope and mission to the Leadership Secondary School, kept me and the other members of the Latino Commission engaged with the public school system on behalf of Puerto Rican/Latino students (see chap. 9 by Rivera & Pedraza and chap. 8 by Caballero, this volume). Clearly, the roles of Puerto Rican educators and community leaders in this reform process are necessarily complex given the nature of the problems and the solutions, given the need to be both external and internal change agents, and given the historical relationships of the Puerto Rican community to other racial and ethnic groups, to other constituency groups such as the United Federation of Teachers, and to the various layers of government.

One of our weakest connections has been to the majority of our elected officials. The traditional wariness, not to say mistrust, between Puerto Rican progressive educators and activists and Puerto Rican politicians, many of whom rose to power through antipoverty and community control struggles, has yet to be addressed or resolved adequately. Too few elected officials (Congressman Jose Serrano, Congresswoman Nydia Velazquez, and Bronx Borough President Fernando Ferrer are stellar exceptions) look beyond the *tira y jala* (give and take) of local machine politics to study the larger picture and support systemic change. Too few Puerto Rican educators and activists have the patience and the foresight to build our agendas from the ground up, from the local to the global, as local politicians are forced to by the exigencies of elections. There is also often an unspoken resentment toward those of us who have attended college and become acclimated to intellectual hierarchies and abstractions. We can seem isolated and out of touch, full of our strategic plans and visions, while local politicians are left to haggle with the power structure to deliver needed services to their poor constituencies throughout New York.

CONCLUSION

In these pages, I have tried to relate my own experiences as a high school teacher, graduate student, researcher and advocate representing ASPIRA of New York, member of the New York City Board of Education, member of various local, state, and national educational organizations (that is another chapter for another book), and, lastly, college professor. Like many of my colleagues on the Latino Commission and in the larger Puerto Rican community, I have played various interconnecting roles. In this chapter, I have argued that these different roles are indispensable to the change process and to advance the vision of quality education for Puerto Rican students in New York City and in the United States. I personally have played many roles at various points in the last 15 years, sometimes simultaneously and often despite my apprehensions and others' sound criticisms. Among the roles are those of teacher, researcher, advocate, administrator, litigant, policymaker, role model, public spokesperson, group facilitator, problem-solver, politician, activist, bureaucrat, coalition-builder, fundraiser, keynote speaker, and public intellectual, not to mention family man and public school parent. I do not for a minute assume I have played all these roles well. My point is not that every Puerto Rican educator has to play all these roles but that we must be able to engage in these activities collectively if we are to realize the vision for the education of Puerto Rican students that we espouse. A value-neutral, unidimensional educational role is illusory and ultimately detrimental to our children's education.

REFERENCES

Association of Assistant Superintendents. (1948). *A program of education for Puerto Ricans in New York City*. Brooklyn: New York City Board of Education.

Banks, J. (1997). Multicultural education: Characteristics and goals. In J. A. Banks & C. A. M. (Eds.), *Multicultural education: Issues and perspectives* (pp. 3–31). Boston: Allyn & Bacon.

Bucchioni, E. (1982). The daily round of life in the school. In F. Cordasco & E. Bucchioni (Eds.), *The Puerto Rican community and its children on the mainland* (3rd rev. ed.). Metuchen, NJ: Scarecrow Press.

Cafferty, P. S. J., & Rivera-Martinez, C. (1981). *The politics of language: The dilemma of bilingual education for Puerto Ricans*. Boulder, CO: Westview Press.

Calitri, R. (1983). *Racial and ethnic high school dropout rates in New York City*. New York: ASPIRA.

Chenault, L. R. (1970). *The Puerto Rican migrant in New York City*. New York: Russell & Russell.

Commission on Students of African Descent. (1998). *Professional development for teachers and administrators of students of African descent*. Brooklyn: New York City Board of Education.

Darder, A. (1991). *Culture and power in the classroom: A critical foundation for bicultural education*. New York: Bergin & Garvey.

Fishman J. A., Cooper, R. L., Ma, R., Hoffman, G., Casiano Findling, H., Terry, C., Greenfield, L., Dindling, J., & Herasimchuck, E. (1971). *Bilingualism in the barrio*. Bloomington: Indiana University Press.

Fitzpatrick, J. P. (1987). *Puerto Rican Americans: The meaning of migration to the mainland*. Englewood Cliffs, NJ: Prentice-Hall. (Original work published 1971)

Freire, P. (1970). *Pedagogy of the oppressed*. New York: Seabury Press.

Glazer, N., & Moynihan, D. P. (1963). *Beyond the melting pot*. Cambridge, MA: MIT Press.

Iglesias, C. A. (1984). *Memoirs of Bernardo Vega*. New York: Monthly Review Press.

Jennings, J. (1988). Future directions for Puerto Rican politics in the U.S. and Puerto Rico. In F. C. Garcia (Ed.), *Latinos and the political system* (pp. 480–497). Notre Dame, IN: University of Notre Dame Press.

Latino Commission on Educational Reform. (1992). *Towards a vision for the education of Latino students: Community voices, student voices* (Vols. 1 & 2). Brooklyn: New York City Board of Education.

Latino Commission on Educational Reform. (1994). *Making the vision a reality: A Latino action agenda for educational reform*. Brooklyn: New York City Board of Education.

Margolis, J. (1968). *The losers: A report on Puerto Ricans and the public schools*. New York: ASPIRA.

Mills, C. Wright, Senior, C., & Goldsen, R. K. (1950). *The Puerto Rican journey: New York's newest migrants*. New York: Harper & Row.

Morrison, J. C. (1958). *The Puerto Rican study, 1954–1957*. Brooklyn: New York City Board of Education.

New York City Board of Education. (1991). *Annual dropout cohort report*. Brooklyn: Author.

Nieto, S. (1995). A history of the education of Puerto Rican students in U.S. mainland schools: "Losers," "outsiders" or "leaders"? In J. A. Banks & C. A. M. Banks (Eds.), *Handbook of research on multicultural education* (pp. 388–411). New York: Macmillan.

Nieto, S. (1996). *Affirming diversity: The sociopolitical context of multicultural education* (2nd ed). New York: Longman.

Ogbu, J. U. (1978). *Minority education and caste: The American system in crosscultural perspective*. New York: Academic Press.

Pantoja, A., & Perry, W. (1993). Cultural pluralism: A goal to be realized. In M. Moreno-Vega & C. Y. Greene (Eds.), *Voices from the battlefront: Achieving cultural equity*. Trenton, NJ: Africa World Press.

Pérez, B., & Torres-Guzmán, M. E. (1992). *Learning in two worlds: An integrated Spanish/English literacy approach*. White Plains, NY: Longman.

Reyes, L. O. (1981). *Power to the people: The process of division of labor in Puerto Rican male and non–Puerto Rican male task groups*. Unpublished doctoral dissertation, Stanford University, Stanford, CA.

Reyes, L. O. (1988). *Su nombre es hoy I: Aspira educational reform agenda*. Unpublished report submitted to Chancellor Richard R. Green, New York.

Reyes, L. O. (1989). *Su nombre es hoy II: Aspira educational reform agenda*. Unpublished report submitted to Chancellor Joseph A. Fernández, New York.

Reyes, L. O. (1993). Bilingual education: Reform for the 1990's. In A. Carrasquillo & C. Healey (Eds.), *Whole language and the bilingual learner* (pp. 200–207). Norwood, NJ: Ablex.

Rodriguez, C. E. (1991). *Puerto Ricans: Born in the U.S.A.* Boulder, CO: Westview Press.

Sánchez-Korrol, V. E. (1983). *From colonia to community: The history of Puerto Ricans in New York, 1917–1948*. Westport, CT: Greenwood Press.

Santiago-Santiago, I. (1978). *ASPIRA v. Board of Education: A community's struggle for equal educational opportunity* (Monograph No. 2, Office of Minority Education). Princeton, NJ: Educational Testing Service.

Sleeter, C. E. (1991). *Empowerment through multicultural education*. Albany: State University of New York Press.

Spring, J. (1993). *Conflict of interests: The politics of American education*. White Plains, NY: Longman.

Urciuoli, B. (1996). *Exposing prejudice: Puerto Rican experiences of language, race and class*. New York: Westview Press.

Walsh, C. E. (1991). *Pedagogy and the struggle for voice: Issues of language, power and schooling for Puerto Ricans*. New York: Bergin & Garvey.

Walsh, C. E. (1996). Introduction. In C. E. Walsh (Ed.), *Education reform and social change: Multicultural voices, struggles and visions* (pp. xi–xvii). Mahwah, NJ: Lawrence Erlbaum Associates.

Zentella, A. C. (1997). *Growing up bilingual: Puerto Rican children in New York*. Cambridge, MA: Blackwell.

II

IDENTITY: CULTURE, RACE, LANGUAGE, AND GENDER

A Strong Sense of Self Is Crucial for Success

Hipolito Baez

As a young man growing up in one of the most disadvantaged, highly congested areas of Springfield, Massachusetts, I know how debilitating poverty can be. My mother passed away when I was 1½ years old, and I was raised by my father, who had only a sixth-grade education and worked in a factory. However, I have always focused on the positive elements of my background, ethnicity, race, and culture, rather than on the problems I faced in a single-parent family. It is through hopeful, articulate discourse, rather than through bitterness, that one can expect to be heard by others. An experience I had as a young man illuminates the social barriers for Puerto Ricans and other students of color entering the high school of their choice. In my case, I chose to attend a public high school known for its excellent college preparatory program. In an interview with one of the high school guidance counselors, I was told that their Latino students did very well in general placement classes. The assumption that Latino students are incapable of doing well in college preparatory classes would have placed me in less demanding classes, and it did not make sense given my previous academic record. After asking for a different guidance counselor, I demanded placement into the honors classes and I quickly progressed into all of the advanced placement classes by my junior year, graduating with summa cum laude honors.

My early decision acceptance at Bowdoin College enhanced these achieve-ments and gave me an opportunity to receive a bachelor's degree from a reputable and prestigious college. Bowdoin College challenged me with a rigorous educa-tion, and in return I gave Bowdoin the kind of diversity that a homogeneous com-munity such as Bowdoin needed. Although it was difficult to adjust from growing up in poverty and being raised by a father who spoke broken English to attending an elite private college, I adjusted well to Bowdoin. Reflecting on my high school experience, I know that had I listened to the guidance counselor who attempted to enroll me in general placement high school courses, I would never have received an acceptance letter from Bowdoin. I wonder how many Puerto Rican students limit their educational opportunities due to ill-advised and presumptuous guidance counseling. High school was a major point in my life from where crucial academic decisions would define the types of work opportunities I would have later in life. I refused to permit anyone to diminish my self-esteem or exclude me from educa-tional opportunities that were rightfully mine. Fears of possible failure were sec-ond to lifelong regrets that so often come in the form of, "What if I had tried?" I would rather learn my limitations than speculate about them or let other people decide how far I could go.

I remember asking for an admissions interview, which was an optional part of the application process. I was referred to one of their local interviewers, a Bowdoin alumnus practicing law in Massachusetts. After we exchanged greetings, the in-terviewer proceeded to explain that Bowdoin was highly selective and he asked about my grades. When I told him that I had straight A's in all of the advanced placement classes, he gave me a look of disbelief, making me feel that I needed to produce an official transcript for him to believe me. After I suggested that this was an interview and not an academic assessment, he reacted defensively, stating that he could ask whatever questions he felt were appropriate. I corrected him by stat-ing that this was my interview, and not his. Needless to say, I politely excused my-self and wished him a good day. I subsequently informed Bowdoin of the incident and asked for another interviewer. Bowdoin assigned another alumnus who also practices law in Massachusetts. He informed me that my first interviewer would no longer be used for area interviews. I was interviewed again and was then rec-ommended for admission.

My encounters with the high school guidance counselor and the Bowdoin Col-lege representatives encouraged me to continue questioning people's assumptions and also motivated me to work more diligently to reach goals that more privileged people take for granted. I become angry when I see educators place intelligent Puerto Rican high school students in less demanding courses that erroneously pre-sume an inability to think in English. The issue of high expectations is clearly linked to the success of Puerto Rican students regardless of whether they are in bi-lingual programs or mainstream classes. A select few Puerto Ricans achieve great success because of high expectations of themselves or from others. The success of a few Puerto Ricans, however, does not equate with an effective secondary school system because there are still far too many Puerto Ricans who fall through the cracks. I personally know Puerto Rican high school students who refrained from applying to reputable colleges simply because they were told that they would not qualify for admission.

The secondary school education that I experienced systematically set Puerto Ricans up for failure. Regardless of the outside legal, political, environmental, and psychosocial factors that also contribute to student failure, the secondary school system needs to more effectively engage with Puerto Rican students. When Puerto Rican students are affirmed and validated as human beings equal to their White counterparts, they have a better chance of succeeding academically and staying in school. The praise that my teachers gave me for my good work helped to counteract the ill advice that I received from my guidance counselor. However successful I become later in life, I strongly believe that the education of Puerto Rican students through high school lacks cultural sensitivity. I always had to work at proving that Puerto Ricans are academically competent and capable of competing with the most advanced White students. Although I spoke English well, the assumption was that the primarily Puerto Rican junior high school that I attended did not prepare me well for the rigors of a mostly White college preparatory public high school. Regardless of my challenging junior high school curriculum and excellent grades, being Puerto Rican somehow symbolized academic incompetence.

I have devoted the most recent years of my life to immersing myself in my Puerto Rican identity and learning more about the diversity of the Puerto Rican experience. Living in a society that views Puerto Ricans as second-class citizens can make being Puerto Rican personally problematic. I find that the problem of being Puerto Rican is not mine; the problem is for those who have limited perspectives on Puerto Ricans. My Puerto Rican-ness is a crucial component of my social identity, but it is not the only one. After I obtained my Master in Education degree, I was accepted to law school. Regardless of what I do later in life, I know that I will enjoy success. My pride in being Puerto Rican and my strong sense of self will carry me through whatever challenges lie ahead.

4

The Struggle of "Imagined Communities" in School: Identification, Survival, and Belonging for Puerto Ricans

Catherine E. Walsh

As the first and most enduring colony of the United States, Puerto Rico and Puerto Ricans on the Island and in the United States have a special status that no other nation, immigrant group, or Latino ethnic group holds. This legacy of colonialism differentially positions Puerto Ricans' relation to diaspora, community, and nation. Grosfoguel, Negrón-Muntaner, and Georas (1997) described this relation for U.S. Puerto Ricans as one of an "increasingly deterritorialized 'ethno-nation' in the United States" (p. 19).

With new migration patterns beyond New York City, which, until a few decades ago served as a kind of Puerto Rican metropolis, and constantly renewed and imagined Island connections, identity for Puerto Ricans in the United States is increasingly understood by Puerto Ricans themselves as transcending territorial boundaries, nation, and place, that is, as both transnational and transcultural (e.g., see Duany, 1996; Flores, 1994; Lao, 1997; Walsh, 1998).

As members of a transnational, deterritorialized ethno-nation in the United States, Puerto Ricans present a distinct challenge to U.S. schools and society where, despite a rhetoric of liberal multiculturalism, the official goal continues to be assimilation into a singular, national, and universal "imagined community" (Zizek, 1997). Within this context and with anti-immigrant, anti-Latino, and English-only policies making schools an increasingly greater contested terrain, issues of identification, belonging, and who imagines community and how they do so become political, not just cultural, concerns.

The notion of imagined community—Anderson's (1991) well-used phrase—conjures up a series of questions related to the space, the place, and the ways that collective identifications are constructed and symbolic boundaries of inclusion and exclusion are drawn. *Imagined* does not mean that these communities are not real. Rather, it refers to the immediately present and rationally discernible; to the visions, shared memory, and desire; and to the images of this community that are fashioned creatively and inventively in individual and group psyches and actions (Flores, 1997).

Imagined communities are used in this chapter to discuss and describe the racialized construction and clash of differentially positioned groups in a northeastern school district, which, for ethical reasons, I refer to as Mill City. In this district, Puerto Rican students are the numerical majority and conservative Whites maintain strong administrative control.

Drawing from school department data, federal court and other documents, meeting notes, as well as interviews that I conducted from 1991 to 1996[1], I discuss the relation between the declining educational condition of Puerto Ricans in this district in recent years and a growing White conservatism aimed, as one school administrator described, at "bringing Whites back to the system." In this context, survival and belonging are key concerns.

By describing the policies, perspectives, and practices that contribute to a reconfiguration of cultural and power relations and by describing the strategies and practices of organized opposition, structured defiance, and

---

[1]This data collection and documentation were done in my role as expert to the plaintiffs and to the court-appointed monitor in a desegregation complaint filed in U.S. Federal Court. In this role, I developed a lengthy report in 1992 based on interviews, observations, and a review of school and state department of education data and documents. In the years that followed, I analyzed school department data and reported on school district progress. Data presented here come from these reports, from my field notes taken during meetings, and from notes taken on various occassions in schools. The quotes from parents and students are from a joint meeting of the Parents Advisory Council and students' group that I was invited to attend.

alliance building and community imagining among Puerto Rican students and their parents, the chapter affords valuable insight into the present-day push-and-pull of colonial relations within the U.S. metropolis. Although the racialized positionings suggest an establishment of binary opposition (White vs. Puerto Rican, colonialized vs. colonizer), the relations as revealed through the words of students, parents, teachers, and adminstrators are actually much more complex and dynamic. As shown in the text that follows, it is not uncommon for individuals from both "communities" to try and understand or momentarily assume the position of the "other" or for White teachers and even some administrators to ally themselves with Puerto Rican parents and students.

Throughout the chapter, my interest is to promote a deeper sociopolitical understanding of the condition of Puerto Rican students in U.S. schools and, in so doing, of the contestatory and changing nature of imagined communities and cultural politics within the current geopolitical reality. Such an understanding provokes a rereading of the colonial situation that clarifies the shifting cultural and power relations and the emergent configurations and strategies at work, a rereading that situates the contemporary reality and condition of Puerto Ricans in U.S. schools within a new and different [post]-colonial[2] conjuncture.

IMAGINING AND READING COMMUNITY
IN THE NATION AND IN MILL CITY

One way to analyze and discuss the play of cultural and power relations and politics in schools and society is to examine who imagines community and how they do so. The ways that individuals collectively identify and position themselves in relation and in opposition to others, the meaning of this positioning for different individuals and groups, and the varying dimensions of collective memory and social experience it recalls are important indicators of the current national, ethnic, and racialized struggles in U.S. schools and society. In other words, struggles over defining identity and belonging through which different groups express their subjectivity and political projects can be understood as constitutive—and constituting the very nature of the national imagined community (Radcliffe & Westwood, 1996).

---

[2]My use of brackets around *post* is meant to highlight the anomalous nature of Puerto Ricans' postcolonial condition—a modern colony that may have transcended the colonial system but not "the ubiquity and primary significance of coloniality" (Williams & Crisman, cited in Lao, 1997, p. 174).

The recent demographic change in the racial and ethnic character of the U.S. population and, in particular, the significant increase of Latinos, have prompted often heated discussion in academic circles, government offices, and public spaces, like schools, about national identity and the social imaginary of the nation. In this context, vexing and often contradictory questions arise: For example, who belongs and what is the relation and substance of this belonging? What happened to universal, national identifications like language and culture, and shouldn't they be restored? How are we to deal with those who maintain double loyalties and are often ambivalent toward the United States? And, what should be done to ensure unity and order? Such questions point to the tensions and fears about what Zizek (1997) referred to as the recent "ethnicization of the national," to issues of hegemonic control, and, in the specific case of Latinos and Puerto Ricans, to new forms of identification and movements that clearly differentiate themselves from those of other hyphenated but integrated "Americans" (Walsh, 1991). They also suggest trouble with the traditionally imagined community of the United States —"the American dream" as it were—evidencing the coexistence of multiple, imagined communities.

Yet, as Flores (1997) cautioned,

> The role of the social imagination and the imaginary in the self-conception of nationally, ethnically, and "racially" kindred groups is of course central, but must always be assessed with a view toward how they are being imagined, from the "outside," and to what ends and outcomes. But the marking off of "us" and "them," though the foundational exercise in "imagining" communities, has its own limits, as it becomes evident that there is as much blurring involved as clear and meaningful bounding. (p. 185)

What are the imagined communities in Mill City? How do we read them? And how do they connect to the national context?

The Mill City community imaginaries described in this chapter are basically three: that imagined and occupied by White conservatives, that created and imagined by Puerto Rican/Latino[3] residents, and that constructed though interracial and intercultural alliances of Whites, Puerto

---

[3]State, city, and school census figures generally count Puerto Ricans as Hispanic without differentiation between various Hispanic groups. Although virtually all of the Hispanics in Mill City are Puerto Ricans, the term *Puerto Rican/Latino* is used here to recognize the Puerto Rican presence and allow for those few individuals who might be of other Latino backgrounds.

Rican/Latinos, and other people of color.[4] Rather than static, permanent structures, these communities can be read as fluid, relational, and still-emergent spaces or groupings that shift and change as they are constantly created, configured, invented, and imagined in individual psyches and in collective practices, actions, memories, and ideals. More than reflexive responses to negative conditions or unfavorably weighted relations (Flores, 1997), these imagined communities weave opposition with the social construction of collective identities, fashioning new and sometimes resurrecting old alliances in a context of markedly changing demographic realities and cultural politics.

As the following pages suggest, the conflicts inherent in the creation and structural positioning of these communities mirror the conflict occurring in society at large. In this sense, the clash of imagined communities within Mill City schools is not just about Mill City per se. It is a localized version of intercultural and postcolonial struggle within the United States: a struggle over the nexus of power and knowledge that still make colonial situations possible (Santiago-Valles, 1994), over the definition and character of the country, and over politics that, because of new structural positionings, cultural dynamics, and transnational identifications for Latinos (as well as for some other groups), call into question the very concept and significance of "nation."

DEMOGRAPHIC CHANGE, RACIALIZED TENSIONS, AND THE MULTICULTURAL IMAGINARY

The relation between demographic change and racialized tensions has been widely discussed, particularly with reference to the desegregation battles of the 1970s. Although Mill City is not substantially different, the rapidness and numerical significance of the shifts, particularly in the schools, coupled with the response of officials provide an interesting case for analyisis.

From the mid-1800s to the early 1970s, Mill City identified itself as a White immigrant, working-class city in which Irish, French-Canadians, Germans, and later Poles and Italians worked together in the city's textile and paper mills. In the 1970s and 1980s, industry declined and the racial/ethnic composition of the population shifted. Puerto Ricans, many who had initially come to the area as farm workers, began to settle in the city. This trend continued into the 1990s. Between 1980 and 1990 the

---

[4]This is not to suggest that these are the only imagined communities in the city. Rather, it is to explicitly name those that are the focus of study here.

Puerto Rican/Latino population actually increased by 120%, growing from 14% to 31% of city residents.

Although the working-class character of Mill City has always been strong, contrasts in the quality of life for Puerto Rican and White residents are particularly apparent. For example, more than half the Puerto Rican population was described as poor in 1990 as compared to 14% of Whites, and unemployment for Puerto Ricans was more than two and a half times greater. Ninety-five percent of Puerto Ricans rent their homes with 80% concentrated in one area of the city where vast overcrowding, declining conditions, and increasing rents are major issues.

Mill City's demographic change is most clearly viewed in the context of schools. There, according to school documents, Puerto Ricans/Latinos grew from 16% of the student population in 1974 to 69% in 1996. In 1974, Whites numbered 7,000 but, in 1996, constituted only slightly more than 2,000 or 27% of the schools. In contrast to other cities in the region and nation that have experienced "White flight" as a response to growing populations of students of color, the numeric decline of Whites in Mill City has not, for the most part, been due to families leaving the city. White parents have instead enrolled their children in private, Catholic schools. Since the early 1990s these schools have remained about 90% White and mostly middle and lower middle class.

State Department of Education figures in the mid-1990s placed Mill City's public school students as the state's poorest economically and among the poorest in terms of educational indicators and academic achievement.

Demographic change has been an important contributing factor to racialized tensions. Numerous examples of animosity toward Puerto Ricans have been documented in recent years, including the rash of apartment building fires in the early 1990s and signs at one particularly heated school committee meeting several years ago that read "Puerto Ricans go home!" In a 1995 brief on a voting rights case in the city, a U.S. District Court Judge argued not only that Puerto Ricans/Latinos experience very substantially lower levels of income, employment, health, education, and housing as compared to Whites but that the city's response to the needs of the community has "often been slow and halting, and at times egregiously neglectful" (U.S. District Court, 1995, p. 919).

Yet, although the city as a whole has generally maintained in its public structures and policies a racialized positioning of "us" and "them,"[5] the schools, particularly from the mid-1980s to early 1990, endeavored to be

---

[5]Examples include the nonexistent support of fair housing programs and enforcement of housing discrimination and the adoption of a city-wide ordinance for English only.

more inclusive. The establishment of two-way bilingual education programs[6] and Spanish-as-a-second-language classes, multicultural teacher training, the hiring of a diverse staff, magnet programs, and other efforts coordinated under the district's desegregation plan began to build what the then superintendent referred to as an integrated school community focused on multicultural learning and acceptance: a new, imagined community.

An environment of change and visions for different relations were set despite negative attitudes of city officials and some staff in the school. As made evident by the comments that a Puerto Rican teacher of Spanish-as-a second-language made to me in the late 1980s, the changing environment and relations were most visible among the children.

> I have really seen a change begin to happen with the students in my school. The White students are excited and enthusiastic about learning Spanish and while at first they were shy about trying to speak Spanish to the Puerto Rican kids, now, after about 6 months, I see White and Puerto Rican kids playing together at recess. The Whites are using their Spanish and the Puerto Ricans are helping them. I can hear both languages present in a real natural kind of way. This never happened before—Whites and Puerto Ricans playing and learning together. It's a sign that something good is happening.

During these years, Mill City schools were often looked upon by other districts as a positive example of efforts to incorporate diversity and create multicultural schools. However, as the section that follows details, by the beginning of the 1990s the imagined multicultural community had come to be seen as a threat by White conservatives in city government, including some officials in the governing committee of the schools. Within 1 year, this imagined community was to be broken apart.

THE DECLINE OF FISCAL SUPPORT
AND THE REPOSITIONING OF WHITE AUTHORITY

As the Puerto Rican/Latino population grew and the White population in the public schools declined, fiscal support of the schools by city government also began to decrease. Although this trend had begun several years

---

[6]Two-way bilingual programs involve roughly equal numbers of language minority and native English-speaking students in an instructional program that teaches academic subjects through both the "minority" language (in this case, Spanish) and through English. The goal of these programs is to develop students who are bilingual and biliterate and who understand and respect one another's cultures.

before, it was made most evident in the 1991–1992 school year when a decrease of $5.7 million in the city school budget and the shift of $2.3 million in ultility, maintenance, and insurance costs from the city to the schools resulted in a 32% decrease of actual funds available for educational services. This meant almost $1,000 less per pupil than the previous year 75% of the state per-pupil average.[7]

Although economic difficulties with city governments and schools were widespread in the state in the early 1990s, the decline in fiscal support in Mill City clearly had a racialized character. The fact that the city's White voters twice approved tax overrides for trash collection rather than schools was one example. Another was the election of several conservatives to the school committee who clearly had a White agenda. One of these officials, shortly after being elected, commented in a meeting I attended that her job was to represent the interests of White voters and not the parents of the Puerto Rican students in the schools. An article in a predominant newspaper cited principals' and teachers' comments that an aging White community had abandoned the schools because of antagonisms toward Puerto Ricans students.

With regard to the city's budget actions, the state Board of Education declared Mill City schools in a state of emergency and cited a "community neglect of education as a responsibility of local government" (State Board of Education, cited in U.S. District Court, 1995, p. 918).

One major impact of the budget cuts was a drastic reduction in the number and diversity of school staff. Approximately 200 teachers with the lowest seniority were laid off, many of whom had been hired as bilingual, ESL, or multicultural teachers. Sixty-six percent of the bilingual administrative and supervisory staff were lost along with staff like guidance counselors, drop-out prevention counselors, and others whose jobs had been to support the student population.

The superintendent who strongly complained to the state about the potential impact of the cuts on services for children was, according to him, pressured to leave along with most of his administrative staff. His comments at that time are revealing:

> What we have done in the last 10 years is to bring two separate systems together—the uptown, underenrolled, power-brokered schools and the downtown, overenrolled, underfunded schools. We leveled the playing field for all kids by giving them equal access. All this is being threatened. (Walsh, 1992, p. 25)

---

[7]These figures and others that follow come from Walsh (1992).

Evidence of the declining educational condition could be seen in severely overcrowded classrooms taught, in many cases, by teachers who had been reassigned to positions, courses, and grade levels for which they had no experience or training; in the absence of textbooks and other teaching materials; and in generalized pandemonium in classrooms and corridors. Puerto Rican/Latino parents expressed their concern by filing a complaint in federal court. This concern did not seem to be shared, however, by the school committee and administration. As one administrator pointed out, this was because the limited resources that did exist had been targeted toward the minority White population. "There is a 'they deserve the cuts' mentality," he said. "The result is that the system has regressed."

During the 1991–92 year, disparities between Puerto Ricans/Latinos and Whites grew in terms of achievement, college preparatory and advanced course participation, and access to full-day kindergarten. Dropouts, retentions, and suspensions among Puerto Ricans/Latinos increased whereas among Whites they declined. External suspensions of Puerto Rican/Latino students increased 63% during the 1990–1991 school year, whereas those of Whites declined by 7%. Special education referrals for Puerto Ricans/Latinos nearly doubled.

The arrival of $3.5 million in emergency educational assistance from the state in March 1992 was too late to remedy the damage that had already been done. As one teacher remarked to me the following year, students had "lost a year that can never be recuperated."

Although funds were restored to the schools in subsequent years through legal pressure and the signing in 1994 of a new Consent Decree between parents and school officials, the 1991–1992 school year was an important turning point in the direction of Mill City education. This turning point is significant not for the budget cuts alone but equally, if not more importantly, for the shift it initiated toward a White conservative administration of the schools, toward deeper racial/ethnic polarization, and toward the decline of educational conditions for Puerto Rican students and their growing exclusion from the educational process.

MONOCULTURAL IMAGININGS

Before, there was an acceptance of the student population, a desire to create a multicultural environment of support and acceptance with funds directed for this purpose. Lots of people who believed in this left the system—they were either laid off in '91-'92 and found other jobs or went elsewhere out of frustration.

—Mill City teacher

For the conservative administration that took the reins of Mill City schools in the early 1990s, a stated goal has been to reestablish "accountability" in the schools, something that current administrators maintain was lacking in the past, multicultural-oriented administration. Equated with standarized testing, curriculum standards, and a "universal" rather than multicultural knowledge base, accountability has become a code word for a strategy that administrators admit is aimed at bringing White students back to the public system. "What White parents want," explained a top administrator to me, "is a good, solid academic program. They are not interested in multicultural education. What we are trying to do is improve the system for all students but especially in ways that will encourage White families to return."

Although accountability could conceiveably improve the system for all students, recent school department data show a decline rather than improvement in recent years of the educational condition of Puerto Rican/Latino students. For example, achievement in math and in English and Spanish reading as measured by standardized tests declined between the 1995 and 1996 school years. Puerto Rican/Latino drop-outs also increased in number and in percentage of the drop-out population. For instance, even though the percentage of Puerto Ricans/Latinos at the nontechnical secondary school has remained at about 50% since 1992, these students went from constituting 77% of the drop-outs in 1992 to 84% in 1995. Similarly illustrative is that Puerto Ricans/Latinos at this high school represented 77% of out-of-school suspensions in 1995 and 80% of the 118 retentions. The problem, as one administrator revealed to me, is that attention is directed toward "taking care of the Whites that have come back and not the kids who really need the help and support."

Puerto Rican/Latino parents and students as well as some teachers and administrators maintain that what is occurring is the reconstruction of a dual system. As Whites have slowly begun to trickle back to the system, they have, despite a desegregation order, been allowed to concentrate in White-neighborhood schools. Evidence of this concentration is documented in school department reports that show increased percentages of Whites in these schools and poverty rate declines. Special magnet programs have been put in place to encourage Whites to return to their neighborhood public schools, and at the nontechnical high school, where the return of Whites has been greater, academic services, advanced classes, and extracurricular activities are targeted toward the White population.

The comments of two Puerto Rican high school students made to me in fall 1996 make clear the growing exclusion:

Cada año me parece que la situación está peor. Además de la gente del programa bilingüe, hay muy pocos maestros y ningún administrador que nos entienden. Hay más suspensiones por cosas pequeñas, por falta de entendimiento cultural. Hemos empezado a vigilar eso y sabemos que no todo el tiempo las suspensiones están reportadas.

[Each year it seems that the situation gets worse. Besides the people in the bilingual program, there are few teachers and no administrators that understand us. There are more suspensions for small things, for a lack of cultural understanding. We have begun to watch this and we know that the suspensions are not always reported.]

Even though we are the majority in the schools, we are constantly made to feel like we don't belong. I'm an honors student and I am still made to feel "rechazada," rejected.

Similarly, Puerto Rican/Latino parents spoke about the decline in support for them in the schools, citing that the parent coordinator no longer had an office; that bilingual parents or students had no representation on the state-mandated school councils; that a lengthy process, including a criminal check, was now required before parents could volunteer in the schools; and that school committee meetings that had once been open to parents were now not announced to the bilingual Parent Advisory Council (PAC), were often conducted in closed sessions, and, when public, provided no Spanish translation.

Cuando pedimos intérpretes, el comité escolar nos dijieron: "están en los Estados Unidos ahora, la cultura de aqui es del inglés."

[When we asked for interpretors, the school committee told us "you are in the United States now, the culture here is English."]

These comments suggest a growing pattern in policy and practice that both ignores Puerto Rican/Latino presence and actively engenders their exclusion.

In essence, it seems that the efforts toward exclusion, "accountability," and bringing Whites back are organized around a vision of a return to the past, the reconstituting of a historical memory that imagines a White community. A teacher's statement verifies this imagining:

This school committee acts as if the Hispanic students are going to go away. That if they ignore the kids' needs and if they wait long enough, the system will be all-White again.

In this present-day imaginary linked to the past, Puerto Ricans/Latinos are conceived as obstacles; Whites and Whites alone epitomize school district progress.

The contradictory reality is that all Whites in Mill City or the schools do not necessarily share this vision or see themselves as belonging to this newly constructed, racialized imaginary and school organization. A number of teachers and several administrators, in fact, have said that they have remained in the system because they believe in the Puerto Rican/Latino students and their parents and in the benefits of a multicultural community. For them, the multicultural imaginary remains their point of reference and ideal.

REREADING THE PUERTO RICAN/LATINO IMAGINED COMMUNITY

Since their initial arrival in numbers to Mill City over 30 years ago, Puerto Ricans have been actively involved in creating their senses of place and community. With the city geographically divided along ethnic and class lines, a Puerto Rican barrio and community are clearly visible. Yet, the geographically situated aggregate of people and their accompanying social and commercial institutions are not the focus here. Rather, it is the imagined community that has been created among in-school youth and, more recently, in alliance with parents.

Puerto Rican/Latino students with whom I spoke in fall 1996 said they have always stuck together because, as one student noted, "We are the only ones who understand and support each other." Another student explained,

> Yeah, there are some teachers who are there for us but they work for the schools so sometimes they can't talk back or defend us in a strong way. *Como las cosas ya están poniendose peor en el high school* [as things are getting worse at the high school], we have started to really stick together and watch everybody's back.

Students identified these worsening conditions as including, among others, the following:

- Suspensions for insignificant infractions or cultural differences, "like not looking an administrator or teacher in the eye or, in my case, refusing to go in the pool when I was menstruating,"
- Comments by administrators in the cafeterias and hallways including that "we are all on welfare,"

- Administrators treating students as children, telling them that "we don't know what we want or need, that we should be told what courses to take and when to study because we won't do it on our own,"
- "Never seeing ourselves or our people in the textbooks,"
- English-only assemblies on topics of major importance like college applications and admissions: *"Es como decirnos que no tenemos derecho o posibilidad a ir a college* [It is like telling us that we do not have the right or the possibility of going to college],"
- Being "constantly made to feel like we don't belong."

In response to the denigrating and unjust treatment they were individually subjected to and of the policies and practices of exclusion, Puerto Rican students organized themselves during the 1995–1996 school year in a kind of loose-knit committee or group, which continued as of the 1996–1997 school year. Students described this group as a space for vigilance and support, to keep on top of the problems at the school, to document and respond to unjust actions by administrators and staff, and to seek solutions. Not surpising, the school administration's response has been to ignore them. As one student recounted,

We have tried to make recommendations about curriculum, courses, and books, we have asked to meet with administrators and with teachers to talk about this—our education—but they [the administrators] say we don't know, that they know best, and that we should just accept the decisions they make for us.

However, as another student explained, the group has remained persistent.

Por ejemplo, en el caso de disciplina, muchos estudiantes hispanos han recibido suspensiones por infracciones insignificantes. Nosotros pidimos una reunión con la administración para exponer nuestro punto de vista sobre eso. Pero alguien de la oficina escuchó nuestra conversación de planear eso. Querían suspendernos por pedir la reunión. Cuando no aceptamos eso, pusieron una mediadora. Pero el principal no quería una reunión. La mediadora contactó el PAC. Finalmente en junio, la directora bilingüe hizo una reunión entre algunos de nosotros y el superintendente. El dijo que iba a investigar el asunto. Los finales de agosto, fuimos con la directora bilingue y el abogado del PAC a una reunión del comité escolar. El propósito de todo era de mejorar la situación y la educación en la escuela. Ellos trataron de evitar la discusión, largando en otra discusión de ellos... Aunque el problema de disciplina como otros problemas, siguen, nosotros nos hemos prometidos que vamos a seguir.

[For example, in the case of discipline, many Hispanic students have received suspensions for minor infractions. We asked for a meeting with the

administration to explain our point of view about this. But someone from
the office overheard our conversation to plan it. They wanted to suspend us
for asking for a meeting. When we didn't accept this, they put in a mediator. But the principal did not want a meeting. The mediator contacted the
PAC. Finally in June, the bilingual director organized a meeting between
some of us and the superintendent. He said he was going to investigate the
issue. At the end of August, we went to a school committee meeting with
the bilingual director and the attorney for the PAC. The purpose was to improve the situation and education in general at the school. They tried to
avoid the discussion, extending another discussion among themselves. Although the discipline problem along with other problems continues, we
have promised one another that we are going to continue.]

The organized resistance and alliances that students have built, although initially focused on countering declining conditions for Puerto Ri-
cans/Latinos at the high school, have served another purpose as well.
They have constructed a newly imagined community in which Puerto Ri-
can/Latino students are both strengthening and rethinking their identities and restructuring notions of belonging in ways that suggest what
Flores (1997) referred to as "the affirmation of cultural and social realities
and possibilities inscribed in their own human trajectory" (p. 190).

An added aspect of the community imaginary construction has been
the inclusion and involvement of parents. Interested in how they could
extend their influence and increase their impact on school policy and
practice, the students began to periodically meet with the Bilingual Parents Advisory Council to inform them of school problems. Alliances were
formed that have led to shared goals, engendered collective and
intergenerational strategic actions, and increased pressure on the
adminstration. As a parent noted at a joint meeting between the two
groups in fall 1996, *"Juntos tenemos que luchar para que la educación se mejore,
para que haya una igualdad.* [Together we have to struggle so that education is made better, so that there is an equality.]"

In addition to producing a shared focus of struggle, these alliances have
further strengthened identity ties and created a more inclusive (in an
intergenerational sense) and shared notion among students and parents
of an imagined school community. One example of this is the changed notion among both students and parents of transnational identification.

Students said that because they had mostly grown up in the United
States, they tended to see themselves as more connected to the United
States than to the Island. For parents, the connections tended to be re-
versed, with most saying that although they now live in the U.S., the Island remains their point of social and cultural association. Yet, as parents
and students together explained, coming together over the issues affecting youth in the schools has deepened the understanding among both

groups and created new ways of imagining transnational and transcultural identifications.[8] As one student shared,

> It's like before we thought we had to just be from here to be accepted. Being Puerto Rican at home but being more American in school. But now we are beginning to see that we are both, that is who we are, that's what makes me "me." And, we are not going to go away from here, it's like Puerto Ricans are here in this city to stay so the administration is just going to have to get used it because I'm proud to be Puerto Rican, I'm proud I have two cultures, two countries, two flags, two languages, and we're going to fight for this.

This new community imaginary that students and parents have together created provides a positional base (and, in essence, an anticolonial project) for confronting discrimination and exclusion in the schools. This base and project need to be understood not merely as a reactive response to White hegemony but as part of a broader cultural politics in which the conditions and situations of subalternity and coloniality are central. In other words, as both subordinate, subaltern majorities in Mill City schools and second-class, colonial citizens of two nations, Puerto Ricans are faced with a cultural struggle that is clearly political in nature.

Whether naive or strategic, some parents argue that part of the task of decolonization (my word, not theirs) has to be to build bridges between different groups and to begin by reeducating school officials to break the stereotypes about Puerto Ricans as well as about poor families in general.

> *Necesitamos cambiar el concepto, el imagen de los puertorriqueños, como también de las otras familias de bajos recursos que este comité escolar y la administración tienen. Tienen que saber que somos responsables, que somos educados, que estamos preocupados por la educación de nuestros hijos.*

---

[8]Lao's (1997) comments regarding the relation between transnationalism, coloniality, and imagined community help situate these identifications historically and politically and make clear the persistance of coloniality:

> To imagine the Puerto Rican national community as a translocal social space (a transnation) is not only to acknowledge how the mutual referentiality between territory and diaspora has always constituted the national, or to recognize the quotidian human flow between colony and metropolis, but more fundamentally it is to refer to the tailoring of a formation of peoplehood that, though hyperfragmented and dispersed, is netted by a web of coloniality (subordinate citizenship, racialization) and interwined by multiple networks and flows to constitute a deterritorialized–reterritorialized "imagined community" and a "social space." As a historical product, constituted and reproduced by specific "social practices," this social space is located beyond the immediacy of place and is intersected by other spaces (subjective, local, state, societal, global) without totally losing its dimension as a locus of identity and association. (p. 176)

[We need to change the concept, the image of Puerto Ricans, as well as that of other families with limited economic resources that this school committee and administration have. They (school officials) have to know that we are responsible, that we are educated, that we are concerned for the education of our children.]

Similarly, even though parents and students named the individuals who they felt were the most problematic, they also indicated that the real problem was not just the administration per se but the adminstration as a reflection of the attitudes, beliefs, and fears of a changing community. Moreover, as they made clear, the problem does not rest with the schools alone; it has to do also with health, housing, and other social institutions. The need, they said, was to work step by step in educating others and in fighting for equality. To paraphrase one parent, "It is not about just us and them, it is about how we can learn to live together."

CONCLUSION

By examining who imagines community in Mill City schools, how they do so, and the inherent struggles in imaginaries, this chapter helps reveal the cultural and power relations and politics that mediate Puerto Ricans' educational condition in U.S. schools. The decline of the educational condition in Mill City cannot be simply described or explained by indicators such as minority status or poverty. Rather, it must be analyzed as an effect of both changing cultural politics and new dispositions of power within postmodern, colonial situations.

In considering who imagined communities and how, it is important to recall that in each of the groupings discussed, socially constructed collective identities linked with resistance to form still-emergent spaces in which symbolic boundaries of "us" and "them" sometimes blurred in response to new envisionings and positionings. The issue then, was not just that conservative Whites, Puerto Ricans/Latinos, and a multicultural grouping each imagined themselves, at different times and places, as "community," but that in the imaginings, each group also had to take into account the "other."

Thus, although the dominion of Mill City's conservative, White adminstration remained strong, they were forced, because of students' and parents' actions, to realize that their imagined community did not exist in isolation. In order to disimagine or exclude Puerto Ricans/Latinos, White administrators had to take Puerto Ricans/Latinos into account. In so doing, they had to imagine a larger, although contestatory, school community in which alliances, loyalties, and associations, as the comments of some teachers and administators made clear, were not always clearly drawn across racialized boundaries or traditional lines of center and periphery. The ultimate recognition within what Hall (1996) referred to as a new "politics of ethnicity" (p. 447), is that the White imagined community cannot survive only by marginalizing, displacing, and forgetting Puerto Ricans/Latinos.

The creation and struggle of imagined communities in Mill City schools are testimony to a new cultural politics, a "war of positions" to recall Antonio Gramsci's (1971) words, focused on processes of identification and otherness that engage rather than suppress difference (Hall, 1996). In this struggle of positionality there is a play of identity and difference in which, to apply the context and groups studied here, Puerto Ricans/Latinos are not just subordinantly positioned as "minorities" (despite being majorities) but are also the object of envy, desire, and imagining precisely because they are Puerto Rican/Latino (i.e., because they have identity). And, as Hall (1996) explained, "This is something the recognition of which fundamentally displaces many of our hitherto stable political categories, since it implies a process of identification and otherness which is more complex than we had hitherto imagined" (pp. 444–445).

As members of a transnational, deterritorialized ethno-nation in the United States, Puerto Ricans, as a group have a distinct relationship to U.S. society and schools and a distinctive place in the public mind and in the Latino imaginary. Although the historical experience of colonialism has made its mark, present-day coloniality as it is expressed in the context of the United States is not, as this chapter suggests, a binary relation of colonizer–colonized. Instead, it is part of a complex, multifaceted, transnational, [post]-colonial, cultural politics, as Lao (1997) suggested,

> A crossroads of unequal exchanges and uneven developments where the imperial and the colonial are intertwined in intricate economies of desire, justice, survival, and freedom, and where social actors are often difficult to delimit on one or the other side of the cultural divide. (p. 175)

And, it is through the new political imaginaries and "wars of positions" which are emerging in this moment that Puerto Ricans can "challenge institutional settings, structural patterns, dominant representations, and power practices that frame [their] many conditions of subalternity and experiences of oppression" (Lao, 1997, p. 184).

The struggles over imagined communities in Mill City schools or in other similar contexts are far from over. Although issues of identification, survival, and belonging will continue to be mapped for some time by hegemonic policies, colonial reconfigurings, and racialized positionings, the practices of structured opposition, alliance building, and community imagining among students and parents are evidence of a new cultural politics that works with and through difference (Hall, 1996). This is a cultural politics that, hopefully, will not let the conservative, White adminstration rest.

REFERENCES

Anderson, B. (1991). *Comunidades imaginadas* [Imagined communities]. México D.F.: Fondo de Cultura Económica.

Duany, J. (1996). Imagining the Puerto Rican nation: Recent works on cultural identity, *Latin American Research Review, 31*(3), 248–267.

Flores, J. (1994). *Divided borders: Essays on Puerto Rican identity*. Houston, TX: Arte Público.

Flores, J. (1997). The Latino imaginary: Dimensions of community and identity, In F. Aparicio & S. Chávez-Silverman (Eds.), *Tropicalizations: Transcultural representations of Latinidad* (pp. 183–193). Hanover, NH: Dartmouth College.

Gramsci, A. (1971). *Selections from the prison notebooks*. New York: International Publishers.

Grosfoguel, R., Negrón-Muntaner, F., & Georas, C. (1997). Beyond nationalist and colonialist discourses: The jaiba politics of the Puerto Rican ethno-nation. In F. Negrón-Muntaner & R. Grosfoguel (Eds.), *Puerto Rican jam: Essays on culture and politics* (pp. 1–38). Minneapolis: University of Minnesota Press.

Hall, S. (1996). New ethnicities. In D. Morley & K-H. Chen (Eds.), *Stuart Hall: Critical dialogues in cultural studies* (pp. 441–449). New York: Routledge.

Lao, A. (1997). Islands at the crossroads: Puerto Ricanness traveling between the translocal nation and the global city. In F. Negrón-Muntaner & R. Grosfoguel (Eds.), *Puerto Rican jam: Essays on culture and politics* (pp. 169–188). Minneapolis: University of Minnesota Press.

Radcliffe, S., & Westwood, S. (1996). Remaking the nation: *Place, identity, and politics in Latin America*. New York: Routledge.

Santiago-Valles, K. (1994). *"Subject people" and colonial discourses: Economic tranformation and social disorder in Puerto Rico, 1898–1947*. Albany: State University of New York Press.

U.S. District Court, Civ. A, 92-30052-MAP (March 27, 1995).

Walsh, C. E. (1991). *Pedagogy and the struggle for voice: Issues of language, power, and schooling for Puerto Ricans*. New York: Bergin & Garvey.

Walsh, C. E. (1992). Report on the Consent Decree Implementation of Hispanic Parent Advisory: "Council v. City."

Walsh, C. E. (1998). Staging encounters: The educational decline of U.S. Puerto Ricans in [post]-colonial perspective. *Harvard Educational Review, 68*(2), 218–243.

Zizek, S. (1997, September–October). Multiculturalism, or the cultural logic of multinational capitalism. *New Left Review, 225,* 28–49.

5

Puerto Rican Identity: What's Language Got to Do With It?

Maria V. Zavala

Language has played a crucial role throughout the history of the Puerto Rican people. History tells of the ongoing attempts at deculturalization[1] through education and the Puerto Ricans' resistance to full assimilation to the American culture (Negrón de Montilla, 1971; Spring, 1997; Walsh, 1991). Substituting English for Spanish was the key to the deculturalization programs attempted in Puerto Rico. Given this historical role, what impact, if any, could language have on the development of the Puerto Rican people? In particular, how might language play a role in identity development?

Almost 100 years after the U.S. flag was planted in Puerto Rican soil, I set out to search for literature connecting language with Puerto Rican identity development. Surprisingly, I found it sorely lacking. I conducted an exploratory study in hopes that it would add an important missing link to the larger picture of the Puerto Rican experience. It is my hope that this study will generate hypotheses that may spark an interest in future larger scale studies. Because of the small number and unique characteristics of this sample, care must be used not to overgeneralize these findings.

---

[1]Deculturalization here is defined as a process of stripping away the culture of a conquered people and replacing it with the dominant culture.

My central aim is to explore the nature of Puerto Rican identity development and to investigate whether language plays any role in Puerto Rican adolescents' search for racial/ethnic identity. To provide a sociohistorical and psychological context, I briefly explore the role of English and Spanish in the history of Puerto Rican education. I also consider the role of bilingualism among the Puerto Rican people, the importance of language in examining racial/ethnic identity as a social construct, and the role of racism and ethnocentrism in the process of exploring ethnic identity for Puerto Ricans. In addition, the current research on racial/ethnic identity development as well as adolescent identity formation is reviewed.

THE ROLE OF LANGUAGE IN THE HISTORY OF PUERTO RICAN EDUCATION

Let's start on October 18, 1898, when the same U.S. forces that had invaded Puerto Rico less than 3 months previously raised the U.S. flag in San Juan and declared the end of Spanish rule and the beginning of U.S. domination. Almost immediately, U.S. educational policy in Puerto Rico emphasized building loyalty to the U.S. flag and institutions and implementing deculturalization (Negrón de Montilla, 1971). Puerto Rican children were educated to shift their allegiance from Puerto Rican nationalism to the symbols of the colonizing country. In much the same way as U.S. and state educational policies attempted to strip Native Americans of their languages and cultures, U.S. educational policy in Puerto Rico attempted to replace Spanish with English as the majority language and introduce children to the dominant U.S. culture (Spring, 1997). This is a classic example of how a nation can use schools to impose its will on a conquered people.

Language is an important part of deculturalization because within it are embedded the culture and values of a people. The imposition of English was tied to building patriotism among the Puerto Rican people. Organized Puerto Rican resistance to U.S. education policies began to appear in 1900, as the language issue continued to be a source of friction between Puerto Rican teachers and U.S. authorities. In 1912, Puerto Rican teachers organized the Teachers Association to resist the policies of the commissioner of education. A teacher's magazine, *La Educación,* stated, "Day after day we have worked for the defense of our mother tongue and at last today we see our efforts and publicity crowned with success by the meeting of the Teachers Association" (Negrón de Montilla, 1971). During this time attempts were made to replace Spanish with English as the language of instruction. Teachers were recruited from the United States, and most of them spoke only English, which meant that by default their instruction was not bilingual (Spring, 1997). The resistance to policies came not only from the Puerto Rican Teachers Association but also from the students. In 1915, resistance to the imposition of English sparked a student strike at Central High School in San Juan (Negron De Montilla, 1971). The strike occurred when a student, Francisco Grovas, was expelled for collecting signatures to support legislation that would require Spanish to be the language of instruction in Puerto Rican schools. The struggle around language continued with mandates enforcing English from President Roosevelt in the 1930s and President Truman in 1946 (Negrón de Montilla, 1971). In 1951, Puerto Ricans voted for commonwealth status despite protests by the minority urging Puerto Rican independence. Commonwealth status gave Puerto Ricans greater control of their school systems than they had before; consequently, Spanish was restored in the schools.

Despite the educational programs of the schools, Puerto Ricans maintained their cultural traditions. They struggled to pass on these traditions and the Spanish language to their children and they resisted any attempts at deculturalization (Culture and Language Policy Task Force [CLPTF], 1978). That resistance to full assimilation through the maintenance of the Spanish language persists to this day. Spring (1997) wrote, "The attempts at deculturalization were eventually countered in the 1950s and 1960s by the great Civil Rights movement. The strong resistance to deculturalization highlights the difficulty, if not impossibility, of deculturalization through educational institutions" (p.). The ongoing attempts at deculturalization and the Puerto Ricans' history of resistance have dramatically affected the education of Puerto Ricans in the United States.

BILINGUALISM AND BICULTURALISM AMONG PUERTO RICANS

One of the most fascinating aspects of bilingualism in the United States is its extreme instability, for it has been viewed as a transitional stage toward monolingualism in English (Hakuta, 1986). Hakuta wrote that "each new wave of immigrants has brought with it its own language and then witnessed the erosion of that language in the face of the implicitly acknowledged public language, English" (Hakuta, 1986, p. 166). Hakuta wrote that at the rate of loss of language diversity observed in other nations, it would take 350 years for the average nation to experience the same amount of loss as that witnessed in just one generation in the United States. Yet among Puerto Ricans, there is a broad allegiance to the maintenance of Spanish as a marker of cultural, social, and political identity (Duran, 1983). It is further evident that young people are retaining their Puerto Rican heritage as a symbol of their identity even when they were not born in Puerto Rico and have little direct connection with the Island and its culture (Colleran, 1984; Rodriguez, 1991). This is evident in the study by the Cultural and Language Policy Task Force (CLPTF; 1978) of the Center of Puerto Rican Studies at City University of New York.

The CLPTF (1978) reported that bilingualism had become a necessity for Puerto Ricans undergoing "circular migration," that is, a constant back-and-forth migration to and from Puerto Rico. It has become clear that even though not everyone is involved in this circular migration, if one is to function in both or either communities, in familial networks and in the general community, one must be both bilingual and bicultural. The CLPTF (1978) study further found that in contrast to the traditional immigrant pattern of transition from the "foreign" language to English over three generations, with grandparents and grandchildren being virtually monolingual in one or the other language, nearly all Puerto Ricans are bilingual to some degree. The second language skills are acquired, for the most part, outside any formal language instruction. There seems to be a life cycle of language use in the community. The younger children learn Spanish and English simultaneously, hearing both languages from those who use them separately and from those who combine them in various ways.

Because identity reflects culture and is a product of the specific culture that creates it, people of different cultures inhabit different worlds, one private and the other public. Jenkins (1993) wrote that "because of the imposition of prevailing White mainstream cultural and social attitudes, members of minority groups have had to develop bicultural identities and skills" (p.). Pinderhughes (1982, p. 114) defined biculturality as "the ability to function in two worlds" as opposed to being caught between them. The ability to be bicultural may lead to a comfort with difference and an integrated sense of self. For those without bicultural ability, the need to function in two worlds may lead to identity confusion and value conflicts. Part of being able to function in two worlds for the Puerto Rican includes being able to speak and understand both Spanish and English. Darder (1995) wrote that when Latino/a students affirm their bicultural existence, they exhibit a greater flexibility and movement in their interactions:

> This is clearly evidenced when a student's particular interaction at any given moment is more likely than not to emanate from a critical assessment of the actual power relations at work. Needless to say, this type of cognitive, physical, emotional, and spiritual flexibility requires a greater sense of

consciousness related to one's identity as both an individual and a social being—a consciousness that supports and nurtures both personal and collective empowerment. (Darder, 1995, p. 326)

How then do Puerto Rican families cope with the need for biculturality?

Zavala-Martinez (1994) proposed that a growing number of Puerto Ricans are born and socialized into an experience that she described as being between two worlds, or *entremundos,* that is, caught between two geographic localities, two languages, two or more identities, and two contending and sometimes dissonant experiences. Can some degree of bilingualism help them function in two worlds? Can bilingualism help in becoming bicultural? Can biculturalism assist in avoiding *entremundos,* being caught between two worlds? Can biculturalism through bilingualism be the road to a more positive ethnic identity achievement outcome for the Puerto Rican adolescent?

ADOLESCENT RACIAL AND ETHNIC IDENTITY DEVELOPMENT

Early adolescence has a unique transitional nature that results at least in part from an interaction between developmental changes at both the individual and social environmental levels (Eccles et al., 1993). As a result, adolescence has come to be known developmentally as the period that can mark tension between conforming to familial and societal expectations.

The most widely recognized framework for conceptualizing the transformation of self during adolescence was provided by Erikson (1968), who appreciated the psychosocial nature of identity and the important role played by the community in recognizing, supporting, and thus helping to shape the adolescent ego. He proposed that the best opportunities for identity resolution occur during adolescence. Erickson defined identity formation as a process dependent on social response.

For minority youth, race and ethnicity are necessary components of identity. Many theorists have concluded that the achievement of a positive ethnic identity must be seen as essential to a healthy personality (Arce, 1981; Baldwin, 1979; Gurin & Epps, 1975; Maldonado, 1975). Phinney (1990) proposed that a commitment to an ethnic identity is an important component of the self-concept of minority youth and mediates the relation between minority status and adjustment. Phinney developed a measure of ethnic identity (1994) used with diverse populations to understand ethnic identity and its role in the lives of youth from all backgrounds. Phinny's questionnaire measure of ethnic identity was administered to 417 high school students and 136 college students from ethnically diverse schools. Reliability, assessed by Cronbach's alpha, was .81 for the high school sample and .90 for the college sample. The relationship of ethnic identity to various demographic variables and to self-esteem was examined. The measure can be used to examine similarities and differences in ethnic identity and its correlates among youth from different ethnic groups. In the current study I used Phinney's Multigroup Ethnic Identity Measure (MEIM), a reliable measure used with ethnically diverse high school and college samples, including bilingual populations. This measure consists of 14 items assessing three aspects of ethnic identity: positive ethnic attitudes and sense of belonging (5 items); ethnic identity achievement, including both exploration and resolution of identity issues (7 items); and ethnic behaviors or practices (2 items). Items are rated on a 4-point scale from *strongly agree* to *strongly disagree*. Scores are derived by reversing negatively worded items, summing across items, and obtaining the mean; scores range from 4 (indicating high ethnic identity) to 1 (low). If subjects have missing items, means are calculated on the nonmissing items. Additional items, not part of the score, assess self-identification and ethnicity of parents.

Although identity development is a complex task for all youths, it is particularly complicated for children and adolescents belonging to ethnic and racial minority groups in the United States. Specifically, the complexity of identity formation may increase as a function of color, behavioral distinctions, language differences, physical features, and long-standing, although frequently unaddressed, social stereotypes (Gibbs & Huang, 1989). The role of family and community environments in positivly identifying with one's own racial/ethnic group has been discussed by many researchers, most notably Cross (1971).

Cross' (1971, 1973) model of racial identity development delineates a personal identity that incorporates personality traits, social and self-evaluation, and a reference-group orientation that includes racial attitudes, group identity, group awareness, and associated esteem. These two domains of personal identity and reference-group orientation may act either in tandem or independently of one another. It is important to consider the limitations of this model. No racial/cultural identity model should ever be viewed as a global personality theory with specific identifiable stages that serve as fixed categories. Other considerations are not taken into account in racial/cultural identity models, including sociocultural forces, class, age, and gender, to name a few. In Cross' model, identity is discussed very globally. Although identity may sequentially move through identifiable stages, affective, attitudinal, cognitive, and behavioral components of identity may not move uniformly. This model should serve only as a conceptual framework to help understand development.

In his model, Cross (1973) hypothesized that there are five stages of development in African-American identity. The first stage is known as *preencounter*, when the individual absorbs many of the beliefs and values of the dominant White culture, including the idea that it is better to be White. The second stage is *encounter*, transition to which is typically precipitated by an event or series of events that forces the individual to acknowledge the personal impact of racism. Anger, confusion, and alienation are common emotions. The individual is aware of rejection by Whites and begins to grapple with what it means to be a member of a group targeted by racism. Initial attempts to define one's racial or ethnic identity may be based on internalized stereotypes about one's own group. Stage three is *immersion/emersion,* which is characterized by the desire to surround oneself with visible symbols of one's own racial identity and actively avoid symbols of Whiteness. Individuals actively seek opportunities to learn about their own history and culture with the support of same-group peers, resulting in a newly defined and affirmed sense of self. The fourth stage is *internalization*, characterized by a sense of security in one's own racial or ethnic identity. One is able to view one's own group, as well as other racial or ethnic groups, more objectively. The fifth is *internalization-commitment,* which is a stage of internalization of a positive personally relevant racial or ethnic identity.

To the extent that this model describes the identity process of a devalued minority group in the United States, that is, Blacks, it may also be relevant for the experiences of Puerto Rican youth. If language is one way in which Puerto Ricans identify as belonging to their ethnic group, but their language is devalued by the dominant group, how is this apparent conflict resolved during their ethnic identity development process? How are racism and linguisism[2] experienced by adolescent Puerto Ricans as they try to develop an integrated sense of self?

THE STUDY

I conducted a small-scale research study to explore the nature of Puerto Rican racial and ethnic identity development and the role of language in that development. Students were recruited through flyers distributed to a variety of colleges and universities in New England as well as by word of mouth. Fifteen self-identified Puerto Rican and bilingual students responded to this recruitment. The first 7 who were contacted and able to schedule appointments were included in the study.

---

[2]Skutnabb-Kangas (1988) coined this term referring to ideologies and structures used to legitimate, effectuate, and reproduce an unequal division of power and resources between groups that are defined on the basis of language.

In-depth interviews were conducted with the participants regarding their socialization process, that is, their home and community experiences and their school and peer experiences during adolescence. I analyzed the interviews thematically, paying particular attention to the role of the Spanish and English languages during socialization and racial and ethnic identity development. In addition, I used Phinney's (1994) MEIM to measure participants' levels of ethnic identity achievement. All students filled out a questionnaire that provided demographic data and measured bilingualism or fluency in Spanish and English. It also measured any change in frequency of Spanish or English language use during college. Because the process of resolving conflicts regarding identity and language usage for these Puerto Rican youth appears to closely parallel Cross' (1991) stages of racial and ethnic identity development, these stages were used as an organizing framework.

As shown in Table 5.1, the participants varied in age, geographic affiliation, socioeconomic status, and racial features; 6 females and 1 male participated in this study. All were pursuing higher education in the United States and all were bilingual to one degree or another. That is, the participants varied from completely fluent in both Spanish and English to understanding Spanish but not feeling comfortable speaking it.

All 7 participants self-identified as Puerto Rican and bilingual. One, José, identified as an Afro-Latino. Spanish language abilities varied, rang-

TABLE 5.1
Demographic Summary

Participant (n = 7)	Age	Language Preference	Geographic affiliation[a]	Racial features (skin color)	Socioeconomics	Community participant was reared in
Esperanza	18	Spanish	IPR	Dark	Low-middle	Puerto Rican
Margarita	19	Spanish	USPR	Dark	Low-middle	Puerto Rican
José	20	Spanish	IPR	Dark	Middle	Puerto Rican
Rosita	20	English	USPR	Dark	Middle	White
Theresa	20	English	USPR	Light	Low	White
Mariá	21	Spanish	IPR	Mestiza	Middle-upper	Puerto Rican
Cristina	22	English	USPR	Light	Low-middle	Puerto Rican

[a]Where participant was reared and received primary education; IPR = Island Puerto Rican; USPR = U.S. Puerto Rican.

ing from being completely proficient to only being able to understand and sometimes speak it. Of all the participants, Rosita and Theresa felt the least confident in their ability to speak Spanish. They were also the only 2 who were reared in predominantly White communities.

Three of the 7 participants were born and, for the most part, educated in Puerto Rico; I refer to them as Island Puerto Ricans or IPRs. Two of the 3 finished their last 2 years of high school in the United States. Four of the 7 were reared and educated in the United States; I refer to them as U.S. Puerto Ricans or USPRs. All of the IPRs and 2 of the USPRs were raised in traditional[3] Puerto Rican households in predominately Puerto Rican communities. One remaining USPR, Theresa, was raised in a predominately White community, although the family's religious affiliation kept them very close to other Puerto Ricans in their town. She also described her home as being very traditional. Rosita grew up in a predominately White community in a less traditional home, though she also attended religious service in Spanish, as did all of the participants in this study. The participants differed in their self-identified socioeconomics: 3 were low-middle class (2 of these were USPRs), 2 were middle class, (1 IPR and 1 USPR), 1 USPR was in the working (low-income) class, and 1 IPR was middle-upper class.

All 7 of the participants reported involvement in circular migration; that is, all had family in Puerto Rico who visited regularly and whom they visited as well. Six of the 7 participants reported that Spanish was still spoken in their homes. Rosita, the USPR from a less traditional home, reported that English was the dominant language in her home. All 7 reported that bilingualism was encouraged as they were growing up.

The IPRs described their educational experiences in Puerto Rico as bilingual. All reported using textbooks in English. English instruction began in the second grade and continued throughout their schooling. As is the case in most public schools in Puerto Rico, only the English class was conducted in English; all other classes were conducted in Spanish.

Three of the 4 USPRs in this study received no formal instruction in Spanish during their early years. Only 1 was enrolled in a Spanish class in the third grade, and 2 reported taking one Spanish class in high school. At the time of this study, 2 of the 4 USPRs were majoring in Spanish or Spanish literature in college. All the USPRs reported actively using their Spanish language. They reported as well an increase during their college years in the frequency of reading, writing, and speaking Spanish as well as listening to Spanish music. The IPRs reported no change in frequency in

---

[3]Traditional here was measured by the questionnaire. It refers to cultural maintenance in the home, such as Spanish spoken; Spanish music, radio, television, books, magazines, and newspapers used; Puerto Rican meals cooked; and cultural celebrations observed.

TABLE 5.2
Individual Ethnic Identity Achievement Scores

Participant (N = 7)	Ethnic Identity Achievement Score (1 = low, 4 = high)
Esperanza (IPR)	2.86
Margarita (USPR)	2.86
José (IPR)	3.43
Rosita (USPR)	3.57
Theresa (USPR)	3.86
María (IPR)	3.57
Christina (USPR)	3.57

these activities; two of the IPRs did report a fear of losing their proficiency and thus they were motivated to continue or increase reading, writing, and speaking the language.

All of the young people in this study were given Phinney's (1992) MEIM, which measures ethnic identity achievement. The items were rated on a 4-point Likert scale from *strongly agree* to *strongly disagree*. The scores ranged from 4 (indicating high ethnic identity) to 1 (low). As shown in Table 5.2, all 7 scores are considered in the range for positive ethnic identity achievement. Can language be salient for Puerto Rican youth? Heller (1987), examining the role of language in the formation of ethnic identity as a social construct, found that shared language is basic to shared identity. More than that, she proposed that identity rests on shared ways of using language that reflect common patterns of thinking and behaving, or shared culture. In essence, language choice and language use play central roles in the formation of these important social relationships, which are necessary to ethnic identity.

In Their Own Words

What familial and environmental factors contributed to this positive outcome? What in these young people's socialization experiences may have contributed to this ethnic identity achievement?

Self-Definitions.   For these young Puerto Ricans, membership in their ethnic group included a pride in their Spanish language and a desire to pass it on to the next generation. Following are some participants' views on what it meant to them to be a member of their ethnic group. The data are presented in terms of socialization factors that most influenced these participants' identities.

María (IPR): Being Puerto Rican means cultural pride, it means the language we speak. I want my children to know Spanish. It's parenting, you know. You cannot forget your roots even like if you're in Russia, you need to know your Spanish. I cannot allow that in my house. I would feel like there is something missing, missing of the culture. I don't want my kids to have identity problems. I don't want them to suffer a lot. I don't want this to happen to them if I can avoid it by telling them they're going to speak Spanish.

José (IPR): I think that the only thing that Puerto Ricans preserve in this country that is Puerto Rican is the language. If we lose that, we are lost. I think that we need to preserve it because it is the primordial basis of our culture. It is the only thing we have to identify ourselves as Puerto Rican. If you do not dominate your own language, then what do you have? You have absolutely nothing because the language is the only thing that says what you are. If you are here or in Puerto Rico and you don't know your language, who are you? Even your own people will stop and ask, "who are you?" So, who are you if you don't know your language? If you are really sure of who you are and where you come from, why wouldn't you know your language? I believe that being Puerto Rican and speaking Spanish go hand in hand.

Margarita (USPR): To me Puerto Rican means a culture, language, religion, living in a Puerto Rican home and being brought up with traditional values, mostly language. I would definitely want my children to know Spanish because it was so instilled in me, "keep your Spanish traditions." So they should always learn where their grandparents, great grandparents are from, where we came from.

Family Influences.   Some of the participants' families were more language conscious than others; that is, some families more actively promoted the use of Spanish in the home. However, all 7 participants reported being exposed to both Spanish and English throughout their youth in the form of television, radio, literature, and music in the home. Regardless of whether the participants were IPRs or USPRs, they all received common messages that English was a necessity for survival whereas being Puerto Rican included the ability to speak and/or understand the Spanish language.

Esperanza (IPR): My mother knew that at some point we would have to come here. That was definite. So we began to press more attention to English. My teachers [in Puerto Rico] always said that it was good to know English because that is something that you need in Puerto Rico no matter what, for a job or if you are going to become a professional, you need English. I began my first semester in high school [in the United States] taking bilingual classes, mixed English and Spanish. I thought I didn't know that much English. I needed to do it for the future but I still spoke Spanish, that didn't change.

Another IPR, María, remembered that although the dominant language in her home and community was Spanish, occasionally "Ma would say phrases in English like 'brush your teeth' or 'come to eat'." María remembered that things changed when they moved to the United States: "In my house you are not allowed to speak English. My dad said, 'You speak English outside and when you come here, you speak Spanish'."

Whenever USPR Rosita's Spanish-speaking family members from New York or Puerto Rico would visit as she was growing up, they teased her, called her *gringa*, and made fun of her inability to converse with them in fluent Spanish: "Yeah, they'd call me 'la gringa, you're such a White girl, look at the way you talk.' " As a result of this teasing and other negative experiences with the Spanish language, Rosita expressed that "sometimes I feel like I'm not Puerto Rican enough, you know, because I don't speak Spanish fluently."

The Impact of School. All 7 participants reported that prior to entering the school system, the use of both languages for the most part was taken for granted. It was upon entering school that the participants first became aware of conflicts between Spanish and English.

Cristina (USPR): All White people were more intelligent than we were That's when I started thinking that they were all rich and stuff like that. They used to wear the little alligators on their shirts and the moccasins. I remember the alligators on the shirts. I didn't know what that meant but then I came to realize that it's something that symbolized something that you wanted to be. I remember pretending I didn't know how to speak Spanish. You know, if you pretended that you were that American, then maybe you would get accepted by the White kids. I remember trying not to speak Spanish or speaking it with an [English] accent.

Margarita (USPR): In school there were stereotypes about the bilingual students, big time. First of all they were bilingual, they don't speak the language, they don't belong here. That's number one. Number two, they were dumb, no matter what, bilingual students, they're just dumb. Everyone said "that bilingual person," but they didn't realize that bilingual means they speak two languages. To them bilingual was not a good thing. There was a horrible stigma attached to them and I think I fell in the trap sometimes of saying "those bilingual people" just because that was what I was hearing all around me.

Unlike the USPRs, the IPRs did not experience language conflicts in school. They learned English in school but used Spanish on an ongoing basis. The USPRs resolved these conflicts by separating their two worlds.

Cristina (USPR): [Spanish was] a private world. Unless you were amongst other Puerto Ricans, then you can let that out, you know what I mean? It was an us thing, you know? I never brought home my friends. I never brought my home to school. It was like I went from one world to another, I started to realize that in my senior year. At home I belonged. Very early on I learned that whenever I do speak in Spanish and I look around and there's another person, I automatically change to English. So it was something that was instilled in me. If I was around Puerto Ricans, it was both, we would talk English, but if we wanted to get something across and we wanted to make it more effective and more personal, we would throw it in Spanish. It would make it ours, it was more like a bonding thing if you threw some Spanish here and there and it still is.

The Influence of Racism and Linguisism. The lighter their skin the more able the participants were to assimilate. Yet they soon realized that their language was devalued as well as the color of their skin. The lighter-skinned USPRs attempted to pass, either physically or linguistically.

Margarita (USPR): I wasn't part of "those" people. They were called "those" people. I wasn't part of "those" people, but I was! It's just that they didn't see me in that light. Whenever they said something which is the wrong thing to do, whenever they said something "those" Puerto Rican people did, I never stood up and said, "well, I'm Puerto Rican too." Why would they say "those" Puerto Rican people and not consider me? I never had a real strong relationship with anyone that was, like me, Puerto Rican. Most of my classes were all White since I was in the advanced classes. I was considered a wanna-be-White person just because I excelled to that level and so there was always that division, which is sad. I knew tons of people in high school but I wasn't part of that majority. I'm light skinned, I guess the color of skin had something to do with it.

Experiences with racism and linguisism added to the conflicting feelings because these young people received messages at home that to be Puerto Rican was to speak Spanish. The IPRs did not encounter linguicism until they arrived in the United States. Interestingly, one of the conflicts experienced by all 7 participants regarded who was the authentic Puerto Rican. Both USPRs and IPRs reported conflicts they experienced with each other in the United States that focused on Spanish language fluency.

María (IPR): I speak English but my friends, they were all Puerto Rican but I remember that there was a distinction because the Puerto Ricans that were from here, they did not want to associate with us. I remember that it was because they thought I was a snob because I didn't talk like them. They used to say that I thought I was better than them because I speak Spanish correctly.

Rosita (USPR): One of my closest friends is Puerto Rican. At first I used to feel intimidated by her because her Spanish is fluent. She'd be like, "I don't understand, why didn't your parents speak to you in Spanish when you were little?" She is from Puerto Rico. I notice a lot of people that are from Puerto Rico that live in Puerto Rico and come here, they don't think that the Puerto Ricans here are Puerto Rican enough.

Not having experienced the same language conflicts as the USPRs, the darker skinned IPRs response to linguicism was anger and resentment toward the dominant culture.

José (IPR): Here, if you are not White forget it, the rest is no good and that's the problem. Why do you think that Puerto Ricans maintain their language? It is a form of telling you, "You don't want me to speak Spanish? Well I'm going to speak it, so you have to deal with it."

The Influence of Postsecondary Education.   For the Puerto Ricans in this study, the college years provided opportunities for self-exploration. Few Puerto Ricans have the opportunity to go to college. The Puerto Rican experience with education has historically involved an imposed system of education, with little or no opportunity for social or economic mobility, self-determination, or fulfillment (Walsh, 1998). The result has been a high number of Puerto Rican student suspensions and high drop-out rates as well as declines in academic achievement rates nationwide. The participants in this study are, therefore, atypical.

The students in this study had access to a culturally relevant and empowering curriculum. That is, they reported taking such courses as Puerto Rican literature and Latin American studies, and they all belonged to at least one Latino organization on campus. Elementary and secondary schools in the United States have traditionally perceived their role to be that of an assimilating agent; the isolation and rejection that come hand in hand with immigration and colonization have simply been left in the school's hallways. Most curriculums in these schools offer only an alien and imposed reality to students. If students feel their culture and/or language to be devalued or invisible, they in turn will feel devalued and invisible. This painfully illustrates the power that education, when seen as a social agent, can have in shaping and developing individual members of a society. For the students in this study, it appears that having a culturally relevant college curriculum to choose from aided in their self-exploration, which in turn aided in their positive ethnic identity achievement outcomes.

For these young people, the college years were also marked by an increased interest in the Spanish language, particularly for the USPRs. All of the USPRs in this study reported an increased interest in becoming proficient in Spanish. Two were taking Spanish or majoring in Spanish literature.

For all participants, the increased awareness and focus on the Spanish language in their college years appeared to be the result of an attempt to integrate their once-divided Spanish and English worlds. Bilingualism, becoming proficient in both Spanish and English, appears to be the bridge by which they were able to accomplish this. For 6 of 7 participants, becoming more bilingual was reported as a need to speak Spanish in public and an increased comfort in switching back and forth between Spanish and English when speaking with another bilingual. For 5 of the 7, it meant accepting both languages as their own.

María (IPR): When I first got to college I only spoke Spanish with one person. Now I speak to all the Latinas in Spanish. If they don't understand, I say things in Spanish and I say, "If she doesn't understand well, that's her problem, I have the right to speak Spanish." Now if they speak to me, I don't go to English, I do both languages but I feel very comfortable speaking Spanish, even like with Americans you know. I go "nena, que te pasa? What's going on?" you know, things like that. My friends, they asked me to teach them words, so I do. The older I get, the more a part of my life Spanish becomes. I need to show you that because I speak Spanish doesn't mean I'm low, you know, this is just me. Something else, now if I am talking with a bilingual, I feel comfortable switching back and forth.

Cristina (USPR): I'm a lot more fluent with English. I struggle with Spanish and it's something that I've been trying to reclaim. I've been reading a lot of literature written by Latinos lately, some Puerto Rican history. Before I didn't even know it existed. Now I'm reading and writing more and more in Spanish and I'm using it more in conversations with other Puerto Ricans. Now I have confidence. I don't feel inferior any more. I used to in high school, I did. People don't want you to speak Spanish and before I was one of those that's very guilty of not speaking it because I didn't want to draw attention to me, but now you can't tell me not to speak Spanish because for me that's the biggest form of oppression. My kids are going to speak Spanish and they're going to speak it loud. They're not going to go with the whispering stuff. As a matter of fact if a White person comes by, we're going to speak it even louder. I am going to ingrain that in them, that you need to be proud of that.

José (IPR): Puerto Rico is a specific area of the Caribbean with a language and culture totally and completely different from other Latin Americans. I think that the more assimilated you are, the less Spanish you speak. The majority of my friends here are Puerto Rican and bilingual. They don't speak English when they are with another Puerto Rican. When a Puerto Rican is part of the group, we force that person to speak in Spanish. If anyone of the group speaks in English and they are Puerto Rican, they are automatically made to speak in Spanish or leave. I feel strongly that if you lose your language, who are you? How do you distinguish your identity from any other group here in the United States?

José self-identified as Afro-Latino and had experienced much racism in the United States. Although he strongly held on to his African roots, he desperately sought to be identified not as African American but as Puerto Rican, which to him meant speaking Spanish. His anger was evident throughout his interview.

DISCUSSION

This study set out to explore the nature of racial and ethnic identity development of 7 bilingual Puerto Rican college students. The results suggest some very important patterns regarding the role of language in these 7 Puerto Ricans' racial and ethnic identity development. Specifically, it appears that the Spanish language may be a very important component in the Puerto Ricans' search for ethnic identity. Bilingualism may, in fact, promote a positive racial and ethnic identity, particularly for the USPRs.

The 7 participants in this study viewed the Spanish language as a way to express their ethnic pride. At the time of the study they reported being actively engaged in their exploration of self and the group to which they belong. There seems to be a parallel here with Cross' (1991) stages of racial and ethnic identity development around language, particularly for the USPRs.

As children, these young USPRs learned that their language was devalued by many and that it was not acceptable to speak Spanish in public. They recalled feeling ashamed of their ethnic group's language and, consequently, keeping the Spanish language private and hidden. The beliefs and values of the dominant culture appear to have included the acceptance of English as the only legitimate language and of those who speak it as the preferred ethnic or racial group. The IPRs experienced the pre-encounter stage of racial and ethnic identity development very differently. On the Island, language was less the issue, and skin color was more salient. For the USPRs in this study, growing up in a world where two languages were heard and therefore learned simultaneously before they even entered school posed a real conflict. They reported feeling caught between two worlds, having become aware that Whites rejected them. Cross (1991) wrote that during this encounter stage the individual begins to grapple with what it means to be a member of a group targeted by racism.

For the participants in this study, the anger felt during the encounter stage led them to the immersion/emersion stage of self-exploration, which included a heightened awareness of their ability to speak Spanish or their limitations with Spanish. At the time of this study, some participants were *just entering*, somewhere in the middle of the immersion stage of their racial and ethnic identity development. Almost all appeared to be emerging with or moving toward a newly defined and affirmed sense of self, which included a pride in their ethnic group as well as a newfound pride in their Spanish language. As the ethnic identity achievement scores show, these young people had begun working through this stage but they were still young and would continue in the process of identity development. Most had not begun the process of internalization.

Clearly the use (or nonuse) of Spanish is likely to be an important issue influencing individual and ethnic identity formation for Puerto Ricans. Belonging to their ethnic group may mean maintaining, reactivating, or becoming proficient in their first language. However, other confounding and intersecting issues influence individual ethnic identity formation. Specifically, the complexity of identity formation may increase as a function of color, behavioral distinctions, physical features, long-standing (although frequently unaddressed) social stereotypes, and language differences (Beal Spencer & Markstrom-Adams, 1990).

IMPLICATIONS

What can be said about the nature of Puerto Rican ethnic identity development? What's language got to do with it? For these young Puerto Ricans, accepting their ethnic identities meant becoming able to bring their two worlds together. It meant rejecting the views of a society that devalues their group and their language. Becoming Puerto Rican meant becoming bicultural, that is, emerging with the ability to function in two worlds as opposed to feeling caught between them. The question remains, Does bilingualism promote biculturalism and does it lead to a healthier psychological outcome? The results of this study highlight the important role that the Spanish language appears to have in these Puerto Ricans' ethnic identity development. The USPRs in this study reported that the more fluent in Spanish they became, the more Puerto Rican they felt. The IPRs felt strongly that full assimilation meant speaking less and less Spanish.

It would be interesting to examine whether trends found with these Puerto Rican participants could be generalized to a larger population of Puerto Ricans from more diverse backgrounds. For example, how might English monolingual Puerto Ricans, reared in homes that were not conscious of ethnicity or language, compare in their ethnic identity development to bilinguals from ethnic/language-conscious homes? How might adolescents who have dropped out of high school differ, if at all, in their identity formation? The IPRs' and the USPRs' experiences differed during the school years. It would be interesting to study these experiences more in depth and their effect on racial and ethnic identity achievement.

Zavala-Martinez (1994) wrote that in this decade, some Puerto Rican adolescents have evolved their own Puerto Rican cultural identity. In New York, Chicago, Boston, and elsewhere, it is an identity that manifests and integrates multiple issues, concerns, and visions of contemporary life. According to Zavala-Martinez, this response has taken the form of a creative surge of musical, poetic, and narrative Puerto Rican voices in the United States that have sculpted meaning out of the disparate and contradictory experience of migration. This historical cultural development embodies and legitimizes the ongoing search for and redefinition of their national identity as it raises critical issues regarding language and culture for the Puerto Rican community both in the United States and on the Island (Barradas, 1980; Campos & Flores, 1979; Sandoval Sanchez, 1992, as cited in Zavala-Martinez, 1994).

Although the dominant society tends to color all Puerto Ricans, variations of color are not as much a problem of identity for Puerto Rican youths themselves as they have been in the past. Zavala-Martinez (1994) suggested that Puerto Rican youth are now constructing their own cultural identity as a bilingual, multicolored group. Puerto Ricans' search for an integrated identity is much more complex than whether one is bilingual or monolingual. For the Puerto Ricans in this study, identity struggles raised critical issues regarding language and culture for the Puerto Rican community both in the United States and on the Island. Yet in the final analysis, the USPR experience is still evolving, and no past experiences of other groups furnish models adequate to its comprehension. In many ways, Puerto Ricans remain very unique.

Many studies (Buriel & Cardoza, 1988; Darder, 1995; Nielson & Fernandez, 1981; Valdivieso & Davis, 1988) focusing on the academic development of Latino students in public schools have identified a variety of barriers and environmental conditions contributing to underachievement. Included on this list are language differences, lack of knowledge by teachers regarding the pedagogical needs of bilingual/bicultural students, and bilingual programs that fail to support the development of genuine bilingualism. The impact of these and many other persistent conditions is quite evident in the grade retention and drop-out rates of Latino students across the country.

Valdivieso and Davis (1988) found that Cuban students have the highest educational level of all Latinos, yet they are the most likely to speak Spanish at home. They are also more likely to come from middle-income backgrounds than any other Latino children. Buriel and Cardoza (1988) focused on the relationship between Spanish-language background and achievement among first-, second-, and third-generation Mexican-American high school students. They found that contrary to conventional wisdom, Spanish is not an impediment to student achievement. Nielson and Fernandez (1981), conducting a large-scale study of Latino high school sophomores and seniors, found that those who were highly proficient in Spanish actually performed better on achievement tests and had higher educational aspirations than those who were not. Even with these findings, many teachers continue to treat students who speak Spanish as a social problem. Nieto (1992) stated that the language dominance of students is not really the issue; rather, the way in which teachers and schools view their language may be even more crucial to student achievement. This devaluation of the Spanish language in school causes the most conflict during the search for an integrated identity among young Puerto Ricans. They learn early that the closer they can get to being Euro-American, including English-speaking, the more valued their position in society. Cummins (1989) claimed that the crucial element in reversing students' school failure is not the language of instruction but rather the extent to which teachers and schools attempt to reverse the institutionalized racism of society as a whole. Therefore, it is not their differences that make them marginal but rather the value that has been placed on those differences by the dominant society (Nieto, 1992).

CONCLUSION

The results of this study may have important implications for both educational practice and counseling methods. There is clearly a pattern regarding the role of the Spanish language throughout the stages of racial and ethnic identity development for the Puerto Ricans in my study, which implies a struggle with two languages. Early in their education participants became aware that their language was devalued by many and that it was not acceptable to be spoken in public. Our society and consequently our educational system, are increasingly multicultural. School systems are faced with the need to address a rapidly growing racially, ethnically, and linguistically diverse population of students. Schools must begin to recognize their unique role as potentially powerful agents for social change. Therefore, preparing all students to become productive members of a democratic society is a major responsibility of schools. The ability to function in two worlds as opposed to feeling caught between them appears to be the road to a positive ethnic identity achievement outcome. Schools, by design, play a powerful role in this process. They not only "dramatically affect the acquisition of knowledge and skills but the creation of identity" for all (Nieto, 1992).

REFERENCES

Arce, C. (1981). A reconsideration of Chicano culture and identity. *Daedalus, 110*(2), 177–192.
Baldwin, J. (1979). Theory and research concerning the notion of Black self-hatred. *Journal of Black Psychology, 5*, 51–77.
Beal Spencer, & Markstrom-Adams, (1990). Identity process among racial and ethnic minority children in America. *Child Development, 61*, 290–310.
Buriel, R., & Cardoza, D. (1988). Sociocultural correlates of achievement among three generations of Mexican American high school seniors. *American Educational Research Journal, 25*(2), 177–192.
Colleran, K. J. (1984). Acculturation in Puerto Rican families in New York City. *Hispanic Research Center Research Bulletin, 7*, 3–4.
Cross, W. (1971). The Negro-to-Black conversion experience: Toward a psychology of Black liberation. *Black World, 20*, 13–27.
Cross, W. (1991). *Shades of Black: Diversity in African-American identity*. Philadelphia: Temple University Press.
Culture and Language Policy Task Force (CLPTF) of the Centro de Estudios Puertoriqueños. (1978). New York: City University of New York.

Cummins, J. (1989). *Empowering minority students*. Sacramento, CA: Association for Bilingual Education.

Duran, R. P. (1983). *Hispanics' education and background: Predictors of college achievement*. New York: College Entrance Examination Board.

Erikson, E. (1968). *Identity: Youth and crisis*. New York: Norton.

Gibbs, J. T., & Huang, L. N. (1989). A conceptual framework for assessing and treating minority youth. In J. T. Gibbs & L. N. Huang (Eds.), *Children of color* (pp. 1–29). San Francisco: Jossey-Bass.

Gurin, P., & Epps, E. (1975). *Black consciousness, identity, and achievement*. New York: Wiley.

Hakuta, K. (1986). *Mirror of language: The debate on bilingualism*. New York: Basic Books.

Heller, M. (1987). The role of language in the formation of ethnic identity. In J. S. Phinney & M. J. Rotheram (Eds.), *Children's ethnic socialization, pluralism and development* (pp. 180–200). Newbury Park, CA: Sage.

Jenkins, L. (1993). African American identity and its social context. In E. P. Salett & D. R. Koslow (Eds.), *Race, ethnicity and self: Identity in multicultural perspective*. Washington, DC: National Multicultural Institute Publications.

Maldonado, D., Jr. (1975). Ethnic self-identity and self-understanding. *Social Case Work, 56*, 618–622.

Negrón de Montilla, A. (1971). *Americanization in Puerto Rico and the public-school system 1900–1930*. Rio Piedras, Puerto Rico: Editorial Edil.

Nielson, F., & Fernandez, R. M. (1981). *Hispanic students in American high schools: Background characteristics and achievement*. Washington, DC: National Opinion Research Center, National Center for Education Statistics.

Nieto, S. (1992). *Affirming diversity: The sociopolitical context of multicultural education*. New York: Longman.

Nieto, S. (1995). A history of the education of Puerto Rican students in U.S. mainland schools: "Losers," "outsiders," or "leaders"? In J. A. Banks & C. A. M. Banks (Eds.), *Handbook of research on multicultural education* (pp. 388–411). New York: Macmillan.

Padilla, F. (1985). *Latino ethnic consciousness: The case of Mexican-Americans and Puerto Ricans in Chicago*. Notre Dame, IN: University of Notre Dame Press.

Phinney, J. S. (1992). The Multigroup Ethnic Identity Measure: A new scale for use with adolescents and adults from diverse groups. *Journal of Adolescent Research, 7*(2) 156–176.

Pinderhurghes, E. (1982). Afro-American families and the victim system. In M. McGoldrick, J. K. Pearce, & J. Giordano (Eds.), *Ethnicity and family therapy* (pp. 109–122). New York: Guilford.

Spring, J. (1997). *Deculturalization and the struggle for equality: A brief history of the education of dominated cultures in the United States*. New York: McGraw-Hill.

Rodriguez, C. (1991). *Puerto Ricans: Born in the U.S.A.* Boston, MA: Unwin Hyman.

U.S. Bureau of the Census. (1985). *Population characteristics: 1991 population reports* (No. 403, p. 20). Washington, DC: U.S. Government Printing Office.

U.S. Bureau of the Census. (1982, August). *Persons of Spanish origin by state* (1980 supplementary report PC80-S1-7). Washington, DC: U.S. Government Printing Office.

Valdivieso, R., & Davis, C. (1988). *U.S. Hispanics: Challenging issues for the 1990s*. Washington, DC: Population Trends and Public Policy.

Walsh, C. E. (1991). *Pedagogy and the struggle for voice: Issues of language, power, and schooling for Puerto Ricans*. New York: Bergin & Garvey.

Walsh, C. E. (1998). "Staging encounters": The educational decline of U.S. Puerto Ricans in [post]-colonial perspective. *Harvard Educational Review, 68* (2), 218–243.

Zavala-Martinez, I. (1994). ¿Quién Soy? Who am I? Identity issues for Puerto Rican adolescents. In E. Salett & D. R. Koslow (Eds.), *Race, ethnicity and self: Identity in multicultural perspective. Washington, DC: National Multicultural Institute Publications.*

Black Pearl Unnoticed

Carlos Mills De Jesus, Jr.

I was more of an observer rather than a participant when it came to school matters. As early as kindergarten, my relationship with school was standoffish. My propensity to be one of the more silent members in my classes allowed me to go through elementary school practically unnoticed. Because my grades were slightly above average, there seemed to be little concern about my lack of participation in class.

For the most part, I enjoyed my days in school. Learning new things fascinated me. I was always aware of what was being taught and I wanted to participate, but I was afraid and felt uncomfortable. Many of the teachers and most of the other students were White. Western philosophies, curriculums, and teaching methods were the rule. The fact that these were unfamiliar to me made me feel alienated. Puerto Rican kids (like me) were often teased because of their accents, and/or because their daily attire made it obvious to others that most of them came from poor or low-income families. Like any other child, I didn't enjoy being teased, and so I went out of my way to become as invisible as possible.

It was the early 1970s. I was one of the darker skinned pupils in my class and this fact in itself made me feel self-conscious. Even at that early age, through the black-and-white television at home, I had become aware of the manner in which people of color were treated by those of lighter skin. It had become evident to me that the less attraction I brought to myself, the more unlikely it would be that I would be-

137

come the subject of harassment or ridicule. Most of the time, even if I knew the answer to the teachers' inquiries, I was too shy in school to raise my hand. Besides, I had been instructed by my mother at home to respond only when I was spoken to. Unfortunately, I took this advice literally and as a result, I ended up speaking to hardly anyone at all. In retrospect, it was highly unfortunate that my teachers never encouraged me to become a more active student through increased participation. Things changed a little by the time I started junior high school.

I was bused to a predominantly White school, and racial tensions were high throughout the year. This manifested itself physically among the students, but even worse, some of the teachers let us know that we were far away from home and that non-Whites were not wholeheartedly welcomed at that school. Although a few teachers were compassionate to our struggles as ethnic minorities, others blatantly told us that we were stupid, acted like animals, and were never going to amount to anything. For the most part, teachers expected very little contribution from us as students. By now, I had almost become accustomed to this unjust treatment and I did whatever I had to in order to get along. Fortunately, puberty welcomed me with a tall, muscular build. This made me feel more secure and it also made some members of the majority group think twice before messing with me. Other Black and Puerto Rican kids were not nearly as lucky. Other than in kindergarten, when I surprised my teacher by counting up to 30 and reciting the alphabet in both Spanish and English, the only time I recall hearing praise for my academic progress from one of my teachers was in the ninth grade. I was the only student in my class to score over a 90 in the New York statewide algebra regents exam. I was now ready to tackle high school.

I chose not to attend my zoned high school because it had a notorious reputation as a war zone for those students who were not White. In fact, my oldest sister, Nancy, attended that school before she was forced to transfer after her first year there. As was the norm with others like her, she had become the target of racial slurs, and when she was physically attacked, she fought back. To this day, I would not be surprised if that boy, who happened to be White, has ever called anyone a "spic" or "nigger" again. I followed in her footsteps and successfully undertook a special entrance exam, which allowed me admittance to Clara Barton High School for Health Professions, in Brooklyn, New York. My sister received an excellent education there. She went on to become a registered nurse and highly recommended the school to me. Although African Americans and Latinos were the majority group in my high school, most of the teachers were White. Although Black History Month was celebrated, the curriculum was definitely skewed. What I have now come to understand as "untruths" about Africa, China, and other parts of the world were disseminated in class regularly, although not all teachers were guilty of this. Except for its climate, music, and cuisine, Puerto Rico was never mentioned.

One day, as a junior in high school, I distinctly remember embarrassing myself when one of the guidance counselors came to our homeroom to talk about the SAT exam and applying to college. I cracked a couple of jokes as I thought about the counselor's audacity in speaking to our mostly non-White class about college. Couldn't this person see that most of us were African American or Puerto Rican and none of us came from wealthy families? We didn't stand a chance. I couldn't understand why he would deliberately attempt to dupe us into believing that if we actually applied to a few schools, some of us would be accepted. I also could not believe how some of the students were actually taking him seriously. Didn't they know that, unless you were financially well off, only White students went to college? Too many of the Puerto Ricans and other ethnic minorities I came in contact with had not even graduated from high school.

Most of my understanding regarding college, erroneous as it may have been, came from commercials, movies, and programs on television. You hardly ever saw a student or professional, for that matter, who was not White and did not speak perfect English. The notion of going to college was hardly mentioned throughout my years as a student. Many of us were not even expected to graduate from high school. It should therefore be of no surprise that I was so ignorant regarding higher education. Aside from my parents, neither of whom were fortunate enough to complete high school, no one encouraged me to perform at my highest capacity in school. Before my aforementioned moment of embarrassment, nobody had ever spoken to me about continuing my education. It simply was not expected, despite the fact that up until that point, I had achieved at above average academic levels.

Today, I think about other school children who look like me and speak a native tongue other than English. I hope that their experience is smoother and safer than mine was. I hope schools today are less threatening to Puerto Rican students and to others who are not White. Additionally, I hope that faculty and other school personnel are more diverse, both philosophically and with their teaching styles, and that they are more willing to include curricula that ethnic minorities can relate to. With so much reform taking place in today's schools, I am hopeful that the message has gotten across that all students, regardless of their socioeconomic status, ethnicity, or academic background, deserve support and encouragement, so that they too dare to pursue academic excellence.

I am certain other potentially gifted students are present in many of the schools around the country. It would be a shame that because of their ethnic minority status, along with educators' low expectations of them, these students do not receive the necessary encouragement all students need in order to accomplish their very best. With today's pedagogical advances in bilingual and multicultural education, the "black pearls" in today's classrooms should not continue to go unnoticed. Rather, their skills, their cultural gifts, and the knowledge they bring to the classroom should be respected, praised, embraced, and further developed. This would instill in them a sense of belonging and community while in school, replacing those feelings of inadequacy that many of them carry along like unremovable scars on their psyches. Education can be everybody's friend. And an unshakable sense of self-worth, knowledge, and appreciation for one's own culture and uniqueness will dissolve whatever harm and ugliness racial slurs may carry.

6

Puerto Rican Female Narratives About Self, School, and Success

Carmen A. Rolón

Puerto Rican female students enter U.S. schools with about the same ability as others to become active learners and successful students, but a significant number of them drop out before graduating from high school. That is, they come to the classrooms with high expectations for their future, but many reach high school with a limited understanding, if any, of their postsecondary educational opportunities (Nieto, 1996; Vázquez-Nuttal & Romero-García, 1989). Puerto Ricans belong to one of the most undereducated ethnic groups in U.S. society (Nieto, 1995), with poor educational attainment at all levels of schooling (Arias, 1986). Puerto Rican females have been further shortchanged by their school experiences because of their gender (American Association of University Women [AAUW], 1992; Sadker & Sadker, 1994). Although these facts may present a dismal picture, there are nevertheless many Puerto Rican female students who are very successful in their educational endeavors. They go to school regularly and overcome the barriers imposed on them on their way to achieving high school graduation. These seeming contradictions prompted me to study the educational experiences of 10 Puerto Rican young women in secondary schools. I was particularly interested in documenting what contributed to their educational success.

In this chapter, the findings of that inquiry are examined. Following the tradition of Gilligan, Lyons, and Hanmer (1990), Nieto (1996), SooHoo(1993), and Zanger (1993), I have sought to portray what young adolescent students say about their experiences as experts of their life conditions, whose insiders' perspective offers useful information to transform curriculum and instruction (Walsh, 1991). At the same time, I have sought to show what teaching, learning, and going to school are like for these students in order to understand the issues affecting their educational experiences and to consider the implications of their insights for improving the learning environment for students like them. This chapter, organized in three sections, focuses on the elements of success among the participants in the study. The first section presents a brief review of relevant literature to frame the context for the interviews. The second section describes the methodology of the study. The final section introduces the participants, offers a thematic analysis of their interviews, and considers the implications of the study.

A BRIEF REVIEW OF RELEVANT LITERATURE

The context of this research is grounded in previous studies documenting the education of Puerto Rican and other Latino students in the United States and the challenges they face in school and society as well as the role that the intersection of gender and other categories of identification plays in female students' lives. A review of this body of literature defines the context of the participants' lives and provides an avenue for exploring the issues and ideas presented in their narratives.

Puerto Ricans represent about 15% of the Latino population in the United States (Nieto, 1995), and Latinos are the nation's second largest minority group (Arias, 1986). According to Morales and Bonilla (1993), between 1980 and 1990, Latinos' demographic growth was nearly 10 times the rate of non-Latino Whites and more than 5 times that of African Americans, accounting for about 30% of the nation's population gain within this time period.

With a median age of 25 years, compared to the national median age of 32 years, the Latino population is younger than the nation as a whole (Morales & Bonilla, 1993). Among Puerto Ricans, the median age is 24.3 years, even lower than that of the overall Latino population (Arias, 1986), which helps explain the high number of Latino students in the nation's schools. For example, in elementary schools Latinos account for 11.3% of all students, and in high schools as many as 10.4% of all students are Latinos (Nieto, 1995). According to Morales and Bonilla (1993), above-average rates of immigration and reproduction among Latinos during the last

2 decades account for their significant population growth and younger median age. These population trends are not expected to change notably in the years to come.

A significant number of Latinos live in cities. Morales and Bonilla (1993) pointed out that the Latino rate of urbanization is 90% compared to 75% for the nation as a whole. Puerto Ricans concentrate primarily in the metropolitan areas of the northeast, especially in New York and New Jersey (Arias, 1986). The representation of Latino students is most significant in large urban areas, accounting for a significant proportion of the student population (Nieto, 1995). Unfortunately, living in the cities hurts Latinos. The suburbanization of goods-producing industries and the increase of highly specialized professional jobs in the cities have reduced job opportunities for Latinos, whose acquired job skills are fewer and whose educational level is lower than the national average (Morales & Bonilla, 1993). For these reasons, the living conditions of Latino families reflect the limitations imposed by poverty, unemployment, inadequate housing, and street violence (Nieto, 1994).

Puerto Ricans share most of the socioeconomic characteristics of Latinos but have some of the worst indices among them (Morales & Bonilla, 1993). Impoverishment among Puerto Ricans is very high. According to Morales and Bonilla (1993), in 1987 the poverty rate among Puerto Ricans was 40.3%, the highest of any racial or ethnic group in the nation. For Puerto Rican children, the rate is even higher at 53% (Nieto, 1995). The unemployment rate is also consistently high among Puerto Ricans. This distressing socioeconomic background frames the educational experiences of a significant number of Puerto Rican students in U.S. schools, and their educational profile provides further information about their school experiences.

As a group, Puerto Ricans have one of the lowest numbers of school years completed and one of the highest drop-out and attrition rates. At the high school level, they are also more likely to be 2 or more years below grade level than their peers, and their enrollment rate in college-preparatory curricula is very low (Arias, 1986; Vázquez-Nuttal & Romero García, 1989). In a comprehensive statistical analysis of several educational factors affecting Latino students in the United States, Meier and Stewart (1991) reported that Puerto Rican students were more likely to be found in low-ability instructional groups and in the most segregated schools in the nation. According to Meier and Stewart, academic grouping was the most significant element discouraging Puerto Rican students. The authors also found that Puerto Rican students were overrepresented among the expelled, that they did not gain access to gifted classes, and that they were overrepresented in special education classes.

Nieto (1995) characterized dropping out of school as an urgent and persistent condition in the educational lives of Puerto Rican students in the United States. Fernández and Shu (1988), after analyzing the High School and Beyond (HSAB) data, found that Puerto Rican students dropped out at higher rates than other students regardless of age, even when they were in academic programs, had average grades, did not have disciplinary problems, and expected to stay in school through graduation. Fernández and Shu's descriptive analysis of the HSAB data further reveals that Latino students felt more alienated from school than students in the national sample. In general, Latino students not only leave school in larger numbers than other groups but do so at an earlier age (Frau-Ramos & Nieto, 1993). Moreover, although in general girls have lower dropout rates than boys, this is not true among Puerto Rican students, where female students' likelihood of dropping out is higher than for male students (AAUW, 1992; Vázquez-Nuttal & Romero García, 1989). An increasing number of studies focusing on the everyday experiences of Latinos and other so-called minority students show how those experiences are constructed within the boundaries of social relations where class (Anyon, 1981; Meier & Steward, 1991), gender (AAUW, 1992; Sadker & Sadker, 1994), race (Fine, 1991; Ogbu, 1991), ethnicity (Bernal, Knight, Ocampo, Garza, & Cota, 1993; Phinney, 1993), and English proficiency (Moll, 1988) significantly limit these students' academic achievement.

METHODOLOGY

A burgeoning field of educational research focuses on the role of students as primary sources of understanding and knowledge about schooling and education (Cleary, 1991; Gilligan et al., 1990; Nieto, 1994; Walsh, 1991; Zanger, 1993). The qualitative research method of in-depth phenomenological interviews (Seidman, 1991) was chosen for this study because the emphasis of the inquiry was exploring, documenting, and understanding the participants' experiences from their point of view. Because I used life-history interviewing techniques (Seidman, 1991), the participants in the study were able to narrate their experiences in their own words. Another reason for selecting in-depth phenomenological interviews was to investigate whether gender was a crucial part of the participants' identities. As is the case with women's oral history, this methodology makes it possible to learn not only their histories and experiences but also the significance of personal relationships in women's narratives (Armitage, 1983). According to Miller (1976), Gilligan (1982), and Margarida (1989), women in U.S. society experience personal relationships not as mere interactions with other people but rather as definitions of who they are. In-depth phenomenological interviews place personal relationships at the center of inquiry, thus revealing the significance of those experiences in the participants' lives and self-definitions. It was, indeed, a useful tool to explore the elements of success among these young women.

There were three criteria for participating in this study: self-identification as a Puerto Rican female student, enrollment in a secondary school in Massachusetts, and an interest in sharing life stories and educational experiences with others. Massachusetts was selected as the site for this study because the socioeconomic indicators for Latinos in the state, as described by the Mauricio Gastón Institute (1994) and Frau-Ramos and Nieto (1993), reflect the heterogeneity of the larger Latino population in the United States. This diversity in the Latino population in Massachusetts provided a rich opportunity to select participants from a variety of socioeconomic levels.

Parents, teachers, and staff from community-based agencies were the primary sources of possible participants for the study. I introduced the project to a meeting of young women in one of the community-based agencies, and 3 of them agreed to take the information with them and think about it. Two of them agreed to participate in the interviews. In addition, I gathered a list of 21 names and phone numbers from the other sources. These students were contacted by phone and given the identity of the person who provided their names, an explanation of the study, and an initial invitation to participate. Ten of them agreed to participate in the interviews for a total of 12 initial participants. I contacted the parents of these young women by phone and provided them with information about the study. A formal letter explaining the study and an informed written consent was sent to them to be signed by both participants and parents. By the end of the first interview, 2 of the participants decided not to continue, and based on the conditions of the written consent agreement, they withdrew from the project. The audiotapes of these two interviews were destroyed.

The structure and content of the interviews were as follows: Each participant was interviewed three times for approximately 75 minutes each time. For most of the participants, there was a 1-week interval between interviews. The first interview concentrated on the participants' experiences since kindergarten; their family background, neighborhood, memories of their teachers, school personnel, and friends; the role of their parents in their education; their participation in ESL and transitional bilingual education (TBE) programs; and the effects of moving from one school to another. Participants described their educational experiences, especially people and events that positively or negatively influenced their academic achievements or made them aware of their gender or ethnicity. In the second interview, the participants offered detailed accounts of a school day, describing their classes and grouping levels, textbooks, peers, homework, and extracurricular activities. I asked them to describe their relationships with their teachers, counselors, parents, and friends, and the role of these individuals in supporting their educational aspirations.

In the third interview, the participants reflected on the meaning of their experiences as Puerto Rican female students. Questions focused on their definitions of themselves, expectations for the future, and issues related to gender, ethnicity, and language proficiency. I also asked questions about problems they faced in schools and recommendations they would make to improve the learning conditions for students like themselves. The participants' narratives revealed three themes that had made a difference in their educational lives. These themes are presented here as findings.

Profiles of Participants

The participants in this study were young women who identified themselves as Puerto Rican students currently enrolled in a secondary school in Massachusetts. Five of them came from a small city where Latinos constitute the largest ethnic group, 31% of the city population. Of all the Latinos in this city, 93.5% are Puerto Ricans, and in the schools, Latinos are more than half the student body. The city is known in this study as Hopeville City, a pseudonym. The other 5 participants came from a midsize college town with a high percentage of middle-class households, where more than half of the student population is of White European descent. This town is called Appletown. In this chapter, I have chosen to portray 7 participants because collectively their narratives best reveal the themes explored in all the other interviews.

Brief Description of Participants

A brief description of each participant follows. All the names used are pseudonyms selected either by the participants themselves or by me.

Natalia Quiñones was a 17-year-old senior at City High School in Hopeville City. She was born in Florida and lived there for about 2 years. She moved to Houston Texas, and lived there for 8 years before coming to Hopeville City 7 years ago. She was the oldest of four children and the only daughter in her family. Natalia lived in a rented apartment in "the south," the heart of the low-income Puerto Rican community. She lived with her mother, a library aide, her father, a truck driver, and three brothers, who were 15, 13, and 12 years old. At the time of the interviews, Natalia was in the process of applying to college. She was the first member of her family to graduate from high school, and her parents were especially proud of her because she would be the first one in their home to have a college degree.

Lulú Cruz was a 16-year-old sophomore at Dearborn Vocational School in Hopeville City. She was born in Puerto Rico and lived there until the age of 7 and she was the second of four children. She lived in a rented house in a quiet working-class neighborhood with her mother, a nurse's aide, and her two younger brothers, who were 12 and 14 years old. Lulú was a good basketball player, and in the summer she enjoyed playing basketball with her brothers. She was the co-captain of the junior varsity basketball team and played other sports as well, including soccer and volleyball. She was also a peer leader educator in a local youth organization and organized information parties for adolescents to talk about AIDS, HIV, safe sex, and other issues of concern to young people.

Juana Alvarado was a 14-year-old freshman at City High School in Hopeville City. She was born and had lived all her life in Hopeville City. The youngest of three children, she was the only sibling living with her parents in their rented apartment. Her father was a security guard in a hospital and her mother a library aide. Of all the participants interviewed in Hopeville City, Juana best expressed how prejudice is experienced in the city.

Alma Soto was a 15-year-old freshman in Appletown High School. She was born in Puerto Rico and lived there until age 3. Her family moved to New York City, where they lived until she was 13. She was the oldest of three children. Her father was a lawyer, and her mother was studying toward an advanced degree in nursing. They lived in a wealthy neighborhood in Appletown. Her sister was 12 years old and in seventh grade, and her brother was 8 years old and in second grade. Alma took private art lessons and had shown extraordinary artistic talent. She was the only participant whose home language was English, and never in the interviews did she convey a strong sense of ethnic identity. Still, like the rest of the participants, her narrative reveals how important aspects of the Puerto Rican culture are lived and cherished in the United States. She best represents what Nieto (1996) and García (1992) respectively defined as "creators of a new culture" and "a new definition of ethnic identity," where elements of different cultures are woven together.

María Hernández was a 13-year-old eighth grader at Appletown Junior High School. She was an only child, who was born in Puerto Rico and lived there until age 11. She lived with her mother and paternal grandmother in a rented apartment in Appletown. They received public assistance, and they moved to the United States when her grandmother was diagnosed with a brain tumor. This is not surprising since better health care is a common reason for Puerto Rican low-income families to move to the United States. Her parents divorced when she was 4 years old but, as is often the custom in Puerto Rico, her grandmother helped raise her granddaughter while her mother worked full time. Her father, who married again and was already living in Massachusetts when they moved, was very involved in María's life, including helping her with homework. María was the youngest participant in the study, as well as the most recent arrival from Puerto Rico. She did the interviews completely in Spanish, and her narrative was colored with both the straightforwardness of a younger voice and the wisdom of Puerto Rican popular sayings.

Denise Figueroa was a 14-year-old freshman at Appletown High School. She was born in the United States and lived there until the age of 3, moved to Puerto Rico until she was 7, and then returned to the United States. She lived with her parents and younger sister in a middle–class neighborhood. Her father was a college administrator and her mother was a psychologist in the schools. Denise was an articulate young woman with a strong awareness of her biculturalism. For her, being bicultural meant to "flip flop between those two cultures." Her narratives best express the dualism of home and school cultures, and they reveal the struggles of demonstrating, to both "Americans" and Puerto Rican peers, that being Puerto Rican does not mean that one has to fit a stereotypical description of that ethnic group.

Jennifer Calderón was a 17-year-old senior at City High School. The third of four children, she lived with her parents and younger brother in a rented apartment in Hopeville City. She was born in Puerto Rico and lived there until age 10, when her family moved to a small town on the eastern shore of Massachusetts. According to Jennifer, they moved to Hopeville City shortly afterward because of the availability of a bilingual program in the school system. Her father had been a refrigerator technician but he had an accident and was now receiving SSI. Her mother was a secretary in a clinic where Jennifer had a clerical part-time job. Jennifer was a talented young woman who was very proud of her academic accomplishments. She won the Junior High School Honor Society Award and was admitted, through the early admission program, to a small private college close to home.

Elements of Success

Three themes emerged from these interviews that seem to define the educational experiences of Puerto Rican female students in the United States. First of all, parents, particularly mothers, were found to be the driving force for encouragement and achievement throughout the young women's educational lives. Second, teachers who made a real difference in these young women's learning experiences were those who most respected and affirmed in concrete ways the students' cultural and linguistic diversity. These teachers were referred to as "a second mother." Finally, all participants defined college education as their foremost educational goal. These themes represent a common thread among all narratives, and they are discussed in the order of significance they seemed to play in the interviews. In what follows, excerpts from the interviews are presented and explored, and the implications for improving learning environments in schools are outlined.

"My Mother Has Been There Through the Good Times and Bad Times"

Parental Involvement and the Mother's Role.   All the participants in this study talked about the role of parents in their educational lives. For most of the participants their parents were "the most important persons" in their education and "the reason to stay in school." Puerto Rican parents continuously stressed the importance of a good education to their daughters, teaching them the value of responsibility with schoolwork, and constructing what Hidalgo (1993) called a framework of high expectations for academic achievement. In all these families, daughters were expected to finish high school, and, for some of them, college was the guiding principle of what they did in school.

In the following passages four participants described the important role their parents played in their education. The first one, Natalia, described her parents and their dream for her to finish high school and go on to college:

> My parents are both Puerto Ricans. My father doesn't have an education. He dropped out of school in sixth grade. He was raised in New York, and mainly on the streets, so he doesn't have like a really good educational background. He's a truck driver. My mother, she was born and raised in Puerto Rico. She barely graduated from high school. She's a library aide. They always have this little goal made out for me to complete high school, complete K through 12, and go off to college. That's their little dream. I think that's excellent! My father will always [tell me] his story, "Look, I got out of school early, and it messed up my life. I never did good, and I will love for you to go to college, and I love for you to have a good education. That's why I want you to stay in school." I think they have this confidence in me.

They're always there for me. They taught me how to be responsible. They support me.

Alma portrayed her parents as concerned about what she needed to better prepare herself for college:

My mother and father, they both went to college and my dad went to law school. My mom is in school right now getting an advanced degree in nursing. I think they have a big role [in my education]. They look at my report card and ask me how I'm doing in classes. If I'm not getting along with a teacher, they go and tell her. They help me a lot. When I needed a tutor they got me one. They encourage me to learn in school and tell me that what I learn now helps me in the future. They basically ask me what I'm doing in classes. I'm getting closer to college so they want me to get good grades. I'm taking advanced science because my parents told me to be in because they feel that in college it's better to have in your record that you were in advanced classes. My dad helps in my homework but I think [my mom] is helping more than him because he's usually not at home after school. She asks me how I'm doing in school and encourages me. She tells me what to do in school.

Juana and Lulú identified their mothers as the reason they had stayed in school. In Juana's narrative, her mother was clearly seen as creating the necessary structure at home for her to be successful as school:

My mother didn't graduate because when she was still in Puerto Rico her mother got sick, [and] she had to take care of her. She just got to ninth grade. My father didn't get much farther than ninth grade. [He] didn't finish school because he needed to work to support himself and us. Now, he's a security guard at the hospital. My mother is a library aide. My mother, she gives me discipline, tells me what to do, at what time to be home. She tells me what is right for me. My mother helps me sometimes [with homework]. Sometimes I'll be on my own. If I don't understand [homework] probably I stay after school for the teacher to help me with it. I don't really ask my father or mother for help [because] it's in English and my mother and father don't know that much English. So, they can't help me. I haven't dropped out because of my mother. She wants us to finish high school. She wants to see that diploma. That's what she wants, that's what I'm going to do.

Lulú best expressed the role of her mother in her education and in her life. Throughout the interviews, Lulú was extremely reflective about her mother and how she had been an example of determination and effort:

My mother works 6 days [a] week. She's a nurse's aide. She works from 7:00 to 3:30. My mother is very proud because she's been my mother and father at the same time, because she always has been with us. I give her credit because she tries hard enough. Everything is depending on my mother. We don't take no welfare. The rent, the telephone, the cable, the light, that's a lot for one person. Two or three years [ago], she went and studied nursing. She wanted to be a nurse's aide, and she took a course and she passed it. Last year she got the license for it. She can work anywhere. That's been good for her. She works hard. I'm trying to get another job, because I want to help my mother with the telephone and stuff like that. I'm old enough to work so I don't feel like my mother [should] do everything, that my mother [should] pay this and that. She helped me, so it's my turn to help her. That's how I see it. Every mother likes her children to help her.

She tries to be there for me. She helps me a lot. Sometimes with homework, she doesn't get things. So, she can't help. She talks to my teachers, she talks to the principal, when I had a problem in school, that I'm a good girl. She's been there behind me all the time, and supporting me for what I do. She wants me to finish school. She wants that, that's what I'm going to give her. She wanted me to take the high school diploma. So, that's what I'm going to give her.

Finally, when asked to name the single most important person in her life who was helping in her education, Lulú had an immediate answer: "My mother! [Pause]. My mother has been there through the good times and bad times. I think it would be my mother. She's been there for me."

In all these narratives, Puerto Rican parents were seen as constructing high educational expectations for their daughters and even using their personal experiences with hardship as examples for their daughters to finish school. They were their daughters' mediators in school and, when possible, they also helped with homework or paid tutors to do so. Their daughters felt encouraged and supported by them. Thus, mothers, especially single mothers, were seen as playing a significant role in the educational lives of their daughters. All participants revealed that their mothers had taught them the basics for school success, discipline, and responsibility, and these mothers were perfect role models because some of them were pursuing their own education or had just finished it. In Lulú's case, her mother was all of that and more, because she had been there for her children as a mother and a father.

To assess the significance of these narratives, the role of the family and the mother in the Puerto Rican culture deserves some consideration. In the Puerto Rican culture, the family is conceived as tightly woven, where family members are mutually supportive and the mother is the thread that holds the family together (Nieto & Rolón, 1997). There is a sense of love, support, and collective responsibility for all members of the family. That is, the well-being of each family member as well as her achievement, concerns, and failures belongs not to the individual but to all members of the family (Nieto & Rolón, 1997). Although this is more an idealized notion of the family than a reality, it is still a cultural frame of reference for Puerto Ricans in the United States, where interdependence is highly valued (Hidalgo, 1993).

The mother is conceived as the embodiment of all these values. Her role is indeed complex. Traditionally, she has been expected to assume most childrearing responsibilities. Today, as the rate of divorce and number of single-parent households continue to grow, the mother's role involves most responsibilities in the family, including those of sole income provider, nurturer, and disciplinarian. Although these multiple responsibilities are sometimes overwhelming for the Puerto Rican mother, they have also been a vehicle for empowerment. In this context, Puerto Rican mothers have become strong role models for their daughters, precisely what is reflected in the narratives of these young women.

The participants in this study were proud of their mothers' achievement in school and at work. As Lulú said, these mothers should be given credit because they tried very hard to provide the best environment for the education of their daughters. Mothers are positive role models, and one implication of this study is that their role in their daughters' lives must be better understood and affirmed by the school system to make Puerto Rican students feel welcome and supported in school. Mothers are major partners in their children's education, and schools must create conditions to make them even more meaningful in that role. As Keenan, Willett, and Solsken (1993) demonstrated in their research, integrating parents into the curriculum enriches it, reduces cultural discontinuities between home and school, and increases understanding of cultural diversity among children. Parental involvement that fosters parallel collaborations between school and home, where parents become effective curriculum partners and active teachers in the classroom, is a successful model (Keenan et al., 1993).

In this study, it is clear that the socioeconomic conditions of the families framed the kind of support Puerto Rican parents could provide to their daughters. Alma's parents, both professionals, were well aware of college entrance requirements, and this knowledge allowed them to guide their daughter more effectively to achieve a college education. They expected Alma to participate in advanced courses, and when she confronted difficulties with the content, they supported her academic success by either helping with homework or paying a tutor to do so. In other words, they not only expected Alma to go to college, but they also knew exactly what needed to be done for her to achieve that goal. This was not true for most of the other participants. Although Juana and Lulú received from their mothers moral support and the strength needed to get ahead in school, they also explained how their parents could not help with homework. For Natalia, a college education was the dream of her parents, whereas for Alma a college education was the guiding principle for school decision making.

These differences reveal how parents from diverse socioeconomic backgrounds have the same commitment to their children's education but very different involvement. One of the most significant implications of this study is that many Puerto Rican parents simply cannot provide adequate academic support for their children in secondary schools. Traditionally, school systems have defined parent involvement based on a middle-class notion where mothers volunteer their time and expertise in their children's classrooms. Also, several studies have demonstrated effective school programs that have successfully integrated Latino parents into the curriculum, mostly at the elementary level (Bermúdez, 1994; Delgado-Gaitán, & Ruiz, 1992; Keenan et al., 1993). But the narratives in the present study reveal that parents are involved in their daughters' education in very different ways. They are seen here as storytellers with cautionary tales about missing a good education; as coaches always pointing to the goal of finishing high school; as sole providers working 6 days a week to meet their family needs; as successful peer students taking night courses and getting their vocational licences; as mediators advocating for their daughter's abilities and aspirations in school; and as dreamers visualizing their daughters with a college degree.

Unlike Alma's parents, who were able to provide direct academic help or pay a tutor to teach her, the parents of Juana, Natalia, and Lulú were not be able to provide academic support to their daughters for various reasons, but not because of a lack of commitment to their daughters' education. This situation has implications for school systems. Schools must learn to differentiate between parents' commitment and involvement in their children's education to carefully assess the role parents can play as collaborators at home and at school, and to design effective interventions that supplement their contributions to their children's education. When possible, as previously explained, a curriculum partnership can be fostered, and at least two strategies might be helpful to supplement parents' contributions to their daughters' education. First, school systems can offer homework clubs, after-school programs where students receive assistance with their academic work from tutors and volunteer teachers. Second, study halls can be structured so that tutors and volunteer teachers are available to students during those periods to clarify content and help with homework. These programs might not have high enrollment rates, but if they also provide free snacks to entice students to attend, they might make the difference in the education of a significant number of students in school.

"School Is Like a Second Home for Students"

***The Role of Effective Teachers in Respecting and Affirming Students'
Cultural and Linguistic Diversity.***   When participants reflected on
teachers who had made a difference in their educational lives, or when
they were asked to define the ideal teacher for students like them, all except Alma used as examples teachers who respected and affirmed in concrete ways their cultural and linguistic diversity in school. Confirming
many studies in the literature concerning effective schools and programs
for Latino students (Commins, 1989; Lucas, Henze, & Donato, 1990;
Moll, 1988), these participants' narratives show that affirming Latino
students' culture and language is necessary to improve their participation
and achievement in schools. The following three excerpts best convey the
issues expressed by most participants in their interviews. They described
the school as "a second home" and effective teachers as those who were
"caring," who were "involved with the students like they were our mothers," and who "love the Hispanic culture."

María talked about two teachers who had made a difference in her life.
One of them, Mrs. López, taught music in Puerto Rico. The other, Mrs.
Pérez, was her ESL teacher in Appletown. Both of them were Puerto Rican:

> The school is like a second home for the students. I had a teacher that was
> like a second mother to me. Her name was Mrs. López. She taught me music
> from first grade to fifth grade. She taught me how to dance folklore [from
> Puerto Rico]. She was really good with all her students. [If I have to choose
> the most important teacher in my life] I would choose either Mrs. López or
> Mrs. Pérez. Those two teachers treated me as if I was their own daughter. I
> share my problems with them. I learn more with them because they really
> care about me. Since they care a lot about me, when I am stuck, they help
> me understand.

As in María's case, Lulú's favorite teachers were those who taught ESL.
In the following excerpt, she emphasized that they knew some Spanish,
which helped them be better teachers for her:

> The only thing that helped me succeed from a lot of things [in school] is one
> teacher that I know from Dearborn. She loves kids. She goes to my basket-
> ball games, she goes to my volleyball games. Mrs. O'Brien, she helps me
> through a lot. This year I got her again. She teaches English, English reading,
> her and Mrs. Barnett. I like them. They are good teachers. Mrs. O'Brien and
> Mrs. Barnett., they're like mothers to me. If I need to talk to one of them, if I

feel depressed, they're always there. I can talk to them about anything. They always go to my games. They have a schedule. They are very involved with the students like they were our mothers. If the kids need any help, they show them that they really care. Both teachers took a Spanish course so they just know a little bit of Spanish. If there is a word I don't understand they just quickly say it in Spanish, or they look for the right word or the right meaning to put to that word. Those teachers, both of them, are best friends.

When asked to define the ideal teacher, Lulú said the following:

If you are a bilingual student, I would like [her] to translate twice, at least once in English and once in Spanish, so that you can understand better. Have a nice, positive attitude. When a student needs you, be there for her. You know, that's your second home. Like I see it, that's your second home because for years and years I'm going to be in school all day, from morning to the afternoon. So I see it that way; that's your second home. The teachers should be like parents to you.

Natalia was very clear about what an ideal teacher was like:

The ideal teacher? [She] can be a male or a female. She has to be very understanding. She has to be very flexible to teach, and to understand everybody's mind because everybody's mind goes differently. A teacher has to try to make everybody understand what she's trying to deliver to the class. A teacher that can explain what's going on, and if somebody don't understand just don't let that kid go out and blew. I like a teacher who gets involved with the students. I like a teacher who gets involved in my business.

Natalia was very close to her Spanish teacher, and her narrative about that teacher best conveyed the significance of teachers who affirmed her culture in school. Throughout the interviews, Mrs. Ferraro was shown in her role as teacher, second mother, and advisor, and as "having a Puerto Rican heart":

I love Mrs. Ferraro! She teaches Spanish, and she's a really good teacher. She's like a mother to her students. She's really caring. She's not Hispanic, but she says she has a heart for Hispanic students. She loves the Hispanic culture. Even though we're native speakers, I think she has taught us more about [our] life and culture. She says she has a Puerto Rican heart. She's always giving us advice that we Puerto Ricans can make something of ourselves and we can become doctors just as well as American people. She wants me to have good records for my school. She has a big impact in my life because all the advice she gives me. She's like our second mother.

According to Walsh (1991) and Zanger (1993), cultural differences between Latino students and school personnel have a major impact on the students' education. Cultural differences tend to marginalize students' life experiences in the school and the curriculum (Bucchioni, 1982) and seem to negatively affect their commitment to finish school. The teachers described in this section impacted the educational lives of these students. The participants perceived them as good teachers, and when asked to explore the reasons for these teachers' effectiveness, participants all clearly articulated that the teachers respected and affirmed their students' home language and culture. This is significant for at least two reasons. First, teachers who speak their students' home language and use it as a legitimate avenue to convey knowledge and abstract thinking positively affect Puerto Rican and other Latino students (Commins, 1989; Walsh, 1991), by helping them to better apprehend what is being taught and ameliorating the affective dilemmas they face while negotiating the different realities in which they live and go to school. Second, that teachers can speak Spanish, or at least understand it, conveys to these students that teachers understand the cognitive and emotional effort undertaken when expressing oneself and learning in a second language. Moreover, they are no doubt more effective teachers because they have experienced the difficulties of acquiring a second language, and they are therefore more likely aware of effective instructional practices when teaching second-language learners. When Lulú said that Mrs. Barnett was "far too good!" and Natalia said that Mrs. Ferraro was "a really good teacher," this was precisely what they meant. As García (1988), Lucas et al. (1990), and Olsen and Mullen (1990) explained, using different communication tools, such as visuals, and using Spanish to ensure clarity of communication and instruction when English skills are not the focus of instruction have been consistently shown to improve the learning conditions and academic achievement of Puerto Rican and other Latino students in U.S. schools.

In all these passages, the allegory of the school as a home and teachers as parents is revealing. It demonstrates how participants used their Puerto Rican cultural frame of reference when describing the meaning of school and effective teachers. They saw these teachers as second mothers who cared about them, were involved in their students' lives and, as Lulú explained, were "best friends" to the students. These teachers were someone to whom these young women could talk about their problems and, as Natalia explained, these teachers had a big impact in participants' lives because of the good advice they offered their students. When these teachers voiced high expectations for their students to "have good records," as

Mrs. Ferraro told Natalia to do, it further reinforced their parents' high educational aspirations. From this perspective, it is not surprising that these teachers and the school were, indeed, second mothers and homes for these young Puerto Rican women because the teachers clearly reinforced parents' high expectations and nurturance.

Finally, Lulú's case also showed how teachers' attitudes toward their Puerto Rican and other so-called minority students made a difference in their lives. Lulú described effective teachers as those who cared enough to go to her basketball games. As I explained before, Lulú comes from a single parent home where her mother works 6 days a week with little or no time to attend Lulú's games. I believe that by going to Lulú's games, Mrs. Barnett and Mrs. O'Brien did more than cheer her team. Rather, they supported her right to do sports in school and affirmed her gendered self-esteem in the process. They demonstrated how teachers, especially in urban areas, must understand how school has become a social institution where students not only learn academic subjects, but also grow emotionally and psychosocially. Whether they are aware of it or not, teachers impact the growth of their students. Similar to what Montero-Sieburth and Pérez (1987) described, effective teachers such as Mrs. Barnett and Mrs. O'Brien take time to better know their Latino students. Although personal time constraints are challenging for many teachers, the role they can play in their students' lives must be addressed when considering how to improve schooling for Puerto Ricans and other minority students.

"I'm Going to Go to College in the United States"

College Education as the Foremost Educational Goal.   When asked about their expectations for the future, all participants talked about going to college. Getting a college education seemed to be the fundamental educational goal of all participants regardless of their socioeconomic backgrounds. However, there were significant differences in the information they had about college, and those differences were directly correlated with their parents' level of education. For participants whose parents were college educated, the information they had was congruent with what is required to enter college in the United States. For those young women whose parents were not college educated, their chances of getting a college education seemed to be curtailed by their lack of understanding about college entrance requirements and the curricular choices needed to be a successful college applicant. Unfortunately, most of the young women described schools as providing little or no guidance to them. Yet, in this study, the aspiration of a college education was a strong element for these young women in continuing their high academic achievement in school.

In what follows, Denise, Juana, and Jennifer talked about their aspirations for a college education. Their narratives show the tentativeness of their young voices as they considered their career options and envisioned their future. Jennifer was a senior who had already been admitted to a small private college. For Denise and Juana, college was years away, but their knowledge of entrance requirements as well as their actual programs of study demonstrated a significant difference that, I suspect, will eventually affect their real chances of getting a college education to match their educational aspirations.

Jennifer had been in the college track throughout high school. In the following passages, she talked about her plan to study psychology, her participation in college-bound programs, and her experience of applying to and being admitted to college while still a junior at City High School:

> I can say that I plan to study. I want to study psychology. I want to be a psychologist, a criminal psychologist. Four years from now, hopefully, [I will be] graduating from college, getting my bachelor degree.

> Pre-College Program, it's a tutoring program. Monday afternoons we meet. They just help us with our homework. They have one person that helps us with our college essays, and if we have problems with the colleges for financial aid. This other guy, he helps us with science and math. We have a senior, she's good at English, so she helps out in English. The program teaches you how to fill out financial aid forms, how to make a good essay for college. It's good!

> In school, they have a college fair. In November, in your junior year, they take you to the college fair. I took information about every single college. I read their information and the ones I didn't like, I took them out. My three choices were Washington College in Washington, D.C., Spring Hill College, and City Community College. I went to an orientation to Spring Hill College and I stayed for the classes. The teachers were nice. The admission office, they treat you like you're a person, not a number. I was there for the whole day, and by the end they knew me already. That was kind of nice. You feel like at home. So, I applied that same day, and three weeks later I got a letter that said that I was admitted to the college. I didn't apply to City Community College.

Denise's aspirations to go to college were matched by her understanding of what she needed to do to get there. In the following passages, she talked about how her grades in ninth grade started counting for college and the fact that she would take a placement test that would go in her college records. Denise was definitively aware of what it takes to get into college:

I have my life kind of planned out, kind of a fantasy. Let see, I'm going to go to college in the United States. I hope that I will be able to go to college, a good college. Between eighth and ninth grade I went to Puerto Rico. I came back in ninth grade, and my grades the last quarter of eighth grade were awful. They were the worst grades they've ever been. As soon as I came into ninth grade I realized, "This is starting to count to college. I have to do something!" So, I don't know how I did it but I pulled them up in the first quarter. I got the best [grades] I ever got. Next year I'll have to go to a college to take Spanish. I'm in the advanced placement in the advanced course. If I take the advanced placement test now, then it will go in my college record.

For Juana, going to college was part of her educational aspirations, but her understanding of college requirements seemed to place her at risk of never achieving that goal:

I think about college. When I finish school, I'm not going to go like a definitive school or college. I want to wait. Probably after a year, I'll go back to college because you've already been 12 years in school, and you have another couple of years in college. You got to have a rest, you know! I'm going to have a rest, and then I'll go to college. I think that it's worth getting an education because I think that if you don't get an education you're going to go nowhere. You're going to be nobody. If you don't finish school, what are you going to do? Work in a factory? I want to be a nurse. That's what I want to be. [In order to be a nurse] I know I got to go to college for 4 years. I see myself finishing school, going to college, becoming a nurse, having a family, having a good job, having a nice car, having everything good because I like everything good.

When asked if she knew what courses she must take in high school to better prepare herself for college, Juana just shook her head. When asked when she would get information about that, she answered,

Probably when you're a senior, that's when they'll be telling you more about college. I have talked to nobody, no counselor, no nothing. I don't know. I don't got no idea because this is my first year [in high school]. I don't know nothing about that school. Probably when I get to higher grades, probably we take trips to City Community College.

As for the role of her guidance counselor in providing information about college, Juana remarked,

[My counselor] didn't tell me much about college. The only thing I know about college is because in the summer I used to work, and some people from college went over there and started talking about college. I got a college book [from] City Community College, and it tells me what courses you can take, what grades you got to have because I think if you got F's, you can't go into college. You got to have good grades.

When asked how school counselors can better meet the needs of students like her, Juana said,

[They should tell you] what you got to do to get to college, get you prepared to college. That's what I think high school is about, preparing me to college because when you're in elementary school they're preparing you to middle school, when you're in middle school they're preparing you to high school, and high school should be preparing you to college. I think that's the way it is.

Juana seemed to understand that her needs as a Puerto Rican female student with aspirations to go to college were not being met. Her experience was similar to those of other young women as reported by Vázquez-Nuttal and Romero-García (1989), who found that the high aspirations of Puerto Rican female students are not met with needed counseling services to guide them through curricular choices. Juana's experience was very different from that of Jennifer and Denise, who not only knew about college requirements but were already making the right curricular choices. What made Juana's experience different from that of Denise and Jennifer? A closer examination of all participants in this study reveals a correlation between their parents' educational level and their understanding of college entrance requirements.

Seven of the participants had at least one parent with some college education. The parents of Juana, Natalia, and María had no college experience. María's narratives about college were very similar to those of Juana. That is, they both talked about going to college, but when asked about college entrance requirements or curricular choices they must make to get there, both said they had no knowledge, but would get that information later on. Their parents could not guide them through that process and their schools had provided no information for these two young women to be successful in their college aspirations.

Natalia's case was different. Natalia had been very successful in school, and like Jennifer, she was one of the few Puerto Rican students in the college track at City High School. As such, she knew that her advanced courses were preparing her for college, and she had been invited to participate in college-bound programs. Still, when compared to Jennifer, whose mother and siblings had gone to college and who was admitted to a small private college, Natalia was still thinking about what college to apply to and seemed convinced that her best choice was City Community College.

Although community colleges provide a wide variety of choices at the associate degree level, Natalia's school records could place her at almost any 4-year college or university of her choice. I suspect that if her parents were more aware of the differences between an associate degree and a bachelor's or postbachelor degree, Natalia would be more likely to apply to a 4-year institution. Again, the role of the school in guiding Natalia to consider her options was missing.

These experiences show the need to restructure counseling services in both urban and suburban schools to meet all students' needs and high aspirations. Neither of the school systems represented in this study had done a good job of informing these young women about college requirements, thereby curtailing their opportunities, nor did professional staff seem to be aware of this situation in their schools. As a result, these school systems were unintentionally discriminating against those students who would benefit most from a college education: first-generation college students.

Juana's recommendation to counselors who want to improve their services to students like her concerned their role in "getting you prepared to college." This is a clear statement that must be taken seriously if we want to improve the learning environments for students in similar situations. This suggestion can benefit all students who dream of a college education but who do not always have the best opportunities to achieve this goal. In addition to providing traditional orientation sessions, counselors can meet individually with all students and can present college and scholarship information and entrance requirements beginning in seventh grade. In this way, students can plan the best course of study and change it according to their academic needs. Parents are part of this process and individual meetings with them need to be advocated as well. Traditional group orientation meetings may supplement individual meetings but should never substitute them, because the impersonal character of those larger meetings makes many Puerto Rican parents reluctant to participate. Scholarship information is of utmost importance for Puerto Rican families. Another recommendation is to create partnerships with college admissions offices to provide these needed services. Public schools and universities can collaborate to create programs that foster academic achievement of students as well, such as the ones portrayed in this study.

Academic Success and Puerto Rican Females: Implications for Students

In this chapter, the elements contributing to the academic success of 10 female Puerto Rican students were examined. Three findings emerged:

1. Parents, especially mothers, were the driving force for encouragement and achievement throughout these students' educational
   lives,
2. Effective teachers who had made a real difference for these female
   Puerto Rican students were those who respected and affirmed
   their cultural and linguistic diversity in concrete ways,
3. College education was defined as their foremost educational goal.

This study has several implications for improving the learning environments for Puerto Rican female students and other underrepresented
groups in U.S. schools. First, fostering parental involvement in the school
and curriculum improves the conditions that make Puerto Rican students
feel welcome and supported in school. To achieve this goal, I recommend a
redefinition of parent involvement to incorporate the concrete ways in
which Puerto Rican parents create conditions for the academic success of
their daughters. Furthermore, collaborations where parents become curriculum partners and active teachers in the classroom, as proposed by
Keenan, et al. (1993), will value and further support that involvement.
Second, to meet the high educational aspirations shared by the participants in this study, tutorial programs need to be created to provide adequate academic support for students whose parents do not have the
academic skills to help their children or the economic resources to provide
private tutors. Third, teachers can more effectively teach Puerto Rican
students by undertaking the enormous challenge of learning a second language, or they can at least master effective instructional strategies for
teaching students learning in a second language. Fourth, supporting their
students beyond the classroom door makes a difference in the educational
lives of these students. Fifth, to meet the high aspirations of a college education among all participants, regardless of their socioeconomic backgrounds, counseling programs should provide guidance about college for
all students and their parents beginning in seventh grade. Finally,
school–university partnerships are suggested as a way to make these recommendations viable in our budget-constrained educational systems.

CONCLUSION

This exploration of the educational experiences of 10 young Puerto Rican
women and their insights into schooling provides insight into the elements that make them successful in school. It also provides an opportunity to reflect about the role school systems can play in creating better
educational environments for students like them. I have presented some
suggestions to that effect in this chapter, but I believe that each school

system has the responsibility to evaluate its resources and priorities to design programs and services that will further foster academic success among Puerto Rican students. To do so is to acknowledge the role that Puerto Ricans in particular, and Latinos in general, will play in U.S. society and its economy during the next century as one of the fastest growing population groups in the United States. To ignore Puerto Ricans and other Latino students is to contribute to the social and economic stagnation that will result from undereducating an ethnic group which Day (1993) estimated will be a fifth of the nation's population by the year 2040.

In this chapter, the narratives of 10 young Puerto Rican women testify to their role as experts on their lives and educational experiences. They demonstrate how aware Puerto Rican students are of what and who can help them succeed in school. Their insights about schooling indicate the role students need to play in school improvement. Students can help to articulate what needs to be done to allow all students to achieve at their highest academic levels. I believe that when school systems listen to students' ideas and implement changes based on those ideas, a more racially, culturally, and linguistically diverse reformation of the school curriculum can be achieved. Otherwise, it will continue to be a challenge to provide equal educational opportunities to all students in the nation's public schools.

REFERENCES

American Association of University Women. (1992). *How schools shortchange girls*. Washington, DC: American Association of University Women Foundation.

Anyon, J. (1981). Social class and school knowledge. *Curriculum Inquiry, 11*(1), 3–41.

Arias, B. (1986). The context of education for Hispanic students: An overview. *American Journal of Education, 95*(1), 26–27.

Armitage, S. H. (1983). The next step. *Frontiers, 7*(1), 3–8.

Bermúdez, A. B. (1994). *Doing our homework*. Charleston, WV: Appalachia Educational Laboratory (distributed by Clearinghouse on Rural & Small Schools).

Bernal, M., Knight, G., Ocampo, K., Garza, C., & Cota, M. (1993). Development of Mexican American identity. In M. Bernal & G. Knight (Eds.), *Ethnic identity formation and transmission among Hispanics and other minorities* (pp. 31–46) Albany: State University of New York Press.

Bucchioni, E. (1982). The daily round of life in the school. In F. Cordasco & E. Bucchioni (Eds.), *The Puerto Rican community and its children on the mainland* (pp. 201–238). Metuchen, NJ: Scarecrow Press.

Cleary, L. M. (1991). *From the other side of the desk*. Portsmouth, NF: Boynton/Cook.

Commins, N. (1989). Language and affect: Bilingual students at home and at school. *Language Arts, 66*(1), 29–43.

Day, J. C. (1993). *Population projections of the United States, by age, sex, race, and Hispanic origin: 1993 to 2050*. Washington, DC: Dept. of Commerce, Economics and Statistics Administration, Bureau of the Census.

Delgado-Gaitán, C., & Ruiz, N. T. (1992). Parent mentorship: Socializing children to school culture. *Educational Foundations, 6*(2), 45–68.

Fernández, R. R., & Shu, G. (1988). School dropouts: New approaches to an enduring problem. *Education and Urban Society, 20*(4), 363–386.

Fine, M. (1991). *Framing dropouts: Notes on the politics of an urban public high school.* Albany: State University of New York Press.

Frau-Ramos, M., & Nieto, S. (1993). "I was an outsider": Dropping out among Puerto Rican youths in Holyoke, Massachusetts. In R. Rivera & S. Nieto (Eds.), *The education of Latino students in Massachusetts: Research and policy considerations* (pp. 147–169). Boston: Gastón Institute for Public Policy and Development.

García, E. E. (1988). Attributes of effective schools for language minority students. *Education and Urban Society, 20*(4), 387–398.

García, K. (1992, January). Gender and ethnicity in the emerging identity of Puerto Rican migrant women. *Latino Studies Journal, 3*(1), 3–8.

Gilligan, C. (1982). *In a different voice.* Cambridge, MA: Harvard University Press.

Gilligan, C., Lyons, N. P., & Hanmer, T. J. (Eds.). (1990). *Making connections: The relational worlds of adolescent girls at Emma Willard School.* Cambridge, MA: Harvard University Press.

Hidalgo, N. (1993, April). *Profile of a Puerto Rican family's support for school achievement.* Paper presented at the annual meeting of the American Educational Research Association, Atlanta, GA.

Keenan, J. W., Willett, U., & Solsken, J. (1993). Constructing an urban village: School/home collaboration in a multicultural classroom. *Language Arts, 70*(3), 204–214.

Lucas, T., Henze, R., & Donato, R. (1990). Promoting the success of Latino language-minority students. *Harvard Educational Review, 60*(3), 315–340.

Margarida, M. (1989). Developmental issues during adulthood: Redefining notions of self, care, and responsibility among a group of professional Puerto Rican women. In C. García Coll & M. L. Mattei (Eds.), *The psychosocial development of Puerto Rican women* (pp. 115–140). New York: Praeger.

Mauricio Gastón Institute. (1994). *Latinos in Massachusetts. Poverty, income, education, employment, and housing.* Boston: The Mauricio Gastón Institute.

Meier, K. J., & Stewart, J. (1991). *The politics of Hispanic education: Un paso pa'lante y dos pa'tras.* Albany: State University of New York Press.

Miller, J. B. (1976). *Toward a new psychology of women.* Boston: Beacon Press.

Moll, L. (1988). Some key issues in teaching Latino students. *Language Arts, 65*(5), 465–472.

Montero-Sieburth, M., & Pérez, M. (1987). Echar pa'lante, moving onward: The dilemmas and strategies of a bilingual teacher. *Anthropology and Education Quarterly, 18*(3), 180–189.

Morales, R., & Bonilla, F. (Eds.). (1993). *Latinos in a changing U. S. economy.* Newbury Park, CA: Sage.

Nieto, S. (1994). Lessons from students on creating a chance to dream. *Harvard Educational Review, 64*(4), 392–426.

Nieto, S. (1995). A history of the education of Puerto Rican students in U.S. mainland schools: "Losers," "outsiders," or "leaders?". In J. A. Banks & C. M. Banks (Eds.), *Handbook of research on multicultural education* (pp. 388–411). New York: Macmillan.

Nieto, S. (1996). *Affirming diversity: The sociopolitical context of multicultural education (2nd ed.).* New York: Longman.

Nieto, S., & Rolón, C. (1997). Preparation and professional development of teachers: A perspective from two Latinas. In J. J. Irvine (Ed.), *Critical knowledge for diverse teachers and learners* (pp. 89–123). Washington, DC: American Association of Colleges for Teacher Education.

Ogbu, J. U. (1991). Low school performance as an adaptation: The case of Blacks in Stockton, California. In M. A. Gibson & J. U. Ogbu (Eds.), *Minority status and schooling.* (pp. 249–285). New York: Garland.

Olsen, R. E., & Mullen, N. A. (1990). *Embracing diversity.* San Francisco: California Tomorrow Immigrant Students Project.

Phinney, J. S. (1993). A three-stage model of ethnic identity development in adolescence. In M. E. Bernal & G. P. Knight (Eds.), *Ethnic identity formation and transmission among Hispanics and other minorities* (pp. 61–79). Albany: State University of New York Press.

Sadker, M., & Sadker, D. (1994). *Failing at fairness.* New York: Macmillan.

Seidman, E. E. (1991). *Interviewing as qualitative research.* New York: Teachers College Press.

SooHoo, S. (1993). Students as partners in research and restructuring schools. *The Educational Forum, 57*(4), 386–393.

Vázquez-Nuttall, E., & Romero-García, I. (1989). From home to school: Puerto Rican girls learn to be students in the United States. In C. García Coll & M. L. Mattei (Eds.), *The psychosocial development of Puerto Rican women* (pp. 60–83). New York: Praeger.

Walsh, C. (1991). *Pedagogy and the struggle for voice.* New York: Bergin & Garvey.

Zanger, V. (1993). Academic costs of social marginalization: An analysis of Latino students' perceptions at a Boston high school. In R. Rivera & S. Nieto (Eds.), *The education of Latino students in Massachusetts: Issues, research and policy implications* (pp. 170–190). Amherst: University of Massachusetts Press.

7

Puerto Rican Mothering Strategies: The Role of Mothers and Grandmothers in Promoting School Success

Nitza M. Hidalgo

> *I am the mother of a new age of warriors*
> *I am the child of a race of slaves*
> *I teach my children how to respect their bodies*
> *so they will not o.d. under the stairway's shadow of shame*
> *I teach my children to read and develop their minds*
> *so they will understand the reality of oppression*
> *I teach them with discipline and love*
> *so they will become strong and full of life[1]*

In a national Latino survey published in 1992, de la Garza, De Sipio, Chris García, and Falcón (1992) reported that 83.5% of Puerto Rican youth in the United States attended public schools. Yet these young people are not well served by the public schools. Puerto Rican educational achievement

---

[1]Excerpt from the poem, "A la Mujer Borrinqueña," by Sandra María Esteves (1997). This poem reveals some of the unique characteristics of Puerto Rican motherhood. It reveals the collective work of building strong Puerto Rican children who can stand up to oppression and other harsh realities.

lags behind other groups: Only 58% of Puerto Ricans have completed 4 years of high school, compared with more than 78% of the total U.S. population. In addition, only 10% of Puerto Ricans have a college degree, compared with more than 21% of the total U.S. population (Institute for Puerto Rican Policy, 1992). Latinos also have higher school drop-out rates than other groups (ASPIRA, 1994).[2] In contrast to the deficit-driven research, current work is reexamining the cultural contributions made by Latino families to their children's schooling (Delgado-Gaitan, 1993; Díaz Soto, 1988; Goldenberg, 1987; Hidalgo & Nevárez-La Torre, 1997; Rivera, 1993; Volk, 1992). Furthermore, recent reports on Latino schooling recommend that schools strengthen their links with Latino families and communities (Great City Schools, 1987; Rivera-Batiz & Santiago, 1994). Although deficit-driven explanations of Puerto Rican school failure have placed the source of educational problems at the family and community level (see Nieto, 1996), the numerous issues related to the low educational achievement of Puerto Ricans include structural factors and within-group elements such as lack of institutional academic support, the existence of discriminatory school policies, the predominance of residence in metropolitan areas, limited English proficiency in school, a high incidence of poverty, and higher rates of attendance in segregated schools (see this volume for numerous examples of this research).

This chapter has a dual purpose: to explore Puerto Rican mothers' socialization strategies related to children's academic achievement,[3] and to reframe the research on parental involvement in schools using ethnic/racial, sociohistorical, and socioeconomic perspectives. The mothers' strategies are understood within the context of a Latino socioeconomically poor community in Boston, Massachusetts, and the mothers' experiences as second-generation, U.S.-educated Puerto Ricans. Within this context, traditional Puerto Rican mothering values and practices employed to promote children's school achievement are reconstructed and analyzed within a sociopolitical theoretical framework.

---

[2]As of 1992, 29.4% of Latino, 13.7% of Black, and 7.7% of White 16 to 24-year-olds were high school drop-outs (ASPIRA, 1994).

[3]This chapter presents findings from a 5-year cross-cultural research project on families' influences on school achievement. The ethnographic study investigated how African-American, Chinese-American, Irish-American, and Puerto Rican families supported their children's school success during the primary grades. Qualitative, longitudinal data were collected on 40 families (9 Puerto Rican families) in Boston, Massachusetts, between September 1991 and September 1994. All the names of family members have been changed. The database for the Puerto Rican cohort consisted of kindergarten, first-grade, and second-grade teacher interviews; yearly classroom observations; review of school records; parent (both mother and father in year 1), grandparent, uncle/aunt, and child interviews in kindergarten, first grade, and second grade; field trip data; and observational and field notes.

THEORETICAL FRAMEWORK

The theoretical framework used in this research employs multiple lenses to examine overlapping spheres of influence grounded in the Puerto Rican family experience. Each sphere contains elements of social structure that interact to produce the context of Puerto Rican family life in the United States. My analysis places families at its center, and the definition of family includes the extended family. Within an ethnic/racial sphere, Puerto Rican family values, behaviors, language, and traditions are explored to reveal how cultural concepts are understood by Puerto Ricans themselves in contrast to how elements of Puerto Rican culture are viewed by the dominant society. For example, Puerto Ricans' construction of race, as a multiracial group, exists on a continuum of multiple racial types, in opposition to the U.S. construction of race along a Black-to-White polarity (Rodríguez, 1995).

My theoretical framework takes into account four other spheres of social structure that impact families: social, educational, sociohistorical, and socioeconomic. The social sphere analyzes the relationship of families to community, friends, other community members, and participation in community institutions, such as schools and churches. How families use their relationships with others within their social location delineates their connections to resources within their community. I agree with Baca Zinn (1990) that a system of stratification is responsible for variations in family structures and their connections to significant community institutions; that is, families adapt to social and economic pressures. The educational sphere consists of parents' educational background (in the United States or in Puerto Rico), levels of educational attainment, and home education-related practices. Being educated in U.S. public schools shapes Puerto Rican families' belief systems differently than experiencing education in Puerto Rico. For example, a U.S.-based education provides little information on Puerto Rican history that parents may pass to their children. The sociohistorical sphere examines Puerto Ricans' colonial heritage, the families' conditions for migration, the historical period in which migration occurred, and families' ties to Puerto Rico. For example, the fact that Puerto Ricans migrate to the United States as citizens creates migration experiences different from those of other Latino groups. Finally, this framework covers a socioeconomic sphere that relates to Puerto Rican families' class position in U.S. society and includes economic status, work history and status, housing conditions, the community's economic vitality, and the adaptations families create in response to the uneven benefits and rewards available to them in society.

The theoretical framework undergirding this research contains the following assumptions (Anderson, 1993):

- Puerto Ricans occupy multiple social locations in the United States.
- Puerto Ricans, as members of a subordinated group, have unique understandings and insights about their experiences.
- The constructs of ethnicity, race, class, and gender influence the cultural knowledge formation of Puerto Ricans.
- The unique viewpoints of Puerto Ricans are not ethnically determined but constructed through lived experiences.

In terms of gender, the role of females in traditional Puerto Rican culture generally has been rigidly constructed. Women are taught the primacy of family obligations (Vásquez-Nutall & Romero-García, 1989). Thus, child nurturance is a woman's responsibility. The ideal Puerto Rican mother is selfless, sacrificing, and subordinate to her husband within the hierarchy of the family. The influence of Catholicism and traditional cultural beliefs, such as *marianismo*, are some of the social forces operating in the construction of Puerto Rican gender roles (García-Preto, 1982).

The Puerto Rican family maintains "close emotional and psychological ties" among its members (Salgado, 1985, p. 31), with mothers being the soul of the family (Elsasser, MacKenzie, & Tixier y Vigil, 1980). Children are taught to have unquestioned respect for parents, especially for the father's authority. Within the hierarchy of power in Puerto Rican families, the mother is the disciplinarian, whereas the father is the final arbitrator (García-Preto, 1982).

Within the U.S. context, American values and educational experiences have influenced Puerto Rican families to transform strict traditional orientations to accommodate the conditions they encounter. Young girls are taught both to be independent and to hold family obligations as primary values (Rosario, 1982). Puerto Rican women under dominant structural pressures create gender role adaptations as survival strategies.

The theoretical framework undergirding this research acknowledges the multiple influences upon the organization of Puerto Rican families and their construction of cultural knowledge. The intersection of ethnicity, race, class, and gender within sociopolitical contexts situates an understanding of Puerto Rican mothers' strategies for their children's school progress. The following section describes the community in which the families and extended families live.

BOSTON AND THE SOUTH END
COMMUNITY CONTEXT

In 1990, Latinos comprised 10.8% of the total population in the city of Boston. Although small numbers of Latinos lived in Boston before the 1960s, most settlement growth happened between 1960 and 1970 (Hardy-Fanta, 1993). The Latino population in Boston increased 71.8% between 1980 and 1990 to its current number of 61,995 (Gastón Institute, 1992). The Boston Latino community is composed of Puerto Ricans (42%), Central and South Americans (29.8%), Dominicans (13.1%), Cubans (3.5%), and Mexican Americans (3.5%; Osterman, 1992).

The South End, a community with a total land area of 1.03 square miles, is home to the largest Latino community in Boston (Coyle & Ganz, 1988). The South End is a diverse community of 28,891 residents with 60% of its population made up of people of color (Blacks 34%, Latinos 16%, Asians 12%, and 8% other; Coyle & Ganz, 1988). The Latino population in the South End grew 35 % between 1980 and 1990.

In the South End, the median yearly income for all households in 1990 was $17,156.00, whereas for Latinos, it was $8,342.00 (Goetze & Johnson, 1992). Forty-seven percent of all Latinos lived in poverty, compared with 14.7% of non–Latino Whites and 29.6% of Blacks (Goetze & Johnson, 1992). Fifty-seven percent of the 16,000 jobs located in the South End are in government and the service sectors (Goetze & Johnson, 1992).

The level of poverty in a community is related to the incidence of crime. Thus, crime is a daily reality for families living in the South End. Crime in the South End[4] accounts for 18.4% of all crimes committed in Boston, although just 5% of the Boston population resides in that community (Boston Police Department, 1994)

More than one third (37%) of all housing units in the South End are public or government-subsidized housing (Goetze & Johnson, 1992). A housing development, which I will call Barrio Betances, symbolizes the Latino community's past struggle against the gentrification of its housing stock. Barrio Betances has 844 housing units, public areas, and commercial space (Uriarte, 1992). The success of the grass-roots fight against the gentrification of the neighborhood led to the distinct Latino identity of the community (Hardy-Fanta, 1993; Uriarte, 1992).

---

[4]The South End is part of District D4, which includes the Back Bay.

FOUR PUERTO RICAN FAMILIES
FROM THE SOUTH END

The remaining sections of this chapter focus on the socialization strategies of four poor to working-class Puerto Rican mothers raising children in the South End of Boston. The strategies are described from the mothers' perspectives.[5] The four families were selected based on three criteria: They were all referred to me by kindergarten teachers as parents of academically successful students, they were all poor to working class, and they shared second-generation Puerto Rican status in the United States.[6] The young parents were born in the United States, either in Boston or New York, with the exception of two fathers (one was born in Puerto Rico and another in Honduras). The Cancel, Collins, and Collazo families were two-parent families, whereas the Rodríguez family was headed by a single mother.

All the parents had been residents of the South End for most of their lives. They all had extended family in the area, and as a result, they spent a great deal of their time in the Barrio Betances community in the South End. All four families had close relationships with their extended families, which included grandparents, siblings, uncles, aunts, cousins, and neighbors. These close relationships were demonstrated through frequent visits, daily contact, and sharing of resources. They relied upon their extended family networks for companionship, financial assistance, child care, housing, advice on childrearing, and socializing.

The Collins and Collazo families resided in a housing development, whereas the Cancel and Rodríguez families lived in government-subsidized housing. All the adults, with the exception of one father, held a high school degree or its equivalent and were employed full time in service or laborer positions. Their household incomes for 1994 ranged from $10,000 to $35,000, placing them from poverty level to slightly above the designated earnings for a middle-class standard of living[7] (Lewin, 1995), yet

---

[5]The focus on mothers' strategies is based on the mothers holding primary responsibility for childrearing and monitoring children's school progress.

[6]Informants for the research project were selected by interviewing kindergarten teachers about the characteristics they sought in potentially successful students. In other words, each teacher defined success. We asked each teacher to refer us to students in her classroom who fit her definition of a potentially successful student. We then contacted individual families to negotiate entry. The children were followed for 3 years.

[7]Class designation was calculated using the parents' level of education, place of residence, and income. Income was delineatd using federal poverty guidelines. Poverty level refers to people earning below the federal poverty level of $14,800 for a family of four in 1994. Low income or working class refers to people earning 100% to 199% of that level ($14,800-$29,452). Middle and higher income refers to people earning more than 200% of the federal poverty level ($29,600 and over; Lewin, 1995).

three of the four family incomes were higher than the 1990 South End Latino median income level.

The four young mothers (Elena Cancel, Natalia Rodríguez, Leticia Collins, and Milagros Collazo) shared a number of similarities. All four women had their first child when they were young (between the ages of 17 and 23), and in each case the child was the first or second grandchild in their families. The maternal grandmothers were the primary caregivers during the early years while the young mothers worked, resulting in close relationships between grandmothers and children. At the time of the study, the young mothers all took primary responsibility for child care and were employed full time outside the home. Some of these similarities are examined in more detail later in the chapter. The following section presents brief descriptive profiles of each family.

PROFILES OF THE FAMILIES

The Cancel Family

The Cancel family (Elena, Bolívar, and their three daughters) lived in the top two floors of a small, three-story apartment in the Barrio Betances section of the South End. The Cancel family previously lived in a high-rise apartment building in the same community. The new residence had two floors with two bedrooms and a playroom for the girls on the second level, and a kitchen, living room, and large bedroom on the lower level. The apartment had access through the back door to a large, fenced-in, community yard surrounded by similar three-story apartments. The children were allowed to play in the backyard without direct adult supervision. In their old apartment, the children were never allowed outside without an adult.

Doña Lola, the maternal grandmother, grew up in Aguadilla, a town on the northwest coast of Puerto Rico. She migrated to Boston with her husband in 1962, where they had four children. Doña Lola and her husband divorced soon after migrating to the United States. Having arrived in Boston during the beginning of enforced school busing, the single-mother family experienced many racially related incidents. For example, Puerto Rican and African-American children, including Elena and her sisters, were bused to South Boston schools. On numerous occasions the school bus was stoned by White protesters to school busing. During that same time, Elena, who had a light complexion, was repeatedly beaten by African-American girls in her neighborhood. Thus, the family found itself in the midst of the White/Black racial tensions of the time.

Elena was 31 years old and worked as a receptionist at a large business firm; Bolívar was 36 years old and worked as head of stock at a department store. Bolívar was born and raised in New York. Both Elena and Bolívar were high school graduates. Their combined yearly income ranged between $30,000 and $35,000. Lillian, the target child in this study, was born on June 6, 1986, and was the middle child. The oldest daughter, Gabriela, who was in the fifth grade, had consistently achieved high grades in school. The youngest daughter, Bethania, referred to by her parents as "the wild one" (which one suspects has nothing to do with her long, curly hair), was in first grade. All three children attended the Bayer Community Elementary School.

The Rodríguez Family

Natalia Rodríguez and her son, David Ocasio, lived by themselves in a well-kept, rent-subsidized apartment in Roxbury, a community bordering the South End.[8] Natalia and David resided in the two top floors of a three-story apartment house. The first floor was occupied by another family. The back of the row of apartments on that block all faced a large, open, community yard in which David played.

Natalia, 26, was born and raised in the Church Street Projects, a housing development in the South End. When I first met Natalia, she listed her education level as eighth grade; since that time, she had earned a G.E.D. Natalia currently worked as training coordinator at a regional hospital, where she earned $10,000 a year. David was born in Boston on April 8, 1986. He was friendly, talkative, and curious about many things and was always neatly dressed in coordinated colors.

Every day Natalia and David spent time with members of their extended family, who lived in the Church Street projects in the South End. Their extended family included Natalia's mother, Doña Mercedes González, Doña Mercedes' husband, and Natalia's sister. David had a close relationship with all of them, particularly with his grandmother, who had cared for him since he was 3 months old. Doña Mercedes grew up in Arecibo, a town in the northwest coast of Puerto Rico. She migrated to Chicago in 1966 and eventually moved to the South End. She was widowed after moving to Boston, and she raised her three children, two daughters and a son, with government assistance.

---

[8]Although the Rodríguez family lived in Roxbury, they spent most of their time in the South End neighborhood where their extended family lived. I describe this phenomenon as "living in two neighborhoods" (Hidalgo, 1997).

The Collins Family

The Collins family consisted of mother and father, Leticia and Miguel, and their son and daughter. When I first met Leticia and Miguel in 1991, they were both unemployed and lived with Leticia's parents in a five-room apartment in the Church Street Projects in the South End. Leticia's older brother also lived there. Her two other brothers visited their parents in the South End almost daily. The first-floor apartment opened directly onto a large parking lot. In the summer, family members would often sit outside their doorway to pass the time and to converse with their neighbors.

Miguel was born in Honduras and moved to the United States as a child. Leticia was born in upstate New York. Both of them had completed high school and were in their late 20s. Miguel, a welder, was currently employed as a night guard. He could not find work in his field because his citizenship application required further documentation,[9] even though Miguel had served 4 years as a U.S. Marine. Leticia worked as a telephone operator for a car repair company. After graduating from high school, she had received a scholarship to a well-respected university in the area. She related why she chose not to attend: During an orientation weekend, she experienced several incidents of racial harassment from the other students in her dormitory.[10] She decided then that she would not put herself in that position again. Instead she took a job as a traveling sales representative and made a living traveling around the country. During her travels she met and married Miguel, who was a Marine based in the South at the time. The Collins family income fell within the $10,000 to $15,000 range.

Doña Sonia Algarín, Leticia's mother, had played an important role in raising Martín. She was born in Guayama, a town on the southern coast of Puerto Rico. She moved to upstate New York in 1958 and eventually to Boston. The grandfather, Don Eduardo, had worked with the Post Office for 25 years. He would retire soon, at which time he and Doña Sonia planned to return to Puerto Rico to live.[11]

Martín was born on October 30, 1985, in Boston. During my first interview with Martín, he drew a picture of his father with a bowl of cherries

---

[9]Miguel Collins' parents divorced before his mother immigrated from Honduras to the United States. The documentation needed for his naturalization as a U.S. citizen was a copy of the divorce decree or a letter from his father acknowledging that custody of Miguel had been granted to his mother at the time of the divorce.

[10]The Collins family were Black Hispanic.

[11]Returning to Puerto Rico is a common dream for many first-generation Puerto Rican families. In part, this dream contributes to the back and forth migration patterns of Puerto Ricans in the United States (Borges-Méndez, 1993; Meléndez, 1993).

next to him, his father's favorite fruit. During the interviews with his family, I learned that Martín admired the fact that his father had been a soldier. All the men who surrounded Martín were strong male figures: his father had been a solider; two uncles were police officers; and a third uncle was a prison guard.

By 1994, the Collins family had moved to their own apartment in a working-class neighborhood in a small city north of Boston. During the summer months, Martín and his sister returned to the Church Street projects to be cared for by Doña Sonia.

The Collazo Family

The Collazo family—Milagros, José, and their two daughters—lived on the third and top floor of a building in the Church Street Projects in the South End. Milagros Collazo, 26, had completed high school and worked as a legal secretary, although recurrent back problems had interfered with her employment. José was 29 years old; he also had graduated from high school. José worked at a hospital in materials management. He was born in Arecibo, Puerto Rico, and came to the United States as an adolescent. The family yearly income ranged between $15,000 and $20,000.

The young family was part of a large extended family, whom they saw every day. The extended family consisted of Milagros' mother and father—Doña Concha and Don Pepe—her three sisters, and their husbands and children. The extended family lived in the Barrio Betances section of the South End, within walking distance of the Collazo's apartment in the Church Street projects.

Doña Concha Colón, Milagros' mother, was a central figure in this family. She was a strong-willed woman in her late 40s, who moved from Rincón, Puerto Rico, to New York when she was about 20 years old, and then eventually moved to Boston. She had four children. Doña Concha became active in the Barrio Betances community during her children's school-age years. She now worked in a local community-based organization and had daily contact with residents of the South End community. Doña Concha described herself as a social activist, and she and her family were well known in the Barrio Betances community of the South End because of her community work.

Carmencita Collazo, the target child in this study, was born on April 19, 1986. According to her teacher, Carmencita was at the top of her class, reading above grade level. Carmencita spent a lot of time with her maternal grandmother, often sleeping over. During such times, they shared a wide variety of activities including doing schoolwork, handing out flyers for community activities, going shopping, and dancing.

MOTHERING STRATEGIES WITHIN
A PUERTO RICAN COMMUNITY

The following section presents the mothering strategies and mobilization of resources for the academic achievement of children based on data from the four low-income families previously described. The strategies are patterns of behavior derived from all four mothers. This section generalizes conceptual categories of strategies from the consistent patterns found in the data and presents illustrative examples of the mothers' descriptions of their strategies.

Sense of Community

The meaning of community for the four low-income Puerto Rican mothers was primarily relational and personal. The presence of other Latinos having similar linguistic, cultural, and spiritual traditions provided the young mothers with a feeling of belonging and identification. The presence of the Spanish language and the shared cultural behavior and expectations found among the community relations sustained the families. Various forms of relations, such as friends, kinlike relations, and immediate and extended family members, formed a common core of people the mothers depended on to ensure day-to-day survival in this economically depressed community.

The community was both a source of strength and a potential risk from which the mothers had to shield their children. The physical survival of children in poor communities where violence is part of daily life was a constant concern for the Puerto Rican mothers (Hill Collins, 1994). The mothers were very aware of the negative influences in their community; their greatest concern was the possibility of losing their children to those street influences, as illustrated in Leticia Collins' comments: "The violence is ridiculous. The drugs. The drug sellers around here, they'll sell in front of the kids, they'll smoke in front of the kids. They have no respect for kids around here at all."

Milagros Collazo also perceived the danger involved in allowing children to play in the streets. She understood the sense of hopelessness that she and her neighbors face.

> [My neighbors] feel the same way I do, but what can you do, kids are kids. They want to go out and play. They want to do things. But some parents around here just don't have the ability to have a car, to go places, to have money and to do things with their kids. So they have no choice but to let them out. And if something happens, you know, what can you do? There's

just no choice around here. There's just no choice around here. There's just no, no way out of it. There really isn't.

Natalia Rodríguez agreed:

And just with all the things in society, all this killing, drugs and all this, everything is so hard. You can teach your kids one thing but once they get older, they tend to get influenced by other friends and neighbors. The parents can only do so much. It's up to the kids sometimes too. The parents can do so much and they can try. You see a lot of kids, their parents are great parents, they're well educated and everything, but then the kids turn out a certain way. A lot of people blame the parents. That's not always true.

The mothers all talked about the possibility of losing control over their children. They believed that external pressures could overcome their best parenting efforts. Their belief was based on countless examples of "good" parents whose children had turned "bad," as Natalia related in the preceding quote. Those children became lost to their families. Thus, there was an unpredictable quality within the mothers' understanding of community: Although their community provided a strong source of cultural identification and familial support, it also contained risk factors for the families who lived there.

The mothers responded to the benefits and disadvantages they experienced in their communities by developing child protection strategies. The mothers used trusting relations with extended family members and friends to sustain their families; they built trust within a small circle of people. By carefully choosing their associates, they could better control the social influences on their children; each family had developed a circle of extended family and friends in which they had *confianza* (mutual trust).

Roles of Grandmothers

The mothers' understanding of community was infused with the many functions that the extended family served, especially the role of the grandmothers, for the young mothers and their children. Their functions were numerous: child care, housing, transportation, companionship, financial assistance, time management, nurturance, and language and cultural maintenance. The grandmothers and the nuclear and extended family worked together interdependently.

Specifically, the grandmothers provided two important services: They nurtured the children, and they mediated with teachers. The grandmothers served the mothering function during the day while the young mothers were at work, they cared for the children after school, and they provided dinner for the children before the young mothers picked them up in the evening. The concept of "multiple mothering" can be applied to these four families. Multiple mothering implies the child's reference to more than one *mami* and the related dividing of mothering responsibilities between the young mother and the grandmother.[12] Natalia Rodríguez and her son David illustrated the concept:

> *Natalia:* My mother basically raised David.
> *David:* *Mamá me crió.* [Mamá raised me.]
> *Interviewer:* *Te crió, sí. ¿Tu la llamas tu mamá o abuelita?* [She raised you, yes. Do you call her mother or grandmother?]
> *Natalia:* He calls her mommy also. I'm big mommy and my mother's little mommy cause she's shorter than I am. But I'm not too tall. He has two mothers, he tells everybody.

In describing the reasons she preferred to remain in her present public housing apartment, Doña Mercedes showed her sense of responsibility to care for David:

> *Yo prefiero quedarme por acá debido a que estoy cerca de la escuela, una llamada, cualquier cosa, se me hace más fácil irlo a buscar. Porque no tengo que estar cogiendo guagua para llevar al nene [David] a la escuela. Y así una llamada, cualquier cosa de la escuela, se me hace fácil pa' ir allá.*

> [I prefer to stay here because I am close to the school, if I get a call, or anything, it is much easier to pick him up. Because I do not have to take a bus to take David to school. If I get a call from the school, it is easy for me to get there.]

Doña Mercedes' desire to stay close to David's school was part of the multiple mothering role. Since she was at home during the day, she would have more flexibility and faster access to the school in case anything should happen.

Second, the mothers' connections to the school were mediated by the grandmothers. The mothers left the children at the grandmothers' homes in the mornings and the grandmothers escorted the children to school. Consequently, the grandmothers became the intermediary between the four working mothers and the childrens' teachers by maintaining the

---

[12]Puerto Ricans may use the term *Mami* to denote mother and *Mamá* to refer to grandmother, although both terms mean mother.

day-to-day contact with teachers and keeping the young mothers informed. In describing how she would take Martín to school before Leticia and her family moved out of her apartment, Doña Sonia said,

> Yo antes lo llevaba por la mañana. Y me iba con él pa' los 'trips' que hacían. Y las maestras me dieron, me dieron un diploma a mí porque yo cuidaba los nenes también con ellas.

[I used to take him in the mornings. And I used to go on trips with the class. The teachers gave me a diploma because I helped them take care of the children.]

The young mothers, because of their work schedules, primarily interacted with the children's teachers during formal open house meetings, although one grandmother, Doña Concha, represented the family at open house meetings when her daughter, Milagros, who had had medical problems, was unable to attend.

> Cuando hay reuniones y esas cosas, sí, eso es lo que yo hago. Ahora mismo hay una reunión que ya yo puse que iba a ir. Porque cuando Milagros no puede ir, yo voy, yo la represento. Sí, si Milagros no va, pues yo voy. Tú sabes, si aquel día, yo no podía ir, pues Milagros hizo el sacrificio. Y eso es lo que hacemos. Nos turneamos, tú sabes.

[When there are meetings and things like that, that's what I do. Right now, there is a meeting that I will attend. Because when Milagros cannot attend, I go, I represent her. If Milagros can't go, I will go. And if one day I cannot go, then Milagros will make the effort to go. And that's what we do. We take turns, you know.]

The grandmothers were also responsible for surmising the conditions in the classroom (for example, whether the teacher was nice to the child, or whether the teacher was in control of the classroom). This type of information became part of the reporting system involved in monitoring between mothers and grandmothers (see monitoring strategy in the following section).

Within this economically poor context, the grandmothers provided social supports for these families. The informal extended family networks were mobilized toward the care and support of the young family and children. The families pooled their resources to derive a range of services, such as child care, which middle income families are able to purchase (Baca Zinn & Eitzen, 1987). Living in an economically depressed community requires family adaptations to accomplish the common goal of child development and to ensure family survival. Adaptations of family patterns are not deficiencies but variations produced by economic conditions and structural pressures.

STRATEGIES FOR ACADEMIC SUCCESS

Puerto Rican mothers, like most parents, function as teachers and models of appropriate behavior for their children. Volk (1992) found that in their homes, Puerto Rican parents employed various formal means (such as reading with their children) and informal learning activities (such as having conversations in Spanish with their children) that fostered child development. Puerto Rican families hold high expectations for their children and create strategies they believe will help their children in school. Díaz Soto (1988), who studied 57 Puerto Rican families of high-and-low achieving children, identified four salient factors in the parenting strategies employed by the high achieving group: Parents communicated in Spanish and English with their children, held high expectations and related those expectations to their children, employed consistent discipline strategies, and vigilantly protected their children.

The Puerto Rican mothers in this study used a number of similar strategies to socialize their children. The strategies were actions related to various areas of socialization, including but not limited to academic orientation, social relations, ethnic/racial identity, and Spanish language maintenance. This section focuses on those strategies geared toward academic success. I have categorized the strategies as: *monitoring, communicating, motivating*, and *protecting*. Monitoring strategies are actions related to academic learning. Communicative strategies are interactions that foster open, nurturing family relations. Motivational strategies are actions designed to stimulate interest in schooling. Protective strategies are actions geared to child safety.

The four sets of Puerto Rican mothering strategies may overlap Epstein's (1995) four types of parental involvement. Motivating and protective strategies correlate with Epstein's Type 1, that is, basic obligations of parents, which include safety and security needs and creating home conditions conducive to learning. Mothers fulfilled their basic responsibilities and ensured the safety of their children. Monitoring and communication strategies correspond to Epstein's Types 2 and 4—communicating with school and helping with learning activities at home, respectively. Mothers kept a close watch on children's work, communicated with the children and the school, and used that information to help with schoolwork at home.

The four types of mothering strategies were constructed out of the social locations of the Puerto Rican mothers, which included the maintenance of traditional Puerto Rican child socialization values, the lived experience of residency in a poor community, a belief in the benefits of schooling for social mobility, internalization of the beliefs and practices promulgated within the U.S. educational system, and the tensions experienced as a person of color in the United States.

Monitoring Strategies

Monitoring strategies were actions that promoted long-term academic achievement, although the short-term purpose was to help children learn subject matter. These strategies changed over time as the children grew older. The changes in strategies employed by mothers were precipitated by the demands, or lack of demands, of teachers and by the level of difficulty of the schoolwork involved.

Various types of monitoring strategies were demonstrated within the Puerto Rican households in this study. Mothers kept informed of what the children were learning in school by asking children for information, checking the children's book bag daily, doing homework with them, receiving daily feedback from grandmothers, and attending open house meetings at school.

The mothers used the information they received to help the children learn school material. They studied the material so they could then teach it to the children. They followed teachers' directions and guidelines whenever those guidelines were provided for working with their children. Mothers read with their children or drilled them in spelling or vocabulary, to reinforce what they perceived to be happening in school to ensure their children's academic success. According to Milagros Collazo,

> I read with her. I work with her, like math and spelling. I try to help her a lot in her homework. I do math, not like the math they do in school, but I try to teach her the times tables, to go a little further than what they teach her in school. Just so she can get a sense of what will come.

Finally, monitoring was interpreted by Puerto Rican mothers to mean teaching school and cultural values. Although I describe cultural values in more detail within the communication strategies discussed later, the two forms of values (school-related values and cultural values) intersected in Puerto Rican mothers' socialization of children. School values and behaviors were related to training in a work ethic. Reliability, organization, consistency, obedience, and responsibility were inculcated to children during their primary school years. In describing how Elena trained Lillian to act appropriately in school, Doña Lola referred to Lillian's behavior in the classroom and to the previous teacher's comment about Lillian:

> *La verdad es, las veces que yo he ido, a buscarla que he llegado, ella ha estado sentadita, calladita. Y la maestra, sí, la del año pasado, ella siempre que yo llegaba, dándome, hablandome bien bonito de ella.*

> [The times that I went to pick her up from school, she has been sitting quietly. And the teacher, last year's teacher, whenever I arrived, she would always have complimentary things to say about her.]

Puerto Rican mothers trained their children in the values they believed were necessary for academic achievement. (Hidalgo, Siu, Bright, Swap, & Epstein, 1995). Being responsible for one's work, being obedient, being organized and neat, handing work in on time, and being dependable to others were behaviors reinforced daily in the Puerto Rican families. The reinforcement of these values increased in intensity as the children entered first grade, where the mothers perceived children would face greater academic demands.

The monitoring strategies operated within the interdependent orientation of Puerto Rican families. That is, no one was expected to do everything perfectly; the children learned to depend upon other members of the family, including the extended family, to assist in the children's endeavors. The interdependent orientation was mediated by the young mothers' second-generation, U.S.-educated status. The four mothers had attended South End elementary schools and they were cognizant of the requirements of the culture of the school, which depends on at-home parental involvement, such as monitoring and helping with homework. The mothers all indicated that their own mothers were unable to help them because of the language barriers the first-generation parents faced. The young mothers' own school experiences had shaped their beliefs in partnership with the school toward the academic success of their children.

Communication Strategies

Communication strategies were actions that fostered open, nurturing family relations. The strategies inculcated cultural understandings, such as the maintenance of cultural values, ethnic identification, and Spanish language maintenance within an interrelational framework. Communication strategies were derived from the need to maintain children close to the family

(family unity) and the important place of relationships within the Puerto Rican culture.

Various actions taken with the children, with the extended family, and as a family fit together to form the communication strategy. For instance, listening to the child was a means to learn about the child's interests, fears, and concerns, and talking with the child socialized her or him into the Puerto Rican culture. Leticia Collins stated: "I talk with him a lot. Both his father and I, we're trying to build an understanding with him. We're both trying to build it." The mothers knew that spending time with children during a get-together, while watching television, or by reading could build trusting, positive relationships. Elena Cancel said,

> I'm always here with them so we talk a lot. We go out. I take them out. In the summer they get a little bit carried away because they'll be outside so much. I spend a lot of time with them. I try to spend time with them and with my sister on weekends, we'll go out together. She has two kids and I have three.

Within the extended family, communication was used to maintain close, daily contact with grandparents, relatives, and trusted friends. The actions included daily visits and phone calls, shopping and recreational trips, and sleepovers. Milagros Collazo stated: "I have a lot of family that do a lot for me. We're all very close in my family. They're really good to me." The grandmothers were enlisted as caregivers for the children after school, which resulted in close relationships between grandmothers and children. For example, in each of the children's kindergarten drawings depicting their family, the grandmother appeared within the drawing as part of the nuclear family.

As a family, the communication strategy attempts to accomplish two purposes, one behavioral and the other symbolic: the maintenance of the Puerto Rican culture through the use of the Spanish language, and the inculcation of the value of having good relations with others. Two of the four Puerto Rican mothers (Elena and Natalia) attended Spanish religious services, spoke to their children in Spanish and in English, and actively taught Spanish to their children. Three of the four young mothers were English-dominant (Natalia, Milagros, and Leticia), yet they used both English and Spanish in interactions with their children. Three out of the four grandmothers spoke to the children primarily in Spanish, whereas the other (Doña Sonia) used English more often than Spanish. The families' maintenance of Spanish provided continuity between generations, especially with the context of an English-dominant society.

The use of Spanish in the children's homes facilitated children's ethnic identification as Puerto Rican because Spanish is at the heart of the

Puerto Rican culture. When asked to identify their nationality,[13] Elena and Milagros identified as Puerto Rican; Natalia initially identified as Hispanic, and upon further questioning, as Puertorriqueña; and Leticia identified as Black Hispanic. All the grandmothers identified as Puerto Rican. This pattern relates to the one depicted by Rodríguez (1995), where first-generation Puerto Ricans tend to hold on to their cultural identity as Puerto Rican. But for later generations there is more acceptance of the non-White or "person of color" categorization to define their status. The later generations who have grown up in the shadow of the civil rights movement maintain their pride in being Puerto Rican but also acknowledge the influence of growing up in the United States (Rodríguez, 1995). Thus, within the biracial classification system that exists in the United States, light-skinned Puerto Ricans do not often identify racially because they don't have to, whereas many Black Puerto Ricans may feel external pressure to do so.

Regardless of how they identified, all the mothers and grandmothers told their children that their identity was Puerto Rican.[14] More is said about this in the discussion of the protective strategy. So the children's primary identification was ethnic, not racial. Puerto Rican mothers gave their children information about Puerto Rico. The grandmothers, especially, were primary sources for information about Puerto Rico, since they had first-hand memories about the Island. For example, the mothers and grandmothers talked about Puerto Rico, visited there whenever possible, and maintained Puerto Rican kitchens and traditions.

At the symbolic, intersubjective level, mothers communicated significant Puerto Rican values to the children. Mothers stressed close family unity and emphasized obligation to family members. They inculcated an interdependent orientation in relation to others. Puerto Rican mothers conceptualized children's school achievements as family accomplishments, not merely as individual attainments. The cultural values of family unity and interdependence were used to counterbalance the external pressures faced by these families within an urban environment.

The Puerto Rican mothers believed that as their children became older, they required more time and attention. In part, this belief was based on

---

[13]My research associate, Gladys Capella Noya, who came from Puerto Rico and attended postsecondary school here, and I agreed that asking the entire cohort of informants to identify racially would be culturally inappropriate since the racial variations of Puerto Ricans do not have the same meaning within the U.S. context. So we asked about their nationality. All 5 first-generation Puerto Rican–born informants identified as Puerto Rican, as did 2 out of 4 second-generation U.S.-born informants, whereas the last 2 out of the 4 second-generation U.S.-born informants identified as Hispanic and Black Hispanic, respectively.

[14]Martín was told by his mother that he was Puerto Rican and Honduran.

the uncertainty that comes from living in an economically depressed neighborhood, where negative influences may affect children. As the children grew older, the mothers related more sophisticated information to them about the importance of school, life in their neighborhood, and life in the world. As Elena Cancel said,

> You have to look out for the older ones now more than you do with the little ones. I think they need more attention than the little ones. The little ones you can keep at home and you could watch over them, but my oldest wants to do more things than she does, it's a little harder.

Later in the interview Elena elaborated:

> I always tell them that if they [child's friends] tell them to do something they don't want to do, you know, say you don't want to do it, don't be scared. Always do what you want to do, not what other people tell you to do. [I] always tell them if someone doesn't want to be your friend because of something that you don't want to participate in, then they are not your friend.

Milagros Collazo stated a similar message she had given her daughters:

> Try to keep away from their friends that try to influence them in other things, being bad. Like drugs, which are a big problem in the world nowadays. Like stealing cars, hanging around, doing things they're not supposed to be doing, because I don't want her to grow up and hang around with these kids.

Leticia's Colins' message was even stronger:

> My son, he knows what reefer is. He knows what cocaine is. It's something that I can't sit here and hide from him, because if he asks me these questions, I will answer them to the best of my knowledge. I explain to him what it is. If he's smart enough to ask me questions, I think he's smart enough to know what's going on, 'cause it's all out there.

Through their daily interactions with their children, the young mothers communicated information couched within the value of close family bonds. The children learned to trust and confide in close family members and to be cautious of outside influences. The communication strategies promoted close family unity, a strength found within Puerto Rican families. The mothers believed that communication strategies developed children's interpersonal skills, especially in relation to family members.

Motivational Strategies

Motivational strategies were actions that stimulated the children's interest in school to support and facilitate school achievement. The strategy took the form of different messages from mothers and the extended family. These messages existed within the context of the efforts poor and low-income parents must exert to ensure the benefits of education for their children. Because living in a housing development, growing up on welfare, having numerous siblings whom parents must provide for, or being from a single-parent family may interfere with school achievement, the mothers in this study conscientiously motivated their children to offset the possibility of school failure.

Motivational strategies included messages of encouragement to work hard, do your best, and keep trying even if you receive low grades. Elena Cancel said,

> Well, I do tell them that if they don't do right, you know, if they don't do well in something it doesn't mean that they're not gonna learn. They just have to try harder. I guess I always tell them to keep trying and, just because they get a bad grade doesn't mean … you get upset, but that you must have not been studying hard. I help her in, you know, find out what the problem is, and try to help her.

By training their children to be determined and to put much effort into schoolwork, the mothers hoped that the children would gain a sense of confidence derived from the accomplishments of hard work and from the support of the family. The young mothers believed that when motivational strategies were used simultaneously with the monitoring strategy, where mothers helped and facilitated the children's work efforts, and the communication strategy, when the relational context was nurturing the children, intervening conditions lost their power to negatively influence the children.

Related to messages of encouragement were messages about the result of good education and expressions of high expectations for their children. Puerto Rican mothers made connections for their children between education and future employment, having more options as an adult, and having a better life. The mothers revealed an idealogy that promotes striving to improve oneself through education, and they taught that hard work and effort lead to success. The mothers maintained a hope that stems from a perception of formal schooling as one of the only (if not the only) route for Puerto Ricans to attain life success. Leticia Collins stated: " I just try to drill into Martín to do good in school. Without school you're not gonna get anywhere." They hoped academic achievement would allow their children to overcome or transcend the parents' socioeconomic position, and they believed that education would allow their children to make it in the United States. They felt the pressure to ensure a good education for their children and, at the same time, they felt a sense of vulnerability from knowing the negative condition of education for low-income Latinos in the United States. Their vulnerability was based on their own problematic experiences in inner-city schools and on the experiences of unsuccessful children of friends and relatives.

Protective Strategies

A sense of vulnerability was at the foundation of Puerto Rican mothers' protective strategies. Protective strategies were actions related to child safety. Puerto Rican mothering was heavily laden with protectiveness as a result of three interrelated factors. Living in an economically depressed area where crime was out in the open developed the first awareness in mothers, a physical danger awareness. Crime in the area was perceived to stem from the different value systems their neighbors held, which resulted in mothers' second awareness. Neighbors' childrearing patterns were unknown to the four Puerto Rican mothers in this study. Thus, they felt compelled to protect their children from negative influences. The final awareness also lay at the root of protectiveness, that is, the awareness of the society's stereotypical beliefs about Puerto Ricans. Thus, the conditions that influenced the creation of Puerto Rican mothers' protective strategies had individual, community, and societal sources.

The mothers clearly compared the difference between Puerto Rican parenting and "American" parenting as one where American mothers allow children many choices and freedom, whereas the Puerto Rican mothers structure children's choices rigidly and maintain tight control. The control protects children from negative influences found within urban, low-income communities in the United States. Leticia Collins made the distinction between Puerto Rican parents and American parents: "Puerto Rican parents are very strict. They pretty much guide their children's way. American parents give children a whole bunch of choices; they pretty much let them decide want they want."

The protective strategies correlated with their various perceived sources. Mothers protected their children from physical danger by restricting and structuring the time the children spent playing outside to only those times when a trusted adult was present to supervise the activity. The play area was restricted to certain geographic locations. This strategy changed as the child grew older to permit more freedom. For example, Leticia Collins had established rules to keep track of her son, Martín, while he played outside. The rules gave him some latitude and provided her information about his play location. Martín could play in different areas of the projects as long as he informed her when he moved from one area to another.

> "You can go there, just make sure you check in the house." He had to check in the house, he had to make sure he made the household a checkpoint. Make sure, if he was going to another place, he had to let us know where he was gonna be at. At any given time, I knew exactly where to find him. Those were the rules. He wasn't able to go as freely, although that's what he wants. But there were checkpoints there. He had to check in.

The Puerto Rican mothers knew that anything could happen at any time in their community, so they tried to control as many of the conditions as possible. They interpreted their role as having to protect children from bad influences, and they actualized the responsibility by choosing the children's friends, keeping the family away from people with negative habits or behavior patterns, and talking to the children about the dangers in the area. The mothers trained their children to be aware of the violence and drugs. Again, the caution was to try to control the children's environment: the social influences, the kind of language they were exposed to, and the ideas and behaviors they learned from others who were not family or trusted friends.

The final protective strategy was directed toward shielding children from the racism in U.S. society toward Puerto Ricans. Puerto Ricans, as a group, occupy various social locations that may be deemed inferior by racist and classist characterizations in this society. Puerto Ricans are multiracial. Not coming from one racial stock, Puerto Ricans have been categorized as being non-White. Yet White is the norm preferred in the United States. Puerto Ricans speak Spanish as a first language, especially if they are recent migrants to the United States. English is the norm in this society, and the English-only movement is evidence of the linguicism[15] that exists today in the United States. Finally, Puerto Ricans are disproportionately poor, a characteristic that is often mistakenly equated with inferior behavior patterns as evidenced by recent debates on welfare reform. These elements, although having no relevance to the character of a people, locate Puerto Ricans near the bottom of the social hierarchy within an unequal system of advantages.

Puerto Rican mothers were painfully aware of the stereotypes about their people. Each of these mothers, as second-generation Puerto Ricans,

---

[15]Linguicism is language-based discrimination (see Nieto, 1996).

had personally experienced the disempowering effects of racism in this society. For three of these mothers, the experiences were a result of teacher behavior or teacher expectations.[16] Although the mothers had faith in the public schools to help their children achieve social mobility, they reserved their trust until they had formed close, interpersonal relationships with their children's teachers.

Although the mothers did not address racism directly with their children, in their children's socialization they actively imparted accurate ethnic information to their children to protect them from the cultural assaults prevalent in the United States.[17] The Puerto Rican mothers actualized the protective strategy by building the children's self-esteem and by developing strong Puerto Rican identities. Elena Cancel said, "I always talk to her about Puerto Rico. I'd like to always try to take them there every year, if I could. So they know. We eat Puerto Rican food. Their Spanish is real[ly] good." Natalia Rodríguez described similar behavior: "He knows that he is Puerto Rican. That's his nationality. I tell him he's gonna need to talk Spanish when we go to Puerto Rico."

The protective strategies were responses to external circumstances the families faced daily. The incidence of crime in their neighborhoods, the accounts of good children being negatively influenced, and the families' personal experiences of discrimination necessitated the close, protective parenting approach taken by the Puerto Rican mothers. They relied on their understanding of Puerto Rican culture and their lived experiences within the U.S. culture to guide their children toward academic success.

"BRINGING HOME INTO SCHOOL:" CORRESPONDENCES TO TEACHER EXPECTATIONS

The monitoring, communicating, motivating, and protective strategies discussed here corresponded to the parental involvement practices described by six kindergarten teachers in their definitions of successful students in this study.[18] The kindergarten teacher interviews revealed the

---

[16]All four of the families had at least one member who has experienced work discrimination also.

[17]"Cultural assaults are systematic attacks on the institutions and forms of social organizations that are fundamental to the maintenance and flourishing of the group's culture" (Baca Zinn & Thornton Dill, 1994, p. 7).

[18]I conducted six kindergarten teacher interviews between March 4, 1992, and April 10, 1992. The teachers interviewed were all White females and, based on the salary scales of the district, were on a middle socioeconomic level. They had been teaching from 12 to 20 years. All the teachers interviewed had taught their entire careers in the same urban district, al-

conceptions they had of the types of home support that foster school success. Home support was defined as the multifaceted influence that families have on their children that develops and nurtures school success. For many of the kindergarten teachers, the children's success in school was closely tied to the amount of support available to them at home. Teachers saw such support as a sign of the parents' interest in children's education, which creates continuity between home and school.[19] Teachers believed that when children knew that someone at home was interested in their work in school, it increased students' motivation to learn. In a supportive home environment, children acquired the right attitude about school. Supportive parents built connections between the home and the school for their children.

Three characteristics of a supportive home were identified by the six kindergarten teachers; First, motivation for learning was fostered through interest and assistance from home. Second, a positive perspective toward school was evidenced by children's social behavior in the classroom, such as being happy, respectful, and responsible. Third, building continuity between the home and school was displayed by the parents' commitment to establishing a partnership with teachers.

All of the teachers believed that children's motivation, the amount of effort that children put into their school work, developed only when there were adults at home who were interested in the children's work. That interest was operationalized by the numerous types of academic assistance children received at home. The communication strategy expressed parental interest when mothers listened and paid attention to children. According to the teachers, the expressed attention helped the develop children's motivation: "Children learn to value themselves when people listen to them." The school work that the mother and child did daily revealed an interest in the child's work. Thus, the mothers in this study helped build children's self esteem by attending to the children's interests.

Furthermore, the monitoring strategy provided concrete schoolwork assistance for children. Teachers expected parents to help their children in developing school skills, such as intellectual and motor skills. One teacher said, "We do a book report club which we have. They have to put the title, draw a picture about what they liked in the book. But the parent has to help them." Many of the activities within the monitoring strategy supported children in their activities at home; for example, helping with homework or reading to children were believed to motivate children toward schoolwork. Reading with children was thought by teachers to fos-

---

[19]All the teachers noted the important role that grandparents play in building a supportive home environment.

ter in children a love of books and good literature: "You know, parents that read to the children, parents that enjoy reading themselves, you know, are more likely to take their children to the library." According to the teachers, successful children "love learning"; motivated children are eager to take in all that the teacher has to offer.

A further characteristic of a supportive home environment for school success was the development in children of the right attitude toward school. Most of the teachers believed successful children enjoy being in school. "Successful child[ren] generally enjoy coming to school, that's probably the first thing I would say. They enjoy books, they're inquisitive. I guess I'd characterize them as pretty enthusiastic." Children were expected to embrace the belief that school would be beneficial. Parental support for schooling taught children to hold values congruent with the values embodied in the school. The mothers' use of motivating strategies reinforced in their children the appropriate belief about how schooling can lead to better life opportunities. In addition to a positive outlook toward school, successful children were responsible in their schoolwork. The teachers believed that parents who ensure homework is completed and brought back to school are developing in their children responsibility toward schoolwork: "being reliable, homework that is sent home always arrives back the next day." The mothers' monitoring strategies described previously developed children's sense of responsibility.

Finally, the teachers expected a partnership with parents. The young mothers in this study assumed a partnership role with teachers. When asked what type of relationship she would prefer to have with parents, one teacher said, "A parent who is open and sees me as a partner. A parent that is willing to let me in as a member of [his/her] team, and realize that I'm not here to pass judgement. I just want to bring out the best that child has. [A] parent that trusts me enough to share what is going on in their own lives." Teachers viewed a supportive relationship as one that closes the gap between children's experiences at home and at school, since what happens at home daily affects children's work and behavior in school. "Successful children usually, they bring school with them, they bring home into school and school into home." In describing the relationship she would like to have with parents, another teacher stated,

A cooperative parent. One that responds, comes in, wants to know how the child is doing! Thanks me, too! One who comes in occasionally and will say "Gee, you know, what is he doing? What is she doing? Show me. What can I do at home for them?"

The monitoring strategy was actualized, in part, by the role that grandmothers played as intermediaries between the working mothers and teachers. Often the grandmothers displayed an interest in the children before the teacher on a daily or weekly basis. Grandmothers related important school information to the mothers, thereby assisting in the operationalization of a partnership model of parental involvement found in the mothering strategies.

The mothers' strategies corresponded to teachers' expectations of parental involvement practices. By nurturing close, family relationships through the communication strategy, by helping children learn within the interdependent framework of the monitoring strategy, by instilling proper work-related behaviors using the motivational strategy, and by building self-esteem and strong identity using the protection strategy, Puerto Rican mothers and grandmothers created a supportive environment that closely related to the teachers' conceptions of school success.

CONCLUSION

The creation of child socialization strategies by a select group of low-income Puerto Rican mothers and academically successful children living in the South End of Boston was the product of the mothers' adaptation to the social, cultural, socioeconomic, and educational conditions of their daily existence. Although I analyzed each of the strategies in isolation, they operated simultaneously within the dimensional web of the theoretical framework. The belief systems that underlie these strategies also overlapped, although for the purposes of the discussion I unmeshed the operating belief system. The strategies were dynamic, modified over time to adapt to the children's growing needs and to the external demands placed upon families. The mothers adapted to the causal and intervening conditions they faced by organizing and structuring their children's environments through actualization of the four strategies and through mobilization of informal networks of relatives and friends, which functioned reciprocally.

Taken individually, each set of strategies corresponds to a dimension of reality within the context of Puerto Rican school achievement in a low-income environment. The monitoring strategies, which ensured that mothers were informed and prepared to aid their children's learning, stemmed from mothers' social sense of partnership in their children's education and their cultural belief in interdependency. The communication strategies, which comprised the relational component within Puerto Rican families, stemmed from the interdependent nature within Puerto Rican culture and the importance of intergenerational continuity. The motivational strategies, which promoted the children's interest in schoolwork and an internalization of a strong work ethic, emerged from a belief in the positive results of schooling. The protection strategies, which attempted to envelop the children within a safe physical and psychological environment, developed from an adaptation against local and societal disempowering conditions, such as low socioeconomic status and stereotypes about Puerto Ricans in the United States.

In this chapter, I have shifted the analytical lens from an at-risk perspective to a theoretical approach that examines the strengths of Puerto Rican families (Swadener & Lubeck, 1995). The close interactions within communities, between members of the extended families, and among networks of friends provided stability for the individual families. The mothers compensated for their limited social bases, resources, and access to institutional opportunities by creating strategies based on cultural strengths. Although social and economic conditions created barriers, limited opportunities, and constrained choices, the Puerto Rican mothers in this study were not just acted upon; they shaped their own lives. Thus, Puerto Rican mothers created strategies essential for child development and academic advancement within a context of economic disadvantage.

REFERENCES

Anderson, M. (1993). Studying across difference: Race, class, and gender in qualitative research. In J. Stanfield & R. Dennis (Eds.), *Race and ethnicity in research methods* (pp. 39–52). Newbury Park, CA: Sage.

ASPIRA. (1994). *The state of Hispanic education*. Washington, DC: Author.

Baca Zinn, M. (1990, March). Family, feminism and race in America. *Gender & Society, 4*(1), 68–82.

Baca Zinn, M., & Eitzen, S. (1987). *Diversity in American families*. New York: Harper & Row.

Baca Zinn, M., & Thornton Dill, B. (1994). Differences and domination. In M. Baca Zinn & B. Thornton Dill (Eds.), *Women of color in U.S. society* (pp. 3–12). Philadelphia, PA: Temple University Press.

Borges-Méndez, R. (1993). Migration, social networks, poverty and the regionalization of Puerto Rican settlements: Barrio formation in Lowell, Lawrence, and Holyoke, Massachusetts. *Latino Studies Journal, 4*(2), 3–21.

Boston Police Department. (1994, October). *Reported part one crime in the city of Boston: By type, time period, and location*. Boston: Author.

Coyle, S., & Ganz, A. (1988). *South End neighborhood profile, 1988*. Boston: Boston Redevelopment Authority.

de la Garza, R., DeSipio, L., Chris García, J., & Falcón, A. (1992). *Latino voices*. Boulder, CO: Westview Press.

Delgado-Gaitan, C. (1993). Research and policy in reconceptualizing family–school relationships. In P. Phelan & A. Locke Davidson (Eds.), *Renegotiating cultural diversity in American schools* (pp. 139–158). New York: Teacher's College Press.

Díaz Soto, L. (1988). The home environment of higher and lower achieving Puerto Rican children. *Hispanic Journal of Behavioral Sciences, 10*(2), 161–167.

Elsasser, N., MacKenzie, K., & Tixier y Vigil, Y. (1980). *Las mujeres: Conversations from a Hispanic community.* Old Westbury, NY: Feminist Press.

Epstein, J. (1995). School/family/community partnerships: Caring for the children we share. *Phi Delta Kappan, 76*(9), 701–712.

Esteves, S. (1997). A la mujer Borrinqueña [To the Puerto Rican woman]. In H. Augenbraum & M. Fernández Olmos (Eds.), *The Latino reader* (p. 384). Boston: Houghton Mifflin.

García-Preto, N. (1982). Puerto Rican families. In M. McGoldrick, J. K. Pearce, & J. Giordano (Eds.), *Ethnicity and family therapy* (pp. 164–186). New York: Guilford.

Gastón Institute. (1992). *Latinos in Boston.* Boston: University of Massachusetts.

Goetze, R., & Johnson, M. (1992, January). *South End planning district.* Boston: Boston Redevelopment Authority.

Goldenberg, C. (1987). Low income Hispanic parents' contributions to their first-grade children's word-recognition skills. *Anthropology & Education Quarterly, 18*(3), 149–179.

Great City Schools. (1987). *Results in the making.* Washington, DC: Author.

Hardy-Fanta, C. (1993). *Latina politics, Latino politics.* Philadelphia: Temple University Press.

Hidalgo, N. (1997). A layering of family and friends: Four Puerto Rican families' meaning of community. *Education and Urban Society, 30(1), 20–40.*

Hidalgo, N., & Nevárez-La Torre, A. (1997). Latino communities: Resources for educational change. *Education and Urban Society, 30*(1), 3–19.

Hidalgo, N., Siu, S. -F., Bright, J., Swap, S., & Epstein, J. (1995). Research on families, schools, and communities: A multicultural perspective. In J. Banks & C. Banks (Eds.), *Handbook of research on multicultural education* (pp. 498–524). New York: Macmillan.

Hill Collins, P. (1994). Shifting the center: Race, class, and feminist theorizing about motherhood. In E. Nakano Glenn, G. Chang, & L. Rennie Forcey (Eds.), *Mothering: Ideology, experience, and agency* (pp. 45–66). New York: Routledge.

Institute for Puerto Rican Policy. (1992, March). *Datanote on the Puerto Rican community* (No. 9/10). New York: Author.

Lewin, T. (1995, March 19). Abortion foes worry about welfare cutoffs. *The New York Times,* Section 4.

Meléndez, E. (1993). *Los que se van, los que regresan: Puerto Rican migration to and from the United States, 1982–1988* (Political Economy Working Paper Series No. 1). New York: Centro de Estudios Puertorriqueños.

Nieto, S. (1996). *Affirming diversity* (2nd ed.). New York: Longman.

Osterman, P. (1992). Latinos in the midst of plenty. In M. Uriarte, P. Osterman, & E. Meléndez (Eds.), *Latinos in Boston: Confronting poverty, building community* (pp. 35-71). Boston: The Boston Foundation.

Rivera, R. (1993). Barriers to Latino parental involvement in the Boston public schools. In R. Rivera & S. Nieto (Eds.), *The education of Latino students in Massachusetts: Issues, research, and policy implications* (pp. 77–87). Amherst: University of Massachusetts Press.

Rivera-Batiz, F., & Santiago, C. (1994). *Puerto Ricans in the United States: A changing reality.* Washington, DC: National Puerto Rican Coalition.

Rodríguez, C. (1995). Puerto Ricans: Between Black and White. In R. Santiago (Ed.), *Boricuas: Influential Puerto Rican writings—an anthology.* New York: Ballantine Books.

Rosario, L. (1982). The self-perception of Puerto Rican women toward their societal roles. In R. Zambrana (Ed.), *Work, family, and health: Latina women in transition* (pp. 11–16). New York: Hispanic Research Center, Fordham University.

Salgado, R. (1985). The Puerto Rican family. In *Puerto Ricans in the mid 80's: An American challenge* (pp. 29–44). Alexandria, VA: National Puerto Rican Coalition.

Swadener, B., & Lubeck, S. (1995). *Children and families "at promise."* Albany: State University of New York Press.

Uriarte, M. (1992). Contra viento y marea (against all odds): Latinos build community in Boston. In M. Uriarte, P. Osterman, & E. Meléndez (Eds.), *Latinos in Boston: Confronting poverty, building community* (pp. 1–34). Boston: The Boston Foundation.

Vázquez-Nutall, E., & Romero-García, I. (1989). From home to school: Puerto Rican girls learn to be students in the United States. In C. García Coll & M. de Lourdes Mattei (Eds.), *The psychosocial development of Puerto Rican women* (pp. 60–83). New York: Praeger.

Volk, D. (1992, March). *A case study of parental involvement in the homes of three Puerto Rican kindergartners.* Paper presented at the annual meeting of the American Educational Research Association, San Francisco.

III

SOCIAL ACTIVISM, COMMUNITY INVOLVEMENT, AND POLICY IMPLICATIONS

A Different Kind of School

Alicia López

If you were to ask me today, I could tell you the name of the woman who led "El Grito de Lares," the Puerto Rican insurrection against Spain in 1868. I could tell you about the Cuban Revolution and slave uprisings in the United States. I could talk to you about the political prisoners to whom I wrote while they were in prison. I could tell you about United States involvement in Latin America and about the dangers of nuclear power. I could talk to you about Mao Tse Tung, Patrice Lumumba, Che Guevara, and John Browne.

I have been lucky to have parents who, as educators, know about education and about the available options, and therefore I have always had excellent educational opportunities. One of these opportunities I participated in from the middle of first grade until the end of fifth grade, when I celebrated my elementary school graduation with the rest of the last graduating class of the Che Lumumba School. Our school was named after two revolutionary figures, Che Guevara and Patrice Lumumba, and although I now jokingly refer to it as "my hippie school," I am serious when I talk about the value of my education there. As an adult, and perhaps more significantly as a teacher, I carry the lessons I learned at the Che Lumumba School with me today.

The Che Lumumba School was founded and directed by parents interested in collaborating in a school whose ideals and values were progressive and multicul-

tural. Initially a project started by graduate students as part of a course focusing on educational alternatives, it became a small school with, at its largest, 13 students. This was in the early 1970s. Most of the teachers were also parents, including mine. Our space consisted of four rooms on the top floor of a university building. Our playground was a large, steep hill behind the building where we would sled in the winter and roll down in the spring. Our cook was Yvonne, a woman from the West Indies who made delicious meals daily and charged us 25 cents each. It was, she said, her contribution to the cause.

The Che Lumumba School was a wonderful place for many reasons. For one, it was almost an extension of my home because I knew many of the teachers and the students outside of school, so it was always a comfortable place for me. The school was comprised of teachers and students from different ethnic and religious backgrounds, and I never felt out of place or like an outsider. Because my Puerto Rican and Spanish background and my bilingualism were always positive attributes at school and at home, I was proud of them and could hold onto that pride when I went on to a public school where I was 1 of 3 people of color among 500 students. At the Che Lumumba School, I had teachers who I had no doubt cared about their students, since many of the relationships extended beyond school walls. Most of the teachers had a personal investment in our education and our future.

Most importantly, the Che Lumumba School was such a valuable experience because of the quality of my education there. Our classes were tiny, at times individual. Our strengths were encouraged and put to use; for example, as early as first grade, I was asked to help one of my friends with her reading, since I was a strong reader. Our education was very hands-on: After we learned about the dangers of nuclear power, our "field trip" was a demonstration against nuclear power. We learned things that public school students never even heard about: When I was in college, I remember being the only person in my African-American history class who knew that Blacks had been counted as "3/5 of a man" in the U.S. Constitution. We studied Puerto Rican political prisoners and the status and history of Puerto Rico in depth. Although I was shy, I was so proud to present a plaque to some of those political prisoners shortly after their release from prison, when they visited our school.

At Che Lumumba, I never questioned not "looking" Puerto Rican. I was never embarrassed about my ability to speak, read, and write in two languages. This was partly due to the people who were my role models, people with whom I could identify culturally or with whom I could relate personally. Lolita Lebrón was one of these role models: a strong, beautiful, Puerto Rican woman who was courageous enough to fight for her beliefs. I corresponded with her while she was in prison, and I was thrilled and awed to finally meet her when she visited our school after being released from prison after more than 25 years.

A picture of me at the Che Lumumba School is one of my favorites. In it, I am wearing a T-shirt that says, "We want girls in Little League!" and although I didn't play baseball, I loved that shirt because to me it was about strong women. An example of one of these strong women was Harriet Tubman, about whom we learned extensively. Because I was fascinated by her escape and by her daring returns to help many other slaves escape, I read in one day a novel telling her story. I also recall being very moved by "The Diary of Anne Frank," the story of a brave young woman in another part of the world. Today it makes sense to me that I chose to attend a women's college, having learned about and become proud of women like these at the Che Lumumba School.

My education was not the typical grammar school experience of most Puerto Ricans. However, I am certain I could not have had a more valuable experience elsewhere. The Che Lumumba School was instrumental in forming the person I am now. Caring teachers, a strong curriculum, a nurturing environment, and hands-on experiences all made it the first of many positive educational experiences that I have been fortunate to have. As a teacher now, I realize the value of the essential things I took away from that school: Question everything you read; go beyond the surface of what you are taught and look for the explanations behind issues; keep an open mind. Most importantly, enjoy the learning process and let it thrill you, because education and learning are gifts.

8

The Puerto Rican/Latino Education Roundtable: Seeking Unity in Vision and Organizing for Educational Change

Diana Caballero

This chapter tells the story of an educational advocacy coalition of New York City Latino community organizations, educators, parents, and activists—the Puerto Rican/Latino Education Roundtable (1983–1997). It discusses how the Roundtable developed and served as a force of political strength for the Latino community through representation and voice in education and as a vehicle for the political education and mobilization of our community. This chapter also illustrates the diversity of some of the issues around which we organized during our 14 years in New York City educational politics and some of the mechanisms and approaches we used to effect change at a grass-roots level as well as at city- and statewide policy levels.

In our quest to maintain and promote a progressive (that is, democratic, tolerant, and just) vision for educational change and to build broader multiracial coalitions, our agenda for educational change was always rooted in our need to develop a Latino educational agenda. Roundtable membership was based on a unity of vision, but the vision was always evolving and changing as we participated in democratic discussion and worked together in a multitude of terrains.

By providing an overview of the stages of our development, what we achieved, and the impact we had on some of the more important educational decisions of the 1980s and 1990s, the chapter offers critical lessons for those dedicated to collaborative work and educational and social change. It chronicles the story of a real-life effort that substantially altered how Latinos viewed educational politics in New York City.

BACKGROUND

The Puerto Rican/Latino Education Roundtable began in the early 1980s as a direct response to the crisis Latino students were facing in the New York City public schools—a school system that has historically been involved in the aggressive destruction of our young people, who make up over 35% of the 1 million students enrolled. The growing inequities, shockingly high retention and dropout data, deteriorated school buildings and overcrowded classrooms, ineffective and compensatory bilingual education, overrepresentation of Latino students in special education, institutional barriers to parent involvement, deficit models of instruction that resulted in blaming students rather than teaching them, minimal support systems for students and families, lack of qualified teachers and bilingual personnel, and inadequate and culturally irrelevant curriculum are just some examples of an alarming educational reality that unleashed resounding cries for educational reform (ASPIRA of New York, 1985; Caballero, 1986; Carrasquillo, 1985; Reyes & Pacheco, 1988).

Local and national reports by the National Commission on Secondary Education for Hispanics (1984), the National Council of La Raza (1986), the National Coalition of Advocates for Students (1988), the New York State Governor's Advisory Committee for Hispanic Affairs (1986), the ASPIRA of New York Report on Racial and Ethnic High School Dropout Rates in New York City (Calitri, 1983), and the Task Force on New York State Dropout Problem (1986) chronicled and sharply criticized the failure of schools to educate Latino and immigrant students. The reports found, for example, that Latinos were the most undereducated group of Americans according to measures of below-grade-level enrollment and number of years of school completed, and that Puerto Ricans had the highest dropout rate of any Latino group. The reports explored why so many inner-city public high schools were not more successful in educating Latinos, and they documented a comprehensive picture of the harassment and victimization of immigrant students. Cited throughout most of the studies were the glaring consequences of tracking and of the inequitable allocation of resources that highlighted what one report referred to as the "dropout epidemic" (Task Force on New York State Dropout Problem, 1986). Another study acknowledged that after numerous reports and millions of dollars spent on research, conditions were worsening (New York State Governor's Advisory Committee for Hispanic Affairs, 1986). The detrimental policies and practices highlighted in the numerous studies in the 1980s reflected the extent to which our young people were being failed by the nation's schools. The evidence indicated a brutal lack of concern for their intellectual, personal, and social well-being, and the entrenched school bureaucracy showed no signs of change.

The educational reality of Latino students was coupled with their social and economic conditions of inequality: Latino youths are one of the most impoverished groups in the city, and their conditions of housing, health, and income supports have declined precipitously over the past 2 decades (Institute for Puerto Rican Policy, 1990; Rodriguez, 1989). The growing xenophobic and anti-immigrant sentiment, giving rise to the "English-only" movement, exacerbated the problems (Crawford, 1992).

The ASPIRA report of 1983 affirmed an 80% high school dropout rate for Puerto Rican and Latino students. Dropping out was a final statement of despair for many of our young people; for others it was a refusal to accept dehumanization. The report highlighted that Latino students' reasons for dropping out had more to do with the school system than with economic and family concerns. As a statement of her passion and anger, Dr. Antonia Pantoja, social worker, educator, and visionary leader, who in the 1950s and 1960s created three of the most significant Puerto Rican organizations in New York City, refused to accept an award from the New York State Board of Regents for her service to education. The founder of ASPIRA, the Puerto Rican Association for Community Affairs (PRACA), and the National Puerto Rican Forum—organizations dedicated to the political, educational, and economic advancement of the Puerto Rican community—stated that in good conscience she could not accept the honor given the continued failure of the public school system vis-a-vis the Puerto Rican community.

Even before *The Puerto Rican Study of 1953–1957* (New York City Board of Education, 1958), recommendations and demands for educational change in the Latino community were articulated in different but consistent ways. Pioneer organizations that began in the 1950s and 1960s, such as ASPIRA, PRACA, the National Puerto Rican Forum, United Bronx Parents, and the Puerto Rican Educators' Association (PREA), and more recent ones such as the Puerto Rican Legal Defense and Education Fund (PRLDEF) that began in the 1970s, have been tireless in their struggle for equal educational opportunities, whether through studying the problems, directly confronting the issues, engaging in community organizing, or working through the courts (Rodriguez, 1989).

Building a Grass-Roots Educational Advocacy Coalition

In November 1982, the Association of Puerto Rican Executive Directors (APRED), an organization created by Puerto Rican executive directors of social service agencies in New York City, held a much-needed and timely conference on the status of Puerto Ricans in New York. Puerto Rican educators who participated in the conference affirmed the need for a forum in which educators and institutions that focus on education could begin holding monthly dialogues on the problems facing Puerto Rican children in the public schools. During that same time, ASPIRA and the PRLDEF found themselves back in court in a legal action against the New York City Board of Education because of an attempt by the schools chancellor to dismantle the court-mandated bilingual education programs that had been in place since the ASPIRA Consent Decree had been negotiated in 1974. As a result of this action, a massive demonstration and a community speak-out on bilingual education (Bisagna-Villafañe, 1985) were organized by many of the same individuals who participated in the APRED conference. Also participating were members of the Haitian, Greek, Italian, and Asian communities. Haitian Creole and Chinese are considered predominant languages in New York City public schools and, with Spanish, are among the 16 languages spoken by 96.2% of all "limited English proficient" students (New York City Board of Education, 1997).

After these events, there was a collective realization that more than just dialogue was needed, especially because the educational situation was worsening. The crisis faced by Latino students in New York City precipitated the need to bring together many of our organizations, educators, parents, legal experts, and researchers to create a community-wide consensus on educational policy and practice that would form the basis for ongoing advocacy and monitoring of the school system in the interests of Puerto Rican and Latino people. Because we viewed education as a vehicle for social and political empowerment, it was time to create and act upon a proactive agenda that would speak to the critical issues as we in the community defined them. We knew that we needed to develop a common vision and agenda so that, rather than always reacting to crises, we would set the tone for the educational debate and promote our vision for educational change. Thus, ASPIRA brought together a number of organizations and individuals, and the Puerto Rican/Latino Education Roundtable was born.

KEY DEVELOPMENTAL STAGES IN OUR FORMATION

The development of the Puerto Rican/Latino Education Roundtable is important, because many lessons can be drawn about how coalitions are built, sustained, and nurtured. In what follows, I discuss the key developmental stages in our formation beginning with how we defined ourselves—our vision and mission. Included is a brief description of our founding member organizations. Because these organizations were created throughout 4 decades, the 1950s through the 1980s, how we identified our priorities and approaches to effect change is particularly significant and highlights the importance of democratic discussion, learning from our history, and consensus building. Following this is a brief description of our organizational and decision-making structure, to which every developing coalition should pay close attention, because a strong foundation enables actualization of the agenda. How we attained our goals is elaborated through a presentation of some of the Roundtable's accomplishments. Finally, lessons are shared through a reflection of how our character and identity evolved and, most important, in what we learned as we created a process for change.

Stage 1: Exploring and Agreeing on the Purpose—Who Are We?

During this stage, the Roundtable developed a conceptual and organizational framework beginning with a statement of purpose, guiding principles, and a membership and governance structure. Following are the founding member organizations:

- Asociación Comunal de Dominicanos Progresistas (ACDP), a grass-roots community organization located in Washington Heights, in the heart of the Dominican community, that provides services to young people and families and is dedicated to community development and empowerment.
- ASPIRA of New York, an organization that provides leadership development and educational programs to Puerto Rican and other Latino youth and stresses the importance of education, community service, and cultural awareness.
- Centro de Estudios Puertorriqueños, a research institution dedicated to the study of linguistic, cultural, educational, and economic realities of Puerto Rican communities in the United States.
- National Congress for Puerto Rican Rights (NCPRR), an activist, grass-roots organization dedicated to securing the human and

civil rights of Puerto Ricans and developing new leadership among youth and women.

- Parent Advocates for Bilingual Education (PABE), a coalition of Latino parents, many with children in bilingual programs, which supports parents in advocating for bilingual programs and gives workshops on parents' rights and parent involvement.
- Puerto Rican Association for Community Affairs (PRACA), a community self-help advocacy organization based on strong self-identity as Puerto Ricans, understanding of Puerto Rican history, and reinforcement of cultural mores as a foundation for group organizing.
- Puerto Rican Educators' Association (PREA), an organization dedicated to the professional advancement of Puerto Rican educators and improving the education of Puerto Rican students.
- Institute for Puerto Rican Policy, an organization that studies the political participation of Puerto Rican and Latino communities.
- Puerto Rican Legal Defense and Education Fund (PRLDEF), which litigates class-action civil rights suits on behalf of the Latino community and which represented ASPIRA in the ground-breaking ASPIRA consent decree (1974) for the New York City public schools (Santiago Santiago, 1986).

The members initially agreed that the Roundtable would have the following goals:

- Advocate on behalf of the Puerto Rican/Latino community at all levels of education with a focus on affecting changes in the public school system from grades K to 12.
- Provide a forum for the debate, discussion, and analysis of major educational problems facing the community.
- Develop strategies to create an educational system that does not reflect the worst aspects of existing economic, political, cultural, and gender structures of inequality.
- Consolidate and build upon resources for educational change from within the community (Puerto Rican/Latino Education Roundtable, 1985).

We also acknowledged that the diversity of the Latino experience had to be recognized, especially because Latino students were no longer exclusively Puertorriqueños but increasingly were from the Dominican Republic, Mexico and other Central and South American countries. This diversity brought with it a variety of backgrounds, social classes, languages, cultures, unique experiences, skills, and problems. With the changing face of the student population came a greater challenge for the

Puerto Rican members of the Roundtable to learn about our extended Latino family to address our unique and distinct educational concerns in a united way. Consequently, we decided that the coalition would not be exclusively Puerto Rican although because of our organizational history and numbers, we continued to be the majority representation in the coalition. We rejected the term *Hispanic* as an oversimplification and distortion of our rich Latino diversity, and because of its Eurocentric essence. We felt the term *Latino* was more inclusive of our African, Indigenous, and Spanish heritages. Thus, our name was born.

Stage 2: Developing the Action Agenda

In Spring 1984, the Roundtable held its first 3-day retreat, which gave us an opportunity to dialogue, begin to build trust and a collective spirit, and develop and take ownership of a common agenda for educational change. This was the first time the group had come together to formally begin building a new relationship. Although some of the individuals had worked together, the sometimes difficult dynamics of building a new collective were present throughout the entire 3 days. Particularly evident was the intergenerational dynamic, which brought together "old" and "young" leaders of the 1960s, 1970s, and 1980s to grapple with the educational problems of our students. How militant should our tactics be? Should our focus be on policy? Should our battle be on the legal front, or should we take it to the streets? Are we activists or advocates? Is there a difference? People who had been actively involved in the Latino community for more than 3 decades struggled over these and other questions to help define who we were to be.

After discussing the merits and effectiveness of different methods to change the school system, we agreed that no single approach would be used exclusively and that our strategy would combine different tactics depending on the issue being addressed and the organizing context. Advocacy, grass-roots organizing, monitoring, lobbying, litigating, policy analysis and development, researching, demonstrating, picketing, testifying at public hearings, and collaborating and coalition-building with other organizations and ethnic groups were all seen as critical strategies for confronting the issues and effecting change. Thus, the pioneer organizations, newer community-based organizations, grass-roots activists, parent advocates, educators, researchers, and lawyers examined how everyone's unique experiences, knowledge, and skills would fit into the entire picture.

From over two dozen issues and problems identified by the group, four areas of work were selected as initial priorities: bilingual education/bilingual special education, student retention, community control, and affirmative action. We developed goals for each area, keeping in mind that we would work both on a policy level and on a grassroots level. Because working with Latino parents was critically important to us, Latino parent involvement became a priority and consequently shaped all of our work. How our goals were put into action shaped our identity and legitimized us as a group with which the school bureaucracy eventually had to contend. It also defined our space within the larger educational advocacy community in New York City, where the Latino voice was invisible. This broader network was primarily White and much more directed at doing policy and legislative work.

Stage 3: Building the Foundation

This period was spent building the foundation of the coalition, implementing and testing the work plan, and becoming known as an educational advocacy coalition and a voice for Puerto Rican/Latino students and parents.

The Puerto Rican/Latino Education Roundtable began as a volunteer coalition. Everyone in the group had a full-time job, many in education or in community and civil rights organizations. Although we started as volunteers, it quickly became apparent that funding was needed for a full-time staff to carry out our mission. Developing proposals for fund-raising, organizing presentations to funders, and seeking funds became a significant responsibility and a time-consuming task. We agreed that members would pay dues according to what they could afford both because it was important that members demonstrate their commitment and, on a more practical level, because funds were needed for more substantial fund-raising. Early on we agreed not to solicit government funding, because conditions would probably be placed on our ability to carry out our mission. Our quest for funding brought us into contact with some of the more progressive foundations and individuals in the city. Inevitably, other organizations doing education advocacy work were seeking funding from the same sources and the competition with them was an obstacle. We did, however, raise close to $1 million throughout a 10-year period (our main support came from the Aaron Diamond Foundation), and we relied on additional resources offered by Latino community organizations, unions such as the Amalgamated Clothing and Textile Workers–ACTWU (UNITE), Health Care Workers–Local 1199, Municipal Employees–AFSCME-DC 37, the Hispanic Labor Committee, and programs within higher education institutions. Individuals provided printing and copying services and transportation, coordinated mailings, donated equipment, contributed the use of their facilities, and volunteered countless hours of people power. The

Centro de Estudios Puertorriqueños became our home, and there we were nurtured and supported. The bilingual programs at City College of New York and Teachers College provided tremendous support, as did Hostos Community College.

During this period, the Roundtable developed an effective working structure as well as a clear definition of the roles and responsibilities of individual members and member organizations. We knew we were not going to be a mass membership–type organization, but nevertheless we wanted individuals and organizations that united around our vision, were grounded in the community, and were reliable and consistent. For example, we counted on people and organizations that could testify at a public hearing and mobilize for a demonstration, but we also needed people who could lick stamps, make telephone calls, and knock on doors. Because many of our members represented organizations, their ability to educate and mobilize their respective organizations was vital for our collective work. Developing community and a "community of mind" was central, and it was at the heart of who we were.

I was hired as the director within a year of the Roundtable's founding. Originally, I had been the representative from the National Congress for Puerto Rican Rights, where I served as president for 4 years. As soon as I was hired, my position was defined and fine-tuned as our agenda was shaped. Organizationally, we decided on consensual decision making, set up a work group structure based on the priority issue areas, and elected a chairperson for each area. Every year we held a retreat to review our work and set goals for the following year. A chairperson, co-chairperson, and board were elected every 2 years. Membership in the Roundtable was by recommendations made by standing members. Eventually, by-laws were developed and 501c.3 nonprofit status was attained.

Stage 4: Building Visibility and Moving the Goals Into an Agenda for Change

For a community to be deeply involved in educational change, members must agree that the public school system breeds both glaring inequities and a standardization of policies and practices that are detrimental to students. Engaging our community in this discourse and developing a common agenda was a major challenge. How do you develop shared values, conceptions, and ideas about schooling? How do you put the agenda out for discussion and feedback (Caballero, 1996)? Because Roundtable members were active in their local communities, they were able to translate grass-roots knowledge into policy and, in turn, to keep community members knowledgeable about citywide educational policy discussion and ensure their input.

We used several strategies to shape the discussion and move our agenda forward. Through joint work, monthly dialogues, and mutual support around common issues, we linked with Puerto Rican/Latino organizations involved in education. Eventually, established and respected organizations such as Educadores del Pueblo (the South Bronx), Parents Coalition for Education, El Puente (Williamsburg), Committee for Hispanic Children and Families, Concerned Citizens of Queens, Concilio de Padres del Distrito 6 (Washington Heights), and El Barrio Popular Education Program became active members of the Roundtable. A number of individuals became members as well, and they contributed in a variety of significant ways to building and forming the Roundtable. The Roundtable also established working relationships with other citywide community, education, and parent advocacy organizations. In addition, establishing relationships with Latino elected officials and other members of city and state government enabled us to educate and encourage them to advocate for specific legislation.

As members of the Roundtable began to understand the critical role played by the media in shaping public opinion about educational policy, we learned the importance of establishing good relations with journalists and media personalities. By being available for interviews, apprising the press of actions beforehand, preparing our information carefully, responding to editorials and press deadlines, and acknowledging the media's coverage, we not only established good relations but also learned how to use the media to our community's advantage. Providing a consistent Latino voice helped to enhance our public image but, most importantly, it provided the Roundtable a vehicle for public discussion and for reaching our community on a broader level.

The policy statements of the Roundtable concerning the role of language in the education of Latino students and on bilingual special education went far beyond the compensatory nature of what existed in the school system and far beyond the ASPIRA Consent Decree: We supported bilingualism and biliteracy. Our work groups in each of these areas tirelessly conducted workshops to raise parents' understanding of bilingual education and advocated for policies and practices that supported quality and enriching programs. We were instrumental in the development and approval of the Language Policy Statement by the New York City Board of Education (February 1987) supporting proficiency in two languages as goals for all students.

Participating in numerous commissions and task forces enabled the Roundtable to be a prominent voice and to raise issues of concern to the Latino community. We contributed to the policy debate on decentralization and school reform, parent involvement, and multicultural education by participating in Manhattan Borough President David Dinkins' Task Force on Education and Decentralization reports published in (1988, 1989); New York State Commissioner of Education Thomas Sobel's Task Force on Minorities: Equity and Excellence, which prepared "The Curriculum of Inclusion" report (1989); New York City Board of Education Multicultural Advisory Board (1994); and the City-Wide Community School Board Elections Committee. The Roundtable unceasingly placed the issues of equity, educational excellence, parents' rights, and language and culture directly on the table in all of these commissions and task forces.

Being on the New York City Board of Education Multicultural Advisory Board, along with such organizations as Advocates for Children, Educators for Social Responsibility, the Martin Luther King Center for Non-Violence, the American Jewish Committee, the Hetrick-Martin Institute, and the New York Alliance of Black Educators, enabled us to consistently promote a progressive view of multicultural education as a process of comprehensive school reform and education for equity and social justice that affirms difference regardless of ethnicity, language, gender, religion, sexual orientation, race, or class. We supported the view that multicultural education must be basic education for all students (New York City Board of Education Multicultural Advisory Board, 1994; Nieto, 1996).

In the area of community school board elections, the Roundtable made major contributions in four elections from 1986 to 1996. In these elections, we saw parent involvement as a way to promote community empowerment, and we consistently promoted the rights of all parents, whether they were U.S. citizens or not, because according to the New York City decentralization law, all parents have the right to register and vote in school board elections (Caballero, 1989).

What consistently characterized our work in this area was our focus on educating about the political process and the need for educational change and on providing candidates' training to parents and community groups. By coalescing with grass-roots organizations as well as "good government" groups, such as the Community Service Society, the ATREVETE campaign of the Office of the Commonwealth of Puerto Rico, United Bronx Parents, the Public Education Association, and the League of Women Voters, we organized workshops, reviewed and proposed decentralization and election reform legislation, and provided testimony at legislative hearings (Caballero, 1992).

We targeted our grass-roots organizing work in three school districts in Latino communities where we worked extensively with parents and community members, organized parent registration efforts, monitored election day activities, and consistently raised the importance of quality and accountability of representation. These districts were the South Bronx, a predominantly Puerto Rican community; Washington Heights, a Dominican community; and Elmhurst and Jackson Heights, Queens, an increasingly Central and South American neighborhood. Because of the work of the Asociación Comunal de Dominicanos Progresistas in Washington Heights in 1989, the greatest number of parent voters were registered in the history of school decentralization (Linares, 1989).

In 1987, a successful campaign for Latino representation on the New York City Board of Education was initiated with ASPIRA, the Association of Puerto Rican Executive Directors (APRED), and the Puerto Rican Educators' Association (PREA), which was directed at former Mayor Koch for not appointing a Latino to the Board of Education. Citywide support from diverse organizations, unions, elected officials, parents, and students fortified our campaign. We organized a massive demonstration at City Hall, and an impending hunger strike by two of our activists was averted when the mayor conceded to the pressure and appointed a Latino (see chap. 3 by Luis Reyes, this volume, for why it turned out to be a symbolic victory). Eventually, by the 1990s, we were able to obtain appointments of a progressive Latino and several African Americans to the New York City Board of Education.

During this same time, the conservative movement calling for an amendment to the U.S. Constitution declaring English the official language was intensified (Zentella, 1988). "English-only" advocates were pushing legislation in over a dozen states, including New York (Crawford, 1992). The Roundtable together with the Asian, Haitian, and other linguistically diverse communities in the city formed the Committee for a Multilingual New York, which developed a public education campaign against the English-only movement, galvanizing large numbers of people in defense of language rights. The campaign raised consciousness about the movement's anti-immigrant and xenophobic essence.

REFLECTING ON OUR WORK: EVOLVING CHARACTER AND IDENTITY

During the initial years of the Roundtable, we developed a very particular character and approach. We focused on building a public presence, ensuring representation and a Latino voice in all issues concerned with education. We also took part in coalition-building, and we made thoughtful and concrete suggestions for policy and practice. Nevertheless, our approach to change was still very piecemeal. Since our inception, we had survived seven school chancellors, four of whom were Latino, and three mayors.

By the early 1990s, we were known and respected but we questioned whether we had really made a difference in terms of systemic change and in the lives of young people and their families.

Our involvement in the Latino Commission for Educational Reform was a turning point in terms of how the Roundtable began to approach school change in the 1990s. The commission was established in 1992 by the Board of Education to make recommendations regarding the education of over 350,000 Latino students attending the New York City public schools. Commission members represented diverse sectors of the Latino community, which included community-based organizations, students, parents, legislators, educators, artistic and cultural advocates, foundations, corporate representatives, the mayor's office, and the teachers' union. Many Roundtable members participated during the 3-years of the commission's work.

During the first year, the commission engaged in research and discussion in such areas as curriculum and instruction, student counseling and support services, parent and community empowerment, factors affecting Latino students' achievement, and the causes of and solutions to the Latino drop-out crisis. The second year's work focused on such issues as equity and funding, bilingual special education, and the CUNY Preparatory Initiative (CPI). The CPI is supposed to strengthen high school students academically to prepare them for successful college outcomes. In reality, it overwhelmingly screens out poor students of color with the least institutional resources, subsequently denying them access to higher education (Rodriguez, 1996). The commission met frequently, reviewed the education reports dating back from *The Puerto Rican Study of 1953-1957* (New York City Board of Education, 1958), and engaged in enriching and stimulating discussion. By building on Latino voices of the past, the commission created a transformative educational vision. The diversity of the commission's representation added to the richness of the discussions and to the final recommendations for change. The commission submitted a two-volume report entitled *Toward a Vision for the Education of Latino Students: Community Voices, Student Voices* (1992) and *Making the Vision a Reality: A Latino Action Agenda for Educational Reform* (1994). For the first time, Latino high school students were represented through student membership in the commission and through a series of surveys and interviews conducted by Latino college students. Their perspectives were an important part of the commission's report and recommendations.

For the Latino community, school change has always been a crucial issue because the student population, rather than the school system, has been blamed for failure. Consequently, although the recommendations made in the past were piecemeal and remedial in nature, primarily addressing the need for bilingual education, the reports released by the Latino Commission for Educational Reform focused on proposals for transforming the school system. It was also the first time that a report articulated a language of hope and a trust in our young people as leaders.

The commission developed a comprehensive and far-reaching agenda to address the failure of the school system to educate Latino students. The challenge was to convince the New York City Board of Education that the commission's agenda had to be addressed, which meant we had to continue to heighten the battle on the policy level and build a grass-roots movement in support of the commission's vision. Participation on the commission allowed the Roundtable and the commission members to reexamine the school system and reflect on what changes had occurred and what obstacles continued to exist.

One of our recommendations called for the creation of a Latino Leadership School modeled after ASPIRA's concept of preparing young people for community leadership and closely tied to the need for expanding the political, social, and cultural empowerment of the Latino community. These goals would be met through the creation of a rigorous and enriched college preparatory academic curriculum characterized by intellectual inquiry and creative expression. Bilingualism and biliteracy in Spanish and English would be developed through a dual-language model, and there would be a focus on Latino history and culture. For many commission and Roundtable members, issues of teaching and learning, innovative pedagogy, and democratic classrooms began to take on a primary focus. This was in keeping with our heightened understanding that to truly transform the schools, we must first transform what happens in the classroom.

During this same time, school reform initiatives that called for replacing the urban school with smaller, caring, community-centered environments organized around educational or community themes were gaining tremendous interest. The school proposed by the commission would become part of the New Visions Initiative (Fund for New York City Public Education, 1992). This initiative was one of the more noteworthy efforts in the school reform movement in New York City, and it has already resulted in the creation of over two dozen small schools. Many commission and Roundtable members became the designers and planners of the school and we were given a planning grant by New Visions to create the Latino Leadership School (Caballero, 1996; Hernandez, 1995).

Although many commission and Roundtable members continued working in the educational policy arena, for some of us, creating our own schools became a focal point. As a result of our involvement, we began to challenge the purpose of schooling and the ways schools should be designed. We also began to craft alternatives to traditional schooling; that is, we envisioned schools with transformative practices and goals created with the communities that the schools would serve.

Since the commission's recommendations were made public, El Puente, a community organization in Los Sures, Williamsburg, Brooklyn, established the El Puente Academy for Peace and Justice, which had its first graduating class in June 1997; la Asociación Comunal de Dominicanos Progresistas (ACDP) created the 21st Century Academy for Community Leadership in Washington Heights, Upper Manhattan; the Leadership Secondary School (originally the Latino Leadership School) proposed by the Latino Commission in Loisaida (the Lower East Side of Manhattan) had its first graduating class in June 1998; and in September 2000, ASPIRA will initiate the Dr. Antonia Pantoja School for Public Policy in the Upper West Bronx. All the organizations creating these schools are Roundtable members and together with two other schools, the Cypress Hills Community School and Our Oasis, have created the Latino Education Network (see chap. 9 by Rivera and Pedraza, this volume). The schools share similar philosophies and are committed to social justice, human rights, and educational excellence that goes beyond traditional standards. Language, culture, and identity are central themes in each school. The schools primarily serve Latino immigrant and U.S.-born Latino students, but they also have African-American and other Caribbean students who choose to attend because of the schools' visions.

Although this small number of schools may not, in and of themselves, change the school system, their creation has moved the system beyond business as usual. These learning environments are based on a paradigm that reveals a profound reorientation in how schools are conceptualized: from traditional to constructivist; from controlling to empowering; from top-down authority to community building; from organizing and managing curriculum to democratically determining curriculum; from alienation to support and caring. Because they offer dramatic changes in policies and practices, these schools give hope to students who have been silenced and marginalized by the school system (Caballero, 1996). Latinos now have an opportunity to create learning environments for young people that reflect a vision which promotes community building. The well-being, academic and intellectual growth, and linguistic and cultural development of our young people—our future generations—are now in our hands.

REFLECTIONS AND LESSONS

When the Roundtable's story is retold, what will stand out? How do we measure our success? What made our process an empowering one? The story presented here may be interpreted in many different ways. Some might say that the Puerto Rican/Latino Education Roundtable had limited success because the system is still basically the same. Yet, because of the educational changes the Roundtable engendered locally and nationally, there is more progressive policy in a number of critical areas. There is still a lot of work to be done, because moving policy into practice is the most difficult challenge. The Roundtable, however, has left a mark on the school reform debate because of our content, tone, and style: assertive, democratic, activist, clear, thorough, and consistent. We were committed to shaping educational policy while keeping ourselves grounded in the community. How else do you represent community and translate grass-roots knowledge and ideas into policy and action? We created a process for change, for people to come together to assess, analyze, and act. We wanted to promote a vision and practice of collaborating and doing. Through this vision of change, both content and process became critical ingredients.

Our process was important because of the people and communities we brought together. Within our own community, the diversity of who we were as Latinos and how we worked out our distinct perspectives was very important. How we expressed our views about education and schooling was particularly significant because the changing U.S. demographics indicated that by the end of the century, nearly one third of all schoolchildren in the United States would be minority—mostly Latino and African American. By the year 2010, there will be about 10 million Latino children in U.S. schools (González, 1994). Although Mexican immigration remains the largest, the numbers from Central and South America and the Caribbean continue to grow (García & González, 1995). As we grow, so do our voices and diversity: We represent a broad spectrum of beliefs, and this will have tremendous implications for school change and for how we create and move the Latino educational agenda.

Shaping a progressive voice in New York City educational politics necessitated coalescing with African Americans, Asians, Haitians, and other Caribbeans, that is, other communities struggling to find their voices. We united around a number of broader issues as well (and with the progressive White community), because they all impact education and schooling. Issues of quality health care, housing, homelessness, AIDS, and police brutality also motivated us to work together. Everyone's knowledge was tapped and brought to the forefront, talent was nurtured, and skills were constantly sharpened.

Roundtable members remain connected to the community and involved in many different ways. Some Roundtable members have taken leadership positions in state and city government and in universities;

some were elected to their local school boards or appointed to the Board of Education; some are heading their own schools as principals or their school districts as superintendents; many are heading their own programs and organizations. All continue to be advocates for change, whether in education or in other areas.

We made many mistakes and we learned many lessons. For example, we learned how to compromise in order to win victories, but we were also very clear about what was nonnegotiable. We learned that when we did not dialogue sufficiently with one another, we sometimes found ourselves taking contradictory public positions. We learned how to agree to disagree. We learned that we could not leave educational change in the hands of the legislators and policymakers. We learned not to support people just because they were Latinos or parents but because they had the best interests of our community at heart. We learned that Latino students have a voice that has gone unheard and that students must be a critical part of any discussion about educational reform.

We learned that we, as a community, need to be involved in all aspects of educational change—advocating for progressive educational policy, organizing parents and community to support change, creating our own schools, monitoring school budgets, developing democratic curriculum, or whatever needs to be done to address the educational crisis and transform the public schools. Ultimately, a critical lesson we learned was that fundamental change takes time because the political forces we need to combat are powerful and will always attempt to restrain progressive movements.

The lessons we learned as educational change advocates and activists in our 14 years together can be applied to any other organizing situation. How that is done needs to be determined by the communities involved and their particular organizing context and social reality. The New York City experience is a dynamic and powerful one, but it is only one of the stories in the volumes that make up our history as Latinos in the major cities of the United States. The Roundtable learned from the Philadelphia, Hartford, Chicago, Los Angeles, Miami, and Boston experiences and from wherever there is a Latino community critically challenging the educational system and proposing directions for change through a multitude of means.

By building on knowledge created by Latino pioneers in educational change, reflecting on our own practice, listening to the voices of our young people, and envisioning the possibilities for change, the Puerto Rican/Latino Education Roundtable shaped an educational agenda for the 21st century and developed as a force that had to be taken seriously, not just in word but in our practice. We did our work with perseverance, determination, and integrity, and we set a fighting example for future generations of Puerto Ricans and other Latinos.

REFERENCES

ASPIRA of New York. (1985). Institutional barriers to Latino students' progress: Policies, procedures and practices. Fact sheet. (Available from ASPIRA of New York, 470 Seventh Ave., NY 10018).

Bisagna-Villafañe, J. (1985). *Speaking out about bilingual education—A community speak-out.* New York: Puerto Rican/Latino Education Roundtable.

Caballero, D. (1986). Puerto Ricans and bilingual education. *Bulletin of the Council on Interracial Books for Children, 17*(3 & 4), 15–16.

Caballero, D. (1989). School board elections: Parents against the odds. *Centro de Estudios Puertorriqueños Bulletin, 2*(5), 87–91.

Caballero, D. (1992). *Community school board elections and parent involvement.* Public comment to Temporary State Commission on New York City School Governance of the New York State Legislature.

Caballero, D. (1996). *Community building in the process of planning a New Visions school—The Leadership Secondary School: A transformative approach for the education of Latino students.* Unpublished doctoral dissertation, Teachers College, Columbia University, New York.

Calitri, R. (1983). *Racial and ethnic high school dropout rates in New York City.* New York: ASPIRA.

Carrasquillo, A. L. (1985). *Hispanic children and youth in the United States.* New York: Garland.

Crawford, J. (1992). *Hold your tongue: Bilingualism and the politics of "English only."* Reading, MA: Addison-Wesley.

Fund for New York City Public Education. (1992). *New visions: Request for proposal.* New York: Author.

García, E., & González, R. (1995). Issues in systemic reform for culturally and linguistically diverse students. *Teachers College Record, 96*(3), 418–431.

González, J. M. (1994). Spanish as a second language: Adding language to the discourse of multicultural education. In F. Rivera-Batiz (Ed.), *Reinventing urban education: Multiculturalism and the social context of schooling* (pp. 257–275). New York: IUME Press, Teachers College.

Hernandez, L. (1995). *Designing and implementing a plan to create an innovative new school to address the high Latino student dropout rates in New York City.* Unpublished doctoral dissertation, Nova University, Ft. Lauderdale.

Institute for Puerto Rican Policy. (1990). Puerto Ricans and other Latinos in the United States 1989. *Datanote, 8.* New York: Author.

Latino Commission on Educational Reform. (1992). *Toward a vision for the education of Latino students: Community voices, student voices.* Report by the New York City Board of Education.

Latino Commission on Educational Reform. (1994). *Making the vision a reality: A Latino action agenda for educational reform.* Report by the New York City Board of Education.

Linares, G. (1989). Dominicans in New York City: The struggle for community control in District 6. *Centro de Estudios Puertorriqueños Bulletin, 2*(5), 77–84.

National Coalition of Advocates for Students. (1988). *New voices: Immigrant students in U.S. public schools.* Boston: Author.

National Commission on Secondary Education for Hispanics. (1984). *"Make something happen": Hispanics and urban school reform.* Washington, DC: Hispanic Policy Development Project.

National Council of La Raza. (1986). *The education of Hispanics: Status and implications.* Washington, DC: Author.

New York City Board of Education. (1958). *The Puerto Rican study 1953–1957: A report on the education and adjustment of Puerto Rican pupils in the public schools of the city of New York.* New York: Author.

New York City Board of Education. (1987, February). *Language policy statement,* New York: Author.

New York City Board of Education Multicultural Advisory Board. (1994). *Making education multicultural: Statement of purpose and recommendations for action.* New York: Author.

New York State Governor's Advisory Committee for Hispanic Affairs. (1986). *A people at risk: Hispanic school dropouts.* Albany, NY: Author.

Nieto, S. (1996). *Affirming diversity: The sociopolitical context of multicultural education* (2nd ed.). New York: Longman.

Puerto Rican/Latino Education Roundtable. (1985). *Statement of purpose.* New York: Author.

Reyes, L., & Pacheco, J. (1988). *Su nombre es hoy.* New York: ASPIRA of New York.

Rodriguez, C. (1996, March). Presentation given at student rally in defense of the City University of New York (CUNY), Hunter College.

Rodriguez, C. E. (1989). *Puerto Ricans: Born in the USA.* Boston: Unwin Hyman.

Santiago Santiago, I. (1986). ASPIRA v. Board of Education revisited. *American Journal of Education, 95*(1), 149–199.

Task Force on Education and Decentralization. (1988). *Improving the odds: Making decentralization work for children, for school, for community.* New York: Author.

Task Force on Education and Decentralization. (1989). *People change schools.* New York: Author.

Task Force on Minorities: Equity and Excellence. (1989). *A curriculum of inclusion.* A Report to the New York State Commissioner of Education.

Task Force on New York State Dropout Problem. (1986). *Dropping out of school in New York State: The invisible people of color.* New York: New York State African American Institute of the State University of New York.

Zentella, A. C. (1988). Language politics in the USA: The English-only movement. In B. J. Craige (Ed.), *Literature, language, and politics* (pp. 39–53). Athens: University of Georgia Press.

9

The Spirit of Transformation: An Education Reform Movement in a New York City Latino/a Community

Melissa Rivera
Pedro Pedraza

What has been the role of Puerto Ricans and Latinos/as in school reform in New York City? How can educational reform movements be directed toward community development? How can we educate young people more holistically—in mind, body, and spirit? How can we practice a critical and creative pedagogy that supports integrated action projects, focuses curriculum on the realities of students and their families, and impacts the social, economic, and educational development of local Latino/a communities? These are some of the questions posed in this chapter.

The underlying assumption of this chapter is that education must impact both the individual and communal level of social life to produce progressive social transformation. As educators, we have to broaden the scope of our vision of education to one in which individual human development and community and social development are perceived as interdependent processes.

223

The goal of community development as an educational objective is implicit in pedagogical approaches that consider the sociohistorical context of students, particularly their daily life experiences, to be of paramount importance. Centering pedagogical practices on issues of language, culture, and identity is an attempt to integrate these two levels, individual and communal, through a program of activities and actions that fosters individual Latino/a student development (Nieto & Rolón, 1997). School reform should also support the development of the local communities in which the students and their families live. Thus, we advocate for education that supports, develops, and transforms both individuals and communities simultaneously. This approach to school reform emerges from and is situated in a broader historical framework concerning the Puerto Rican community in New York City.

This chapter focuses specifically on (a) the Puerto Rican community's involvement in education reform movements in New York City, (b) a small schools reform movement that has caught the imagination of many progressive educators in New York City, and (c) an innovative community school in Williamsburg, Brooklyn. The thread that braids these three stories together is an inclusion of and commitment to community, economic, and social development as part of school reform strategies in New York City's Latino/a neighborhoods.

SCHOOL REFORM
IN THE PUERTO RICAN COMMUNITY

The Puerto Rican community has historically been and continues to be a social force for progressive change in the New York City school system, basing its advocacy efforts on a community perspective. For instance, there is a connection between the struggles for social justice in the Puerto Rican community and the current movement for educational change in New York City, whose model was partially developed within the sociopolitical context of a particular Puerto Rican neighborhood. That is, what is now being contemplated as a citywide reform strategy by some progressive educators was modeled in part by District 4 in the East Harlem section of New York City for more than 20 years. In what follows we briefly review that history.

Community Control

East Harlem has had a tradition of progressive educational innovation and reform since the 1920s. This history is exemplified by Leonardo Covello's work with Italian immigrant children at that time and in the

1950s with Puerto Rican children.[1] The East Harlem Block School (EHBS), formed by African-American and Puerto Rican parents in the 1960s, is an example of a school designed to provide an alternative educational experience for children of color in *El Barrio* (the local name for East Harlem). Consequently, in the 1960s, amid the debate about community control, a campaign was organized in East Harlem to create a local school district. Puerto Rican, African-American, and progressive White struggles for school improvement, coupled with the Ford Foundation's support for experiments in community control, created a political climate for effective school reform. The New York City school reform legislation that was proposed mandated the creation of 32 local school districts that divided East Harlem into two districts. Parents, educators, and community members were opposed to this division and thus organized a campaign, demanding one district encompassing the entire East Harlem community. The parents and activists of the community won that struggle, and East Harlem maintained its identity as School District 4 of Manhattan.[2]

Furthermore, in its second school board election in 1973, District 4 obtained its first (and the city's first) majority Puerto Rican school board. One of the newly elected local school board's first actions was to hire Anthony Alvarado, a young, innovative Puerto Rican educator, as superintendent of District 4. Alvarado, in collaboration with other community educators and activists, immediately initiated three reforms relating to pedagogical practice and school organization in the district that would directly respond to the needs of East Harlem's largely Puerto Rican student population. First, the school board was encouraged to pass a resolution declaring District 4 a bilingual school district (the first district in the city to take such action).[3] Second, a district-wide reading program was instituted to promote literacy development, and third, with input from a collective of educational innovators, a network of pioneering schools was developed for the district.

---

[1]See Covello's reports on the education of Puerto Rican children (Covello, 1946–1947, 1953). For more information about Leonardo Covello's work, see Meyer (1985).

[2]The struggle to create a Puerto Rican/Latino school district also occurred in other parts of New York City such as District 32 in Brooklyn. However, the creation of this district did not lead to a Latino/a majority school board because other interested parties controlled the electoral process in communities without the East Harlem activist tradition and experience (Alice Cardona, former ASPIRA parent coordinator, personal communication, December 1996.)

[3]The Language Policy Task Force at the Center for Puerto Rican Studies wrote, at Alvarado's request, a short position paper giving the social, legal, and pedagogical rationale for this move. Alvarado distributed the paper to all the local school board members because he wanted the vote on this matter to reflect, for political reasons, a consensus rather than a Puerto Rican majority opinion. (Language and Policy Task Force, 1975).

The first of these schools, Central Park East, was established in 1974 by Deborah Meier (Bensman, 1987; Meier, 1995). It would become, for some in New York City and the nation, a model for urban public schooling, particularly for communities of color. Nevertheless, from the perspective of progressive Latino/a educators and activists, issues of language, culture, identity, and community were still not adequately addressed because the movement for change within the school system was driven by professionals. They shared many community concerns; however, since they were not from the community, they approached the issues from a strictly pedagogical perspective rather than from historical, sociocultural, economic, and political perspectives and did not elaborate young people's role in community self-determination and development.

Nonetheless, as a result of the educational and structural changes in East Harlem described previously, by the 1980s, District 4 had moved from last place in reading test scores to midranking among New York City school districts. These reform efforts demonstrate a community commitment to establishing innovative schools to address the academic and cultural needs of young people in East Harlem and illustrate the potential impact of community control over local institutions.[4]

Puerto Rican and Latino/a-Created Educational Community Organizations

The massive failure of the public school system and the vision of community development, centered on certain pedagogical principles, have mobilized the Puerto Rican and Latino/a communities to design educational programs and develop organizations to address the academic, physical, and socioemotional needs of its children and young people. These educational organizations, most of which are grounded in local neighborhoods, developed programs that have provided training and generated a knowledge and resource base for Puerto Rican and Latino/a community members, supporting the perspective that education should be designed for both individual and community development.

Some of these include, for instance, the Puerto Rican Forum, which developed ASPIRA in the 1960s as an educational and youth development organization. In addition, the United Bronx Parents organized parents and community members around the need for school reform, and the Puerto Rican Association of Community Affairs (PRACA) created preschools and bilingual day-care centers. The East Harlem Block Schools (mentioned ear-

---

[4]For more information on the history of Puerto Rican community participation in New York City school reform, see Pedraza (1997).

lier) started day-care centers and an alternative elementary school, and
ASPIRA, later in the 1960s, expanded its work to include student leadership
training and legal advocacy. The Puerto Rican and Latino/a Education
Roundtable, a consortium of community educational groups, organized for
education advocacy in the 1980s (see chap. 8 by Diana Caballero, this volume, for more information on the Roundtable).

After attempts to implement desegregation, decentralization, affirmative action, bilingual education, and more recently multicultural education to address persistently poor school outcomes, a more multifaceted
approach is now being advocated by some progressive educators. These
educational activists are adopting the strategy of educational reform begun in District 4s El Barrio, in the early 1970s (i.e., the creation of small innovative schools) as a solution to the New York City school system's
failure to holistically educate Latino/a students.

THE LOCAL SMALL SCHOOL REFORM INITIATIVE: NEW YORK NETWORK FOR SCHOOL RENEWAL

Support for a broad-scale effort in New York City to create small schools
received significant assistance from a $25 million Challenge Grant from
the Annenberg Foundation in 1995, providing New York City and four
other sites (the San Francisco Bay Area, Chicago, Los Angeles, and Philadelphia) with financial support for a 5-year initiative to reform public
schools. The New York Network for School Renewal (NYNSR) project
(the official title for the Annenberg initiative in New York City) is an out-
growth of the school reform work of four organizations.[5] These organizations—the NYNSR sponsors—had been working separately on a
common set of initiatives: small schools, school-based budgeting, greater
school autonomy, school-based forms of accountability, and collaborative
decision making. As sponsors of the NYNSR project, they combined their
individual efforts to achieve a broader goal, leveraging their efforts into a
systemic reform strategy for the New York City school system.[6] The goals
of the NYNSR project are to create a critical mass of small, effective
schools that equitably serve the full range of children in New York City
public schools and that create a model for public education and ultimately
influence the public school system.

---

[5]The four organizations include the Association of Community Organizations for Reform Now (ACORN), the Center for Collaborative Education (CCE), the Center for Educational Innovation (CEI) at the Manhattan Institute, and New Visions for Public Schools.
[6]Information taken from NYNSR Research Collaborative (1997).

New Visions for Public Schools

Throughout this NYNSR project, we have worked most closely with the New Visions for Public Schools organization. For instance, Pedro served on the Advisory Board for 5 years, and was a member of the group that devised an open process for creating these new small schools. The idea at New Visions was to encourage groups, particularly from outside the school system, to submit proposals for small innovative schools organized in any manner consistent with the purposes and goals of New Visions' mission statement. The impetus for this effort came from the success of some of the new high school programs created since 1984 within the Board of Education's high school division alternative programs project to address the needs of low-performing students. Another inspiration, as mentioned previously, was the District 4 experiment in small school innovation.

By Fall 1998, this effort by New Visions resulted in the creation of more than 40 new schools. One cofounder of The Leadership Secondary School (the first public dual-language high school in New York City) wrote,

> The New Visions initiative has been very important for the Puerto Rican and Latino community in New York City since it has provided an historic opportunity for experimentation and innovation in education not previously available. New Visions' view of schooling offers dramatic changes in policies and practices that give hope to students who have been marginalized and silenced by the prevailing system. In the struggle to create these schools, issues of access, educational excellence, equity, and linguistic and cultural diversity have been put on the front burner. Our mutual challenge is to assure that these become defining characteristics of school change, particularly within the New Visions initiative. (Caballero, 1997, p. 1)

Although New Visions was initially funded by the Aaron Diamond Foundation, the Annenberg grant has allowed this work to continue through the NYNSR program, though the process for creating new schools will vary according to the sponsoring agency.

The Learning Zone

At present there are more than 140 small schools in the NYNSR project within the public educational system, at both the primary and secondary levels. This proliferation has led some reform advocates to suggest a "learning zone," a distinct citywide school district with its own administrative regulations, within which these schools can operate, freeing them from most of the bureaucratic constraints limiting experimentation. The hope was that as this zone grew, it would create a critical mass that could drive system-wide reform.

In 1996, Rudy Crew, the chancellor of New York City schools, embraced the idea of improving the schools within the system that are threatened by a state takeover (because of their abysmal records of noneducation) by reconstructing them into small schools like the innovative NYNSR schools. Compared to other approaches to improve the school system, the attempt to focus reform within this city at the local school level is viewed, at least among the progressive educational community, as a positive and effective strategy to implement pedagogical change and improve student outcomes.

The schools in New York City that were scheduled to be taken over in 1996 by the state education department as a result of substandard performance for more than 5 years without improvement, also known as SURR schools (Schools Under Review and Revision), are overwhelmingly populated by students of color. Of the 16 schools on the SURR list threatened with immediate state takeover, 11 were majority Puerto Rican and Latino/a, 9 had significant "beginning English learner" student populations, and 7 were in the South Bronx, currently the largest Puerto Rican community in New York City.[7]

The chancellor's plan to create a citywide district or learning zone (as previously described), combining the failing and innovative schools, may focus attention on the need for adequate education for Puerto Rican children, because this approach is based on the interplay between systemic reform, school reorganization, and classroom instructional practices. The idea is that a multifaceted strategy would support a holistic approach to nurture and sustain effective teaching and learning practices in the classroom and community.

As part of the Annenberg initiative to create small schools and networks, the Challenge Grant specified that an evaluation be conducted. Thus, in July 1996, the NYNSR project contracted with New York University's Institute for Education and Social Policy (IESP) to evaluate the NYNSR project in cooperation with a group of other researchers and research organizations that make up the Research Collaborative. The research includes four studies:

1. An Outcomes Study analyzing demographic information on NYNSR and non-NYNSR public schools.

---

[7]There are more than 100 schools on the SURR list in New York City. Most are not threatened with immediate state takeover (Ferrandino, 1996).

2. An Implementation Study investigating to what degree the NYNSR project is being implemented and what the implementation looks like.
3. A teacher-inquiry study.
4. Our collaborative project with El Puente Academy for Peace and Justice, which is the subject of the section that follows.[8]

OUR PARTICIPATORY PROJECT: EL PUENTE ACADEMY FOR PEACE AND JUSTICE

As part of our involvement in the NYNSR evaluation, we are collaborating with faculty, staff, young people, and community members at El Puente Academy for Peace and Justice in Williamsburg, Brooklyn, to learn about developing and sustaining community-based schools. For more than 10 years, Pedro has had a close working relationship with the founder and cofounder of El Puente, and Melissa has worked for more than 3 years with a number of staff members at El Puente on youth and community development projects. In spring 1997, we entered into this project with El Puente Academy both as researchers and as coparticipants with El Puente staff in the struggle for visionary, community-centered education and social justice. We became integrated into the El Puente family through our participation in staff development sessions, various organizational committees, discussions and development of bilingual/biliteracy programming, and celebrations and special events. Through our involvement in these committee meetings and program development sessions, we, as coresearchers with El Puente faculty and staff, have explored notions of education and transformed practices in the classroom and the Williamsburg community. In addition, we have interviewed staff members and observed facilitators in their classrooms.[9]

In collaboration with El Puente Academy staff members, we have focused our investigation on two specific concepts of education: the effectiveness of a critical pedagogy and an action-based, community-oriented curriculum built upon the realities of young people of color and their families and centered on issues of identity, culture, and language; and the impact of a small, public school emerging from and braided into a youth and community-development organization.

---

[8]The Outcomes and Implementation Studies are being conducted by researchers at New York University's Institute for Education and Social Policy, and the teacher inquiry by a university researcher from the New School for Social Research.

[9]El Puente Academy staff members refer to teachers as "facilitators." This practice is connected to their philosophy and educational principles, as described later in the chapter.

Our participatory project with the community at El Puente Academy draws on a number of approaches to research, including research as praxis (Lather, 1991), activist research (Cancian, 1993; Fine & Vanderslice, 1992), collaborative and participatory action research (Maguire, 1987; Park, 1989; Torres, 1991; Young & Padilla, 1990), and the Centro's own experience in implementating its mission.[10] This collaborative investigation is grounded in principles of participatory inquiry that is

> educational and empowering for the participants, with outcomes that include action on attitudes and structures that inhibit self-worth, social justice or liberation. The criteria of successful research in this framework are related more to empowerment or social justice than to generalizable knowledge. (Maguire, 1987, p. viii)

We decided to use this participatory action research approach because we believe that methods where "people themselves investigate their reality in order that they may transform it as active participants" (Park, 1989, p. 1) are the way to change the current conditions in Williamsburg, Brooklyn, and the field of education for marginalized communities.

As mentioned previously, we have worked with members of the El Puente community prior to this project and respect and admire their dedication to the development of young people and multicultural communities. We therefore embarked on this journey with El Puente Academy staff members to investigate their practices as a way to reflect on and continue to develop new methods for implementing a vision of progress that integrates the individual and community in human development.

History of El Puente's Community-Based Organization

Former Young Lord[11] Luis Garden Acosta founded El Puente and assembled a group of community leaders and professionals, including professional dancer and long-time arts educator Frances Lucerna. Together they organized in 1982 to create a community "safe space" to address the persistent educational crisis and the increase in violent crimes in Williamsburg, Brooklyn. The group named the new space El Puente, Spanish for "the bridge," which is a metaphor for the physical presence of the Williamsburg

---

[10]The Centro de Estudios Puertorriqueños at Hunter College, CUNY was established in the 1972–73 academic year with the mission of producing knowledge about the Puerto Rican experience in the United States for that community's own use.

[11]The Young Lords Party was a political organization whose mission was focused on personal, community, and economic development in Latino/a communities across the United States. For more information, see Morales (1996).

Bridge, connecting Brooklyn to the lower east side of Manhattan, as well as the commitment to helping young people make connections and build bridges in their lives. The cofounders rejected a service-provider ideology and instead sought to provide Williamsburg residents (who are mostly Latino/a) with opportunities, spaces, and experiences so that they can determine what is best for them to live holistic, healthy, and productive lives. In essence, El Puente founders embraced a belief in and practice of self-determination and community development.

For years, members of El Puente have worked on issues directly impacting Williamsburg residents' lives. For instance, in 10 days in 1993, in response to critical health and well-being issues, El Puente members surveyed community residents' health care needs, established a vaccination clinic, and led a campaign to vaccinate more than 1,200 people in the community and others throughout New York City. In education, El Puente members have provided tutoring programs and Spanish and English literacy classes for young people and adults. In the arts, mural painting, dance, and theater classes have been offered, and in-house repertory companies, such as Teatro El Puente, have provided creative outlets for young people to address critical issues in their lives such as youth culture, racism and sexism, the AIDS epidemic, environmental justice, violence, interpersonal relationships, and others. Community members have also struggled persistently for environmental justice by planting trees in the neighborhood, turning vacant lots into community gardens, addressing issues such as lead pollution and garbage transfer stations for nuclear and chemical waste, and joining forces with the diverse population of Williamsburg (African American, Polish, Hasidic and Latino/a residents) to protest the placement of an incinerator for garbage disposal in the community (Rose, 1995).

El Puente Academy for Peace and Justice: Principles, Pedagogy, and Curriculum

After working with the Williamsburg community for 10 years, Frances Lucerna and a group of El Puente educators, parents, and community activists united to create a public school in their neighborhood.[12] They shared a vision that education must happen in the context of community, and they believed that one of the most effective ways to reach young people and unite their individual and collective development is through edu-

[12]Some of the founding members of El Puente Academy for Peace and Justice include Hector Calderón, Luis Garden Acosta, Frances Lucerna, Maribel Lizardo, Rossy Matos, Joe Matunis, and Josephina Santiago.

cation. They believed that by developing new knowledge and implementing a more holistic way of learning, school could be connected to a larger context of family and community. El Puente submitted a proposal to New Visions for Public Schools in 1992 and 1 year later became 1 of the initial 16 New Visions schools to embark on a journey toward liberatory education and community development. The Academy opened in March 1993 with one 9th-grade class, and in fall 1996, there were more than 120 students in all four high school grades (9th through 12th), 34 of whom graduated in El Puente Academy's first class in June 1997.

The Academy's vision is grounded in four cornerstone principles: love and caring, collective self-help, peace and justice, and mastery. From this set of values relationships are built and sustained and holistic learning happens within the context of community. El Puente's principles are integrated into the Academy's daily life through a creative, critical pedagogy (Park, 1995). By incorporating students' realities and communities into the curriculum (i.e. housing, health, employment, and violence) and by utilizing emancipatory educational practices "by which the oppressed are equipped with the necessary tools to re-appropriate their history, culture and language practices" (Freire & Macedo, 1987, p. 157), schools can emerge as "cultural spaces" that support both personal and intellectual growth as well as community development (Freire, 1970; Giroux, 1988; hooks, 1994; Walsh, 1996).

The creative and critical educators at El Puente Academy believe that learning requires participation and inquiry, supported best by collective modes of dialogue, investigation and production. In contrast to teachers who use the "banking model" of education, which considers students' minds to be empty accounts into which teachers deposit information through didactic lectures and texts and which focuses on mechanical, lower order skills (Freire, 1970), the critical and empowering educators at El Puente Academy recognize the participatory nature of learning. They incorporate both the cognitive and affective into activities, use problem-posing and dialogic methods, value anti-racist multiculturalism, and emphasize critical inquiry across disciplines by implementing action research projects. We describe five of these principles in action in the following sections: student-centered curriculum, activist projects, integration of the arts, emphasis on holism, and dedication to ritual and celebration.

Student-Centered Curriculum. El Puente Academy faculty and staff believe that learning begins with the lives of the students, that young people should author their personal life stories, and that students' lived experiences should be connected to academic learning. For instance, means "going back to the source." This integrated curriculum provides young people an opportunity to go back to their sources, including their personal knowledge and families' experiences. For the first 6 weeks of class, El Puente Academy students investigate their historical, sociocultural, and familial traditions and legacies in their global studies, English, science and art classes. The culmination of this unit is the creation of "Who Am I?" books, which are developed in global studies and English classes and designed and crafted in art class. Their science class supports this project by centering on the "science of self."

An example of the participatory nature of our research with El Puente Academy staff members was a course that we developed. The course emerged from the sociocultural and linguistic backgrounds of the student population. This course, an Afro-Latino/a elective, was developed by members of the biliteracy collective, including the authors.[13] We provided collective members with history, readings, and resources on cultural and linguistic theories and practices, and together we engaged in study, developed an internal language assessment tool to research the language backgrounds of the young people at El Puente, and designed the Afro-Latino/a course. The class studied Afro-Latinos/as' experiences through a series of workshops. A team of facilitators explored this theme through at least one of the following lenses or disciplines: Latin Caribbean dance and music, literature (poetry, fiction), oral and written history, and the visual arts. This class was conducted in English and Spanish, and the young people who participated included both Spanish dominant and English-dominant students. In addition to addressing the history and culture of the young people through the content of the class (Pan-Africanism in Latin America and the Caribbean), the dual-language component also exposed the students to another language and provided them with literacy skills in both English and Spanish.

Activist Projects.   Because the ultimate goal of El Puente Academy's curriculum is to connect young people's academic and personal lives to community development, there is a concerted effort to integrate and focus parts of the curriculum, projects, and other activities on community issues, especially those directly impacting the lives of the students and staff members at El Puente Academy. Because the majority of the staff members also live in the Williamsburg neighborhood, they work collaboratively with young people and their families to improve their own com-

---

[13]1997–98 Biliteracy collective members included Jessica Abrussezze, Sonia Bu, Hector Calderón, Evelyn Erickson, Nequi González Martínez, Adjoa Jones de Almeida, Frances Lucerna, Pedro Pedraza, Melissa Rivera, Paula Rojas, and Steve Suffet.

atively with young people and their families to improve their own community's environment, housing conditions, and educational opportunities. They are not outsiders looking in, but rather insiders finding ways to collectively address the issues that impact their own lives.

For example, the ninth-grade English facilitator integrated into the curriculum the threat of a waste transfer station being placed in the Williamsburg community. As part of the ninth-grade English curriculum, students are required to learn grammar, various writing techniques, and essay development. The facilitator created a writing unit focused on the impending environmental issue. Two community educators were invited to speak to the class about the current environmental conditions in the neighborhood as well as the upcoming local City Council meeting. Students were then asked to think critically about issues relating to garbage in their community and to state their personal concerns in writing. Some students mentioned bad smells, rodents, air pollution, persistent asthma related to environmental conditions, dirty streets, and abandoned building and lots. Young people then drafted individual testimonies, documenting their personal experiences and stories and reporting on the conditions they had witnessed. Once completed, drafts were circulated for peer review, were revised, and ultimately were submitted as testimony at the City Council meeting on the waste transfer station initiative. This project encouraged young people to integrate academic learning with community issues and to "make broad connections between individual experiences and social issues, between single problems and the larger social system" (Shor, 1992, p. 127).

Integration of the Arts. El Puente Academy faculty and staff strive to broaden the understanding of education to include the visual and performing arts. The commitment transcends merely decorating the walls with pictures of local, national, and international Latino/a and African-American community activists who struggled for justice. The faculty and staff are dedicated to weaving this commitment to the arts into the students' study. For instance, students research and study their own cultures as well as others in their history, English, and art classes through projects that integrate the arts, critical literacy, and community activism.

For the entire 1996-97 academic year, El Puente Academy's sophomore and junior classes participated in an integrated project on sugar. The Sugar Project was an interdisciplinary cultural and academic collaboration among artists, community organizers, and educators active in Williamsburg, Brooklyn. It was inspired by a local landmark, the Domino Sugar factory. Young people studied the history of sugar and its social and economic effects (i.e., slavery and colonial economies based on dependent monocultivation in the Caribbean and Latin America) as well as the patterns of sugar consumption in the United States. The sophomore class took an integrated course entitled "Voices of Liberation: The Culture of Resistance." Students explored the ways in which Caribbean, Brazilian, and African-American peoples have interacted with sugar throughout their histories. Then, the young people studied and created various cultural expressions of resistance to colonialism, slavery, and oppressive labor (i.e., music, dance, theater, visual art, video, oral history, fiction, and poetry).[14]

In the class "Participation in Government: The Politics of Resistance," El Puente Academy juniors investigated "how people participate in the governing of their own lives by demanding social and political change either from inside the system or from outside the system, including the creation of manifestos, slavery and maroon societies, the legacy of the Black Panthers and Young Lords, and youth in prison and welfare reform."[15] The culmination of the Sugar Project was the the Sweet Freedom Sugar Feast, a performance and parade with student stilt-walkers, Afro-Caribbean dance, spiritual songs, a skit, and a presentation of short videos about race and identity produced by young people. This community celebration took place outside in El Puente's garden, which was decorated with student-created murals. Foods made with white sugar substitutes were also provided to expose young people and Williamsburg community members to less processed, more natural sweeteners, including brown sugar, honey, and sweet juices.

During the 1997-98 school year, another arts-rich, interdisciplinary project in which juniors participated focused on garment workers and factories. The Garment Project at El Puente was based on the historical connection between the Puerto Rican community in Williamsburg (one of the first Puerto Rican communities established in New York City at the turn of the century), factory workers (who migrated in large numbers to Williamsburg during the 1920s and 1930s to work in garment factories), and the garment industry (where many women skilled in needle trades labored).[16]

An integrated design team of artists, academic facilitators, and community organizers developed a curriculum that explored the world of fashion from cultural, social, economic, political, and human rights per-

---

[14]Paraphrased from the "Voices of Liberation" syllabus prepared by Adjoa Jones de Almeida and Alfa Anderson.

[15]Excerpted from the "Participation in Government: The Politics of Resistance" syllabus prepared by Adjoa Jones de Almeida and Alfa Anderson.

[16]For more information on the garment industry and "pioneras," see Benmayor, Juarbe, Alvarez, and Vázquez (1987).

spectives. Students researched factory conditions with workers from a labor union, interviewed factory workers (many of whom were students' relatives) and young designers, studied and analyzed marketing data and techniques, wrote monologues with guest artists Danny Hoch and Martín Espada, created a dance piece about factory work, designed a fashion show, wrote and shot a video, created stage sets and life-size stage puppets, studied the conditions of child labor in other countries, and met with adolescent workers from the Dominican Republic. All of this culminated in a spectacular multiarts, outdoor performance for the community and an art exhibition in a community art gallery, Momenta Art.[17]

Holism.   El Puente Academy facilitators and staff members strive for holism in all of their endeavors, that is, an integration of body, spirit, mind, and community. The following examples illustrate the wide variety of activities, group sessions, and human and material resources available to support young people's holistic development. For instance, young people at El Puente learn about those who have struggled for human rights (such as Martin Luther King, Jr., Evangelina Rodríguez), and the students use the inspirational words and images of these leaders as the backdrop for their learning. The environmental team's herb planting events, the Wellness Center's classes with Academy seniors on meditation and holistic healing techniques, and the Holistic Individualized Program (HIP) where young people address issues through one-on-one support, men's and women's groups, and group activities exemplify the school's commitment to holism. College preparation, the sports program, and performing arts classes provide spaces to develop the mind, body, and spirit. In addition, El Puente Academy young people participate in interdisciplinary projects, summer internships (such as "Yo! Youth Organizers"), and collaborative programs and conferences at the local, state and national levels. Students' family members participate in the life and culture at El Puente Academy through the Parent Action Center (which offers classes on parenting skills and leadership development) as well as in educational activities and community projects (such as a local high school restructuring effort and an environmental asthma outreach initiative). These activities support a home–school–community alliance. In sum,

---

[17]The description in this paragraph was excerpted from El Puente Academy's 1997–98 End of the Year Report written by Frances Lucerna. Facilitators and staff members involved in this project included Jessica Abrussezze, Alfa Anderson, Bill Blechingberg, Sonia Bu, Hector Calderón, Jackie Chang, John Fleming, Nequi González Martínez, Jessica Green, Adjoa Jones de Almeida, Frances Lucerna, Joe Matunis, Patricia Montoya, Alexios Moore, Paula Rojas, Josh Thomases, and Beth Wehner.

this focus on holism encourages young people's social, emotional, spiritual, and intra- and interpersonal development.

Rituals and Celebrations.   The following events, awards ceremonies, rituals and celebrations, and performances also illustrate the commitment to holistic development and community devotion, the fifth element of the El Puente Academy's principles in action.

Each year El Puente Academy holds a Cultural Bazaar, an event dedicated to expressing and sharing the multiple cultures represented at the school. For instance, in November 1997, six classrooms were transformed into cultural spaces, including a Bomba and Plena workshop, where students learned the history and movement of the two traditional music/dance forms in Puerto Rico; the women's group room, where young women recited original poetry and prose about being females of color in the United States; an art studio work-in-progress puppet performance about maquiladoras in Mexico; a Dominican room, where young people performed an original skit about the intergenerational issues impacting young Dominicans in the United States; a Taíno nation lecture demonstration on Puerto Rico's indigenous community; and a Harlem Renaissance club scene with spoken word, jazz music, and dance performances. During the first part of the day, young people presented their research through creative modes of expression and visited the other cultural rooms, engaging in various activities. In the afternoon students participated in or observed the main program, consisting of spoken word, short thematic dramatization, and dance and hip-hop performances. This event is traditionally scheduled before the Thanksgiving break so students can recognize the many cultures with which they are blessed and for which they should be grateful.

At the Senior Class Show in 1997, which was dedicated to the memory of a student who died an innocent victim of street violence during his senior year, Academy students performed a skit, original poetry, and a rap. This was followed by three concurrent workshops facilitated by Academy seniors for all El Puente students to discuss violence (including date rape, domestic abuse, and gang-related street violence) and its impact on young people and the community.

The "Academy Awards" is El Puente's annual ceremony to recognize the development and achievements of young people in the academic disciplines, visual and performing arts, community service, and El Puente's principles. Awards are presented to young people for their academic achievement and intellectual progress by discipline; their talents, skills, and expressions as creative beings; their contributions to the Williamsburg community through organizing and outreach efforts; and their embodiment of the spirit of El Puente Academy's principles (i.e., love and caring, collective self-help, peace and justice, and mastery).

El Puente Academy held its first graduation in June 1997. This 2-hour bilingual and multicultural celebration included an African drum and dance performance by a local company, Forces of Nature, and speeches and performances (song/rap, poetry, dance) by the graduating seniors. Other speeches and spoken word activities included an awards presentation by Congresswoman Nydia Velázquez, a keynote speech by the renowned Puerto Rican poet Martín Espada, and a personalized poem and tribute to the graduating class performed by El Puente facilitators, titled "34 names, 4 years and a life." El Puente also developed its own personal symbolic traditions, including an altar ceremony for the senior who was with the class in spirit, a sash-robing ceremony, a legacy ritual where seniors passed on a quilt to junior class representatives, and a choral performance by the senior class. It was a moving and inspirational celebration of life, love, and community.

These examples provide a snapshot of the integrative and innovative projects El Puente Academy initiates with the school community as well as the entire Williamsburg neighborhood to educate holistically, collectively, and for the purpose of community development and social change. The connection of pedagogy to community needs and social action is inherent in the structure of this movement at El Puente Academy

El Puente Academy's Vision for a 4-Year Process

Following in this tradition of holism and commitment to community, a group of staff members at El Puente Academy has been developing a 4-year vision for the Academy.[18] This vision is described as a 4-year process where young people come to understand themselves in the context of their community and the world. Facilitators are working together to create an integrated program where the entire curriculum each year will be designed around a question or theme.

The first year at the academy would be young people's introduction to El Puente. For many, it is a marked difference from other "schooling" experiences (i.e., no bells, students as the subject of learning, facilitators addressed by their first names). Anticipating this drastic shift, the first year is dedicated to answering the question, "Who am I?" It is about self-awareness and creating community among peers, facilitators, and other staff members. The *Sankofa* curriculum (described previously) focuses on going back to your roots to know who you are. Young people in-

---

[18]This effort has been led by a senior facilitator, Hector Calderón.

vestigate their personal histories and those of their ancestors, situating themselves within a broader context.

The second year's focus would be on the group or community level. The question guiding learning is "Who are we?" Membership in multiple groups is explored (i.e., family, youth, race/nationality, culture, gender, class, sexuality, religion, etc.). The final 2 years would be spent exploring the questions "What is the nature of the world we live in?" and "What can we do about it?" The goal is that by the 4th year, young people would organize their academic work around a community project, through an internship with a local organization. Thus, in addition to receiving an academic diploma upon graduation, young people will also have the skills and experiences to be community organizers.

Three philosophical principles ground this 4-year process, as described by one of El Puente's facilitators at a staff development session (Calderón, 1997). First, there is a divine human spirit. We live in a world that often dehumanizes and violates, and because the Academy is dedicated to peace and justice, it must stay true to its commitment to the human spirit within the Williamsburg community and the world, hence the focus on a community project. Second, learning is naturally focused on community needs. Disciplines are ways of understanding that were created to address the needs of people in communities and that developed as a result of human experiences. Because disciplines were created to address community needs, schools should integrate community issues into the curriculum. Third, knowledge is holistic; therefore, learning should not be compartmentalized. At El Puente, the principle of holism is grounded in the belief that the mind is located in the body and spirit. They are not three separate entities, but rather integrated parts of a whole being. Learning thus should emerge from community needs, should be directed toward developing people holistically, and should remain true to the human spirit.

El Puente Academy's Challenges and Struggles

As with all transformative, grass-roots, community movements, El Puente Academy is also struggling with some difficult issues, including the need for a leadership development and mentoring process that will ensure the future viability of the institution; a dual-language model at the secondary level to develop biliterate young people; and tools to balance national standards (i.e., standardized requirements and exams) with more holistic, project-based curricula and forms of assessment.

El Puente staff members recognize that struggle is inevitable if transformation and liberation are the goals, and they address these complex issues in their daily work. For instance, staff development workshop sessions are designed for all El Puente members to address issues of leadership, the process of decision-making, and the infrastructure of the organization. An Interim Leadership Circle has been formed with staff, student, and family representation to develop systems of mentorship and training based on a holistic vision. Second, given the shifting demographics in the Williamsburg community, growing numbers of young people are entering high school dominant in Spanish. As a result, El Puente staff members have created a biliteracy collective (in which we are involved) to critically examine issues of language, culture, identity, and literacy and to develop an integrated model that will support dual language development for young people, their families, and El Puente staff. During the 1997–98 academic year, we worked with staff members of this group in four areas, including study, research (a survey and language assessment tool for internal use), training of other facilitators, and program development (activities, units, and classes to address multiple language and literacy acquisition such as the Afro-Latino/a class mentioned earlier). Third, El Puente representatives are working with a coalition of schools to obtain a waiver from state-mandated standardized exams, proposing instead rigorous assessment standards for more holistic development for young people. The charge El Puente faculty, staff, and administrators have taken recently is to create a unified, full-day program that will serve young people and their families, including those who work at El Puente. The vision is becoming a reality in a community with few resources but with much dedication, passion, vision, commitment, and love.

CONCLUSION

Innovative small schools like El Puente Academy for Peace and Justice serve their communities by developing a relationship between classroom pedagogy and community needs. Educational goals that address individual needs in the context of the broader social conditions of the community, and schools that are part of a strategy for social change, could help transform young people and their families as well as develop communities socially, economically, and culturally.

The Puerto Rican and Latino/a community in New York City can now, with these new and future innovative schools and programs, implement a vision of education that goes beyond the minimalist criteria of adequate achievement as measured by standardized tests and develop a strategy that coordinates action at the political, economic, sociocultural, artistic, and pedagogical levels. That is, the Puerto Rican and Latino/a community can explore the connections between curriculum, governance, organization, the arts, parent involvement, and social change within the community, creating links to community, economic, and social development as well as to political participation and active citizenship. Having the space and freedom to experiment with these ideas is a critical process that we can build on and learn from as practitioners, administrators, researchers, and critical citizens. We should seize the opportunity.

Education focused on youth and community development within a concrete sociohistorical context is to us a much more productive way of understanding our collective mission and task as educators, advocates, organizers, artists, and researchers. For poor and working-class, culturally and racially diverse communities, an educational model that integrates the learners' cultures, languages, and identities, recognizes the mind–body–spirit connection within creative beings, and commits to braiding learning to community development and social action helps develop critically thinking, community-minded, justice-seeking, artistic young people and adults as well as increases opportunities for holistic growth, human development, and community building. In essence, as El Puente Academy's motto expresses, this sociocultural and educational journey helps "inspire and nurture leadership for peace and justice."

REFERENCES

Benmayor, R., Juarbe, A., Alvarez, C., Vazquez, B. (1987). *Stories to live by: Continuity and change in three generations of Puerto Rican women.* New York: Centro de Estudios Puertorriqueños, Hunter College.

Bensman, D. (1987). *Quality education in the inner city: The story of the Central Park East Schools.* New York: Community School Board, District 4.

Caballero, D. (1997). *Latino Education Network proposal to New Visions.* Unpublished report, Latino/a Education Network, New York.

Calderón, H. (1997, August). *El Puente Academy's four-year vision.* Presentation at El Puente staff development session. (Unpublished manuscript).

Cancian, F. M. (1993). Conflicts between activist research and academic success: Participatory research and alternative strategies. *The American Sociologist, 24*(1), 92–106.

Collins, P. H. (1991) *Black feminist thought: Knowledge, consciousness and the politics of empowerment.* New York: Routledge.

Covello, L. (1946–1947) *A program of education for Puerto Ricans in New York City.* Report of the Assistant Superintendents, Board of Education of the City of New York.

Covello, L. (1953). *Puerto Rican pupils in New York City public schools.* New York: Board of Education of the City of New York.

Ferrandino, J. J. (1996, April 11). *Data for new high schools.* Memorandum to Dr. Luis Reyes from John J. Ferrandino, Supervising Superintendent, Division of High Schools, Board of Education of the City of New York.

Fine, M., & Vanderslice, V. (1992). Qualitative activist research: Reflections on methods and politics. In F. Bryant, J. Edwards, R. S. Tindale, E. J. Posavac, L. Heath, E. Henderson,

& Y. Súarez-Balcazar (Eds.), *Methodological issues in applied social psychology* (pp. 199–218). New York: Plenum.

Freire, P. (1970). *Pedagogy of the oppressed.* New York: Seabury Press.

Freire, P., & Macedo, D. (1987). *Literacy: Reading the word and the world.* South Hadley, MA: Bergin & Garvey.

Giroux, H. (1988). *Schooling and the struggle for public life: Critical pedagogy in the modern age.* Minneapolis: University of Minnesota Press.

Hooks, B. (1994). *Teaching to transgress.* New York: Routledge.

Language and Policy Task Force. (1975). *Statement in support of bilingual education.* New York: Centro de Estudios Puertorriqueños, Hunter College.

Lather, P. (1991). *Getting smart: Feminist research and pedagogy within the postmodern.* New York: Routledge.

Maguire, P. (1987). *Doing participatory research: A feminist approach.* Amherst, MA: The Center for International Education, School of Education.

Meier, D. (1995). *The power of their ideas.* Boston: Beacon Press.

Meyer, G. (1985). Leonardo Cavello: A pioneer in bilingual education. *Bilingual Review, 12,* 55–61.

Morales, I. (1996). *Pa'lante siempre pa'lante* [film]. Latino Education Network Services; Columbia University Station, P.O. Box 250073, New York, NY 100250.

New York Networks for School Renewal (NYNSR) Research Collaborative. (1997). *Who we are: Students and schools in the NYNSR project (1995–1996).* New York: New York University.

Nieto, S., & Rolón, C. (1997). Preparation and professional development of teachers: A perspective from two Latinas. In J. J. Irvine (Ed.), *Critical knowledge for diverse teachers and learners* (pp. 93–128). Washington, DC: AACTE.

Park, P. (1989). *What is participatory research? A theoretical and methodological perspective.* Northampton, MA: Center for Community Education and Action.

Park, P. (1995). The creative moment in critical pedagogy. In J. Frederickson (Ed.), *Reclaiming our voices: Bilingual education, critical pedagogy and praxis.* Ontario: California Association for Bilingual Education.

IV

CLASSROOM AND SCHOOL STUDIES

The Counselor
by Shaggy (a.k.a. Jaime Flores)

Mrs. Andino
we regret
to inform you
that your son is perfectly
fine
for someone with a spanish
surname.
He is just too smart
for his
own good.

P.S.
TELL HIM THANK YOU
for the advice
on my marital problems

10

Social Action Projects: Apprenticeship for Change in School and Community

Milga Morales
Elvira R. Tarr

Puerto Ricans have a long history of settling and raising their families in New York City. For example, in 1940, 85% of all Puerto Ricans in the United States called New York City their home (Sánchez Korrol, 1994). Although the Puerto Rican population is not as densely concentrated in New York City as it was in the past, Puerto Ricans still comprise over half of the Latino population of the city. Nearly 1 million Puerto Ricans still reside in New York (Institute for Puerto Rican Policy, 1998). A steady stream of new Spanish-speaking immigrants contribute to the continuity of the Puerto Rican culture and language. Puerto Ricans have made some socioeconomic gains and have increased their participation in the daily affairs of New York City, but for the most part the potential political strength of the Puerto Rican people is not commensurate with their numbers in the population.

As teachers of prospective teachers, many of whom will teach in Brooklyn, we consider it our responsibility to open our students' eyes to these realities. The lack of visibility in the political and social processes of the city makes it imperative to teach preservice teachers the potential of their Puerto Rican students as participants in those processes.

BACKGROUND

We have taught social studies methods together for more than 10 years in a public urban university, and although each of us has personally participated in political and community activities, until recently we had not made a concerted effort to include our preservice students in these activities. We faced several challenges in attempting to do so, including our students' limited experiences outside their local neighborhoods. Although our preservice students often participated in cultural and religious activities, these were mostly confined to the students' immediate communities. The mission of the City University of New York, which has traditionally been to educate the children of the working class (although one can question whether this continues to be its role), is reflected in the other challenges that our students present: a lack of economic resources and limited early opportunities to develop their full academic potential. These limitations can result in a parochial mindset that mitigates against social activism. Additionally, many of our preservice teachers have family responsibilities, and the majority must work to augment family income.

The continued impoverished conditions of Puerto Ricans in the United States, combined with attacks on the new immigration, shrinking welfare, and "English-only" policies, made us aware that the battle for full participation in the political process necessitates preparing teachers for deliberate and sustained participation in that process. Civic participation is especially urgent for students whose communities are the targets of English-only policies and immigrant bashing. As a consequence, we decided to infuse our course work with social action projects by fostering community connections with cultural and social institutions.

Given the current reactionary political conditions in the United States, we believe that preservice teachers need to understand the sociopolitical processes that affect their lives and to develop the tools that can bring about change. A strong knowledge base and a critical understanding of the historical and cultural aspects of society can help teachers comprehend the consequences of proposed legislation and policies that affect both the larger community and the Puerto Rican population. We have found that when preservice teachers engage in social action activities in the community, they develop the confidence to become critical thinkers and they bring a unique vision to their teaching.

PURPOSE

In this chapter we describe the process we used to engage our preservice teachers in understanding civic affairs and the political and social milieu in which they would work as educators. It seemed to us that engaging them in this way would help them develop a consciousness as agents of change, a stance we believe is crucial in forming a critical and reflective perspective about teaching. This perspective helped us to revamp our social studies curriculum. Consequently, during summer 1996 we redefined our course objectives as follows:

1. To help preservice teachers of all backgrounds become aware of the culture and strengths of the Puerto Rican community.
2. To understand the institution of education as embedded within the larger social and political world.
3. To create an educational environment in which preservice teachers could explore what it means to become agents of change in their schools and communities.

We describe our planning and the thematic projects that emerged, namely, The City as Mosaic; The Museum Project; The Triple A Process, based on Paulo Freire's philosophy; Child Labor; Labor History; and Fighting for Our Rights. Finally, we briefly describe some of the projects our students designed for their work with elementary school students.

Although our objectives were targeted primarily toward our Puerto Rican students, we expected the objectives to apply to all preservice teachers. We focused on the Puerto Rican community because of our close historical affiliation with many Puerto Rican community organizations and our strong ties to the Department of Puerto Rican Studies at our college. Also, the current controversies surrounding the maintenance of ethnic mother tongues and cultural pluralism presented both an opportunity and a challenge that could include all our students.

We used classroom and field experiences to promote the development of social action projects. We also hoped that the preservice teachers would carry their new skills over to their future work with young children. An initial evaluation of this model has suggested that it was successful: Puerto Rican students were able to break down the wall that had formerly separated some of them from their community, and the curriculum enabled all our preservice students to realize their potential as agents of change.

Profile of Preservice Teachers

An overwhelming number of our university students come from working-class backgrounds, and they are beset by many financial and social problems. These conditions pose serious limitations on their ability to participate in activities outside of their college work. Because of these constraints, they have also found it difficult to become engaged in political and social activities. Our students' backgrounds are diverse: They are Puerto Rican and non–Puerto Rican, and they have had a range of educational experiences, although most have been educated in New York City. Our Puerto Rican preservice teachers account for approximately 35% of our student interns, and many are first-, second-, and third-generation immigrants.

In order for preservice teachers to participate in the democratic process, they must first have opportunities to engage in political and social activities. They must serve as role models for the young children they will teach and must model the skills needed to engage in social action.

Social Action

Before describing our work it is necessary to explain what we mean by social action. In our classes we teach about social, economic, and political events and how those events affect the people who experience them. We do this by encouraging our students to see through the eyes of the participants. Consequently, our students have worked on projects that have helped them delve more deeply into multiple aspects of the subject matter. Presentations of their work have involved group reports, map making, debates, and role playing. However, until we initiated social action projects, the students' work generally ended in the classroom. We began to see that it was vitally important to go beyond the classroom experience to engage preservice teachers in social action projects that might lead to change outside the classroom. This would enable our students to follow through on projects they had begun in the classroom. As the work progressed, we also asked them to devise social action projects for elementary school children. Every class project required participants to reach out to the world beyond the classroom, whether a college classroom or an elementary school classroom. Some of the projects included writing letters to protest child labor conditions in Honduras, interviewing family members to produce a family tree, and contacting a labor union in the community.

UNIVERSITY PROJECTS

What follows is a description of some of the activities in which we engaged preservice teachers in the university setting during one academic year.

The City as Mosaic

New York City provided a fertile site for much of our curriculum. In one project, The City as Mosaic, our students developed a genealogical study of their own families. Several of them had not talked with members of their families for years, and others reported making long-distance calls to grandparents and family friends to gather as much information as possible. With a sample diagram of a family tree in hand, students interviewed family members. The research that evolved and the preparation for class presentations allowed students to explore topics in geography, political science, history, and the social sciences.

The students found interesting ways to visually represent their extended families, and many were able to document their genealogy as far back as four or five generations. For some, representing their family using the image of a tree did not work. One student used a culturally embedded image, small bohíos(dwellings of the Taínos, the indigenous inhabitants of the Island of Puerto Rico), placing the names of her ancestors on the entrance to the bohíos. During her presentation, she shared her extended family history. At the same time, she discussed the political and social issues related to the migration of Puerto Ricans to the United States, particularly during difficult economic times on the Island. Other students were better able to understand why Puerto Ricans had left the Island in large numbers during the late 1940s and why so many of them settled in New York State, where jobs were available.

The second part of the assignment required students to investigate the larger community. We suggested they choose a physical structure, such as a school, church, or civic building, that was significant to the people of the community. They needed to document the history and social significance of the structure by photographing or drawing it, developing a map focusing on the surrounding areas, and reporting on their research. As future teachers, they would have to learn to make social studies more engaging and dynamic. Because material in the social studies is often presented in a static manner and is therefore uninteresting to children, we suggested that creativity in designing their presentation was important.

Our students responded to this assignment in a variety of ways. Some chose to research school buildings (private, parochial, public), hospitals, and also apartment buildings in their communities. A student who focused on a public school in Sunset Park in Brooklyn, a primarily Puerto Rican/Latino community, not only reported on the history of the school building itself but shared information about the programs housed in the school and the rationale for those programs. This project led us to a discussion of bilingual education. She indicated that due to the linguistic needs of the students, many of the staff were conversant in both English and Spanish, although some teachers in the school were monolingual. The preservice teachers became very curious about how instruction was carried out in the bilingual classes. Several of them had never worked in a bilingual setting, yet they understood the importance and the benefits of developing proficiency in another language. The pedagogical practices of the school were discussed. The project also helped the students understand that a knowledge of the vision and underlying philosophy of bilingual education would help them understand the function of the school in the larger community.

This project also led to a discussion and assessment of New Vision schools in New York City (see chap. 9 by Rivera and Pedraza, this volume). Several such schools created by community representatives and parents, developed from ideas and proposals generated after many meetings and activities where diverse groups of people discussed the philosophy and goals of the school they envisioned. An example of such a school is El Puente Academy for Peace and Justice, in Williamsburg, Brooklyn, located in a Puerto Rican and Dominican area of the borough. As part of our course work, we visited the school and met with members of the staff who were creating a rich and culturally embedded curriculum.

The City as Mosaic theme provides many possibilities for social action projects and activities. It draws the students out of their neighborhoods, helps them to accept and share the diversity of their communities, and teaches them about other ethnic and racial groups. It takes preservice teachers into unfamiliar neighborhoods and communities, where they are hesitant or reluctant to go. In one case, the project brought Puerto Rican students in contact with Orthodox Jewish students who lived in the Williamsburg community, and it provided both groups with the space and time to dialogue about commonalties and differences.

Several of the readings for The City as Mosaic project focused on the lived realities of Puerto Ricans in the United States. The first reading was a novel by Piri Thomas, *Down These Mean Streets* (1967), a description of the life of an Afro–Puerto Rican male who grew up in Harlem, New York, in the 1940s and 1950s and who moved to the suburbs of Long Island as a teenager. This book was particularly enlightening to many of our students because they had never read an autobiographical account of any Puerto Rican or Latino writer. Key themes in this book—language, culture, ethnicity, gender, and race—became part of our discussions.

A second reading was *Family Installments* (1982), by Edward Rivera, a book that provided an interesting comparison to *Down These Mean Streets*, by describing the life of Puerto Rican students in a parochial school setting. Using Venn diagrams, we identified the differences between the childhood experiences of Thomas and Rivera. One significant similarity was how Puerto Ricans were treated by the larger society. In both cases these authors, as young men, faced discrimination because their language, skin color, and culture were different from the majority. We asked students to respond to the readings by creating a collage. The resulting art projects symbolized the discrimination and violence suffered by both Thomas and Rivera.

A third reading was *The Puerto Rican Struggle: Essays on Survival in the U.S.* (Rodriguez, Sánchez Korrol, & Alers, 1980). Because many of the autobiographical works of Puerto Ricans written in English focus on their experiences in schools and communities, we wanted our students to have a more comprehensive picture of factors contributing to the socioeconomic conditions of Puerto Ricans in the United States today. The various essays in the book clarify the political, social, and economic situation of Puerto Ricans, particularly in the northeast region of the United States. The conclusion reached by our preservice teachers from these readings was much in line with a publication of the U.S. Commission on Civil Rights (1976) that described the future of Puerto Ricans in the United States as "uncertain." Although large numbers of Puerto Ricans reside in the United States, only a small minority of them have entered the middle class; in addition, the drop-out rate continues to be very high; AIDS, drugs, and violence permeate these communities; and more recent anti-immigrant attitudes contribute to this uncertain future.

The last assigned reading was the play *The Oxcart* (1969), by Rene Marques. This play draws on the experiences of Puerto Ricans in the 1940s and 1950s who migrated to the cities of the eastern U.S. (primarily New York City, but also Philadelphia and agricultural areas of New Jersey). The play begins in a rural town in Puerto Rico, and it describes the journey of a Puerto Rican family as they moved from the town to the impoverished district of San Juan known as La Perla. The poor economic conditions of that area motivated them to continue their journey to the United States, but in New York City they faced all the tribulations of poor people in urban areas. Several of the preservice teachers identified with this sojourn, as they themselves had migrated to the United States, mostly for economic reasons, although some for political reasons as well. This play allowed our students to begin to understand the journeys of many immigrants and migrants who have come to the United States due to the exploitation of their native countries, the conquest of their national territory (as in the case of Puerto Rico), or the enslavement of the people at the hands of those more militarily powerful.

The Museum Project

To further encourage our preservice teachers to become familiar with other neighborhoods and communities, we asked them to visit either the Brooklyn Museum or the Museum of Natural History in Manhattan. For many students, this visit was their first trip to Manhattan. Although some students had family in other areas of the city, they rarely were able to use the cultural or educational resources the city has to offer. In some cases, our preservice teachers were genuinely surprised that so many resources were accessible not only to them but also to the children who they would eventually teach.

In addition to the museums mentioned previously, several students went to El Museo del Barrio, located in East Harlem, where they saw the work of Puerto Rican artists previously unfamiliar to them. Others visited the Metropolitan Museum of Art in Manhattan, and they reported on the section housing the American Wing. Still others were fortunate to view an exhibit called "The Convergence of Cultures" at the Brooklyn Museum, which documented the connection of Spanish and indigenous cultures.

Not all children have the opportunity to visit museums, and our students discussed this possibility. If children cannot visit museums, they might not understand the concept of the museum as history. Our students discussed projects such as creating a museum in the classroom to duplicate the experience. A museum corner could be designated and artifacts brought from the children's homes. It was suggested that family pictures and other objects brought in by the children for the museum could lead to a discussion of how artifacts are selected to constitute history. The discussion of a class museum also helped address the notion of stereotyping cultures.

A Freiran Philosophy:
The Triple A Process of ASPIRA

As a result of the readings and the knowledge they acquired through the projects, our students began to analyze how they could be more directly involved in social action projects. Because one of us (Milga) was conversant with the process used for social action projects by ASPIRA (see chap. 3 by Nieto, this volume, for a brief description of ASPIRA), we decided to use it with our preservice teachers. The process, referred to as the Triple A Process: Awareness, Analysis, and Action (ASPIRA, 1991), has been copyrighted and is nationally recognized for motivating Puerto Rican/Latino youth to become community and government leaders. *Awareness* refers to the need to know the factors—economic, educational, political, and social—that affect the daily lives of preservice teachers as well as the lives of the children they are going to teach. *Analysis* is the ability to collectively study a situation from a variety of perspectives and clearly understand its component parts. *Action* refers to the strategies and tactics that must be discussed, reflected on, and rediscussed in order to address an issue and successfully move forward. This process was discussed within the framework of Paulo Freire's *Pedagogy of the Oppressed* (1970/1995). Freire suggested a paradigm for working in the community that includes the concept of dialogue. He proposed that a relationship of equality must exist between the subjects involved in change, because progressive change can occur only when the oppressed can free themselves of the notion that they cannot control and shape their own lives. For a highly religious community, such as the Puerto Rican/Latino community, which often is reluctant to contradict the powers that be, it is especially important to learn how to address problems from a radical perspective. The Triple A Process is a clear, distinct, and simple elaboration of Freire's ideas.

The Triple A Process helped the students prepare and shape a Citizenship and Immigration Fair in collaboration with the Department of Puerto Rican Studies in a Puerto Rican community in Brooklyn. Because many of the students were enrolled in a course that required field activity, with our supervision they collaboratively organized the fair at a local junior high school. Parents and community members, including the press, came to obtain information about citizenship, and many also registered to vote at a booth set up in the same area by a member of the local school board.

A second project in the same community was *Arriba Los Niños*, a college-supervised mentoring project involving our bilingual preservice teachers with the young people of the Sunset Park community in Brooklyn. The preservice teachers met with elementary school students to give them information about careers and opportunities to attend college. With one of the elementary school principal's support, students organized parent discussions and workshops in the classrooms. A small grant from a local company allowed *Arriba Los Niños* to bring in an anthropologist to speak about her profession with the children. To help them appreciate the kind of work in which urban anthropologists are involved, she taught them anthropological skills such as conducting oral histories. Parents were included at all levels of program planning to ensure parental involvement and community support. Many community members contributed recipes for a parent recipe book of Puerto Rican/Latino dishes. Each parent received an *Arriba Los Niños* T-shirt designed by one of the preschool teachers who worked on the project.

Finally, the elementary school students visited Brooklyn College. As a result of this visit, the preservice teachers coordinated a multicultural conference with the parents that featured Alma Flor Ada, one of the most prolific Latina writers of children's books in the United States. In her workshop with the parents, Ada encouraged them to keep journals and to write their own books.

Child Labor

Bob Herbert's columns in the *New York Times* sparked another idea for social action projects among our preservice teachers. His op-ed articles describing the brutal labor conditions under which young children in
Honduras, primarily girls, worked sounded an alarm regarding the oppression of women and children. Herbert depicted the long hours of work,
the harassment of children by factory managers, and the paltry pay these
children earned. In addition, the children were unable to go to school.
What was most troubling was that the clothes these children made were
sold in the United States for prices far above the manufacturers' cost and
they were purchased by consumers who were unaware of the conditions
under which the clothes were made.

Because we thought understanding this problem would help students
realize the impact of social studies on their daily lives, we contacted Herbert's office in the hope that he would be able to speak to our students. He
was unavailable but suggested we contact Charles Kernaghan, the executive director of the National Labor Committee. Kernaghan sent brochures
describing the devastating effects of child labor and a video taken in Honduras. Although most of our students were from Latin American backgrounds, they were shocked at what they read and saw on tape. Our
discussions about the global economy took on new meaning for them.
They were surprised to read that the clothes made under sweatshop conditions were sold in the stores they frequented. The labels of Gap, Liz
Claiborne, and K-Mart were all too familiar to them.

We also invited Kernaghan to the college to talk about his work in com-
bating child labor throughout Central America. Kernaghan is an eloquent
speaker, and as he talked about the long hours that the girls worked for the
usual pay of 35 cents an hour, the connection to young children became
clearer to our students. He and his assistant came with two very young female workers. After Kernaghan spoke, he turned the meeting over to the
young women. His assistant translated as they told the poignant stories
of their experiences. They spoke of barbed wire around the worksite that
kept outsiders from visiting the factory. They were given a daily work
quota and if they did not complete it, they were forced to work long into
the night. Sometimes they had to sleep in the factory to be on time for
work the next morning. They also described the sexual harassment and
insulting language they endured. They were forced to undergo examina-
tions to determine if they were pregnant, and were forced to take birth
control pills. These young girls, 15 or 16 years old, were usually the sole
breadwinners of their families, which explained why they were willing to
comply with the demands of the factory managers. The girls also told our
class that workers who engaged in union activities were fired.

At the end of the meeting, Kernaghan announced that there was to be a major demonstration in front of a Gap flagship store near Macy's in Manhattan. It was being mounted to put pressure on the store because it sold clothing produced by child labor. The purpose was to force Macy's contractors to pay decent wages to their employees. In the class discussion that followed, the students expressed their concern for the workers. One student said that the companies were too large and powerful and that nothing could be done to fight them. But some students said that if people remained silent, they were complicitous in the inhumane conditions that had been described. We told them that we were going to participate in the demonstration to bring attention to the plight and suffering of child workers in Latin America, and we encouraged students to join us.

Our students wrote letters to the owners of Gap, and several reported that they spoke to salespersons in Gap stores. The events of the next few weeks exceeded our expectations. The pressure that had been applied by groups all over the country forced the owners of Gap to agree to have their plants monitored for child labor abuses. There has been concerted pressure on other large corporations who use cheap labor in other Latin American as well as Asian countries to observe fair labor practices that do not hurt either the workers in those countries or our labor force in the United States.

This activity made students aware of some of the social effects of globalization, the need for individuals and groups to protest wrongs, and how their actions could contribute to change. This activity also led to lessons in our classroom in geography, economics, political science, and history. Social studies took on new meaning for our preservice teachers as it became alive for them.

It became apparent to us, in the course of class discussions, that the students knew very little of labor history and the historic struggle of workers to obtain decent working conditions. They knew little of terms such as *boycott, arbitration, lockout,* and *blacklist.* In short, the problems of labor, for them, were problems of another economic class, and they did not feel those problems pertained to them. They felt that because they were becoming "professionals" they did not identify with "workers." This narrow view led us to consider additional activities for classes. The two of us talked about the necessity for preservice teachers to understand the plight of workers in economically troubled areas of the world but also to know about the labor conditions in the United States. Most of our preservice teachers will work in the inner city and the children they will teach are primarily children of workers, many of whom come from countries where exploitation is pervasive. An understanding of the difficulties the parents of inner-city children face helped to increase our students' sensitivity to the social and economic conditions prevalent in these communities.

Labor History

As a result of the experience with the National Labor Committee, we developed a separate unit focusing on labor history. We identified four areas of concern that would be investigated cooperatively. The first group researched the history of labor movements in the United States, Central America, and Puerto Rico, including the relationship between the United States and the Island. The second group investigated the history and current conditions of women in the workplace. Because of the overwhelming number of women in education, we decided that gender was an important category for investigation. The third group focused on a particular labor union by learning the history of that union and its current activities. The national headquarters of the International Ladies Garment Workers Union, the Municipal Workers Union, Local 1199, and the Hospital Workers Union are all located in New York City. Because of the huge amount of material available, we suggested that the students focus on one of those unions. The fourth group interviewed workers at the college and at neighborhood stores about the current conditions and attitudes of workers in their local communities. We expected that by engaging in these activities, students would begin to consider some of the problems and appreciate the strengths of the parents of children they would teach. We expected these experiences to provide some insight into the current labor conditions of the global economy.

To start the students on their projects, we listed some people and events with which they should become familiar: The March of the 10,000, Luisa Capetillo, Dolores Huerta, Frances Perkins, Walter Reuther, Sacco and Vanzetti, the Triangle Fire, Bread and Roses, the United Federation of Teachers (the local teachers' union), the Teamsters Union, Local 1199, and Unite. We showed the photographs taken by Lewis W. Hines of child labor in the early part of the century, and we referred to the murals of workers by Diego Rivera.

The students spent many hours preparing for their class presentations. Students were surprised at how much they learned through this project: that so many women were part of the labor movement; that Puerto Rican, Polish and Jewish women worked together in sweatshops in New York City in the early 1900s; and that Sacco and Vanzetti were executed not only for their political views but also because of prejudice against immigrants. Finally, as the students reflected on current labor conditions, they understood the power of government and corporations over the lives of workers, including their own lives.

Fighting for Our Rights

Many of our students were second-generation Latinos, and they began to understand the connection between the rights their parents had fought for, such as bilingual education and bilingual ballots, and the ongoing need to maintain and improve these programs. We began a project on the civil rights laws passed in the 1960s, legislation of which many of the younger college students were unaware. We first asked the students to research language rights in the United States, including the legislation to declare English the official language. To really address this problem, the students needed to learn about the laws that govern the United States and the context in which they were passed. We asked them to read the Constitutional amendments and choose one that they found particularly important to their communities. Most students focused on the 13th, 14th, and 15th amendments. We then asked them to create lesson plans on the 1st amendment to teach a social studies lesson at a public school.

To provide a context for understanding the significance of the Constitution, we described how it developed out of a revolutionary movement not very different from the Cuban Revolution (although this revolution is presented in very negative terms to North Americans). We asked students to read the Preamble as a revolutionary document and to dramatize the reading so that the document would come alive. The discussion and reading of the Constitution led them to address Supreme Court decisions of special significance to them. These included PL92-154, which affects the schooling and education of children who are differently and/or physically challenged; Brown v. the Board of Education, which in 1954 ended the legal racial segregation of schools; and, Lau v. Nichols, a 1974 Supreme Court decision that allowed the use of languages other than English as the medium of instruction in U.S. public schools.

The focus on rights led us to conversations about "powerful citizenship" and the idea that many of us only respond passively to our responsibilities as citizens; we often do not question decisions made by the local or federal government about our lives. We discussed the concept that the "good" citizen is also the "powerful" citizen who achieves a level of consciousness that allows him or her to collaborate and develop strategies that encourage others to become activists. We began to discuss persons who were not passive, individuals such as Martin Luther King but also women, particularly Puerto Rican/Latina women, of whom students knew little. We discussed a number of Latinas: Dolores Huerta, a Mexican-American organizer for the United Farm Workers; Julia de Burgos, the

Puerto Rican writer–poet and anticolonialist activist; and Antonia Pantoja, who along with other progressive Puerto Ricans constructed a network of organizations which today are the bulwark of activism on behalf of Puerto Ricans and other Latinos in the United States. The students also created a mural that included women in the union movement as well as others about whom they had read.

PROJECTS WITH CHILDREN

The preservice students were now ready for their first official field visit to the elementary school where they were to observe social studies being taught in the classroom. We chose a school that had a significant number of bilingual classes. The Puerto Rican and other Latino preservice teachers were especially excited about being placed in bilingual classrooms and working with children from their own language and culture. We asked the students to visit the school, observe the surrounding community, and write their observations in journals. They worked with us to develop a model for transferring some of the ideas we had discussed in our course into the school setting with children.

Global Village: Issues and Images

Drawing on their previous course work in the social sciences, the preservice teachers prepared an exhibition focused on global issues. We divided the participants into groups, each of which was assigned a continent. Each individual then identified a city within the continent to study. After some initial research and much discussion, the students developed a set of questions they would investigate for each city. The propensity to identify only the "tourist" aspects of the city became easier to resolve when participants focused on problematizing issues they had studied in class.

Another exercise required students to create an imaginary island, within specific lines of latitude and longitude. Students were required, given the particular geographical and demographic makeup of the island as they designed it, to describe the problems and issues (and possible solutions) that the island's inhabitants would face. Our students thought this exercise was depressing, and they did not seem to want to focus on problems. Connecting the real issues of a community with the leisure or recreational aspects of the island was one of the most complex and difficult areas we addressed. Many of our preservice teachers thought this issue was too complex for the early childhood grades. Others, although anxious to teach these issues, held some preconceived notions as to what children were capable of comprehending. For example, they thought that the children they were going to teach would not readily understand the concept of a city. It was only after they had experience in the elementary classroom that they understood how smart the children really were.

Collecting and Creating

Two other activities that emerged from this project included the design of scrapbooks with information about the city that participants were studying and the cooperative creation of a quilt representing the global village. To engage our preservice teachers in developing the city scrapbook, we described it as a book like a family album that tells a story about the city and its people. It could include news articles, current and historical data, artifacts that could fit in the scrapbook, photographs, and many other bits and pieces that together tell the story of a particular city and teach it in a visual and exciting manner.

To prepare the scrapbook, we encouraged our students to read the newspaper daily and to collect magazines, flyers, and newsletters from the community. We asked them to visit consulates and the United Nations Library and use the Internet to learn about significant events in that city and country. They were also required to develop a bibliography of the city and country and include at least 20 references of books and other appropriate materials. They also had to research and prepare a list of trade books for children. Using the whole-language approach and including literature to teach social studies was an area with which only some of our students were familiar. Using a number of books from around the world, we demonstrated how they could teach about people from different countries. We also discussed how people from all over the world sometimes treat each other with prejudice.

The final activity was to create an international quilt reflecting the issues and problems of the cities. Students produced a large, colorful quilt representing 32 cities. It was shown on campus and became the focal point of the exhibition. Today, the quilt hangs in the Bilingual Multicultural Resource Center for viewing by the next generation of preservice teachers.

EVALUATION OF THE SEMESTER

The evaluation of our work centered on the achievement of our initial objectives and the intellectual and personal growth of the preservice teachers. Their study of the history, culture, and, most importantly, stamina of the local community contributed to their appreciation of Puerto Rican communities in the United States. Their study also helped shatter the stereotypical images that the non–Puerto Rican preservice teachers had of Puerto Ricans. As they mentioned in class discussions, they had usually pictured the community as a very close-knit, clannish group that was barely connected to the larger community. They thought of Puerto Ricans as a marginalized group suffering greatly from the many problems of the urban environment with few resources to ameliorate their condition. In short, they had bought into the one-dimensional stereotype of Puerto Ricans as victims that is portrayed in the media.

Our students learned about the many organizations and activities that had developed from family and neighborhood support networks within the Puerto Rican community. They also learned that families in need could call on not only relatives but local community organizations and neighbors and were able to draw strength and vital information from their assistance. The isolation that many non–Puerto Rican preservice students experienced in their own communities was in decided contrast with the support experienced in many Puerto Rican communities. For their part, the Puerto Rican preservice teachers brought brochures and leaflets to class that described forthcoming events in their communities, and they shared this information with the other preservice teachers. Some of them later participated in these events.

Understandably, the initial concern of the preservice teachers was to learn about being a classroom teacher. The questions early in the year focused on classroom management, teacher guides, student discipline, and school administration. We responded to their concerns, but we also believed that their forays into the local communities and their work in the elementary schools would broaden their vision of the teacher's role. Studying the history of the community and meeting with parents and politicians helped them understand the political and social forces that affect schooling in the United States. These activities also contributed to their understanding of the critical need for collaborative action and strategic planning to achieve social justice. It is difficult to change attitudes, but we believe, based on the preservice teachers' comments, that more than a few of them began to see themselves as agents of change in their work as teachers.

One of the goals of education is development of a sense of dignity and self-worth. Our belief that "telling is not teaching" made us move from the usual method of simply telling our students that they are worthy. Instead we provided opportunities to test their ability to confront the challenges they will face in their classrooms. Through their course work, they found they had strengths of which they were often unaware, and this contributed to their feeling of empowerment. A significant implication of our work is that students need to have opportunities to realize their strengths and the strengths of their communities by participating in projects that demonstrate those strengths. Involvement in social, political, and educational experiences can also provide knowledge of the many ways that people can participate in civic affairs. For those preservice teachers who have an awareness and connection to community, as is the case with many of our Puerto Rican preservice teachers, supporting these links and building upon their relationships are critical.

The semester was trying because it was labor intensive. We had to spend more time contacting community organizations and arranging meetings with political and community leaders. There is a dearth of materials in this area, which has led us to begin compiling materials for other teachers. But to say that the semester was rewarding for us, the faculty, is an understatement. Not only were we able to observe our students participate in community action, but we also saw some of them assume a leadership role. Most of the preservice students grew not only in conceptual understanding but also in political savvy. They began to talk of the need for making alliances and networking, words that they now incorporate into their daily speech.

Last, we had the opportunity to concretize one of our firm beliefs, that is, that educators should be social activists. We believe we have taken an important, exciting step in that direction and we will continue to pursue that goal. We are now developing guidelines and corresponding projects and activities to distribute among teacher educators and others interested in the education of children. Part of this process will include the development of a manual or set of guidelines to help preservice teachers understand the politics of grass-roots organizing and how to "fight City Hall." We are also compiling a list of all Puerto Rican organizations, nonprofit community groups, social activists, and public listener- and viewer-controlled media to give to our preservice teachers.

We have concluded that there are many ways to demonstrate social activism and community empowerment. We now know that many of the Puerto Rican preservice teachers are willing to become more involved, but very often economic conditions do not allow them to participate. We expect to develop internships that build on community links. These projects will differ from those that assume participants have no relation to their communities. Finally, the semi- "invisible" status of the Puerto Rican community is of concern to us. That is, how the Puerto Rican community differs from immigrant populations is often missing in history and social studies curricula and texts. Building on this need, we expect to publish a paper that gives non–Puerto Rican preservice teachers the information and insight they need to collaborate with the community and work toward community empowerment.

CONCLUSION

As we evaluated the semester's work with our students, they expressed enthusiasm in learning about the world around them and the world beyond their local community. Although not all the students were ready to label themselves as agents of change, it was clear that they were asking questions that all teachers must face: Why am I becoming a teacher? How will I change the conditions under which my community lives? What resources will I need? Our preservice teachers thought that the semester's work had positively influenced their preparation for teaching and for contributing beyond the classroom to their community. This can in turn heighten their ability to convey to their students the importance of civic action to achieve social justice, a primary goal of a truly democratic society.

REFERENCES

ASPIRA. (1991). *The ASPIRA story: 1961–1991*. Washington, DC: Author.

Freire, P. (1995). *Pedagogy of the oppressed*. New York: Seabury Press (Original work published 1970)

Institute for Puerto Rican Policy. (1998, February). Puerto Ricans and other Latinos in the United States. *IPR Datanote, 19*.

Marques, R. (1969). *The oxcart (La carreta)*. New York: Scribner's.

Rivera, E. (1982). *Family installments: Memories of growing up Hispanic*. New York: Morrow.

Rodriguez, C. E., Sánchez Korrol, V., & Alers, J. O. (Eds.). (1980). *The Puerto Rican struggle: Essays on survival in the U.S.* New York: Puerto Rican Migration Research Consortium.

Sánchez Korrol, V. E. (1994). *From colonia to community: The history of Puerto Ricans in New York, 1917–1948*. Berkeley: University of California Press.

Thomas, P. (1967). *Down these mean streets*. New York: Knopf.

U.S. Commission on Civil Rights. (1976). *Puerto Ricans in the continental United States: An uncertain future*. Washington, DC: Author.

Teachers Don't Care

José Manuel Caraballo

I don't think teachers care about students. For example, once I asked my social studies teacher to explain a test question that I didn't get. He took 20 points off my test. I ended up failing the test because of those 20 points. I asked him why he took 20 points off the test and he said, "I did it because I don't answer questions during tests," and he walked away. But when a White girl asked him questions during the test, he answered them. I don't think that is fair because he should answer everyone's questions. I'm Puerto Rican and he should answer my questions too. Sometimes I want to say something to him but I'm afraid he will tell the principal I was not respecting him. One day it happened to my friend David and he was sent to the principal's office. The social studies teacher was always taking 20 points off David's tests because he kept asking questions. One day David started to yell at him and he got sent home and couldn't come back to school until his mother came in. David is Puerto Rican, like me.

There is another teacher I have named Mr. Gonsalves. Every time you ask him a question, he makes a big speech. That's why we don't ask questions in his class, even when we don't understand something. For example, when you ask him how to do a problem he will say, "Didn't you just hear me say how to do it?" But he never said anything and he never told us how to do the problem. I hope someday this problem will be fixed and kids can ask questions again without being treated unfairly. That's why I don't do the work: because I can't ask questions on how to do it and I don't understand it so I don't do it!

There is one good teacher, my English teacher, Mrs. Harris. She helps me and shows me how to do things like spelling, nouns, and punctuation. For example, I failed a written test and I stayed after school for extra help. She explained what I did wrong and she let me take the test over and I got an A+. I wish all the teachers were like her. Then there would not be so many problems in our classes.

It makes me feel angry because teachers are supposed to help students. But they don't pay attention to what you say and they don't care. That is their job and I don't think they are doing their job. It is our education teachers are messing with and we're not going to take it anymore. I hope one day someone has the guts to step forth and take a stand and then maybe someone will realize that this is not a game and start listening to us. Maybe that someone will be me or someone I know. But I hope it happens soon because if it doesn't, it will become even worse than it is now. I would not like to see that happen.

11

Puerto Rican/Latino Student Voices: Stand and Deliver

María E. Torres-Guzmán
Yvonne Martínez Thorne

The urgency to account for student voice in understanding the schooling of American youth in the current reform efforts emerges from our insistence in understanding the shifting role of students. The concept of students as passive learners has shifted to one of students as cocreators of their learning environments. Students are perceived as active mediators of instructional events and interpreters of classroom reality (Sheets, 1994; Weinstein, 1982). Thus, it is our contention that one cannot adequately address and understand the schooling experience of American youth or fully understand the process of educational change embodied in school restructuring without engaging the voices of students.

Despite the growing awareness of the importance of student voice in educational reform, it has not emerged as a focus of educational research. The lengthy process of helping students find and elicit their voice, the mistrust of and lack of confidence in adults' desire to hear their voice, and the potential threat that student voices pose to the way schools are governed and to the ideas that teachers have about the role of students in the school (Straus, 1992) are but some of the reasons for the absence of student voice in the lit-

269

erature on the schooling of American youth and educational reform. Furthermore, emphasis has historically been placed on seeking the perceptions of outside experts and ignoring the importance of student voice when considering educational reform.

Even fewer studies have addressed the perceptions of Latino youth as they pertain to their American-schooling experiences (Nieto, 1994; Latino Commission on Educational Reform, 1992; Rodriguez, 1992). These studies have examined the personal and family characteristics associated with underachievement and school failure. Few studies have asked students about their thinking, their attitudes, and their beliefs about school. Similarly, few studies have investigated the structures of support that help to perpetuate the underachievement and school failure found in Latino communities, such as the insidious effects of oppression and racism on the education of Latino adolescents. Fine (1991) proposed that the absence of young people's voices in the debate on educational reform served to further silence the oppression and racism that continue to exist in their communities. Studies investigating the voices of Latino students are therefore critical to educators and policy makers interested in educational reform and restructuring schools to serve all students. Latino student voices may also provide insight into the very structures that perpetuate the underachievement and school failure found within Latino communities.

In this chapter we examine the voices of adolescent Latino students at Esperanza High School,[1] an alternative bilingual–bicultural high school located in a poverty-stricken, urban Latino neighborhood. The neighboring schools were all cited as deficient and were ranked in the bottom 10% of all schools in the state. The zone school that served this community was also found to have a dropout rate of 60% to 65%.

ESPERANZA HIGH SCHOOL

Esperanza High was established with three goals in mind: develop leadership skills in students and foster a commitment to community service, establish a maintenance bilingual–bicultural model in which family and culture are prominent, and develop an alternative educational model that could be integrated into the local high school as a school within a school that would be of greater benefit to Latino youth. Of major concern was the engagement of educationally neglected Latino students in a process

---

[1]The names of the school, the students, and the teachers were changed to ensure anonymity.

that enabled them to undertake care-for attitudes (Noddings, 1984) and undertake leadership roles in the community.

Esperanza was administratively under the local educational agency as a small, alternative, high school for students who were unable to complete their zoned school experience. The school was housed in a community-based organization that was well-known for promoting Latino youth and community empowerment and for its advocacy programs for youth, after-school program, drug prevention, and community involvement in issues of equity, police brutality, and so forth. Adolescents (ages 12–20) residing in this geographical area represented the largest concentration of Hispanic youth in the city and were perceived as the highest at risk for dropping out of school, unemployment, teenage pregnancy, child abuse, criminal behavior, and violent death. The problem was further compounded by the absence of integrated services within the neighborhood that could consistently address these risks. It is within these conditions, and in response to them, that the alternative school for high-risk Latino youth was established.

Students at Esperanza High School

Thirteen students were officially enrolled at Esperanza High school when it first opened its door the second half of an academic year. During the fall semester of the second year, student enrollment rose to 40. Although the enrollment requirement was almost reached by the mid-fall semester, within a few months the numbers of enrolled students decreased. Eighteen students were taken off the roster for a variety of reasons; some had moved, and others had an inordinate amount of absences. Most of the students were referred to the school by the neighboring high school. About half were transfers from other schools and one discharge from another school. Some students never attended high school and were out of school for several years before deciding to return to school. One student returned to school because the high school diploma she received from her country of origin was not accepted in the United States. Many students were not accepted by their neighborhood high school because they were overage. The students ranged in age from 16 to 20.

Most of the students at Esperanza High were labeled at risk by the local school district authorities. All were from Latino homes with at least two-thirds of Puerto Rican heritage and the remaining from Dominican, Cuban, Nicaraguan, and Ecuadorian ethnic backgrounds. About half of the students (45%) were born in New York or other parts of the United States. We were able to see the files of 15 students, most of whom we interviewed. At least 10 had stopped attending the zoned high school, 3 were new arrivals to the United States, all were from barrios of poverty, living in a neighborhood with a high incidence of drugs, violence, and high levels of dropping out before completing high school. Spanish was the language spoken in the home; only two reported that English was also spoken at home. Of the 15 students we were able to attain language test scores, seven had scored below the 21st percentile of the language proficiency test given by the district, signifying low levels of English proficiency. Three fell in the gray area of 22nd to 40th percentile, and 5 were, according to the test, proficient in English. The school was housed in a community-based organization that selected the master teacher and determined the curriculum goals.

Teachers and Support Staff

During the time of our study, the teaching staff consisted of three teachers: a female Latino master teacher who taught at the school since its inception, a White English monolingual teacher, and a Latino male teacher. Support staff were also involved at the school and included a part-time education specialist/college-and-career-advisor, an intake coordinator, a dance coordinator, social worker, a counselor/staff developer, and several counselors and tutors.

Although many aspects of the lives of Latino students were captured as part of a larger ethnographic study of the school (Torres-Guzman, 1989), we limited our focus to what the students had to say about teachers and their teaching, and about how the students said what they had to say. We specifically wanted to find out what they had to say about their experiences in school at Esperanza and elsewhere. We were particularly interested in how Latino students were similar to and different from non-Latino students in their perceptions about their schooling experiences as portrayed by the literature. Moreover, because our conversations about teaching with these youth occurred over a year, we wanted to know how their talk about teaching developed throughout this period. We assumed that their way of expressing their ideas about teaching in an atmosphere of empowerment would change over time.

Eliciting Student Voices

Research Methods Used.   A review of the literature on students' thinking about school revealed several research methods for eliciting student perceptions: paper-and-pencil measures, teacher–student dialogues, and ethnographic research. The most common were the paper-and-pencil measures, in which students were asked about a predetermined domain of interest such as teacher performance (Benninga, Guskey, & Thornburg, 1981; Meighan, 1978), teachers use of power in the classroom (McCreskey & Richmond, 1982); teacher competencies (Vollmer, Creek, & Vollmer, 1990), and teacher communication and effectiveness (Scott & Nussbaum, 1981). These domains and the questions asked were often preselected by educators or researchers, leaving little room for students to determine more salient dimensions for evaluating their teachers and schooling experiences.

Teacher–student dialogues offered greater flexibility for students to mediate and interpret relevant topics than the paper-and-pencil measures. This method, however, placed a greater emphasis on surface language (what the students said) to the exclusion of students' social and cultural linguistic expressions (Walsh, 1987). Teachers who differed from their students' social and cultural realities were often vulnerable to this tendency. In order for teacher–student dialogues to be effective in eliciting Latino and other ethnolinguistic students' perceptions, sensitivity and trust need to be established between students and teachers (Mercado, 1993).

Ethnographic research also provided the opportunity for students to voice their perceptions about their schooling experiences. Student perceptions about their thoughts, attitudes, and beliefs about schooling were elicited through individual and group interviews. In contrast to the paper-and-pencil measure, the ethnographic interview allows for students to respond to open questions about their personal experiences in U.S. schools, their classroom environments, curriculum, pedagogy, and other factors associated with school success and failure. Collaborative ethnographic research projects between teachers and students, in which students actively engaged in determining the focus of research and the methods of data collection and analysis, allowed for students to have a greater voice about their educational concerns (Mercado, 1993).

The data used in this chapter was collected as part of a larger ethnographic study that focused on how teachers defined and created empowering environments for their students throughout the curriculum, school policies, and the relationships they established with their students. Field notes of our conversations and observations are used within. Our main focus, however, is on two specific events that called our attention to what students had to say about their educational experience and specifically about teaching: a student strike with follow-up interviews, and a film viewing.

The Student Strike.   The students' concerns about teaching were first manifested during a student strike that occurred toward the end of the fall, the first year of our study. The master teacher was concerned about a high level of student absenteeism and other unacceptable behaviors of students and subsequently changed the schedule of classes. Students protested the change in schedule by declaring a walkout and a strike. The researchers, which included the two authors, were in the school on that particular day in December. One of the authors quickly integrated herself with the students by asking the students if she could sit in during their meetings. She was granted the role of observer. The other author sat in the meetings of the teachers as they processed the student strike.

Follow-up interviews were conducted during the winter months when the researchers asked students to reconstruct the events leading up to the strike, the significance of the strike and the outcomes, and what they thought about teachers and teaching. In these follow-up interviews, the students were asked to talk about their educational experiences at Esperanza and in other schools and how they defined good teaching.

The Film-Viewing   The second event was designed collaboratively by the researchers, teachers, and students. It was an open-ended dialogue about good teaching between the researchers, one of the teachers, and a group of eight students, immediately following the viewing of the film *Stand & Deliver*. Because the storyline of the movie was about the efforts of a brave, effective teacher by the name of Jaime Escalante, we all felt that an open-ended discussion about the film and the thoughts it provoked would be a good way to get at students' perception of good teaching. We based our premise on the fact that since the strike the students were active participants in determining our research focus. We had listened to them, talked with them, helped them think through school tasks and sharpen their presentation skills, and offered a supportive ear.

The events of the student strike and the film viewing revealed many of the Esperanza High School students' thoughts about good teaching. As Mercado (1993) proposed, when students were involved in determining the direction of what researchers attend to, the results were a broadening of opportunities for students to voice their many concerns and to be heard. When given the opportunity to share their perceptions about their schooling experiences, students had much to say and their voice was a powerful way to learn about school and classroom practices.

Student Voices at Esperanza High School

Causes of the Student Strike.   In early December, during the fall semester of the second academic year of school, the master teacher made a decision to change the school schedule. This decision was the direct consequence of a meeting between the administrators of the community-based organization and the teaching staff of Esperanza to address the growing concerns over student tardiness, alleged drug use, and absenteeism. Just a few days prior, a decision was also made to combine the three classes in the gym. The master teacher announced to the students that their school day would be extended. It was this change in the schedule that became the catalyst for the student strike.

One of the Puerto Rican student leaders, Victoria, offered her explanation of the underlying conflict precipitating the students' decision to strike:

> *Victoria:* So, we decided, let's make a strike because it can't always be like that.... Isabel (master teacher) can't be bossing us around.... You know, like, we gotta do what they wanna do. Because we wanna do what we feel comfortable with. So, Isabel started saying that, no if y'all don't like it, well that's too bad. So we said, hold up, we're gonna have to win this case.... Like the teachers have to be more comfortable with the students so that we could talk and communicate with each other.[2]
>
> *Interviewer:* So it wasn't just about the time, it sounds like it was about the teachers' attitudes.
>
> *Victoria:* It was ... about everybody's attitude, and hanging out. That is why Isabel changed the schedule, because everybody was hanging out. They'd seen a couple of people in the park and cutting out of school. So we had made a promise that we wasn't gonna cut out if she changed the schedule. I was talking to everybody, so we all went to the front and we all started saying we want a strike.

The importance of the quality of student–teacher relationships emerged as a salient issue in the schooling experience of the students at Esperanza High. They expressed a desire for open communication between the students and teachers and perceived the action taken by the master teacher to change the school schedule without engaging the students in discussion as a breach in communication.

---

[2] The quotations are as close as possible to what was said. Some of the background noise associated with oral speech events (the uhm, the you knows, etc.) were deleted.

Inside the Student Meeting During the Strike.   Following their declaration of a strike, the students were asked by the teachers to clarify their issues. The students met in one of the classrooms to discuss their concerns. The following is a summary of the fieldnotes kept by the researcher who was granted permission to observe the student meeting.

The students were in the room. Victoria, one of the student leaders, was standing up. She held a pink sheet of paper in her hand and was writing down what the students had to say. She opened up the student discussion by focusing on the issue of alcohol and drug abuse and exhorted her classmates to take responsibility for their actions, "You were drinking your 40s in the park, you know who you are." Several students expressed hurt over being falsely accused. Victoria encouraged them to speak up and let the adults know that they should be careful in making assumptions about the students.

The discussion turned to absenteeism and morning tardiness. One of the students talked about how he experienced the teacher's approach to his lateness as disrespectful. Victoria intervened by letting the student know that she felt he was wrong during an incident that occurred between him and the teacher a few days prior. No one elaborated further about this incident nor did anyone offer any explanations. The importance of this interaction was the acknowledgment by Victoria that the students were not always right.

They shifted to a discussion of academics and teaching. An issue they talked about at great length was the absence of connection between the curriculum and their preparation for the GED. They also expressed surprise over the inconsistency in teaching. A student elaborated further by talking about how one of the teachers would get excited about the topic and then deviate to another midstream.

Finally, the discussion centered on how teachers sometimes disrespected the students by not permitting them to speak and how the teachers often misunderstood them. They concluded with a list of items they wanted to address with the teachers:

- the curriculum, graduation, and passing the GED;
- student participation in classroom decision-making process;
- the school governance structure and their representation; and
- objections in the areas of scheduling, grouping, and discipline.

Victoria asked all the students present at the meeting to sign the list. As they signed, they acknowledged the historical importance of their actions with a solidarity slogan in Spanish. After all, they had staged the first student strike in their barrio. They also proposed that the entire community of teachers and students was to be held accountable and that the conflict was everyone's to solve. This was made poignantly visible when Xavier, one of the teachers, approached the classroom where the students were meeting. He addressed Victoria, "Should I wait outside?" She responded without hesitation, expressing surprise and annoyance. "You are making a division between you and us. Hey man, what's the matter? *Tu eres familia* [You are family]. Stay seated." Shortly after this incident, Isabel, the master teacher, came into the classroom, and they began a school dialogue. Ray, who was the local school agency-appointed teacher, remained distant from the process.

The strike was a powerful mechanism for the students to voice their concerns about their schooling experience. Under other circumstances the student strike could have been construed as a highly antagonistic and conflictive situation. This, however, was not the case for the students organized the strike in a caring way. They stayed within the ethos of caring and empowerment created by the school personnel and the community-based organization and within the parameters of the teacher–student relationship they were familiar with at Esperanza High, that of family:

> *Aida:* Thank God everything came out O.K. because not everybody could have a strike like we did. Like hitting teachers. Because I heard of strikes that they be hitting teachers and treating them wrong. We treated them right; you know what I'm saying? We treated them real good and we just told them. "Excuse us. Get out of the room. We wanna talk it out because we don't have this and that." And Isabel was proud, you know? The teachers and staff, they were all proud about it because they know we did it right. If it was somebody else, "Oh, let's hand out, let's get some bats, let's beat them down" you know. We're talking like human beings.

The results of the student strike were positive for all. The school schedule prior to the strike was reinstituted and the three classes were no longer held in a one-room location. As the following excerpt of a staff interview following the strike indicated, the students experienced an immediate victory, and the strike came to be perceived by all concerned as one of the student body's most powerful actions.

> It kicked the whole ass of Esperanza. Everything happened from then on … everything went into motion … we realized we have to get organized, we realized we have to start meeting, we realized a whole bunch of things and we really started acting on it … everyone became aware that this alternative school is a big issue. (Excerpt from Esperanza staff interview)

Students, teachers, staff, and administrators began to reassess the needs of the school and to work on student contracts, governance structures, and leadership in a different way.

The students' decision to strike was an act of empowerment that allowed for caring to be demonstrated by the students for each other and for the school. When asked how they came to the idea of a strike, they spoke about a valuable lesson they vicariously learned about human rights from the master teacher's experience with a parent takeover of an elementary school: "When you want something, you all get together and agree on it. Go for it until someone listens."

The leaders of the student strike were convinced that the issues of the strike were relevant to the entire school community and therefore took responsibility for their actions in order to create change.

Prior research investigating student voice found that the interaction between teachers and students was essential for student learning (Galbo, 1986). Students who perceived their teachers as caring were more likely to succeed (Latino Commission on Educational Reform, 1992; Straus, 1992). When students were asked to describe characteristics of caring in teachers they reported demonstrated patience, interest in the needs of all students, praise for student efforts and applause for student success, and sensitivity toward the situation and problems of their students (Kramer & Sclosser, 1992; Latino Commission on Educational Reform, 1992). They described a desire for teachers to recognize who they are, to listen to what they have to say, and to respect their efforts (Phelan, Locke, Davidson, & Cao, 1992). Teacher caring was also associated with students' willingness to put more effort in their work (Mercado, 1993). The ethos of caring by teachers was found to be important to student learning (Greene, 1986; Mercado, 1993; Noddings, 1991).

Caring as a Central Value

Within the month following the student strike, two-thirds of the students who were enrolled since the beginning of the school year and were part of the student strike and its aftermath were interviewed by the researchers. Given the reality of the student strike, we assumed that continued dialogue with the students was necessary. Although the students were engaged in dialogues with the teachers around their contracts, we

---

[3]The others were impossible to recuperate due to technical difficulties with the audio of some interviews that were videotaped.

also wanted to get a deeper sense of what was happening independent of our observations.

The following is based on an analysis of 12 of the interviews.[3] The students were allowed to determine the language (English or Spanish) to be spoken in the interviews. When given the opportunity, the students at Esperanza High had much to say about the characteristics of "good" teachers and were quick to launch critiques of teachers who did not meet their standards, both in their past and present schooling experiences.

Caring in the Teacher–Student Relationship. Noddings (1984) stated the following about the relationship of "caring for and being cared for" in the teacher/student relationship. She said:

> Teaching involves two persons in a special relationship. Usually, there is a fairly well defined "something" in which the two engage, but this is not always true. Sometimes teacher and students just explore. They explore something, of course, but this something is not always prespecified; nor need it remain constant or, for that matter, even lead somewhere definite. The essence is in the relationship. In the relationship, the teacher has become a duality; she shares a view of the objects under study with the student. (Noddings, 1984, p. 195)

For the students at Esperanza, their ideal of a good teacher was embodied in the teacher–student relationship. They described good teachers as those who were caring, showed respect, and were supportive of them.

Caring Through Communication. The students gave examples of the caring communication they had with teachers outside the classroom at Esperanza High. Students commented that the master teacher would call their homes to give them their homework assignments, to speak to their parents, or to speak to them about other nonschool related matters.

> *Elizabeth:* She called my house after I gave birth and reminded me that I had to come here.

Students stated that when teachers were accessible, the student/teacher relationship was richer for them.

> *Julia:* It's a good relationship. Like … if anyone have a problem, you can call Isabel at home. You can't call a teacher at home in the

other school. She gives you her phone number; she gives you her address, if you have to talk to her.... If she's not here, like you wanna talk to her and she's sick, and she's not here and you could give her a call and ask her how she's feeling.

Open teacher–student communication gave students a sense of being listened to, understood and cared for. It is what Noddings (1984) explained as being "totally and nonselectively present to the student" (p. 180) or prioritizing "those matters at the heart of human existence" (p. 184).

And if [students] have any problems, they could talk to [the teachers] about them, help us out with problems, 'cause if a student has a problem, it's gonna be that much harder to concentrate on the school work. So, I think if the teacher has a close relationship with the student, he could ... work better with school. (Julia, Interview, lines 1439–1452)

[The teacher] can be a good friend and a good listener when you need one. (Jose, Interview, lines 2021–2022)

Good communication was something students valued. They felt teachers had a role in creating an open environment with students. This sense of teacher control with respect to communication with students also came through in their comparison with other schools:

Angelo: Over there I wasn't able to communicate with the teachers as I do here.
Elizabeth: Everybody's comfortable with one another [here] because it's, you know, I guess teachers sometimes they understand ... how a student feels when they don't feel well.

The students also felt that teachers who showed they really cared for their students' future promoted good communication. They felt that when they were challenged from the base of caring, students responded by doing more than what they would have otherwise.

Juan: The teacher that cares, that will always look out for you.... And teach you very hard.... Like if you don't want to do something, they force you to do it.
Elizabeth: She's pushy and stuff at times, but it's good because sometimes it makes me see what she's talking about

and I'll sit there and do the work. And Xavier, he's
pushy, but he's always telling you, 'Look, if you don't
do this, this and that will happen and you're gonna
need it. In your future you're not gonna know what to
do because you didn't do it.'

Julia: Giving time. Caring means following up and giving students
time. Here [meaning Esperanza High] was different 'cause
here if you really wanted to learn some of the teacher would,
would care, and they would teach you and that's how it ...
kept you from ... going to hang out.

When students perceived their teachers as not caring, this created disin-
centives for them. One student spoke about an experience in a zoned high
school he attended.

Julia: It's like (brief pause) they ... really don't care. It's like they
just give you the work and whether you do it ... or not it's the
same with them. They don't really care.

Research findings provided support for the importance of demonstrated caring through open teacher–student communication as voiced
by the students at Esperanza high school. Students in prior research studies also voiced a desire for open communication with their teachers and to
view their teachers as having thoughts, feelings, and experiences that en-
livened and went beyond the academic content of the classroom (Phelan
et al., 1992). Humor and openness were perceived by students as helping
to bridge the age and status barriers between teachers and students and
helping build relationship (Phelan et al., 1992). Latino high school students identified a need for more caring teachers that engaged in fam-
ily-like relationships with their students (Darder & Upshur, 1993).
Underachieving students also expressed their need for direct and personal
interactions with their teachers, and explicit statements affirming their
value and self-worth and that demonstrated they were liked personally
by their teachers (Phelan et al., 1992). Teacher caring through communication was found to legitimize the personal concerns of the underachiever
and to help them to refocus their energies on long-term goals, such as high
school graduation. Similarly, adolescents from culturally diverse backgrounds, identified as at-risk for dropping out, described good teachers as
those who were aware of their students and inquired if they were in trouble; included in classroom discussions topics of interest to students; made
themselves available after class; and listened to students without pre-
judging them (Schlosser, 1992).

Caring as Demonstrated in the Valuing of Language and Culture. Another aspect of caring that students identified as a characteristic of a good teacher was the teacher's value of the students' language and culture and their efforts to bridge the differences. A student conveyed this as she compared her previous school with Esperanza High.

> *Julia:* This is a Spanish-speaking community, and over there [previous school] ... those teachers are not from here. They live somewhere else and then they just come here, and they don't care. They are like, "So what if you speak Spanish." And they don't care.... They're not Spanish, you know. They don't care if we learn how to speak Spanish and how to write it, and our culture, or what happened, or about the slavery in Puerto Rico, all that.

Although the goals of Esperanza High embodied bilingualism, the native language component of the program was not structurally designed. The two Spanish-speaking teachers were able to use English and Spanish as necessary to assist students with understanding the subject or message. Students commented not so much about language use, but moreso on symbolism. When Spanish was heard, the students felt respected.

> *Jose:* Well, here, Isabel talks a lot of Spanish. Xavier tries. He tries.

And, caring was related to respect for diversity.

> *Jose:* Yeah ... here you don't discriminate. At least in that point of view, everybody is the same.

Esperanza students were not alone in their expressed desire for the inclusion of their culture and language in the curriculum. High school students across racial and ethnic backgrounds also voiced their need for the inclusion of their native language in the curriculum and for their teachers to learn about their culture and acknowledge the difficulties they encountered adapting to a new culture and learning English as a second language (Nieto, 1994). Similarly, Latino students from other high schools also voiced their need for the integration of Latin American culture in the curriculum as a way to mediate their strong sense of marginalization and exclusion by their teachers and non-Latino peers (Darder & Upshur, 1993).

Caring as Receptivity. Esperanza high school students were clear in their desire for their teachers to maintain the authority associated with being a teacher. They were also certain of the importance of a mutual relationship with their teachers or what Noddings (1984) called "receptivity," where each is caring and respectful and can live with the others' strengths and weakness. Noddings stated: "It is not primarily happiness in either the sense of fulfilling pleasure or avoiding pain or trouble.... The primary aim is ... [caring and being cared for], despite pain, deprivation, and trouble—filled at least occasionally with joy, wonder engagement, and tenderness" (p. 174). Understanding this receptivity, living with strengths and weaknesses came forth in the students' comments about their teacher, Isabel. They did not refrain from criticizing her and the other teachers at Esperanza High when they felt it was necessary. The issue of receptivity was embedded in their reason for striking.

> *Juan:* Sometimes we're in class and Isabel, like she comes in a bad mood. She takes it out on us.... And then that's pissing us off. Hmmm. Then we don't give a fuck.
> *Julia:* Some of the bad things have been because of Isabel's moods.

They were also able to appreciate the importance of Isabel as a role model and for establishing real relationships with them. They considered her a friend.

> *Interviewer:* So how did you learn to negotiate that way?
> *Elizabeth:* Isabel taught us ... she was talking about striking ... it was what she said. When you want something, you all get together and agree on it and go for it until someone listens.

They also perceived her and the other teachers at Esperanza as trustworthy.

> *Gabriela:* Los maestros son siempre maestros, claro. Pero quizás porque aquí la, eh, la clase es muy pequeña, hay más comprensión, más confianza, más ayuda, y eso. Entonces aqui lo que más me gusta de aqui es que se comparten los problemas de cada uno, que sea de un maestro o sea un alumno se comparte todo, y se discute todo en cualquier tema que sea. (Teachers are teachers. But perhaps because of the small class, here you find more understanding, more confidence, more help. What I like best about this school is the sharing, be it a teacher problem or that of a student. Anything can be discussed).

Esperanza students' desire for teachers to show caring through receptivity is supported by the findings in the literature. When students were asked for their perceptions about teaching they indicated a desire for teachers to assume power and control over students (Kramer & Scholosser, 1992; Sheets, 1994). They also expressed a need for teachers to decrease the mechanisms by which teachers tended to demonstrate overt control. They offered as examples intervening less and trusting them to do the work (Mercado, 1993), being treated in an equitable manner (Galbo, 1986), and providing continuous encouragement and assistance with improving their understanding of the subject matter. Students also voiced the need for adults to negotiate with the students acceptable standards of behavior (Phelan et al., 1992).

Good Teaching

The students at Esperanza High wanted teachers who were knowledgeable about the subject matter and their students, demonstrated effective pedagogy, and teaching methods, and encouraged them as students. They identified a good teacher as one who was knowledgeable of subject matter and of his or her students.

> *Jose:* Well, he knows, he has to know what kind of work he can assign you 'cause he has to know whether or not you're capable of doing it.

A good teacher was someone who would help students comprehend the work and was patient with them. He or she would be available to them to review the material and help them do the work.

> *Jose:*   Somebody who will explain the lesson as many times as necessary for you to understand them.
>
> *Elizabeth:*   And Xavier, if I don't understand something, he'll sit there and he'll explain to me until I get it. And, he'll take his time. He has patience.

One student spoke about the challenges that a good teacher presents to his or her students. She described what Noddings (1984) spoke about when she said:

> The one-caring teacher is not necessarily permissive. She does not abstain ... from leading the student, or persuading him, or coaxing him toward an

examination of school subjects. But she recognizes that, in the long run, he will learn what he pleases. We may force him to respond in specified ways, but what he will make his own and eventually apply effectively is that which he finds significant for his own life. This recognition does not reduce either the teacher's power or her responsibility.... The teacher's power is, thus, awesome. It is she who presents the "effective world" to the student. (p. 176)

Aida appreciated her teacher for placing her in a natural language learning situation that forced her to speak English as a second language, something she really wanted.

> *Aida:* De los maestros ... hay veces que me ponen en el frente para atender al teléfono y muchas de las llamadas son en inglés, entonces esto me ayuda bastante. [The teachers put me up front to answer the phone and there are many calls of people speaking English. This helps me a lot.]

With respect to sensitivity to second language learning, it was not so much the methodology of second language learning, but that the teachers gave them meaningful opportunities for engaging in second language use.

Good teachers were also those who also believed in the students and their potential. Students viewed as important teachers encouraging them to think about their future.

> *Jose:* She encourages me because of want, I want, of going to college and everything, And she's like, always like, 'where you wanna go?'

Esperanza students' conceptualization of good teaching was similar to those of other students. Researchers found that students in general wanted teachers who demonstrated effective pedagogy, knowledge of subject matter, and used effective teaching methods (Heroman, 1990; Samuels & Giffiore, 1980). They reported preferences for instruction that were active and transactional (Phelan et al., 1992). They perceived teaching methods in most classrooms as emphasizing teacher-centered models of learning with role learning generally favored over creativity and critical thinking (Nieto, 1994). Students preferred a variety of dynamic pedagogical methods that encouraged active student participation. Good teachers were described as those who were able to make course content comprehensible and that could discuss a subject from alternative points of view and were critical of teachers whom they perceived as weak in knowledge of subject matter (Darder & Upshur, 1992).

The student strike served as an important data source for making visible the voices of the students at Esperanza High School. When given the opportunity, they had much to say about their schooling experience at Esperanza and their ideas about effective teaching. Clearly, caring emerged as a central theme and was seen as manifested in the teacher–student relationship. Caring was conveyed by both teacher and student through the process of open and honest communication in and outside of the classroom. Good communication between teacher and student was perceived as related to academic success and failure. Caring was also demonstrated by the inclusion of Spanish language and Latino cultures in the curriculum while encouraging students to learn English as a second language. Receptivity, or a caring and respect for each other's strengths and weaknesses was also important. Good teaching emerged as important to the schooling of Esperanza students and was identified as effective pedagogy, knowledge of course content, and encouragement of students. These findings also emerged as central themes, but in a different way when we viewed the movie, *Stand & Deliver*.

Stand & Deliver: The Relationship Between Caring and Other School Tasks

In April, toward the end of the first year of our ethnographic study, we viewed, with one teacher and a group of students, the film *Stand & Deliver*. After the viewing, we walked to the college with which the researchers were affiliated, located a few blocks away from the theatre.

Although Noddings (1984) and the Latino Commission on Educational Reform (1992) proposed that teacher caring superseded teacher knowledge of content domain as essential to student learning, the students seem to make a connection between both caring and content knowledge that suggests a more intimate relation between the two. They also connected these aspects to how a good teacher communicates respect.

One of the researchers started asking a probing open-end question when a student assertively took the floor.

Iliana: Yo lo que pensé fue que deberían de llevar a Ray para que viera la película ... [laughter from the group]. No, no, no, que el viera de una manera que el pueda enseñar, porque el no enseña. El no enseña. El no sabe enseñar y siempre esta relajando y no sabe enseñar. No sabe dar clases, nada. (What I thought was that you should take Ray to see this movie ... [Laughter]. No, no, no, so that he could see one way he could teach, because he does not teach. He does not teach. He doesn't know how to teach, he is always fooling around , and he doesn't know how to teach. He does not know how to give classes, nothing).

One after the other, the students launched their complaints about this teacher. He was appointed by the local educational agency and was the only non-Latino (Anglo) teacher at the school. He was the teacher that had remained distant during the strike. The students described him as delighting in "getting one over on them" and reminding them of how little they knew. According to the students, he lacked the sensitivity to issues of second language learning and the different ways of knowing. Some students said they sometimes knew the content but could not demonstrate it in English. He, in turn, did not know Spanish. He sometimes told them that although they had gotten the right answers, they were not acceptable because the procedure was not "the right way." The students' concluded that the teacher did not have sufficient content knowledge or cultural sensitivity to perceive their answers as acceptable or to explain to them how his methods differed from theirs. He was the opposite of the Jaime Escalante, the Latino teacher portrayed on the screen. The students strongly felt that Ray did not respect their intelligence or their ability to learn or to see things differently. This perception was significant because it illustrated the relationship between pedagogy, the content knowledge of the teacher, and the teacher–student relationships, and student learning. The way in which these factors interact together in the classroom communicated a lack of caring and respect to the students.

This initial discussion led to more talk about teaching–what the researchers had hoped. In the dialogue, one of the researchers asked for the students' expectations of their teachers. Their first response pertained to content knowledge.

Alfredo: They're supposed to know what they're showing us.
Researcher: Right.
Iliana: The minimum.

They moved to talk about one of the teachers who they felt had shown respect.

Hector: Que hace como Xavier. Cuando Xavier nos da estudios sociales y nosotros no entendemos algo, y nos los da, y nos los da [other students join in chorus] y nos los da, y nos los da, hasta que nos cansamos [laughter]. [It's like Xavier, when Xavier is teaching social studies and we don't understand something, he gives it to us, and gives it to us (students join in), and gives it to us, and gives it to us, until we are tired (laughter)].

Iliana: Y lo da, hasta que lo aprendemos. Esto hace un buen maestro [And he reinforces it, until we learn. This is what makes a good teacher.]

Hector: Entonces nos dedica mucho tiempo también [He dedicates a lot of time to us].

Iliana: El se asegura que nosotros aprendemos de lo que no entendemos primero. [He makes sure that we learn what we don't understand the first time he gives it.]

The students did not attribute everything to the teacher. They acknowledged their own lack of attention to school tasks. They reflected on the interactive nature of teaching by using the concept of *ganas* [desire], a term taken from the film.

Pilar: One thing I learned was having the desire, because it's not just the teacher having the desire. But suppose that you were the teacher and you have the desire and all the students, and we [meaning the students] don't care, we don't want to learn?

He went on to speak about the role of the teacher's patience and belief in students.

Pilar: Look, he [Escalante] tried to bring it out. And when he started to get results, then he knew they had *ganas.* If you [the teacher] would have not tried, [if the teacher] look at them and look and just by the expression on their face and say these people don't want to learn and don't bother teaching them, then you would never really know if they had the desire to learn. So, he [Escalante] tried first. And he seemed to be able to get a response. It keeps on going.

In analyzing what the students had to say, we realized that most of the topics that emerged after the film viewing were not new; they were part of our conversations throughout the year (i.e., what students said in their interviews about the importance of caring was echoed in this discussion). There were, however, two differences: the students spoke about teachers more directly (with names attached to critiques or praise) and they spoke using a collective language. Their experiences with the strike and negotiating the contracts and the film offered the students a new language (i.e., ganas) and new images (i.e., Escalante) to talk about the issues of teaching and instruction.

These differences can be explained in various ways. Because the film viewing was toward the end of the academic year, it would be reasonable to make the argument that the joint planning of the film influenced what they had to say and how they said it. It reflected the relationship they had with us. We were regularly at the school, we participated in a variety of school events, and we helped the teachers and the students prepare for public presentations in conferences. In other words, we built enough trust for them to feel more comfortable in talking with us as researchers and with their teachers. The mutuality and bidirectionality of the relationship was embodied in this event.

Another possible explanation is that the difference in the way they said what they did after viewing the film was a reflection of their personal growth and development. They become more confident and sophisticated in how they expressed themselves throughout the year, reflecting a degree of empowerment of voice.

By studying students in action (the strike) and engaging them in meaningful dialogue (through the interviews and after the film viewing) about their schooling, we were able to capture what they had to say in a robust way and gained a deeper understanding of what they believed good teaching entailed. The students had set the tone of the conversation with the strike in the fall. It was a critical conversation that they invited the adults to have with them. The researchers engaged in the conversation as much as the teachers. We were both participants in and observers of their development. We participated by creating spaces for their conversations (interviews, group conversations, etc.) and by encouraging teachers to continue with the intellectual and governance structures that would create the conditions for student empowerment. As observers, we were able to provide on-going feedback and periodically highlight the reoccurrence of themes throughout the year.

We found that the voices of Esperanza High students did not differ dramatically from the perspectives of other American students documented in the literature. Esperanza students wanted caring relationships with their teachers that were characterized by open communication and time. They also desired teacher–student relationships that were trustworthy and human. The students required of their teachers to be caring and to possess pedagogical competence and knowledge of content areas. All three, in their view, were vital to their ability to assume the role of students as learners. The students at Esperanza differed from non-Latino in their value and pride in their language and culture and status as second language learners. They expressed a need for Latino culture and the Spanish language to be integrated in the school curriculum.

We also found that although the topics throughout the year were on going and recurring, a difference was noted in the posture and language of students. The students of Esperanza High eventually named the teachers and described their teaching competence. And, there was a sense of collectivity in what they said and how they said it.

REFERENCES

Benninga, J. S., Guskey, T. R., & Thornburg, K. R. (1981). The relationship between teacher attitudes and student perceptions of classroom climate. *Elementary School Journal, 82,* 66–75.

Darder, A., & Upshur, C. (1993). What do Latino children need to succeed in school? A study of four Boston public schools. In R. Rivera & S. Nieto (Eds.), *The education of Latino students in Massachusetts: Issues, research, and policy implications* (pp. 127–146). Boston: Gastón Institute for Public Policy and Development.

Fine, M. (1991). *Framing dropouts: Notes on the politics of an urban public school.* Albany: State University of New York Press.

Galbo, J. J. (1986, March). *The teacher of adolescents as significant adult.* Paper presented at the First Biennial Conference of the Society for Research on Adolescence, Madison, WI.

Greene, M. (1986). In search of a critical pedagogy. *Harvard Educational Review, 54,* 427–441.

Heroman, D. S., (1990, April). *Student perceptions of the learning environment assessments of teacher performance and student learning.* Paper presented at the annual meeting of the American Educational Research Association, Boston, MA.

Latino Commission on Educational Reform. (1992). *Toward a vision for the education of Latino students: Community voices, student voices* (Interim Report). New York: Columbia University.

McCreskey, J. C., & Richmond, V. P. (1982, May). *Power in the classroom: Teacher and student perceptions.* Paper presented at the annual meeting of the Eastern Communication Association, Hartford, CT.

Meighan, R. (1978). A pupil's eye view of teaching performance. *Educational Review, 30,* 129–137.

Mercado, C. (1993). Caring as empowerment: School collaboration and community agency. *The Urban Review, 25,* 79–104.

Mitchell, V. (1991). African-American students in exemplary urban high schools: The interaction of school practices and student actions. In M. Saravia Shore & S. Alvizu (Eds.), *Cross cultural literacy: Ethnographies of communication in multiethnic classrooms* (pp. 19–35). New York: Garland.

Nieto, S. (1994). Lessons from students on creating a chance to dream. *Harvard Educational Review, 64,* 392–426.

Noddings, N. (1984). *Caring: A feminist approach to ethics & moral education.* Berkeley, CA: University of California Press.

Noddings, N. (1991). Caring and continuity in education. *Scandinavian Journal of Educational Research, 35,* 3–12.

Phelan, P., Locke Davidson, A., & Cao, H. T. (1992). Speaking up: Students' perspectives on school. *Phi Delta Kappan, 73,* 695–704.

Samuels, D. D., & Giffore, R. J. (1980). Students' perceptions of the characteristics of "good teachers." *Journal of Instructional Psychology, 7,* 28–34.

Scott, M. D., & Nussbaum, J. F. (1981). Student perceptions of instructor communication behaviors and their relationships to student evaluation. *Communication Education, 30,* 11–53.

Schlosser, L. K. (1992) Teacher distance and student disengagement: School lives on the margin. *Journal of Instructional Psychology, 43,* 128–140.

Sheets, R. (1994). *Discipline: Chicano students' perceptions. Ethnic integrity or dysfunctional behavior?* ERIC Document 389361.

Straus, I. W. (1992, April). *Restructuring school practice through students' voices.* Paper presented at the annual meeting of the American Educational Research Association, San Francisco, CA.

Torres-Guzmán, M. (1989). *El Puente/Teachers College Collaborative Research Project: Final Report.* Washington, DC: Hispanic Policy Development Project.

Torres-Guzmán, M. (1991). Stories of hope in the midst of despair: Culturally responsive education for Latino students in an alternative high school in New York City. In M. Saravia Shore & S. Alvizu (Eds.), *Cross cultural literacy: Ethnographies of communication in multiethnic classrooms.* New York: Garland.

Vollmer, M. L., Creek, R. J., & Vollmer, R. R. (1990). *Student perceptions of teaching competencies.* Paper presented at the annual meeting of the American Association of Colleges for Teacher Education, Chicago, IL.

Walsh, C. (1987). Language, meaning, and voice: Puerto Rican students' struggle for a speaking consciousness. *Language Arts, 64,* 6–15.

Walter, E. M. (1987). Schooling and minority adolescents' mobility goals: A casual model. *Journal of Educational Equity and Leadership, 7,* 109–128.

Weinstein, R. S. (1982). An editorial statement. *The Elementary School Journal, 82,* 397–398.

Teachers Who Made a Difference

Elizabeth Capifali

My first recollection of school dates back to the early 1950s in the South Bronx when I entered first grade at P.S. 25. I never attended kindergarten, and I went to school speaking only Spanish. My first grade teacher was kind and gentle, but this did not deter me from running away from school shortly after the first day. Although home was a good five blocks away I ran back there as fast as I could. I recall my concentration on getting home, a place where I wasn't a stranger, a place where safety awaited me. I arrived home scared and crying. We didn't lock our doors so I quietly went into the house and hid behind the door. My abuelita (grandmother) heard my whimpering and discovered me. For the next 2 weeks, my mother left her job to accompany me to school every day. It was the only way I would return to school. It was comforting to be able to look to the back of the room and see my mother there.

Not only was my mother asked to stay with me in school, but she was also asked to speak to me in English only. My mother was Filipino and my father was Puerto Rican. We lived with my father's mother, and at home we spoke to one another only in Spanish. Unfortunately, speaking Spanish was seen as a deficit and not as a resource in the school system. I quickly learned to speak English, and my phobia of school diminished. My first-grade teacher was a passionate teacher. I remember her excitement every time a student learned a new fact or a new word or simply recited the alphabet. Learning became infectious and it was rewarded with cheers, not only from the teacher but from the other students as well. Because Miss Goldstein treated us like individuals, I was able to adjust and flourish in that environment.

Miss Davis, my seventh-grade English teacher, was gentle in her manner but firm in fostering the importance of a good education for all of us, although the makeup of the class was 95% Puerto Rican and 5% Euro-American. She would tell us the importance of understanding and enjoying literature. Words became alive in her class because she was able to relate, for example, Homer's "Odyssey" to our lives. She engaged us in our learning, and we wanted to learn more. There was no room for us to fool around or do poorly. It was expected that we would be successful, and we were. This was not a coincidence, because Miss Davis used her energy and belief in us as a conduit for our accomplishments. I felt so special in her class although I really had to work hard in order to understand and achieve the goals she set for us.

Her engagement in our education had a ripple effect on me because I was able to enter other classes and have the same expectations for myself in other subjects. She planted that seed within us that told us that we were special and intelligent and that we had the capacity to do exceptional work. It is probably no accident that most of my peers did go on to college and that we have been successful.

In 1975 I went back to visit Miss Davis. I didn't know if she would remember me because it had been 18 years since I had been in her class. Why did I go to see her? She was often in my mind because now that I too was a teacher, I looked back at the high expectations she had for us. Miss Davis did indeed remember me; she was even able to tell me where I sat. I was amazed and pleasantly surprised. She was not surprised that I became a teacher; she expected us to do well. I remember and treasure that visit to see Miss Davis as much as I treasure the year I spent in her English class.

Both Miss Goldstein and Miss Davis acknowledged my presence and set high standards for me. The result was success in their classes. These two situations describe what success can be. Many students are not as fortunate as I was to have had such supportive teachers in my formative years.

What is the common thread that weaves throughout Miss Goldstein's and Miss Davis' teaching? It is their belief that every student is important, and the responsibility they felt to create an environment where students can flourish and bloom into their own fields of genius. Teachers have the potential to be catalysts for many success stories. Would I have succeeded in school without the support of Miss Goldstein and Miss Davis? I probably would have because of my parents, but with the support of these teachers, school became a place where curiosity was encouraged, where learning was presented as a challenge, and where discovery was the prize that kept you going.

These two teachers stand out in my mind as stars that provided a light for my journey as a student. But still I have asked myself, what was missing from my education? I sometimes wonder what would have happened if I had had Puerto Ricans as teachers earlier in my education. From first grade through high school, I never had a teacher who was Puerto Rican. That is quite significant for me, because it wasn't until my late 40s that I had a Puerto Rican professor. The analogy I can use to explain how I felt after I was exposed to a teacher from my own culture is that of a car that is finally aligned and drives smoothly and straight ahead. My sense of loss, only made apparent after being exposed to someone who is Puerto Rican, was heightened, and the experience catapulted me into wanting to connect more with the Puerto Rican culture. I have a clearer understanding of who I am and of the richness of my culture and language. Reflecting back on my experiences, I can truly say that my education was misaligned and I was not cognizant of the incongruences between how I felt as a student and how I perceived myself in this society.

Having a Puerto Rican teacher was fulfilling for me and it has made an indelible mark on my educational experience. I wish that every child could have role models from their own culture, teachers who affirm their language and traditions and who understand firsthand the experiences unique to that child. I treasure all of my good teachers, including Miss Davis and Miss Goldstein. But I also feel that something was missing in my early education because it can be so meaningful to have teachers who look like us, come from our culture, and speak our language.

12

Student Agency Through Collaborative Research in Puerto Rican Communities

Carmen I. Mercado
Luis C. Moll

As a collective, Puerto Ricans have the highest poverty rate, lowest household incomes, and lowest labor force participation of all Latino groups in the United States. Few educators are aware of this stark reality. This lack of awareness has been documented by those within the community (Mercado & Moll, 1997) and by those outside of it (Bigler, 1997). Over the past 20 years, conditions have worsened as a result of a changing economy, the loss of manufacturing jobs to cheaper labor markets, and a changing social policy (Cordero-Guzmán, 1996). Bonilla (1985) suggested that the poverty afflicting the Puerto Rican community, with its attendant effects on health, housing, and education, results primarily from the lack of living wages. These conditions shape and constrain the lives of children and youth just as family status and the characteristics of ethnic communities influence students' school experiences and educational attainment (Portes & MacLeod, 1996).

The lack of knowledge about the collective experience of Puerto Ricans and their mode of incorporation into the host society (Portes & Rumbaut, 1996) has resulted in distortions and misrepresentations concerning the lower social, economic, and educational status of members of this group in the United States. One pervasive belief is that the low status of Puerto Ricans results from an unwillingness to work and a deliberate refusal to learn English. Unfortunately, mainstream social science research has helped to perpetuate this belief (see, e.g., Chávez, 1990), which the media (Pérez, 1990; Vázquez, 1990) and schools (Walsh, 1991) continue to reinforce. This is an issue of special urgency, as the beliefs students have about themselves are part of their identity, mediating their activities and relationships with others. Thus the beliefs exert powerful influences on students' learning and development (Salazar, 1989).

Given these conditions, teachers and students need to develop new representations of their school's community that reflect the strengths and resources of its residents, as well as the strategies and knowledge that help families survive even under very difficult financial conditions. These representations counter negative perceptions and erroneous beliefs about the abilities of the students or the communities in which they reside. Two illustrative cases show that a change in representation can be facilitated by the active engagement of teachers and students in research within their communities.

In the first example, bilingual teachers, predominantly first- and second-generation Puerto Rican women who were reared in El Barrio (East Harlem in New York City), and now are teaching there, engaged in research to learn about cultural resources for learning that are present in students' homes and communities. In the process, they learned about the lives their students actually live (Mercado & Moll, 1997). Although the ultimate goal of these efforts is to use research-generated knowledge to create academically challenging learning environments, far more is involved. In constructing knowledge through collaborative research, teachers confront implicit and unexamined beliefs and assumptions guiding their pedagogical actions, which have consequences for the treatment of Puerto Rican students in schools. When teachers visit students' homes as researchers, they begin to question the pervasive belief that these homes are lacking in cognitive resources for learning or that they are places from which students must be rescued. Complex social and structural forces, such as the difficulty of earning a livable wage, have an impact on family life. Even so, these households have a certain resourcefulness and adaptive strategies for responding to these forces. Through their research experiences, teachers gained a new respect for students' families, new appreciation of how they can contribute to classroom activities, and renewed vigor to work against social and educational inequities.

In the second example, first- and second-generation students of Puerto Rican ancestry attending a low-performing middle school in the Bronx,

New York, apprenticed as educational ethnographers. In this manner, they gained access to forms and social practices of literacy that are central to the knowledge construction process and that constitute cultural capital in our society. Collaborating in the study of their own questions extended students' social networks considerably and allowed them to enter into qualitively different relationships with their families, friends, and individuals from different professional communities.

Weaving back and forth between past, present, and future worlds—the world of the home, the school, and the university—students were provoked to question the conditions of their lives even as they began exploring new social and academic identities. The crossing of physical and psychological borders that these activities required elicit beliefs that students had about who they are and what they are capable of accomplishing in academic contexts. Addressing these beliefs, which affect students' participation and learning, required sensitive mediation. Nonetheless, over time, students' scholarship enabled them to amass evidence that demonstrated to them and to others the high standards of academic excellence that they were capable of accomplishing when the conditions permit.

Youngsters whose academic experiences have been socially constrained harnessed the power of literacy, including familiar and new social practices and communicative resources to understand and improve the conditions of their lives. Schools "don't teach them what they need to learn," in the words of one student-researcher. Students also learned to value the knowledge that resides in their homes and to care about and understand the social problems of their community. In effect, the collaborative research activities featured in this chapter illustrate how research can become an important cultural tool for human and community development, even for those who may have reason to suspect its motives and uses.

BILINGUAL TEACHERS AS RESEARCHERS

Increasingly, over the past 20 years, there is growing awarreness that schools are not the only settings in which children learn. Homes and local communities constitute important contexts for learning. Researchers at the University of Arizona proposed the theory of *funds of knowledge* as a way to think about and describe this learning (see Moll & González, 1997). Specifically, the stock of knowledge and practices that result from a household's activities and experiences are its funds of knowledge. Children acquire specific knowledge and skills through activities with family members and others who form part of the family's social network. However, these funds of knowledge usually remain untapped for learning in school both because teachers may not know they exist and because gaining access to them for teaching requires support. Understanding these funds of knowledge, a form of social capital, and harnessing them as resources for learning in schools is more essential now than ever before given the dramatic shifts in the school-age population that have occurred as a result of immigration.

Teachers in Arizona did precisely that. They participated as research collaborators, developing the theoretical and practical means to identify, locate, and document funds of knowledge that reside in the homes of low-income students of Mexican ancestry (see González et al., 1993; Moll et al., 1992). They also developed the pedagogical implications of this work, important in light of the growing presence of Mexicans in the southwest. In New York City, where the Latino population has grown considerably in the last 10 years, bilingual teachers are engaging in a similar effort (see Mercado & Moll, 1997). Because Puerto Ricans constitute about 50% of the Latino population in New York City, this research is presenting an unusual opportunity to learn about the oldest and largest Latino community, a community about which little is known but much assumed (Zentella, 1997). This is significant because the Puerto Rican community in New York City has been the focus of much social science research, which Puerto Ricans have described as giving an unbalanced emphasis on dysfunctionality of family life (Zentella, 1997).

One unusual exception was *The Puerto Rican Study*, a study that bears some similarity to the study of funds of knowledge. *The Puerto Rican Study* (Morrison, 1958) commissioned 50 years ago by the New York City Board of Education sought, to understand the impact of the mass migration of Puerto Rican families during the late 1940s and early 1950s, primarily from an agrarian economy to a large urban school system. This action-research project found, as we discovered in our research that "there is much in the lived experiences of Puerto Rican students that can be drawn upon profitably for instruction" (p. 61). Perhaps we need to ask why there has been so little progress in educational attainment and socioeconomic status of Puerto Ricans over several generations. However, unlike *The Puerto Rican Study*, the funds of knowledge study engages teachers in field research in the homes of students. Through their efforts, these teacher-researchers contributed to the knowledge base for teaching by broadening our understanding of Latino families living in New York City. The specific purpose here is to highlight some of the dramatic shifts in teachers' thinking that have resulted from the systematic study of Puerto Rican households.

Entering students' homes with the view that culture is the way people live their lives, teacher-researchers were surprised to learn that each household is distinct in composition, living arrangements, and beliefs and practices. There is no typical Puerto Rican household (see Appendix A for a summary of the characteristics of the households we studied). In the process, they confronted the popular view guiding teachers' pedagogical practices: that all members of a group share a normative and an integrated view of their own culture.

Teachers also came face-to-face with the reality that the income of Puerto Rican households we studied falls far below the national and state medians, shockingly evident from the living conditions of many households and their need to supplement incomes through entrepreneurship and public assistance. Teachers found this economic reality most affecting when they first visited students' homes. As these quotes reveal, teachers were jolted by the realization that although they thought they knew where their students came from, actually, they did not. This is true even though many were former residents of El Barrio, where the majority of the households we studied resided.

- "I've often said I know my students' stories because I've been there. Well, I was wrong…. Times have changed and the conditions for many of these children are worse than expected."
- "There exists a poverty I only thought existed in other places in the world, but not in America."
- "Children … live in fear of what could happen to them and their families."

Variability in adaptive processes was also evident as we compare experiences across households. That is, families living under modest and restricted incomes may lead very different lives as a result of the social networks to which these households are connected and the quality and diversity of potential resources for learning that reside in each household (see Appendix B for a summary of the funds of knowledge that have been identified). Consequently, there are differences in the degree and kinds of funds of knowledge that reside in different households. These findings suggest the pitfalls of simplistic and stereotypical characterizations of students' homes and families that obliterate important differences among families. For almost 20 years social scientists affiliated with El Centro de Estudios Puertorriqueños at Hunter College in New York City have argued that Puerto Rican culture is undergoing major transformations that neither the melting pot metaphor nor theories of cultural pluralism adequately capture. Even so, little research has been conducted from this theoretical stance. As Pousada and Greenlee (1988) said:

If we are to frame appropriate research questions and utilize our research findings to formulate policy that reflects the needs and concerns of people upon whom it will impact, then we must face squarely the variable nature of consciousness, social practices, and language patterns that exist in the community. We must find the means by which to incorporate this richly variegated day-to-day existence into generalized statements that in some sense embody the experience of the people we work with, as well as to help them better understand their situation and see ways to improve or change it. (p.16)

Zentella (1997) conducted extensive sociolinguistic research in El Barrio and found that "migration and economic history, gender, race, education, and age-related norms and activities shape each network, and consequently, children's linguistic and cultural development" (p. 39). This may explain why some of the households we studied do not seem to be connected to the extensive and rich social networks that Zentella found and which teachers familiar with the Arizona study expected to find. For now, we can only speculate that the differences may also be due to the limited time teachers spent with the households. In addition, household members seem to be under increased pressure to engage in multiple income-producing activities to earn even a modest income. They seem not to be inclined to solicit the assistance of neighbors as fears of child molestation and abuse intensify or to create additional obligations that are part and parcel of the exchange of favors. As indicated in a previous article (see Mercado & Moll, 1997), this apparent isolation needs to be examined further, particularly as it has implications for shaping the socialization experiences of children.

Nevertheless, broad unifying themes across households reflected a shared history. Teachers also learned a very key point: Within the poverty, there can be an abundance of riches. For one, there is love, the essential emotional support that nurtures and sustains human beings in stressful times and drives the will to survive.

- *"Hay mucho humor y risa que facilmente contagia ... Ita [a pseudonym] hace todo con dulzura y con amor. Sus hijos reflejan lo que ella refleja ... Ita es un guia en la vida de sus hijos aunque ella no lleva una vida tradicional."* ("There is humor and laughter that are contagious ... Ita does everything with tenderness and love. Her children reflect what she reflects ... Ita is a guide in the lives of her children, although she doesn't have a traditional life.")
- "I learned from the García family about love, despair, pain, hope, survival and happiness. Mrs. García is a fighter, a woman of tremendous courage."

There is also "a lot of learning taking place at home." The following examples show how literacy in English and Spanish are interwoven, to a greater or lesser extent, throughout the learning opportunities present in these households. The influence of school-related literacy appeared to be particularly strong in the households we studied. According to some of the teachers,

- "Learning is constantly taking place in Ita's home. She is a collector of antiques, photographs, tools, paintings, books, magazines, people, language and culture. She is a historian and a storyteller."
- "My greatest surprise in this research was not that the family had much to offer, it was that Jacklyn [a pseudonym] had a virtual classroom in her home. With the phonics cards and blackboard and her teaching and management skills.... I feel she adopted the classroom model for home management."
- "Star Leaf [a self-selected pseudonym] has an extensive collection of books in both English and Spanish. This is because her aunt works for Barnes and Noble [a well-known bookstore]. She would depend on Star Leaf's input on whether certain books would be enjoyable for children her age."
- "Mrs. Castillo [a pseudonym] works on academic activities from books but she doesn't seem to know other types of learning that go on in the home.... While I was interviewing her, one of the things that I came to admire about her is the relationship she has with her children.... She acknowledged all their comments and restated them when she was unclear. Throughout the interview, Mrs. Castillo's son answered many questions directly.... You can really tell she talks to her kids."

Admittedly, some teachers needed to look closely to find the funds of knowledge that reside in particular households. This is not always an easy task considering the limitations the teachers imposed on themselves out of respect for the family's time and space.

- "Going through the experience and listening in class ... made me feel something was missing or I was doing something wrong. Everyone was finding and reporting rich experiences and funds of knowledge while I seemed not to be looking at what was probably there. *No podía ver lo que estaba ahí.* [I could not see what was there.]"

As teachers engaged in these activities, their perceptions of students began to change as they interacted with them in their home. That is, teachers came to realize that the view they had of students in the classroom was at best limited and incomplete:

- "I see [Roy] as a family member who has roots and identity.... He's a brand new person in my eyes."
- "I've seen my students go from being a class to individuals in my mind. I try to approach them in this way. As a new teacher this is very difficult, as everyone in the system tries to deal with numbers and categories."
- "I discovered that Ita's children read at home in English and Spanish because the material she provides draws attention, but not in school."

Why are [Ita's] children facing problems in reading?

- "I know that when I look at my students now I wonder what kinds of funds of knowledge I would find in their [homes] and how I can use them in the classroom."
- "Throughout the interview, Mrs. Castillo's son answered the questions directly.... It was ... easier ... to view [his] language competencies in the home setting than in the school."

Furthermore, as home visits gave teachers a better understanding of the members of their classes, teachers developed new concepts of their responsibilities to students.

- "This experience has helped me to learn that although my student has a caring and loving mother, he is not stimulated.... Therefore it is up to me the teacher to provide ... experiences that will motivate."
- "Charles and his siblings all seem hyperactive children, having some difficulty with learning. Through this research, I found that they are very bright children that are lacking some social skills because of the lack of social activities outside the home."

Teachers also expanded the repertoire of pedagogical resources they can use to improve the conditions for learning in school, as these comments revealed:

- "I have learned that I can't pass judgment; I don't know what's happening in the home."
- "Parents seem more like allies now ... I wouldn't think twice about involving the parents in the classroom."

- "Now I see things differently when I walk through my community."
- "The use of funds of knowledge inches its way into my curriculum, at times even unnoticed. Population density, culture, customs, religion, language, technology, and other topics in the students' social studies books became almost mystically intertwined with the funds of knowledge research."
- "I learned from this project by doing. Children learn that way, too."
- "I would like to engage in a similar project with all of my students acting as researchers. I want them to be involved in a community study."
- "In order to help children (overcome) the fears they live with, we cannot dismiss their experience.... We must be willing to validate these experiences and help children find solutions. We also have to be careful that we just don't teach children to ignore a problem and run away from their communities."

The following is perhaps the most significant insight gained from this study: *Knowledge gained through participation in research that involves getting to know students and their families strengthens the teachers' identification with their students.* The teachers gained an increased awareness not only of the commonalities they shared with their students' families but also of the injustices that many of these families continue to experience. Salazar (1989) argued that this kind of awareness is essential to fuel a commitment to work for the betterment of a group. The emotional impact of these experiences on the teacher, who began to see his or her students' homes and families in relation to their own, is evident in these statements:

- "The home reminds me of my home when I was growing up—flower sofas, curtains, plastic covers—tons of family pictures, a lot of plants. It gave me such a warm feeling."
- "My mother's life and [my student's mother's] life are very similar."
- "She was very similar to me."
- "I see my own mother in a different light."
- "I used to think, I made it; why can't they? Now I realize it's more complex."

A current concern among educators is how the teacher education curriculum may be reformed so as to address the needs of diverse learners. Research that engages teachers as researchers is a powerful means of creating educational reform at two levels simultaneously, in public schools and in institutions of higher learning. As this discussion makes clear, the funds of knowledge project illustrates how "to include information concerning students' experiences, culture, how to effectively teach language minority students, and ... how to work with parents" (Nieto & Rolón, 1997, p. 116). Specifically, through guided home visits, teacher-researchers examine beliefs they hold about their students and their students' families. Knowledge about students and students' homes as learning contexts is fundamental to creating quality curriculum and instruction that will increase the likelihood of attaining high standards of academic performance for all students. Most importantly, through these activities, teacher-researchers develop qualitatively new social relationships with their students' homes and families that will support learning in school. We continue to study more intensively and over an extended period of time the impact of these experiences on classroom teaching and student learning.

MIDDLE SCHOOL STUDENTS AS ETHNOGRAPHERS

The middle school represents a critical juncture in the development of a sense of purpose and commitment to educational goals (Schonhaut, 1988); it is also the juncture at which many students "reject schooling" (Solá & Bennett, 1991). This is a serious problem at a time when a college education is essential for economic survival (Reyes, 1994). Both nationally and for the Puerto Rican community in New York City, dropping out is an issue of particular seriousness. In New York City, even conservative estimates indicate that Puerto Rican youth have a disproportionately higher dropout rate in an educational system that has been predominantly minority (36% Latino, 38% African American, and 20% White) for the past 30 years (Reyes, 1994). Puerto Ricans are likely to attend underachieving, segregated schools—possibly the most segregated in the nation (Trueba, 1998)—and by the time they enter high school, if they make it, these youngsters are far behind others in terms of academic achievement (Reyes, 1994).

Even when Puerto Rican students are on grade level, the majority are underprepared to pursue academic studies, given the instructional emphasis on basic skills and remediation (Cole & Griffin, 1987). An immediate means of addressing this situation is to provide rigorous and accelerated preparation in disciplines that will enable youth to become academically competitive in areas that respond to the demands of our society. Research has already documented the pedagogical value of ethnographic research for accelerating the academic preparation of special education and English as a second language (ESL) high school students (Heath, 1985). Through activities with young adolescent students in the Bronx, the borough with the largest concentration of Puerto Ricans in New York City and possibly the nation, we have found that ethnographic research has the same potential for younger learners (see Mercado, 1992, 1998).

The middle school–college partnership that is described in this section was initiated by Carmen (CM) and Marceline Torres (MT), a bilingual teacher in a mainstream program, to understand and address the reading underachievement of students in Marceline's classes. The majority of these students were Latino, predominantly first- and second-generation Puerto Ricans, some of mixed ethnicities and many overage because of retention. Engaging in authentic research gave students access to forms of literacy that constitute cultural capital in our society and consequently, they were unimaginable to these learners. As Bennett (1991) reported, "It is commonplace that literacy is differentially distributed among classes and ethnic groups in U.S. Society" (p. 14).

The outcomes of these efforts are frequently impressive. Students consistently made statistically significant gains on standardized tests of reading, typically within a 7-month period (from September to March). This pleased students because it demonstrated that they could succeed. It also pleased members of the administration of a school at risk of corrective action by the district superintendent and by the State Education Department. However, Marceline and I were more impressed with outcomes that tests cannot measure. Students demonstrated increased confidence to harness the power of literacy to take control of their own development, and to broaden their learning opportunities in and out of school. They were learning to recognize, value, and use the knowledge that resides in their homes, and they were relating to family members in different ways. Also it was evident to us that, over time, students gained self-confidence to participate in academically rigorous activities in unfamiliar settings, which required them to interact with and relate to adults from other professional communities. Most importantly, students who previously had made fun of the homeless developed a serious interest in addressing the ills of society. A number of teachers in the school confirmed these changes, emphasizing students' readiness for learning, meaning that students seemed more inquisitive, alert, and prepared to learn in comparison to others who had not participated in these activities.

Several years after this research experience, we continue to ponder, What was it about these activities that responded to specific needs and concerns affecting the education of Puerto Rican youth? These understandings are especially relevant now that an emphasis on raising performance standards for all students elicits questions about how this may be accomplished with populations who have been historically underrepresented in college and in the professions. In the narrative that follows, we describe how our approach responded to these specific issues and concerns.

A Collaborative, Inquiry-Based Approach to Learning

The model of learning that we created with our young collaborators, more from instinct than from study, corresponds to what Rogoff (1994) described as a "community of learners." According to Rogoff, children learn through side-by-side and face-to-face participation with others in the everyday activities of their community. In these purposeful activities, the participation of less experienced members is usually guided by supportive adults and peers and by a variety of accessible cultural tools, such as talk, print and texts of various kinds, writing, computers, and television.

A specific focus of our community was that of broadening students' uses of literacy to learn. According to Langer (1987), literacy learning is a form of social learning that emerges from engagement in activity rather than from direct instruction. Children are socialized in their community's literacy practices through observation of and participation in activities requiring purposeful reading and writing. Viewed from this sociocultural perspective, literacy is a socially shaped behavior rather than an individual ability or skill. Socializing middle school students into the literacy practices of ethnographic researchers enabled these students to acquire the cultural tools (the ways of learning) of a high-status community in our society to which they typically do not have access.

Because of the challenging nature of these activities for sixth graders (even mature sixth graders), the beliefs students held about who they were ("I come from a bad family") and what they were capable of accomplishing in academic contexts ("I can't do college work") required careful attention and mediation. These beliefs, which form part of students' sense of self, are a potentially negative influence on their participation and learning, particularly their willingness to invest time and energy in intensive and occasionally boring activities. Although schools typically separate affective–emotional development from cognitive–intellectual development, they are actually inseparable, forming a seamless whole that is human development. For all learners, but more so for learners with sensitivities about who they are and what they know, providing physical, emotional, and intellectual support was essential to accomplish challenging academic goals. However, as made clear later in the chapter, the character of this support varied widely.

In our community of learners, we all served as resources to one another and assumed different roles according to the activity at hand and the needs that evolved (Rogoff, 1994). Thus, students had flexibility to assume roles that corresponded to evolving interests and needs. Students were also encouraged to seek answers to research questions they found compelling and to organize research teams that included friends and peers of their choice. Under conditions that were more favorable to students, we were in a better position to ascertain what students could accomplish with and without support. This is important as students' knowledge and skills are very often invisible within the contexts of classrooms, particularly students who lack confidence in what they know and whose expressional means (e.g., nonstandard varieties of English and Spanish) are different from those valued by the school (literate English). Prevailing views of learning usually limit students' opportunities to learn as those who are perceived to lack the basics never seem quite ready for exposure to more challenging work. We took the opposite approach. That is, we introduced students to research without a lengthy preparation, which enabled us to learn what students knew through direct participation in activities. Because of their novelty, research activities initially generated a great deal of enthusiasm. As expected, students' strengths and creativity became apparent through their participation, as did their vulnerabilities. However, what could not be anticipated was what these specific strengths and vulnerabilities would be.

Although we considered this to be a far more efficient and powerful approach to teaching and learning, and assumed students were competent and had the support to meet the challenge, students had needs we did not anticipate. Specifically, students needed a great deal of encouragement and assurances from their adult guides to take risks and to validate their efforts. We tried to make the time to provide each student with a personal word of encouragement, but this was no easy challenge given that a class size of 26 to 36 students seriously limits opportunities to provide individual attention. However, writing took on a whole new purpose as students discovered the power of this medium for informing us of their needs and for eliciting pleasurable reactions from us, and this guaranteed our attention. Thus, for students who were said to be very poor at writing and who did not like to write, writing became instrumental in changing our personal and pedagogical relationship.

What was also distinctive about our community of learners is that it was future oriented, both as a means to compensate for years of underpreparation or neglect (as one student said, "They don't teach us what we need to learn!"), and as a way of stirring students' imagination, to envision other future possibilities at a critical juncture in their development. Our concern was not simply to address past gaps or to improve current scores on reading tests, a worthy but limited emphasis in our estimation. Our activities were designed to enculturate students to possible future worlds, for example, the world of post-secondary education and the world of research. Thus, the work of student-researchers was not just another form of schoolwork.

Enculturating students to the world of research meant going to authentic settings in which researchers gather to discuss their work. This presented unimagined learning opportunities for students, beginning with the proposal submission process, preparation for the event, travels to and from professional gatherings at college and university campuses, conference centers, and hotels, culminating in a conference presentation. This proved a powerful experience for adolescent learners who spend most of the time at home or on their block, apart from an occasional family outing or, for some, a visit to relatives in Puerto Rico. Formal presentations gave a concrete purpose to our activities and provided a goal that paced our work; they also created multiple opportunities to be in each other's company and with individuals from other communities. Being together in different places in and out of school augmented the possibilities for learning from and about each other as human beings and deepened our emotional bonds. Consequently, our activities created qualitatively new contexts for learning and for relating to each other as human beings, which is why a number of students likened us to "a family."

Observing students as they interacted with unfamiliar others in potentially intimidating college settings enabled us to understand what they were learning. We could see how they were broadening their social uses of literacy, as well as how they were being prepared for participation in possible future worlds, (Rogoff, 1994). According to Rogoff, learning means a change in participation. Thus, we attended closely to indicators of change in self-confidence (e.g., eye contact, voice, body posture), changes in students' uses of communicative resources for oral presentations—presenting information and making points through means such as voice modulation, transparencies, charts, and speeches—and changes in students' social skills.

In addition, our approach built on and extended students' communicative resources developed through participation in social worlds outside of school, resources that are typically devalued in school (Zentella, 1997). We also promoted qualitatively different relationships between children and families as research became a family affair. Finally, because of the segregation that characterizes schools attended by Latino students, we also sought to extend students' social worlds. Each of these is described in greater detail in the narrative that follows.

Broadening Students' Communicative Resources for Learning

As Van Manen (1990) observed, research is the work of writing, and ethnographic research requires creating and interacting with texts of all kinds in ways that exploit the symbolic representation of meaning. In assuming the role of researcher, the texts students write are, in effect, a means of representing themselves within the various social worlds in which they interact. Consequently, these are heteroglossic texts that represent students as they interact within various discourse communities. However, because the words of others are filtered through students' words, these texts are potentially powerful tools for reflection and understanding, particularly when examined in relation to other texts and in relation to students' life experiences. Not surprising, students are more willing to enter in or to create new social practices that involve the production and analysis of academic texts that represent their word and the world (Freire, 1995) and their world in their words.

Formal presentations created additional opportunities to put these texts to new uses, as students assumed and anticipated the role of other, thinking critically about what others might want and need to know within the time limitations of a typical presentation. Rereading and reflecting on the meanings of the collection of observational notes, interviews, and summaries of activities contained in students' research folders and notebooks engaged students in data reduction. They learned to synthesize essential information to prepare speeches, chronologies, handouts, and transparencies to guide their public talks.

These presentations also created opportunities for students to display competence in oral performance that form part of the popular culture of adolescence among Black (King, 1994; Ross Baber, 1987) and Latino youth (Flores, 1993; Solá & Bennett, 1991). Some students used an animated presentation style to give talks using the overhead projector, talking and reading from a large screen the illustrative examples and data they projected. Students rarely used index cards, preferring to speak extemporaneously, with or without the aid of handouts and charts, or to speak from prepared texts (speeches). We did not attempt to change or correct students' language, a heteroglossic combination of standard English, Puerto Rican English, working-class Spanish, and codeswitching. However, we willingly responded to those who sought out such corrections, particularly when students saw their words projected on large screens. Although students' ways with words (Heath, 1983) were respected, legitimized, and valued, a message that was reinforced by the ethnographic procedures we employed, it was evident that this was occasionally problematic. These students are astute observers who are sensitive to and knowledgeable about the value attached to certain forms of English over others in academic contexts.

Students' forms of self-representation became the substance of all activities, but as the year progressed, students appropriated the discourse of research, a fusion or hybridization of the different social and academic communities in which they were participating. The students' use of technical research terms led some adult audiences to confront, if not alter, their expectations of students. Some insisted that students were especially picked for this project, as a means of explaining unexpected articulateness associated with intelligence. Others were moved to tears when confronted by the person of the symbolic student who may have been invisible in school. Still others appreciated the fact that students' ways with words had improved the quality of communication in academic communities not known for lively exchanges. Pleased by the attention they received, students shifted easily to discourse styles that yielded positive effects—deliberately representing themselves in language forms that led others to perceive them as intelligent, capable beings.

Strengthening the Bond Between Children and Families

Research activities brought the school into the home and the home into the school. Accomplishing academic work became a family affair. Although we know that schools introduce activities in the home by way of homework (Moll & Díaz, 1986; Taylor & Dorsey Gaines, 1988), the emphasis of these research activities was different. Students learned about and from family members in order to understand social realities that concerned and affected them directly. Thus familiar social practices that reinforce literacy were given new purposes, as occurred when students engaged in focused conversations or interviews with parents, communicated through letters, or sought out information together as the family went about daily activities such as going to a medical appointment, visiting an ailing relative, attending a church service, or watching television.

Students suggested to family members that they give talks on topics of common interest and invited them to attend monthly research celebrations to learn about their research accomplishments. Thus, activities associated with research created unusual opportunities for students to relate to their families in qualitatively different ways at home and at school. These activities contributed to altering the perceptions of those students who had learned to be ashamed of who they are and what their parents know within the context of school. They strengthened the bond between young adolescent learners and families, and also between homes and schools, particularly significant for a number of parents who had limited interactions with schools because of their own negative experiences as students.

Extending Students' Social Worlds

As previously discussed, by engaging in research students crossed physical and psychological borders, sometimes even within the same building. They entered diverse adult academic communities in which they were regarded as authorities who were there to share their findings. In interacting with members of these communities, students came face-to-face with the imagined "other." Seeing themselves in relation to these others caused students to think about how they had represented or imagined them (really smart) in relation to the way they experienced them (just like me). Students now had a wider range of others that they could use to imagine possible future selves. According to Anderman and Maehr (1994), this aspect of the self-concept constitutes a powerful link between cognition and motivation.

As we have come to realize, our activities also created opportunities for students to interact with institutional agents who provide access to key resources and information essential to success in mainstream institutions. Stanton-Salazar (1997) argued that racial and cultural minorities often encounter obstacles in establishing relationships with these potential mentors, a serious problem that affects their ability to negotiate mainstream institutional settings such as schools. Therefore, on a number of different levels, activities associated with ethnographic research played a potentially decisive role in mediating the formation of new academic identities.

Further, the opportunity to visit college campuses enabled students to see these settings as they are and not as they are imagined, and to extend their web of relationships to include many of Carmen's professional colleagues ("Dr. Mercado's friends"). These experiences also contributed to qualitative differences in the way students engaged in social practices that now had a different texture, as students witnessed their actual use in legitimate communities of practice. As is evident, our community of learners blurred distinctions between and among what are generally constructed as three distinct worlds or communities: the world of the home–community, the world of the school, and adult academic communities.

Our approach is similar in many ways to the culturally relevant pedagogy described by Cummins (1989), Ladson-Billings (1996), Nieto and Rolón (1997), and effective instruction for middle schools (Schonhaut, 1988). In all of these approaches there is an emphasis on students as collaborators in the construction of the curriculum; assisted learning (or social mediation); using familiar communicative resources as tools for learning; and the inclusion of students' homes and communities as resources for learning. This contrasts sharply with the "adult-run" learning model that characterizes middle schools, in general, and the middle school in which our activities took place, in particular. In the next section, we present an extended case study of one student, "Indio" (a pseudonym), which brings this approach to life.

ONE STUDENT'S EXPERIENCE
OF THE CURRICULUM

Indio, some day you will be a teacher or an ethnographer.... I was glad to have met such a good ethnographer.
—Postcard from a researcher attending the NABE conference (January 1991)

Known for his compassion for the homeless and for his skillful presentations at conferences, locally and nationally, Indio was 12.3 years old when we embarked on these activities. He was born in Puerto Rico and came to New York at the age of 5. His mother, however, was born in New York City. Indio entered school in New York City, and after he was held over in the first grade, his mother agreed to place him in a bilingual program. Indio traveled regularly to Puerto Rico to spend summers with his grandfather. His speech is a form of Hispanized English marked by transfer of Spanish phonology and grammar, which Zentella (1997) explained is common among those who have been reared in Puerto Rico. Although he was in a mainstream, English monolingual class, Indio continued to use his bilingualism as a resource for learning. He shifted between Spanish and English to discuss writings in English that are accented by Spanish phonology. Interestingly, it was Indio's maturity and confidence in public speaking, sometimes from a prepared text and sometimes extemporareously, that brought him to the attention of his peers and to adult audiences.

First drafts of writing from Indio's research notebook and fieldnotes of interactions with Indio constitute an unusual chronicle of Indio's uses of literacy over a span of 3 years, from September 1989 to May 1991. However, this chronicle is most compelling for what it reveals about the active and creative agency (Duany, 1995) that ongoing participation requires for students from stigmatized groups. As Trueba (1987) correctly pointed out, traditional measures of academic achievement are incapable of capturing this active and creative agency.

We are Doing Things We Didn't Even Imagine

From the beginning, Indio demonstrated both a disposition and an ability to use writing to establish relationships with significant adults for whom this is a meaningful way to relate. Indio was skillful at capturing personally significant details of our conversations, but more than that, he sustained our interactions through writing. This was evident when he made clear his intent to follow up on CM's invitation to call her for help and when he signaled approval to have his writings shared with the teachers in CM's graduate course. He highlighted CM's interest in collaborating on a book with the student–researchers and then established his intent to author his own "little book."

Possibly not unrelated, Indio also began experimenting (on his own) with the discourse of research, including the writing of a fake report, an interesting linguistic ambiguity. Imaginative play, a form of symbolic activity and an early form of writing (Vygotsky, 1978) provides a safe vehicle for rewriting our lives, even for young adolescent learners. In playing at being researchers, students demonstrated a willingness to imagine themselves differently, assuming a role they had come to know primarily through images of mad scientists or academic nerds. However, Indio also playfully reminded us that students were just pretending to be researchers, despite what his teachers may have imagined. Indio displayed rather sophisticated skills at accomplishing complex relational work through writing, as he discovered its potential to allow him to imagine himself differently as a learner and to elicit the attention, approval, and encouragement from respected teachers. These excerpts document Indio's initiation to research. (Carmen asked students to indicate what they wanted to study if they could learn about anything they wanted, and Indio considered two topics he found compelling before deciding on studying the homeless.)

∼

CM: What do you want to learn about?

I: Where do diseases come from and what can we do to prevent them? (September 15, 1989)

How can he help the government with his problem and the homeless? (September 29, 1989)

~

I look over my notes three times.... I did a fake report so I could get used to it. I put all the information I have put together. Before Friday I will call Dr. M. so she could help me. (Indio's progress report, October 24, 1989)

I'm planning to interview people and make a discovery. But first I'm going to get data. I will observe and take notes. I will interview a homeless woman so I could make like a little book. Mrs. T could try and tell Dr. M. and she could do it over her computer. She could also take it to where she works so she could show it to the people [the teachers in CM's classes]. (Indio's progress report, October, 1989)

"Research Is Work to Be Taken Seriously, Not as a Joke"

Although earlier writings (not included) suggested that Indio had a close relationship with his mother, his writings show signs that this relationship was undergoing qualitative changes. Extended conversations about the homeless were enabling Indio to learn more about his topic and, more importantly, to see his mother in a new light. This new appreciation provoked Indio to question why she dropped out of school because their research collaboration proved how smart she really was. Indio's question was at once an attempt to understand the beliefs he held about this reality and a means to reassure himself that he was not ashamed of his mother because she was a high school dropout.

Through oral presentations and speeches, another form of self-representation, students also made transparent beliefs and perceptions that did not surface in class, as occurred when Indio proclaimed that at first he thought research was boring. These public confessions are disconcerting for those of us who believe that we are sensitive to students' needs. Yet, they are an important and powerful reminder of the need to constantly question beliefs and assumptions we hold about students, no matter how sensitive or knowledgeable we believe we are. As the level of activity intensified, we saw glimpses of Indio's approach to challenges research presents—activities that also forced him to confront and question beliefs and assumptions he had about school dropouts, as these excerpts suggest:

~

My group is a difficult one.... Please observe us and tell us what we are doing right and wrong. (Indio elicits CM's assistance in his progress report,
December 8, 1989)

My mother helps me.... She told me she dropped out of school but I tell her
why? She knows this! (CM's fieldnotes of conversation with Indio, December 22, 1989)

Well I am working on a survey and questions. I watched TV shows about
my topic even books. I also ask my relatiffs questions about being homeless
and what would you do? I got different answers. I didn't just do it with my
family. I also asked other people. When I ask my classmates for help, they
help me out. Miss. T gave me ideas and specially Dr. M. Before I leave I want
to give special thanks to Dr. M and to her assistance Miss. T. (Indio's progress report, December 26, 1989)

~

Indio's presentation at Fordham University

Good afternoon teachers and parents. Thank you for welcoming me ... and
some of my classmates.... At first I thought research was boring. I even told
my mother how boring I thought it was.... My ... project is about the
homeless. I picked this project cause not only adults get homeless cause
young people like me and you get homeless.... I have learned lots of
things.... I learn that homelessness is no joke or to laugh at the homeless ...
give them a hand help them.... I learn to don't drop out of school and to follow your dreams.... I'm planning to put everything together and make a
book. Research brought us closer together. I talked to people I didn't know
about the homeless. I want to thank Dr. M and Miss. T for making me believe in myself. (Text prepared by Indio for our first conference presentation
at a local university, January 9, 1990)

"Research Brought Us Closer Together"

From the very beginning of our collaboration, Indio focused on the special
bonds that united us, insisting that research brought us closer together.
This became dramatically evident when, 6 months into this academic
year, Indio was willing to travel longer distances to remain in this school
after his family relocated outside the boundaries of the district. This is not
surprising if we consider that participation in this exclusive community
of learners creates opportunities to engage in interesting and important

work that brought with it attention and recognition from high- status adults from prestigious academic communities. This enabled Indio to broaden his social ties, which includes classmates but also well-known researchers and educators from other settings.

However, changes are complex and take time. Late in the school year, when confronted with a group of students from an elite private school, Indio felt compelled to make public some of the obstacles members of his family have encountered in realizing their dreams of a college education. Claude Steele (1997) argued that academically successful students from stigmatized groups are plagued by feelings of inadequacy and may act in ways that reflect fear of being treated in terms of racial stereotypes. In general, however, experiences associated with research provoked Indio to challenge beliefs and assumptions he had about his capabilities as a learner and about his family's circumstances. They also provided him with a new means to secure attention and respect and to establish his worth as a human being.

~

> I am writing this letter because ... when I past to seventh grade I won't be able to do research with my teacher. I got so excited to work on research I don't want to stop.... I am even writing a story about ... how it changed my life. (Indio's letter to Principal, June 1, 1990)

> "There's a lot of homeless peoples. Some people call them bums.... You should really call them homeless.... My sister is very smart. She wants to go to college but has 2 children. I feel very sad. It's not my fault ... sometimes I cry. I need your help." (CM's notes of Indio's comments at a meeting with private school students, June 8. 1990)

> Q: Do any members of your family have special abilities and interests that may help us with this project?

> I: Yes, my mother and my sister could talk about teenage pregnancy. (Indio's response to a question on end-of-year project evaluation, June 15, 1990)

It is evident that Indio experienced many dramatic academic, social, and emotional changes within a brief period of time. However, it was his reading scores that gain him entry into the school's gifted program.

Doing Research With Indio as a Research Assistant

In the second year, Indio volunteered to serve as research assistant (his term), which meant that he committed to doing research on his own.

This is an act of courage or defiance on his part, as seventh graders are not scheduled for research despite their efforts to organize their own program (see the first entry in June). Research was now regarded as disruptive and an obstacle to learning. As one of the assistant principals in the school observed: "All these kids want to do is to do research!" Despite this, Indio was willing to challenge what at best was misplaced priorities on management and control over student motivation and interest. Although he was now in the school's gifted program, it was our activities that continued to compel him.

In assuming the role of research assistant, Indio became more deliberate in helping to document our activities. He also helped to prepare younger students for conference presentations, alleviating fears associated with this intimidating activity. Indio wrote a narrative in which he reintroduced the homeless woman he interviewed, who was now working like a "normal lady." Indio revealed for the first time that the homeless woman was a family friend. Writing can be a powerful tool to construct alternative worlds and a means to cope with or to change the conditions of one's life.

~

Miss T. asked me to be a scribe and observe her class. I am a seventh grader now. Last year I was in Miss T's class and I knew about scribing.... She asked them what is scribing and the class happily answer "scribing is observing and writing. (Indio's fieldnotes, October 15, 1990)

Maria Varela (MV) visited me.... MV was the homeless woman who lost her two kids and her mother took them. I interviewed MV since my mom and I know her. After I interviewed her I did not see her until October 12, 1990. She came straight to my door and knocked.... My mother went to my room and told me to go to the living room that she got a surprise for me. When I got there MV was sitting down on the sofa. I was very happy because when I saw her she was dressed like a normal lady.... She told me that she has a job and her mother finally decided to help her. (Indio's fieldnotes, October 26, 1990)

~

(Indio's talk to sixth graders in MT's current class)

Some people may think that one person doesn't make a difference.... I made a difference. I helped a lady out.... I got to do a lot of things I didn't expect to.... We had a lot of guest speakers because MT wanted us to get involved in our research.... Last years was one of the best years in school.... I

grew much more mature. (Indio's presentation to the sixth graders introduced to research during the 1990 to 1991 school year, December, 1990)

CM: How has research helped you to be a better learner?

I: Research helped me find my true inside ... the one that cares. (CM's
fieldnotes of a conversation with Indio in preparation for our first conference presentation of the year, December, 1990)

Indio was especially skillful at provoking students' thinking, as CM's
fieldnotes from a train ride to Boston on our way to a conference suggests.
During these intimate and relaxed moments outside of school, with fewer
students and fewer interruptions to worry about, we got to know more
about the students personally—about their emotions, their thoughts,
and their actions in other social worlds that are invisible within the classroom. In listening to Indio relate to younger students, we had glimpses of
the teacher he was becoming.

~

On the train to Boston, we ask each other questions.

Indio: The information you're getting, do you think it will help you through
life? Please explain why.

Indio says that he comes from a "bad family" because there are many drop-
outs.

Several days later, in the privacy of an empty classroom we revisit the topic.
CM explains that the same pattern exists in her family and also in MT's.
CM asks Indio to ponder: "What do we have in common?" (CM's
fieldnotes, February 15, 1991)

~

The "Save" Conference [the acronym SABE stands for State Association for
Bilingual Education] was very nice.... Before we went to the presentation,
Dr. M. show us some of her researcher friends. In the conference, the student researchers were doing fine and spoke so professional. Well, the students researchers also got stuck in some words. After that conference the
audience asked the researchers questions. After the questions, the researchers went to another one but the difference was that the conference was in
Spanish. That conference was nice and experenceful to me. C.M. did lovely
in her speech the only thing I remember was the word "L.E.C.T.U.R.A." I
also forgot what it meant. After CM finish, Heidi's mother went up to talk.

She had said to the parents in the audience that when parents hear and let their kids talk and express themselves that the parents then will understand their kids problems.... At the end Indio took the stand and talk to the parents about how the program "Research" has help him and his mother get closer.

Comments: CM you did great!!! Mrs. G. I think you did a wonderful speech! I love it! Student researchers you all did wonder, marvelous, great!!!! (Indio's fieldnotes, March 9, 1991)

I Let My Problems Get in the Way of My Life and My School Work

We consider ourselves to be sensitive educators, yet we were oblivious to powerful forces influencing Indio's life that caused him to disappear for extended periods of time. Although in our view these struggles were a consequence of living with limited financial resources, the belief that they are the result of individual problems, including family dysfunctionalities, is not easily alterable. As we confronted the reality that our research activities were incapable of addressing the formidable obstacles that students like Indio encountered, we also confronted the resilience and preserverance that students display. Indio was undaunted by life's obstacles, as these excerpts suggest.

∿

6th period today I met with MT, Dr. M., Pamela and the other two women researchers [graduate students from Hunter College]. Today we talked about why I don't visit Miss T. any more and get aquainted with my students. I felt very embarrassed because I let my problems get in the way of my life and school work. Today I will start doing research, I don't think after all the work I did I should throw it all away. Indio is back to the starting pointed and work yourself up again. (Indio's fieldnotes, April 17, 1991)

∿

CM: Indio, what did you do this year?

I: I help them excel in their presentation.... I was acting like a role model.... Chris wants to know how I scribe.... I'm going to give him lessons ... when they have a problem, I help them out.... I'm their big brother (CM's fieldnotes May 10, 1991)

We embarked on this research project to enable young adolescents to harness the power of literacy in order to take control of their own development and go beyond the limitations schooling may impose. That we succeeded on a short-term basis is supported by qualitative and quantitative evidence accumulated over several years. Whether these efforts have been successful on a long-term basis depends on the criteria we use to measure success. We are convinced that our children have a kind of brilliance born out of struggle and adversity, but it is often dimmed by their schooling and the conditions of their lives. However, as Indio's struggles suggest, it takes more than broadening the range of literacy practices to support the academic preparation of students from stigmatized groups. Assistance is needed in coping with formidable obstacles, some created by the school, some resulting from debilitating ideologies, but all reflecting the student's (and their family's) position in society. Drawing strength and support from the symbolic community we created through research, we share a bond which enables us to be hopeful about the future.

DISCUSSION

The two collaborative research studies described in this chapter are essentially ethnographic experiments through which we imagine alternative possibilities for teachers and students. Both studies emphasize the agency or will to take action that is born of collaboration with others. They also emphasize the value of entering the school's community with the goal of defining it as a valuable resource for teaching and learning.

In the first study, teachers visited local households as learners, seeking to understand and document the knowledge and experiences of families. The study was successful in helping teachers discover fundamentally new understandings of families by building explicitly on the funds of knowledge found in the households. The goal, up to now at least, was not necessarily to create new classroom practices but to accomplish something that may be more difficult: to challenge and alter long-held perceptions that families living in poverty somehow lack experiences that are worthwhile for schooling. By collecting first-hand data on these families, through interviews and fieldnotes that they later analyzed as a group, teachers helped to form new representations of the community. Through the act of writing and reflection, they were able to redefine in new theoretical terms what they observed in the households. Van Manen (1990) explained how research on lived experiences of the sort described previously contribute to the formation of new understandings: "Research is the work of writing, but in writing, the writer ... produces more than text. The writer produces himself or herself.... Writing is a kind of self-making or forming" (p. 126).

Similarly, in the second study the students created new identities as learners primarily through the uses of writing. These uses of writing included fieldnotes, reflections, letters, reports, and presentations. Each of these writing activities became a different way of relating, interacting, and learning about the surrounding realities and about the students' social world. For both the student-researchers and teacher-researchers featured in this chapter, thinking through writing became the central mechanism by which knowledge about students' homes and communities was constructed and through which all participants gained increased consciousness of the barriers that impede students' progress and the resources available for overcoming these obstacles.

However, because the activities summarized previously are academically challenging and involve research on lived experiences that evoke strong emotional reactions, the support they require is not fully captured by Rogoff's (1994) theory of guided participation. For young adolescent students, but also for bilingual teachers, it requires the creation of social-learning contexts where participants feel a sense of belonging (community) and the encouragement and support that enables them to confront the challenges they experience.

Introducing these changes also necessitated the use of resources beyond those available in schools within marginalized communities. Basically, especially with students as coresearchers, we sought to increase the number of individuals from a variety of contexts who were willing to engage in meaningful and purposeful interaction with youngsters concerned about understanding and helping to resolve some of the critical social issues affecting them and our society. However, we did not limit participation to members of professional communities as we accessed funds of knowledge from our different worlds—the home, the community, and the university. In this manner, we also acted against one of the greatest limitation these students confront—the isolation and segregation that characterizes teaching and learning in large cities. As Wells (1995) suggested, "what we learn depends crucially on the company we keep, on what activities we engage in together, and how we do and talk about these activities" (p. 238). These collaborations are essential, whether one is a teacher–researcher analyzing households or a student–researcher learning about the homeless in the most affluent of societies.

APPENDIX A: CHARACTERISTICS
OF PARTICIPATING PUERTO RICAN HOUSEHOLDS

Residence

- 53% El Barrio
- 27% Bronx
- 13% Brooklyn
- 7% Lower East Side
- 73% live in public housing or tenements

Male–Female headed households

- 53% male–female heads
- 47% single female heads

Age of female head

- Median age = mid-30s (range = 27 to 47 years old)

Ages of children

- Median age = 10 (female); 8 (male) (range = 2 [male] to 24 [male] years)

Size of household

- Smallest = 3, largest = 8 (median size household = 4.5 members; average no. of children = 2)

Birthplace of female head

- 47% Puerto Rico
- 40% mainland (New York = 33%; Wisconsin = 7%)
- 13% Latin America

Educational attainment of female head

- 36% never completed high school
- 29% high school or GED
- 29% 2 or more years of college
- 7% business school

Labor force participation

- 33% New York City employees
- 27% other steady employment
- 40% on public assistance
- 100% other income-producing activity selling goods and services

Involvement in schools

- 47% school volunteers
- 27% paid teacher assistants

APPENDIX B
A SAMPLE OF FUNDS OF KNOWLEDGE
IN PUERTO RICAN HOUSEHOLDS IN NEW YORK CITY

Material and scientific knowledge

Education/pedagogy, health education/nutrition, electricity, domestic pets/animals, Latin America, music and dance, computer technology, business, negotiation skills

Formal education

Teacher: music, dental hygiene, technology; assistant teacher: school volunteer, clerical assistant; Adult ed: GED, ESL, didactic teaching at home

Communications

Bilingualism, translation and interpretation, letter writing, journalism

Health care and medicine

Nutrition, dietary planning as preventive medicine and for treatment of diabetes

Performing arts

Classical, jazz, Latin; cello, piano, trumpet; solo and ensemble; salsa singer; composing and arranging; ballet

Religion and rituals

Baptisms, communions, weddings, Bible studies, moral knowledge and ethics, charity work with elderly and disabled

Recreation and hobbies

Computer games, trips, quilting, needlepoint, sewing dolls' clothes, framemaking, painting, toy and figurine collecting

Business entrepreneurship

Business management: Pizzeria, bodega; Sales: Avon, Amway, Tupperware; Food: *piragistas*; babysitting; jewelry; crafts; tailoring; needlework; fund-raising

Household management

Child care, comparative shopping, budget and finances, appliance repair, cooking, sewing

Home/building maintenance and repairs

Wiring, plastering, painting, wallpapering, plumbing, insulation, window installation

Activism

Advocacy work in community, challenging school policies and practices

Institutional

Board of Ed./district/school structure, policies and practices, parents' organization, students'/parents' rights, hospitals

Folklore

Oral traditions: verbal play, jokes, storytelling, sayings, proverbs; celebrating traditions; music: songs, dances, games; religious beliefs and practices; traditional foods.

REFERENCES

Anderman, E. M., & Maehr, M. L. (1994). Motivation and school learning in the middle grades. *Review of Educational Research, 64*(2), 287–309.

Baber, R. C. (1987). The artistry and artifice of Black communication. In W. L. Baber & G. Gay (Eds.), *Expressively Black* (pp. 75–108). New York: Praeger.

Bennett, A. (1991). Discourses of power, the dialectics of understanding, the power of literacy (pp. 13-33). In C. Mitchell & K. Weiler (Eds.). *Rewriting literacy. Culture and the discourse of the other.* New York: Bergin and Garvey.

Bigler, E. (1997). Dangerous discourses: Language, politics, and classroom practices in upstate New York. *CENTRO, Journal of the Center for Puerto Rican Studies, 9*(1), 8–25.

Bonilla, F. (1985). *Contemporary Marxism.* San Francisco: Synthesis.

Chávez, L. (1991). *Out of El Barrio.* New York: Basic Books.

Cole, M., & Engeström, Y. (1993). A cultural-historical approach to distributed cognition. In G. Salomon (Ed.), *Distributed cognition.* New York: Cambridge University Press.

Cole, M., & Griffin, P. (Eds.). (1987). *Contextual factors in education. Improving mathematics and science instruction for minorities and women.* Madison: Wisconsin Center for Education Research, University of Wisconsin.

Cordero-Guzmán, H. (1996). *Puerto Rican poverty in New York City: A review of the main trends and proposed explanations.* Unpublished manuscript.

Cummins, J. (1989). *Empowering minority students.* Sacramento: California Association for Bilingual Education.

Duany, J. (1995). Common threads or disparate agendas? Recent research on migration from and to Puerto Rico. *CENTRO, VII*(1), 60–77.

Flores, J. (1993). *Divided borders. Essays on Puerto Rican identity.* Houston, TX: Arte Público.

Fordham, S. (1993). Those loud Black girls: (Black) women passing in the academy. *Anthropology & Education Quarterly, 24*(1), 3–32.

Freire, P. (1995). *Pedagogy of hope* (rev. ed.). New York: Continuum Press.

González, N., Moll, L. C., Floyd-Tenery, M., Rivera, A., Rendon, P., Gonzáles, R., & Amanti, C. (1993). Funds of knowledge for teaching in Latino households. *Urban Education, 29*(4), 443–470.

Heath, S. B. (1983). *Ways with words.* New York: Cambridge University Press.

Heath, S. B. (1985). Literacy or literate skills? Considerations for ESL/EFL learners. In P. Larson, E. L. Judd, & L. S. Messerschmidt (Eds.), *On TESOL '84: Brave new world for TESOL* (pp. 15–28). Washington, DC: Teachers of English to Speakers of Other Languages.

King, J. E. (1994). Teaching diverse populations. In E. R. Hollins, J. E. King, & W. C. Hayman (Eds.), *The purpose of schooling for African-American children: Including cultural knowledge.* (pp. 25–26). Albany: State University of New York Press.

Ladson-Billings, G. (1996). *The dreamkeepers: Successful teachers of African American children.* San Francisco: Jossey-Bass.

Langer, J. A. (1987). A sociocognitive perspective on literacy (pp. 1-20). In J. A. Langer (Ed.). *Language, literacy, and culture: Issues in society and schooling.* Norwood, NJ: Ablex.

Mercado, C. I. (1992). Researching research: A student, teacher, collaborative project. In A. N. Ambert & M. D. Alvarez (Eds.), *Puerto Rican children on the mainland* (pp. 167–192). New York: Garland.

Mercado, C. I. (1998). When young people from marginalized communities enter the world of ethnographic research: Scribing, planning, reflecting, sharing. In A. Egan-Robertson &

D. Bloome (Eds.), *Students as researchers of culture and language in their own communities* (pp. 69–92). Cresskill, NJ: Hampton Press.

Mercado, C. I., & Moll, L. C. (1997). The study of funds of knowledge: Collaborative research in Latino homes. *CENTRO, Journal of the Center for Puerto Rican Studies, 9*(1), 27–42.

Moll, L. C., Amanti, C., Neff, D., & González, N. (1992). Funds of knowledge for teaching: Using a qualitative approach to connect homes and classrooms. *Theory Into Practice, 31*(2), 132–141.

Moll, L. C., & Díaz, E. (1987). Change as a goal of educational research. *Anthropology & Education Quarterly, 18*(4), 300–311.

Moll, L. C., & González, N. (1997). Teachers as social scientists: Learning about culture from household research. In P. M. Hall (Ed.), *Race, ethnicity and multiculturalism* (Vol. 1, pp. 234–244). New York: Garland.

Morrison, J. C. (1958). *The Puerto Rican study, 1953–1957*. Brooklyn: New York City Board of Education.

Nieto, S., & Rolón, C. (1997). Preparation and professional development of teachers: A perspective from two Latinas. In J. J. Irvine (Ed.), *Critical knowledge for diverse teachers and learners* (pp. 89–123). Washington, DC: American Association of Colleges for Teacher Education.

Pérez, R. (1990). From assimilation to annihilation: Puerto Rican images in U.S. films. *CENTRO, Journal of the Center for Puerto Rican Studies, 2*(8), 8–27.

Portes, A., & MacLeod D. (1996). The educational progress of children of immigrants: The roles of class, ethnicity, and school context. *Sociology of Education, 69,* 255–275.

Portes, A., & Rumbaut, R. G. (1996). *Immigrant America* (2nd ed.). Los Angeles: University of California Press.

Pousada, A., & Greenlee, M. (1988). Toward a social theory of language variability. In C. Alvarez, A. Bennett, M. Greenlee, P. Pedraza, & A. Pousada (Eds.), *Speech and ways of speaking in a bilingual Puerto Rican community* (pp. 11–92). Language Policy Task Force. Center for Puerto Rican Studies, Hunter College, City of New York: Research Foundation of the City of New York.

Reyes, L. O. (Chair) (1994, March 23). *Making the vision a reality: A Latino action agenda for educational reform*. Final report of the Latino Commission on Educational Reform. (Available from New York City Board of Education, 110 Livingston St., Brooklyn, NY)

Rogoff, B. (1995). Observing sociocultural activity on three planes: Participating appropriation, guided participation, and apprenticeship. In V. V. Wertch, P. Del Rio, A. Alvarez.

Salazar, J. M. (1989, December). La investigación acerca de la identidad cultural, nacional, y supra-nacional y su importancia en el proceso educativo. [The investigation of cultural, national, and super-national identity and its importance in the education process]. *Cuadernos de investigación en la educación,* No. 1, 12–17.

Schonhaut, C. I. (Chair) (1988). Middle School Task Force report to the New York City Board of Education.

Solá, M., & Bennett, A. (1991). The struggle for voice: Narrative, literacy, and consciousness in East Harlem. In C. Mitchell & K. Weiler (Eds.), *Rewriting literacy: Culture and the discourse of the other* (pp. 35–55). New York: Bergin & Garvey.

Stanton-Salazar, R. (1997). A social capital framework for understanding the socialization of racial minority students and youth. *Harvard Educational Review, 67*(1), 1–40.

Steele, C. (1997). A threat in the air. How stereotypes shape intellectual identity and performance. *American Psychologist, 52*(6), 613–629.

Taylor, D., & Dorsey-Gaines, C. (1988). *Growing up literate. Learning from inner-city families.* Portsmouth, NH: Heinemann.

Trueba, H. T. (1998). The education of Mexican immigrant children. In M. M. Suarez-Orozco (Ed.), *Crossings: Mexican immigration in interdisciplinary perspectives* (pp. 251–275). Cambridge, MA: Harvard University Press.

Trueba, E. (1987). The ethnography of schooling. In H. T. Treuba (Ed.), *Success or failure? Learning and the language of minority students.* Cambridge, MA: Newbury House.

Van Manen, M. (1990). *Researching lived experience.* Albany: State University of New York Press.

Vázquez, B. (1990). Puerto Ricans and the media: A personal statement. *CENTRO, Journal of the Center for Puerto Rican Studies, 3*(1), 4–15.

Vygotsky, L. S. (1978). *Mind in society.* Cambridge, MA: Harvard University Press.

Walsh, C. E. (1991). *Pedagogy and the struggle for voice: Issues of language, power, and schooling for Puerto Ricans.* New York: Bergin & Garvey.

Wells, G. (1995). Language and the inquiry-oriented curriculum. *Curriculum Inquiry, 25*(3), 233–269.

Zentella, A. C. (1997). *Growing up bilingual.* Malden, MA: Blackwell.

V

DIRECTIONS FOR THE FUTURE

Afterword

Janice Petrovich Beiso

This book deepens our understanding of the personal and collective struggle of Puerto Ricans in U.S. schools and communities. It is a struggle that paints compelling triumphs over adversity but also recognizes that intolerance of racial, cultural, and language difference still presents formidable barriers to many Puerto Ricans. From Gillian Rivera's account of her school experience as a young student who moved from Puerto Rico to the United States, experiencing racism and discrimination yet continuing to pursue her education, to Nitza Hidalgo's account of the role of mothers and grandmothers in promoting school success, the chapters of this book are a testament to the resilience and resources of the Puerto Rican people. They demonstrate that the Puerto Rican community has been an agent of change, actively promoting educational policies and practices to enhance their children's success.

Like many marginalized groups, Puerto Ricans have mobilized resistance in response to exclusion from established institutions. The authors of this book document and portray many manifestations of collective action such as the establishment of Puerto Rican organizations that respond to the community's needs. For example, Luis Reyes recounts the development of ASPIRA, which promotes educational access and develops youth leadership to sustain the movement toward equity and was founded through an organized movement of concerned parents, students, and civic leaders. The Puerto Rican community's fight for bilingual education, as María Zarala, Diana Caballero, and Sonia Nieto describe, is another example of mobilizing for change. In this case, the desire has been to promote children's educational success in an English-speaking society while preserving their active participation in the language and culture of their parents.

The struggle of Puerto Rican students in the United States finds parallels with the struggles of other nondominant groups excluded from power because of gender, race, ethnicity, language, culture, or sexual orientation. The efforts of Puerto Ricans to receive an excellent education can be strengthened by insights into what distinguishes them from, and joins them to, the struggles of other marginalized groups. For example, the Philippines changed from a Spanish colony into a U.S. colony in 1898. So did Puerto Rico. Since that time the language of teaching in the public schools in the Philippines has flip-flopped from English to Tagalog to bilingualism. A similar situation has occurred in Puerto Rico, where teaching occurs primarily in Spanish, although English was imposed in 1898 and is still taught in school. Clear parallels exist between the history and the language issues of the Philippines and Puerto Rico even though they are half a world apart. In both places, people hang on to their native language as a vital part of their culture. In both places massive migration is a social and economic reality. In both places jobs are scarce, and knowing how to speak English opens up job opportunities abroad. Many highly skilled engineers, medical doctors, and other professionals leave for the United States, as do less skilled workers.

We have much to learn about how other educational and political systems address the needs of nondominant groups. Although histories of migration and marginalization may differ, comparative cross-national research on nondominant groups would deepen our understanding of common barriers and may spark new ideas for addressing them. There are many areas for further research that can help us move beyond outdated approaches and point to new strategies for collective action. Research that is comparative, cross-national, and cross-ethnic is needed to help build our understanding on a variety of topics relevant to the achievement of Puerto Rican children.

---

[1]Tagalog is just one of many native languages in the Philippines. Puerto Rico had no other native language groups when the United States invaded the Island.

TOPICS FOR FUTURE RESEARCH

In reviewing current research on Puerto Rican students in the United States, three topics stand out as needing more attention: language and power, colonialism and educational opportunity, and coalition building for school reform.

Language and Power

As Rényi (1993) noted, "social rewards for taking on the language of power is a worldwide phenomenon" (p. 140). This fact does not escape immigrant groups in the United States. Indeed, one could argue that Latinos who voted in favor of California's Proposition 227 [2] did so because of their belief in the importance of learning English. Advertisements built on that conviction to argue that bilingual education programs were not the best way for children to learn English. Bilingual education has been under attack, and many Puerto Rican leaders are concerned over the lack of a coherent response, of a new formulation that can galvanize support. To enrich the dialogue on bilingual education in this country, we need a greater public understanding of the benefits of language diversity, the development of language policies, and the history of language struggles in other countries.

The effort to establish the language of those in power as the language used in public schools is not unique to the United States. Nations around the world are struggling over language issues. There are over 4,000 languages in the world, but fewer than 200 nations. Thus, most countries contain various native language groups. In countries where multiple languages are spoken, such as Indonesia, the government has declared one "official" language in an attempt to promote national unity. Interestingly, South Africa's approach to promoting unity as a country that recently transitioned out of a politically mandated system of forced marginalization (apartheid) has been to declare 11 of the country's languages as official. Each of these countries has chosen to deal with language diversity in a dramatically different way. Their challenge is to develop educational systems that translate these policies into a practice that helps all children achieve, no matter what their language background. Research on student achievement and educational approaches in each of these contexts could help inform language policy in the United States.

---

[2] Proposition 227 ruled that all children in California will be taught in English unless their parents specifically request otherwise.

One of the strongest arguments for educational change in the United States is the economic benefits of education. In an increasingly globalized economy, common sense dictates that multilingualism is an asset. For example, multinational firms may be global but their work happens locally. Customers need to be addressed in their own language. Employees who can speak the local language as well as the multinational's operating language are likely to command higher positions and salaries. However, we do not know enough about the relationship between fluency in various languages and income. If multilingualism is found to have economic benefits, these findings could be used as an argument to promote bilingual education. History shows that the introduction of languages other than the dominant one into schools all over the world has required political power. In the United States, where Latinos are projected to shortly become the most numerous ethnic group, mobilizing and harnessing our potential political power to improve education for our children is one of our greatest challenges and one of our greatest opportunities.

Colonialism and Educational Opportunity

Colonial conquests have had a variety of manifestations, not the least of which is the imposition of the culture and language of the colonial power. In Puerto Rico, as in all places that have become U.S. possessions, English became the language of schooling after the U.S. takeover. By the same token, Spanish was the dominant language during the 400 years when Spain was the colonial power. The struggle over what language to use for teaching in the public schools has been a characteristic of education in Puerto Rico as well as in the Philippines. These struggles evidence the difficulty that dominant groups have in imposing new cultures and languages. However, advantages arise for those who learn the language and culture of those in power: such knowledge provides some access to more powerful jobs and increased economic opportunity for the colonized population. It becomes evident to people living in colonial situations, particularly to the wealthier sectors of society who aspire to maintain their economic advantage, that those who learn English are rewarded with better jobs and higher salaries. Thus, many who wish to succeed in a colonial situation and improve the class status for their children quickly seize opportunities to learn the culture and language of power.

In Puerto Rico, as in the Philippines, students who wish to become fluent in English typically attend private schools where teaching is in English. Most private schooling in both Puerto Rico and the Philippines, as in many other parts of the world, occurs in religiously affiliated schools. Private religiously affiliated schools have played an important role in educating the native elites of the world's colonies. With the growing interest in school privatization, the role of private schools in the education of Puerto Rican children appears to be a timely research topic. The purported success of parochial schools in educating minority children is often used as an argument in favor of vouchers. However, hard evidence to support this position is lacking. Research is needed to document the achievement of comparable cohorts of students in public and private schools.

History is rich with examples of the role of religious institutions in spreading the language and culture of the new regime. However, the relations between colonialism, cultural imperialism, and religion need to be better understood. An example is the case of Mexico during Spanish colonization. Part of the Spanish conquest involved building churches on top of Aztec temples to co-opt native places of workshop. The priests wisely capitalized on the native population's reverence for the particular geographic location since that reverence could be rechanelled into the new religion. The role of religious institutions included teaching the language, values, and culture of the colonial power. In this way, native populations could acquire the customs, dress, and manner of those in power. Nevertheless, their native origins were used to bar them from actually acquiring power.

Linguistic differences have contributed to educational stratification in the education systems of current and former colonies where private elementary and secondary schools that teach in English occupy the higher levels of the educational hierarchy. The highest level of the educational hierarchy, the most highly prized education, becomes that obtained in the colonizing country itself—the United States for Puerto Ricans and Filipinos, the United Kingdom for Indians and Nigerians, France for Algerians, and so on. This is one example of how the educational situation of Puerto Ricans parallels that of other colonized people. Understanding this history, the differences, and the commonalities not only may allow us to interpret our reality more fully but also may help us find solidarity with those in distant parts of the world.

Constituency Building and School Reform

A quick review of history yields many examples of educational reforms–bilingual education, school finance reform, and special education–where people have acted together and achieved changes in schools. Broad coalitions that connect people of different ages, ethnicities, occupations, and levels of influence have great potential to make change, if mobilized. In fact, what is perhaps the most comprehensive systemic education reform effort in this country, that of the State of Kentucky, was initiated and has been sustained by engaged citizens. Citizens of Kentucky pressed for the reform of a school finance system that provided less funding to schools in poor communities. When the court mandated that a new, more equal, system be put in place, an active citizen's coalition helped fashion the Kentucky Education Reform Act (KERA), which totally revamped the financing, governance, and teaching systems to promote high-quality education for all children.

Examples such as that of Kentucky demonstrate that the key to successful and sustained citizen action is to constantly redefine the strategy needed to pursue the defined goals. Recent rollbacks in the affirmative action gains of the 1970s and 1980s are testament to the need to continue to redefine strategies. Solid data obtained through research and evaluation are needed to help inform the public dialogue required to sustain a reform effort over time. Sustaining a reform requires being able to assess the performance of an intervention such as affirmative action or bilingual education and developing capacities for learning, reconceptualizing, and acting strategically. Comparative research on language and power, colonialism and educational opportunity, and constituency building and school reform can help inform our practice and strategy in our pursuit of excellent and equitable public education.

In the United States, India, and South Africa, as in other democracies around the world, schools, universities, and governments are struggling to make real the idea of democracy. The groups in power—males, Whites, the wealthy—are not typically the majority of the population. Puerto Rican students in U.S. schools are part of the international quest for enfranchisement of marginalized groups. In the next decade, changes in the educational systems that promote the progress of Puerto Rican students will increasingly depend on establishing coalitions with others. Broadening educational opportunities for Puerto Ricans will require greater understanding and dialogue about the manifestations and impact of inequity on all children of the world and a greater effort to build broad-based constituencies to support reform.

REFERENCE

Rényi, J. (1993). *Going public: Schooling for a diverse democracy.* New York: Norton.

About the Contributors

Hipolito Baez, Jr., received an AB from Bowdoin College and an MEd from the University of Massachusetts at Amherst. He began his candidacy for a Juris Doctor at Western New England Collefe School of Law in the Fall of 1998. While attending law school, he also works as a paralegal for the Hartford, Connecticut office of the national law firm of Jackson, Lewis, Schnitzler & Krupman. This law firm specializes in labor and employment law on behalf of management. His focus at this firm is writing federally mandated affirmative action plans on behalf of employers and pension plan work. Prior to that, he worked as a Case Manager for the Massachusetts Department of Mental Health. His past activities include, but are not limited to, serving as a Human Rights Officer, participating in Human Rights Committees, advocating for the human rights of dually diagnosed adults involved in mental health services, and ensuring that the local community meets the needs of Latinos.

Diana Caballero is an educator, community activist, and crusader for bilingual education. For over 25 years, she has worked extensively with parents, educators, students, and community organizations in promoting educational and social change. Born and raised in the South Bronx, she attended New York City public schools and recently earned her doctoral degree in educational administration/bilingual education from Teachers College, Columbia University. In September 1998, she became assistant professor in the Bilingual Education Program at the City College of New York. Here she hopes to create learning environments that are democratic and empowering and that create a passion for teaching, learning, and social change.

Elizabeth Capifali is a doctoral student in language, literacy, and culture at the School of Education, University of Massachusetts, Amherst, majoring in multicultural education. She has taught an undergraduate introductory course in multicultural education at the university, and prior to that she taught elementary school in Harlem for 16 years. Her research interests focus on children's literature, the writing process, and the education of Puerto Ricans. She has coedited a children's anthology of writing, *Kaleidoscope: Many faces, many voices* (Community Service Society of New York, 1988), and she has worked with high school students to create a forum for antiracist schooling. She is married and has three children.

José Manuel Caraballo is called Manny by his family and friends, but at school he likes to be called José. He is 14 years old and lives in Springfield, Massachusetts. José has a cat named Suzy and he likes to swim, take walks, fish, and play with animals. He also likes to play video games, read poetry, and perform magic tricks. When José grows up, he wants to be a wrestler, but if he cannot be a wrestler, he wants to be a lawyer because they make a lot of money and help people at the same time. He hopes that when he grows up, he will not have to worry about money.

el Cortés, a Williamsburg Puerto Rican Brooklynite who has also lived in Rome and now lives in Manhattan, has been writing all her life—in her head. A few years ago it got too cluttered up there, so she started putting the writing on paper. She has also been a bilingual special educator for many years. Within the last few years she has been awarded, for her writing, a MacDowell Fellowship, an NEA Fellowship at Virginia Center for the Creative Arts, and a residency at Fundación Valparaíso, an international artists' colony in Spain. She has published work in fiction, nonfiction, and poetry. el Cortés has been working on a collection of interrelated stories that she would love to finish so she can get on with her life guilt-free.

Jaime Shaggy Flores is better known as Shaggy the Poet, modern-day griot, Nuyorican, Massarican, bilingual-speaking, revolutionary santero poet of the University of Massachusetts. Finishing his thesis titled *African Diaspora* in May 2000, he is founder of the Annual Voices for the Voiceless poetry concert and the Urban Arts project. Shaggy works using the arts, culture, politics, and history to empower youths and the Black and Latino community. His book, *Sancocho*, is published by his own company, Dark Soul Graphics. A resident of Springfield, MA, he was born in Nueva Yol on January 21, 1973.

Nitza M. Hidalgo received her doctorate from Harvard University and is presently associate professor of education at Westfield State College, Westfield, Massachusetts. She teaches multicultural education, foundation of education, and ethnic studies. Dr. Hidalgo was appointed research associate during the 1994-95 academic year at the Five College Women's Studies Research Center, Mount Holyoke College, Massachusetts. She was the past chairperson of the *Harvard Educational Review* and the coeditor of *Facing Racism in Education*. She also coedited an issue of *Education and Urban Society* entitled, "Latino Communities: Resources for Educational Change." Her research interests are in the areas of Puerto Rican family involvement in education and multicultural pedagogy.

Alicia López teaches French and Spanish at a Manhattan private school for girls. She very much enjoys working with young people, in the classroom as a teacher and outside as an advisor. She will be pursuing a master's degree some time in the near future in the anthropology of education. Ms. López lives in Williamsburg, Brooklyn.

Yvonne Martinez Thorne is executive director and psychologist at the Creative Living Counseling Center, an interfaith counseling center in New Jersey. She has published several articles and provided presentations on the achievement motivation of successful, high-achieving Latina women. Dr. Martinez Thorne has also served on the faculty at Hunter College and Drew University as multicultural specialist in counseling. She holds a doctorate in Counseling Psychology from Teachers College, Columbia University. Dr. Martinez Thorne lives with her husband, Dr. Leo S. Thorne, in New Jersey.

Carmen I. Mercado was born in Puerto Rico and brought to New York at the age of four. She has been affiliated with New York City public schools her entire life, as a student and more recently, since 1988, as a faculty member in the Department of Curriculum and Teaching at Hunter College of the City University of New York. She teaches courses in English and Spanish on literacy, teacher research, bilingual education, and diversity. She was also an elementary school teacher in one of the first dual-language programs in the Bronx. Her most personally and professionally affecting experience has been that of collaborating with teachers, students, and families in constructing knowledge together. She continues to learn about herself and others from activities focused on identifying and building on the vast wealth of sociocultural resources for learning in nonmainstream communities. Her current interests include understanding how writing mediates the formation of personal and social identities.

Carlos Mills De Jesús, Jr., is director of ALANA Student Services at the College of Saint Rose, Albany, New York. He is a graduate student in the Educational Administration and Policy Studies Program at the University of Albany. His first publication appeared in the Spring 1997 issue of *Multicultural Education*, the magazine of the National Association for Multicultural Education. Mr. Mills plans to continue his studies in Ireland, where he will pursue a postgraduate degree in ethnic and racial studies at the University of Dublin, Trinity college. Upon his return to the United States, he will seek admission into a doctoral program in multicultural education.

Luis C. Moll (UCLA, 1978), born in Puerto Rico, is a professor in the Department of Language, Reading and Culture of the College of Education at the University of Arizona. His most recent research involves the analysis of biliteracy development, how children acquire literate competencies in two languages, and the classroom and community conditions that facilitate and support such development.

Milga Morales is dean of student life at Brooklyn College of the City of New York where she was previously associate professor of education at Brooklyn College of the City University of New York. She obtained her PhD from Yeshiva University's Graduate School of Psychology and studied under Dr. Joshua Fishman and Dr. Ofelia Garcia. Dr. Morales was born in Puerto Rico and raised in Brooklyn. She has studied and written about language and the Puerto Rican/Latino community in the northeast. As an educator, she regards the politicization of teachers as indispensable and works to ensure that her students have the knowledge base and the critical know-how to work closely and meaningfully with inner-city children.

Sonia Nieto is professor of language, literacy, and culture in the School of Education, University of Massachusetts, Amherst. Her research focuses on multicultural and bilingual education, the education of Latinos, and Puerto Rican children's literature. Her publications include *Affirming diversity: The sociopolitical context of multicultural education* (2000, 3rd ed.) and *The light in their eyes: Creating multicultural* *learning communities* (1999), as well as many book chapters and articles. She serves on various national advisory boards that focus on educational equity and social justice, and she has received many awards for her community service, advocacy, and scholarly activities.

Pedro Pedraza has been the director of the Language and Education Task Force at the Centro de Estudios Puertorriqueños at Hunter College, City University of New York, for the past 25 years. He has published work on issues of language, culture identity, and education within the Puerto Rican and Latino communities in New York City, Puerto Rico, and Cuba. He has designed and developed programs in the Puerto Rican community for children and adults, including the Young Scientist Club and El Barrio Popular Education Program. In addition, he has served on many boards of educational, advocacy, youth, and community organizations such as Advocates for Children, Educators for Social Responsibility, the Puerto Rican/Latino Education Roundtable, and New Visions for Public Schools.

Janice Petrovich Beiso is director for education, knowledge and religion in the Education, Media, Arts and Culture Program of the Ford Foundation. She was formerly national executive director of ASPIRA, director of Research Studies at the American Council on Education, and director of the Research Institute of the InterAmerican University of Puerto Rico, where she founded the Center for Research and Documentation on Women. She has a Bachelor of Science degree in chemistry and a master's degree in teaching and chemistry from the University of Puerto Rico in Río Piedras. With a Ford Foundation fellowship, she obtained a doctoral degree in educational policy research at the University of Massachusetts at Amherst. She serves on various nonprofit boards including the White House Commission on Educational Excellence for Hispanic Americans.

Luis O. Reyes, PhD, is an associate professor of education at Long Island University, Brooklyn Campus. Between 1990 and 1998, he served as a member of the New York City Board of Education and chaired the board's Latino Commission on Educational Reform. He has held teaching positions at Baruch College and Brooklyn College, CUNY. Dr. Reyes was deputy director for Research and Advocacy at ASPIRA of New York, a youth leadership organization serving Puerto Rican and Latino youth. Dr. Reyes has gained a reputation as an articulate and outspoken advocate for educational reform, especially in the areas of bilingual and multicultural education, drop-out prevention programs, and equal educational opportunity.

Xaé Alicia Reyes is associate professor with a joint appointment in the Department of Curriculum and Instruction and The Puerto Rican and Latino Studies at the University of Connecticut at Storrs. Reyes was born in Puerto Rico, where she received most of her schooling. Both her undergraduate and master's degrees are from the University of Puerto Rico in Rio Piedras, and her PhD is from the University of Colorado at Boulder. Before her current appointment, she was at Rhode Island College in Providence, and in the Spring 1997 she was visiting professor at Brown University's Center for the Study of Race and Ethnicity. Her research focuses on issues of identity and critical pedagogy. She is the mother of two sons.

Gillian Rivera was 19 years old and a junior at Amherst Regional High School in Amherst, Massachusetts when she wrote this. She lived with her mother and younger sister. Her two older brothers were instrumental in influencing and encouraging her to continue her studies. She was copresident of Latinos Unidos, an after-school club that works with the Latino community and sponsors cultural events in school. During her spare time, she made a special effort to interact with the youth in her community in a variety of ways.

Melissa Rivera has worked as an educator and activist on many participatory research, evaluation, and design projects with youth programs, community-based organizations, public schools and universities, teacher-training courses, and prisons. Her work has encompassed issues of race, gender, culture, language, identity, education, media, and the performing arts as well as youth, adult and community development in the Washington D.C., Providence, Boston, and New York City Metropolitan areas. She received her doctorate in Human Development and Psychology at the Harvard University Graduate School of Education in June 1999 and continues to work on various educational, literary, and arts projects.

Carmen A. Rolón is a visiting assistant professor in the Department of Psychology and Education at Mount Holyoke College, where she teaches courses in teaching and learning in secondary schools and issues in bilingualism. Her research interests include the educational experiences of students from diverse cultural and linguistic backgrounds, the education of females, and parent involvement. She has written a number of book chapters on these topics. She also taught Chapter I math at junior high schools in Puerto Rico and coordinated the Multicultural/Multilingual Resource Center at the University of Massachusetts School of Education.

Elvira R. Tarr is a professor of education at Brooklyn College, where she has taught courses in social studies, educational philosophy, and multiculturalism. She coedited *The re-education of the American working class* and has presented papers at the American Educational Research Association and the National Association of Multicultural Education on topics such as the workplace, multiculturalism, and feminism. Her interest in Japan led to a Sasakawa Fellowship in 1995. Her current research is a comparative study of women workers in Japan, China, and the United States at the turn of the century. She received her doctorate at New York University for her thesis on the epistemology and social philosophy of Chas. S. Peirce.

María Torres-Guzmán is associate professor and director of the Program in Bilingual/Bicultural Education at Teachers College, Columbia University. She has published numerous articles and chapters, coauthored *Learning in Two Worlds*, and developed computer-based and curricular materials in Spanish.

Catherine E. Walsh is professor in the graduate program of Latin American Studies at the Universidad Andina Simón Bolívar in Quito, Ecuador, where she teaches courses and conducts and supervises research related to issues of interculturality. She also is senior advisor of urban research at the Northeast and Islands Regional Educational Laboratory at Brown University. Dr. Walsh has extensively studied and written about school related issues for Puerto Ricans for almost 20 years. She has also served as federal court–appointed expert and monitor in a number of northeast school districts, representing Puerto Rican plaintiffs.

Maria V. Zavala is a private consultant with her own consulting business. She has a master's in psychology from Mount Holyoke College. Her consulting provides training, workshops, and presentations around topics such as diversity in the workplace, team development, leadership development, diversity and counseling, and group facilitation. Her work has been cited most recently in Dr. Beverly Daniel-Tatum's book, *Why are all the Black kids sitting together in the cafeteria? and other conversations about race* (1997). Her study, *A bridge over divided worlds: An exploration into the nature of bilingual Puerto Rican youths' ethnic identity development*, was a master's thesis done for Mount Holyoke College in 1995. Her paper, *Who are you if you don't speak Spanish?* was presented at the annual meeting of the American Educational Research Association in New York, April 1996.

Author Index

347

Subject Index